An Earth-Shattering Event

What I received I passed on to you as of first importance:
that Christ died for our sins . . . that he was raised
on the third day . . . and that he appeared.
1 CORINTHIANS 15:3-5

In Word

The Jews were split on the issue. Some believed that God would one day resurrect human beings, others did not. The Greeks believed in the immortality of the soul, but certainly not in a physical resurrection. For everyone, however, the issue was a mysterious, one-day-we'll-understand issue. No one—absolutely no one—expected to see a resurrected human in his or her lifetime.

Not until Jesus came, anyway. He raised a few people from the dead Himself—Jairus's daughter and Lazarus, to name two—but those were temporary resurrections. Everyone knew Jairus's daughter and Lazarus would die again one day. Still, the fact that they could be raised for a time gave hope to eyewitnesses that permanent resurrection was at least theoretically possible. And then when Jesus appeared after being in a tomb for three days . . .

This was the earth-shattering foundation of the church. Jesus' teachings were profound, His miracles spectacular; but they didn't define the church. The new movement that began in a small Roman outpost was based on a revolutionary, shocking truth: The specter of death had lost its power. A man, certifiably dead, was now alive. And He promised life to everyone who believed in Him.

In Deed

It's impossible for us to understand, two millennia later, how utterly radical the idea of resurrection was. It was not an illusion of prescientific people; Jesus appeared to a lot of people, for many days, and displayed His eternal body. Many who saw Him were later martyred for admitting it. That doesn't happen en masse with illusions. It only happens with historical fact.

If you think about it, this fact changes everything. It changes how we live, how we think, how we plan, how we work—everything! Let it change you; no, let it define you. Resolve this year to live a resurrected life.

> Jesus has forced open a door that had been locked
> since the death of the first man. . . . Everything
> is diffe

An Essential Sign

*If Christ has not been raised, your faith is
futile; you are still in your sins.*
1 CORINTHIANS 15:17

In Word

The Resurrection validates everything we believe in. Without it, the Bible is bold
enough to say, our faith is worthless. Those who think Christianity is worthwhile for
life in this world alone are disagreeing with Paul; he thought we were pitiful creatures
indeed if our faith is only a this-world faith (v. 19).

No, God gave us the Resurrection—Jesus' and ours—for a reason. It's a promise,
a pledge, a validation that our life on this fallen planet is but a tiny fraction of the life
we were meant to live. While the rest of the world goes about living for the here and
now, we live for eternity. While they make investments hoping for good returns in a
matter of years or decades, we make investments hoping for good returns in a matter
of timeless "ages." While they interpret their trials as things that will make or break the
quality of their lives, we interpret our trials as events that are shaping us to understand
God and inherit His riches. The Resurrection makes all the difference in the world.
And beyond.

This, in fact, was the point of creation from day one. Genesis is the account of
God's creation, but the cross of Christ and the empty tomb are the account of the re-
creation. The early church was suddenly aware that they were living in the regenesis,
the fulfillment of all God had promised, the Kingdom that does not pass away. And
that knowledge guided everything they did.

In Deed

We often think of the Resurrection as an Eastertime phenomenon—a past miracle
that gives us faint hope for the future. It is so much more.

The Resurrection validates our faith in the redeeming work of our High Priest,
who has taken away our sins. It allows us to live with a sense of risk and adventure,
because it makes us part of a new order of creation that ultimately cannot fail—our
lives are grounded in Someone who reigns in eternal victory.

No resurrection, no Christianity.
—MICHAEL RAMSEY

THE ONE YEAR®

WONDER
of the CROSS
DEVOTIONAL

**365 DAILY BIBLE READINGS
TO RENEW YOUR FAITH**

CHRIS TIEGREEN

WALK
THRU THE
BIBLE®

TYNDALE HOUSE PUBLISHERS, INC.
CAROL STREAM, ILLINOIS

Visit Tyndale's exciting Web site at www.tyndale.com

TYNDALE and Tyndale's quill logo are trademarks of Tyndale House Publishers, Inc.

The One Year is a registered trademark of Tyndale House Publishers, Inc.

The One Year Wonder of the Cross Devotional: 365 Daily Bible Readings to Renew Your Faith

Designed by Beth Sparkman

ISBN 978-1-4143-2396-1

Printed in the United States of America

15 14 13 12 11 10 09
 7   6   5   4   3   2   1

WALK
THRU THE
BIBLE

Helping people everywhere live God's Word

For more than three decades, Walk Thru the Bible has created discipleship materials and cultivated leadership networks that together are reaching millions of people through live seminars, print publications, audiovisual curricula, and the Internet. Known for innovative methods and high-quality resources, we serve the whole body of Christ across denominational, cultural, and national lines. Through our strong and cooperative international partnerships, we are strategically positioned to address the church's greatest need: developing mature, committed, and spiritually reproducing believers.

Walk Thru the Bible communicates the truths of God's Word in a way that makes the Bible readily accessible to anyone. We are committed to developing user-friendly resources that are Bible centered, of excellent quality, life changing for individuals, and catalytic for churches, ministries, and movements; and we are committed to maintaining our global reach through strategic partnerships while adhering to the highest levels of integrity in all we do.

Walk Thru the Bible partners with the local church worldwide to fulfill its mission, helping people "walk thru" the Bible with greater clarity and understanding. Live seminars and small group curricula are taught in over 45 languages by more than 80,000 people in more than 70 countries, and more than 100 million devotionals have been packaged into daily magazines, books, and other publications that reach over five million people each year.

Walk Thru the Bible
4201 North Peachtree Road
Atlanta, GA 30341-1207
770-458-9300
www.walkthru.org

R. Kamsler

Introduction

When God's Spirit burst on the scene at Pentecost, Spirit-inhabited believers were in awe and onlookers were amazed. The power of the Cross had been unleashed, and lives were being changed. The Kingdom of God was breaking into the empires of the world.

The early church was an enigma to virtually everyone, even its own members. The new movement continued to make waves across the empire throughout the first century, and no one, not even its own proponents, could figure it out. How did God's new work fulfill old Scriptures? Where did it fit within Judaism? What was this new creation supposed to look like? What, ultimately, was God doing with His people?

Much of the New Testament was written to answer these kinds of questions. But Acts, the apostolic letters, and Revelation were more than a record of theological struggles; they were a testimony to the inexplicable work of God through the death and resurrection of Jesus.

The devotional readings in this book are based on the experiences and testimonies of the early church. You'll find some readings based on Old Testament passages that figured heavily in the church's understanding of God's purposes, but the majority of devotionals are taken from Acts, the letters of the apostles, and Revelation. These are the writings that have shaped church history for the last two millennia and continue to inspire us today. They build up our faith by testifying to the still-surprising power of God. And, by encouraging us to keep our focus on the Kingdom that is and is to come, they show us how we may experience the wonder of the Cross ourselves.

A Powerful Process

Just as we have borne the likeness of the earthly man,
so shall we bear the likeness of the man from heaven.
1 CORINTHIANS 15:49

In Word

The first-century Christian lived with an eye on the coming Kingdom. More than that, he or she lived with an eye on the new creation taking place within. It was a marvel to behold: a sinful heart taking on the likeness of Jesus.

True, Paul had to remind his readers that this was happening. Some were ignorant of the process, sometimes even of the goal. Some, like a lot of Christians today, accepted the Resurrection as a future reality but not as a present dynamic. They forgot what Paul emphasizes in Ephesians 1:19-20—that the very power that raised Jesus from the dead is the power that is working in those who believe. The magnificent force that overcame death is at work in the hearts and minds of those for whom He died.

We can't take that for granted. The Jesus we read fondly of in Scripture really is alive, and He makes His home within us. We may not be aware of His presence, but that's our fault, not His. When we gather as a corporate body in our churches, He is there, bringing all parts of the whole together. When we are alone in our moments of crisis and need, He is there, reminding us, if we will let Him, that sealed tombs are no match for His creative power. Sinful hearts, too, are no match for Him. Whatever frustrates us in this world, He has overcome it. We can live with that blessing not only in the future physical resurrection but also in the present spiritual one.

In Deed

We need to live with an eye on the coming Kingdom. There are corporate elements of that; God is building His church for a glorious purpose. But there are individual elements as well. Deep within your soul, His Spirit has rebirthed you. He is growing you to maturity, and you are being shaped into His image. One day, you will look just like Him. It's inevitable.

That's going to happen whether we're aware of the process or not, but what a blessing to be aware of it! Examine what He's doing deep within you, and participate in it wholeheartedly. It's what you were made for.

> The resurrection is a unique manifestation
> within this world of the transition God makes for
> us out of this way of being into another.
> —AUSTIN FARRER

A Permanent Support

Therefore, my dear brothers, stand
firm. Let nothing move you.
1 CORINTHIANS 15:58

In Word

Our lives are grounded in eternity. That realization made the early church bold and adventurous. It kept them from cowering at the hands of the Romans and the roar of the lions. It kept them from running from Pharisaical zealots and savage stonings. It motivated Paul, who had been dragged out of one city and left for dead, to get back up and walk into the same city with a powerful message (Acts 14:8-20). It inspired Stephen to proclaim the risen Jesus with his dying breath (Acts 7:56). It made the church an in-your-face contradiction to the reigning culture.

Oh, for such boldness today. The power of eternity will not make us aggressively offensive, as some misguided Christians become, but it will cause us to be unmoved in the face of the world's fickle opinions. It will give us perspective.

Think about the influence of an eternal perspective. It won't let us write off relationships as insignificant; they have "forever" implications. It won't let us be indifferent to our responsibilities; we will be accountable in judgment. It won't let us interpret our trials as defeats; they never last as long as our lives do. It won't let us spend our resources of time, money, and talents frivolously; they are opportunities for everlasting investments. And, perhaps most profoundly, it won't let us live in fear of death; the wages of sin have been dealt with, and we have nothing to fear when this body wastes away. We are more secure than the mountains and the seas. Our feet are planted on imperishable ground.

In Deed

Knowing that we are grounded in eternity—really knowing it deep down inside—will transform a neurotic, fearful soul into a powerful, courageous servant of the most high King. It will drive us to live our adventures with meaning and purpose.

Learn to live with the perspective of eternity. Be faithful in this world, but crave the day this temporal dwelling is shed for heavenly glory. That craving ought to shape everything we do. The power of an eternal perspective changes lives—beginning with our own.

Christ has turned all our sunsets into dawns.
—CLEMENT OF ALEXANDRIA

An Urgent Message

The last enemy to be destroyed is death.
1 CORINTHIANS 15:26

In Word

Our world is dying. Many of its citizens know that; others live under wild illusions. The existentialists of past ages, for all their hopelessness, at least got one thing right: If God isn't real, life is pointless. You live and you die. And no one, in the long run, remembers you.

That's the hopelessness that shapes a lot of societies today. Cultures cut loose from spiritual absolutes are drifting aimlessly, pointlessly toward death and meaninglessness. The world's citizens try to make the best of it, much like the band on the Titanic that kept playing even as the ship began to sink. Those who do not know Christ invest their lives in pleasure, relationships, work, status, possessions, and a host of other things, none of which lasts. But they give the illusion of meaning, and sometimes illusions are better than nothing. At least in the minds of those who hold them.

But Christianity offers a Kingdom without illusions. We have meaning, purpose, truth, and an ultimately worthwhile Person to point to. Our world clutches its deceptive trinkets—false philosophies and pursuits—because it's afraid to own up to the sin that separated us from the Creator. But owning up leads to immense blessing, and we're the only ones who can point the way. The world needs the knowledge of the Resurrection more than it knows.

In Deed

That's why Jesus commissioned His disciples to go into the world and be witnesses. Witnesses of what? Of a once-dead Savior standing before them with holes in His hands and a promise in His mouth. That alone—that above every word this world has ever uttered—is the meaning to life.

You have a holy purpose. By accepting the risen Savior, you accepted the risen Savior's mission. Perhaps you did not know that at the time, but now you do. A desperate, blind world waits for truth. Be a witness of the Resurrection, which pulls us from this sinking ship into the regenesis. The world needs that knowledge. It is dying without it.

> Jesus' resurrection makes it impossible for man's story to end in chaos.
> —CARLO CARRETTO

Intimate Union

Since we live by the Spirit, let us keep in step with the Spirit.
GALATIANS 5:25

In Word

For centuries, God's people watched the Spirit work. They saw the Spirit lead through the wilderness, inspire the prophets, fill the Temple, and empower the kings. Still, He was a phenomenon, not a way of life. No, the prescribed way of life was the law of Moses. And though the law was good and complete in itself, it never provided a complete relationship.

That changed after Jesus ascended. The law that was written on stone tablets became the law that was written on hearts. And the Writer was more than an abstract principle; He was God Himself, the Spirit from eternity past, the very Breath of the Almighty. Just as God exhaled into the first Adam, He breathed Himself into those who have faith in the second Adam—Jesus. Flesh once made from dust and destined to return to dust became a holy habitation; God came to live in very human, very earthen vessels. The Temple of stone became a temple of flesh—organic, dynamic flesh.

Jesus is the prototype, of course. He was the very definition of the temple of God on earth. But after His ascension, what temple was left? The one on Mount Zion, with its tattered veil and its spiritually blind guardians? No, not good enough. God had ordained a better dwelling: us.

In Deed

We had no idea that all past tabernacles and temples were pictures of Jesus and blueprints for the human heart, did we? Both nervous and infatuated, we once wondered if the God of our dreams would pay us any attention, only to find that He now approaches us in an intimate union beyond anything human flesh has ever experienced. It's the greatest romance the world has ever known.

The question for us today is whether we're even aware of the intimacy. Has the marriage grown comfortable—maybe even distant? If so, go back to the beginning. It's astounding that God dwells within. Rekindle the flame, and let Him burn.

Breathe on me, Breath of God.
—EDWIN HATCH

Destined Lovers

If you are led by the Spirit, you are not under law.
GALATIANS 5:18

In Word

Our Bridegroom was never after a slavishly obedient bride to begin with. Sure, He loves it when His people conform to His standards, but no groom with even an ounce of passion wants a cold, calculated servant for a bride. No, God's purpose from the very beginning was a people for Himself—who lived, breathed, and loved in sync with Him. He wanted hearts that beat His rhythms, companions with whom to share His secrets and His deep longings. Rules never accomplish that; only freely given love and intimacy do.

That's why the law of Moses is not at the end of the Bible. It's a start, a lesson in the futility of human sin. It existed, according to Paul, to lead us to Christ (Galatians 3:24). It saved no one; it only showed us our need for a Savior.

The fulfillment of the plan, the early Christians realized, was the staggering truth that God made us not to know Him through obedience, but to obey through knowing Him. The romantic embrace from our holy Suitor comes first; then our character can be transformed to look like Him. And the evidence of the romantic embrace came in Acts 2, as the wind blew and the fire fell. The Holy Spirit claimed His true love. We will never be the same.

In Deed

It's a genuine shame that many Christians have turned this holy intimacy back into religion. Perhaps it's too close, too personal. Religion is easier; it keeps God at arm's length. But if God were satisfied with arm's length, Jesus never would have died and the Holy Spirit never would have descended. He made us to crave intimate union, and then He offered Himself for the craving. Religion isn't enough. An exhilarating, thriving marriage is.

If that's not your experience with God, something needs to change. Draw close to Him in complete trust and desperate love, and He will draw close to you in holy passion. This union is your fulfillment, planned from eternity past. Embrace it by letting His Spirit embrace you.

> What else are the laws of God written in our hearts but the very presence of the Holy Ghost?
>
> —AUGUSTINE

The Deeper Passion

*Live by the Spirit, and you will not gratify
the desires of the sinful nature.*
GALATIANS 5:16

In Word

You will follow your passions. Yes, there may be times when you compel yourself to
say, "Not my will but Thine," but the sustaining drive of your life will be somewhat in
line with the deepest loves you treasure. So when the Bible tells us to live by the Spirit
and not by the desires of the sinful nature, it is also implying an important relationship
issue: our love for the Spirit must run deeper than our love for the world.

The contrast really is that simple. We have a constant choice: whether we are
going to be in love with God or with the world, the flesh, or the sins we once held dear.
That should be an easy choice—after all, God is far more worthy than any other—
but our other suitors know just how to dazzle us with empty words and false promises. Sometimes we're far too easy prey. And when we are, we gratify the desires of
the sinful nature, just as Paul warns. We do so not because we have evil intent, but
because we've misdirected our love. We've let the intimacy with the Spirit grow cold
and turned our eyes in other directions.

Turn back. The blessing of living by the Spirit—basking in His love and returning
His embrace—is far greater than anything the sinful nature can deliver.

In Deed

You may have thought of your life as a series of moral choices, some pleasing to God,
others not. While that's true—there are moral choices that God has very strong opinions about—that's not to be our focus. Our focus is not to be on banishing sin from
our lives but on falling deeply, passionately in love with the One who redeemed us
and has made a home with us. If we get that right, the sinful nature doesn't stand a
chance.

Cultivate love. Develop your relationship with the Spirit. Spend time with Him,
praise Him, ask Him to have His way with you. The closer you get to Him, the further
from sin you will be.

> Being changed and sweetly breathed upon
> by the Spirit of God, the will desires and acts
> not from compulsion, but responsively.
> —MARTIN LUTHER

Love Shows

*The fruit of the Spirit is love, joy, peace, patience, kindness,
goodness, faithfulness, gentleness and self-control.*
GALATIANS 5:22-23

In Word

The Spirit lives within us, but He has an external agenda. From the warm fire of fellowship in our hearts, He expects to shine. The description in Galatians 5:22-23 about the fruit of the Spirit is not about productivity. It's about character. Furthermore, it's not simply about attitudes; it's about Him.

Have you noticed that? These are not traits to cultivate. This is not a description of what we are supposed to look like, per se. This is a description of what He already does look like. The fruit of the Spirit is supposed to come forth from us because the Spirit comes forth from us. The New Testament is not a covenant to reform fallen flesh; it's a covenant to plant the life of God in His people. Paul didn't mean to provide us a to-do list here. This verse is not about who we strive to be, but about who we display.

That's why when we ask God to help us with patience, joy, self-control, or any other fruit, we're a little off base. He doesn't mind so much; He applauds the desire. But He would prefer that we not partition His Spirit into distinguishable traits to acquire. His desire is that His life in us be visible. When we ask, we simply need to ask that He magnify Himself in us and help us to take a backseat to His leadership. He doesn't want us to focus on our improving character, but on His constant virtue.

In Deed

Scripture provides this list of fruit, not so much so we can check off the areas in which we need improvement, but primarily to indicate whether our fellowship with the Spirit is as deep as it ought to be. If we find ourselves lacking in love, for example, we need not seek more love. We should rather seek more closeness to the Spirit of love. Our insufficiencies should never lead us in search of more fruit, but in search of the fruitful One. In His arms, under His leadership, and given over to His influence, the fruit will come.

> When we allow the love of God to move in us, we
> can no longer distinguish between ours and His.
> —AUSTIN FARRER

What the World Needs Now

*The acts of the sinful nature are obvious . . . those who
live like this will not inherit the kingdom of God.*
GALATIANS 5:19, 21

In Word

Galatians 5:19-21 contains a frightening list of sinfulness; it's even more frightening when we realize that it describes our natural selves, at least in spirit if not in behavior. We have all been participants in fallen humanity at its ugliest and can only bear good fruit by having a fruitful Spirit within us. The tragedy for our world, however, is that the list of sinfulness still describes us today. Fallenness is the natural state of unredeemed humanity, which drives the world we live in.

That's why the list of the fruit of the Spirit in Galatians 5:22-23 is so remarkable. It's countercultural. The early Christians who discovered this amazing presence of God within them were separated further and further from the corruption around them. They became a pariah to some, a witness to others. Either way, they were a statement that fallen flesh doesn't have to reign. There is an incredibly worthwhile alternative.

That's the role we play. That's what Jesus meant when He told His disciples they were lights in the world and the salt of the earth. Though the fruits of the Spirit do in fact make us a pariah to some and a witness to others, in both cases we are a statement that fallen flesh doesn't have to rule. Our culture can do with that knowledge whatever it wants: love us, hate us, try to explain us. Regardless, it needs to know: life in the Spirit of God is an alternative.

In Deed

Displaying the Spirit is one of our primary functions in this world. Our job is to get self out of the way and let Him shine. Why? Because a dying world needs to know that its corruptions are not the norm. Our friends and relatives need to see that the ways of the world are not the ways of God. The status quo of the human rebellion simply must be challenged.

If you needed a mission in life, this is it: to be countercultural to the world, to be the evidence of your holy Companion, and to display a love the world needs to see.

There is not a better evangelist in the
world than the Holy Spirit.
—D. L. MOODY

The Intrusive God

They were filled with jealousy and talked
abusively against what Paul was saying.
ACTS 13:45

In Word

For years, Israel had heard the stories: God bringing His people out of Egypt, guiding them to the land of promise, pruning the nation through kings and prophets, disciplining them for rebellion, and lavishing upon them promises of restoration in the last days. And what promises! These were no modest hopes, not by any means. They were predictions of ultimate fulfillment and of eternal peace and prosperity. Israel, it surely seemed, would be magnificently blessed.

That's the context that Jesus' ascent and the Holy Spirit's descent burst into. The amazing things God was doing were clear indications that the fulfillment of promises past had come. The prophets were being proven right. The Kingdom was arriving in its glory.

The problem was that the Kingdom didn't look like the kingdom many people expected. Some marveled at the intricate, awesome plan of God, but others preferred the status quo. They rejected the message of Paul and Barnabas at Antioch, as elsewhere, because their personal world was too well constructed to be modified, even by the Almighty. It's a curious phenomenon of strictly religious folks: God can be honored in the past and hoped for in the future, but He can never, never be allowed to intrude in the present.

In Deed

It's a tragic shame when the status quo is more relevant to us than the work of God, but that's often the case. We get complacent, and as much as we complain about our circumstances and hope for better, we just can't handle the surprising intrusions of our God.

But we must. His intrusions are fulfillment of promises past and the purpose we seek. We should always open up to His plan, whether it fits our expectations or not. We serve a God who loves surprises. He surprised first-century Jews with the Messiah and the Spirit, He surprised the early church with miracles and missions, and He will surprise us with the blessings we crave today. When you least expect Him, expect Him.

We block Christ's advance in our lives
by failure of expectation.
—WILLIAM TEMPLE

The Faithful God

What God promised our fathers he has fulfilled for us.
ACTS 13:32-33

In Word

Paul's sermon in Antioch, recorded in Acts 13, was compelling. Many Jews were intrigued by it, and many Gentiles rejoiced over it. It shows God's work throughout the ages, unifying a strange, varied history under one overarching purpose: salvation through Messiah Jesus.

For us, Paul's sermon is like an aerial photo taken at thirty thousand feet. It shows the whole landscape, including the glorious peaks of salvation. Even more than that, it demonstrates the abiding faithfulness of God—from the choosing of Abraham to the resurrection of the Savior. Every step of the way, this God has watched over His people, cultivated their loyalties, purged their rebellions and sins, and secured their redemption. God had invested centuries in His plan. He never abandoned it or even diverged from it. He had a remedy for the Fall from day one. And when the Holy Spirit had come, believers knew just how perfect the remedy was.

In Deed

That should be profoundly comforting to those of us who wonder if God is still with us. Not that we doubt His faithfulness in principle, of course. No, our doubts are more subtle. We wonder if He is faithful to us right now, in our current circumstances—in our nation, in our families, in the details of our daily lives. We know He would never abandon His plan for the world, but we suspect He might abandon His plan for us. We appreciate the view from thirty thousand feet, but we really want Him at ground zero in our lives.

God's story in the Bible is not simply told for the sake of Israel or the church. It is told in order to reveal His character. And one undeniable observation from the story in Scripture is that God is faithful, both in master plans and individual lives. Always has been, always will be. Remember that when you doubt. There has been a remedy from day one, and it is perfect.

> Be still my soul, the Lord is on thy side.
> —KATHARINA VON SCHLEGEL

The God of Promise

He has fulfilled for us. . . . As it is written.
ACTS 13:33

In Word

Fulfillment. Everyone wants it; no one claims to have obtained it. The desire is written deep within our hearts, and it drives us all our lives. Underlying all the things we do, all the decisions we make, is this craving to be whole—fully satisfied and at peace. We want to be complete.

There's a significant answer for us in the writings of the early church. Over and over again, the apostles' letters point to Jesus as the fulfillment of the Scriptures. From Peter's first sermon on Pentecost to the voices of angels in Revelation, the gospel is described as the completion of all God had ordained. Jesus rose "according to the Scriptures." The Kingdom is coming because "it is written" that it would. Nearly every aspect of the new creation is identified with some inscription penned centuries before. Why? Because, as Jesus had once said, "The Scripture cannot be broken" (John 10:35).

What's the connection between the prophecies of Scripture and our craving for fulfillment? Simply that God has demonstrated Himself trustworthy. If He spoke it, it will happen. That means that when the Bible says that no one can comprehend what God has planned for us, it's true. When it says that we will be raised into everlasting glory, it's true. When it says that all things work together for the good of those who love Him, or that we can legitimately rejoice in all things, it's true. Whatever Scripture has promised you, it cannot be undone. The Word is inviolable.

In Deed

There's a close connection between the fulfillment of the prophecies about Jesus and the fulfillment of the promises given to you. If God has been reliable in one—and the witness of the apostles is that He most certainly has—then He will be reliable in the other. It's inconceivable that God would promise His people, both collectively and individually, His fulfillment and then not deliver it. When His Word speaks, it speaks truth. The God who has relentlessly pursued His plan for Israel and the church will relentlessly pursue His plan for you.

> Every promise God has ever made
> finds its fulfillment in Jesus.
> —JONI EARECKSON TADA

The Confidence of the Believer

They were glad and honored the word of the Lord.
ACTS 13:48

In Word

Knowing that God's plan is inviolable is not only incredibly comforting, it's also the ultimate source of confidence. There is nothing accidental about our salvation, and there's nothing accidental about the way God is working it out in our lives. The zeal of the Lord accomplished God's plan for the ages, and His Spirit applies it individually. We are His because He claimed us for Himself.

That means that we stand on very solid ground. We don't have to live in fear and doubt, anxiously wondering whether we're walking in His will. We don't need to stress over every little setback, hoping it didn't get us off His perfect path. The sovereign God of all history is the sovereign God of our day—today. Knowing that means the difference between insecurity and godly confidence.

Think about that. The God who promised Abraham many descendants—and delivered—is the God who promises you ultimate meaning in your life. The God who promised David an everlasting Kingdom has promised you an inheritance in it. The God who promised to raise Jesus from the dead promised to raise you from the dead. His track record is impeccable and inspiring. His sovereignty has never let anyone down, and we can be assured we won't be the first.

In Deed

Do you live in such confidence, or are you insecure with God? Deliberate sin may have set you in the latter frame of mind, but even that, after repentance and restoration, is redeemed by God for His purposes. The overwhelming testimony of Scripture is that we who believe in the gospel are in sync with God's underlying design for history, and that we are safely guided by the same hand that guided Abraham, Isaac, Jacob, Joseph, David, Isaiah, Daniel, Paul, and especially Jesus.

If you live a nervous life, relax. God's faithfulness applies to His Word, and it applies to you. His plan for the ages is yours. Rest in it always.

> We must make [God's promises] ours by
> embracing them in our hearts.
> —JOHN CALVIN

The Direction of History

The word of the Lord spread through the whole region.
ACTS 13:49

In Word

The world doesn't understand the direction of history. Many cultures believe we live in cycles, repeating history over and over again. Others have embraced randomness, thinking that we wander aimlessly through this universe, from one ignorant generation of evolution to the next. The Bible is believed by many cultural historians to be the first record of a people who believed history was moving in one direction and had a point. We know the reason for that, of course: the Bible was inspired by a God with a plan.

It's a remarkable testimony: fulfilled prophecies, consistent themes over multiple writers and vastly different centuries, and a Messiah who unifies the Word from beginning to end. It's unique in the world of religious literature, and we're unique in the world of religious consciousness. We see history as purposeful and meaningful, and we refuse to drift through life. A world that has given up hope needs to see that as often as it can.

Just as the early church preached that it was the fulfillment of God's plan, the church of our generation needs to preach the same. We alone can provide order to random cultures and absolutes to relative societies. We alone have been entrusted with the truth of the ages, as Paul preached in Athens (Acts 17). We alone are commissioned to point to judgment as a coming reality. Our God has called us to be participants in His plan, and His plan involves reaching an aimless world. We who know the target of history have a holy responsibility to point to it.

In Deed

The remarkable sense of fulfillment felt by the early church needs to be ours as well. Our Savior, the Bible tells us, is the apex of history, and His Cross stands as the central event. We are assured that every knee will eventually bow to Him, and every tongue— even the most blasphemous—will eventually confess Him as Lord. Our world hungers for the purpose we've realized, and there's only one appropriate response for us: feed them.

The only possible answer to the destiny of man is to seek to fulfill God's purpose.
—PAUL TOURNIER

Amazing Grace

As for you, you were dead in your transgressions and sins.
EPHESIANS 2:1

In Word

There's scarcely a better summary of the plan of salvation than Ephesians 2:1-10. Not only is it the spiritual history of mankind, it's also ours individually. We were dead in our sins—thoroughly dead—and God rescued us. We were, as Paul tells us, without hope in this world (Ephesians 2:12), completely helpless and unaware of the way out of our condition.

And what a dreadful condition it was. Paul's assessment of the human condition is nothing like the "I'm okay, you're okay" philosophies of our culture's gospel of tolerance. In fact, he's terribly blunt in his political incorrectness: we were compatible with the spirits of disobedience, living in our lusts and deserving of God's wrath. We were destined for judgment if God had not intervened. We may not like to admit that, and we may shudder at the harshness of the idea, but we cannot deny that this is a soundly biblical assessment. Humanity, in its rebellion, was completely, utterly lost.

This was the gradual realization of the early Christians. In light of the Cross, the human condition could not be sugarcoated. One does not observe the agony of Jesus, interpret it as a payment for sin, and then minimize the sin. If a bloody, beaten Savior hanging from a crude, splintery stake is a picture of judgment, the sin under judgment must have been enormous, catastrophic, and deadly.

In Deed

Why is that important to know? Because we don't understand grace until we understand sin. Most early Christians had been content to follow Jewish law or Greco-Roman deities, not knowing their desperate condition. But the Cross was not only a statement of God's great mercy; it was also a statement of how much that mercy was needed.

The Christian who remembers the dreadful nature of sin is the Christian who understands the magnitude of grace. Only then are we equipped to live, breathe, and share the gospel of salvation. Meditate on your salvation, and let the mercy of God sink in.

> The grace of God does not find men fit
> for salvation, but makes them so.
> —AUGUSTINE

Forever Mercy

It is by grace you have been saved, through faith.
EPHESIANS 2:8

In Word

The first Christians could hardly get their minds around the gospel of grace. We have trouble with it ourselves, but at least we've had centuries of preaching and theology to lay it out for us. Not so in first-century Ephesus, or anywhere else the gospel was taught. That's why Paul spent so much time in many of his letters explaining that mercy was God's way from the beginning. In the relationship between God and people, grace has always been the key.

Think about it: God could rightly have taken Adam's and Eve's lives on the day of the first rebellion or flooded the world without saving Noah's family. He could have never called Abraham, never rescued Israel from Egypt, never established David's kingdom, and never promised a Messiah. He could have let the law render judgment on our stubborn ways, never hanging His Son as a sacrifice. The wages of sin was death, even from the beginning. Yet God let us live.

When that realization dawned on the first Christians—that our sin was so bad that it deserved the judgment so nauseatingly visible on the cross—it became the unquenchable inspiration of martyrs and missionaries. Christians were so convinced of the advent of the Kingdom of God that they counted their lives in the kingdom of this world as a temporary bother. Many in the early church saw the magnificent grace of the gospel and abandoned all self-righteousness, self-dependence, and self-will. Nothing else mattered.

In Deed

That's the will of God for all of us. The grace that underlies our salvation is humbling and precious. It is the way God has always operated with His people, in every age. Grace through faith saves. Nothing else ever has.

If grace has always been God's modus operandi with His people, and we are His representatives on this earth, what does that say about our attitude toward others? It should be gracious. Always. Nothing else reflects His character like a heart of mercy.

> The grace of God is infinite and eternal. As it had no beginning, so it can have no end.
> —A. W. TOZER

Deep Foundations

*God, who is rich in mercy, made us alive with Christ
even when we were dead in transgressions.*
EPHESIANS 2:4-5

In Word

Understanding God's love and mercy is the foundation of the Christian life. If we don't have that down, we aren't going to get the rest of it right. Even so, this love and mercy are often the things we distort most easily. We simply can't believe God would love us so much, because we know we're not worthy of such love. And yet that's what mercy is all about—undeserved love. We find that the most critical truth of Christianity is the hardest to sink in.

Why do we have such a hard time basing our lives on absolute mercy? Because it's foreign to us; we don't operate that way. We don't forgive people easily while they are still in a state of hostility toward us. We don't make the first move to extend grace; we wait for an apology or a sign of regret. We don't love our enemies and go out of our way to embrace strangers. We don't cut people much slack.

But we serve a God who has done all of that. Not only did He cut us a lot of slack, He made us sons and daughters, heirs of His eternal wealth. We struggle to accept such lavish love because we've never seen it before. It's simply amazing.

In Deed

If we do let His mercy sink in, however—if we ever can let it be the unshakable foundation of our lives—it has incredible power to transform us. It makes us secure enough to extend love to offensive people, it keeps us from the tendency to act out of guilt, and it connects us with the heart of the God who is really there, not the God we think we imagine.

Do not try to build a Christian life on anything but this. Every motivation, every impulse, every attitude ought to spring from an awareness that we are irrevocably loved and forgiven by a magnanimous, merciful God. That foundation is the only one that can calm our fears, relieve our worries, and allow us to live life in perfect joy and peace.

Grace is God Himself: His loving energy at work
within His church and within our souls.
—EVELYN UNDERHILL

Powerful Prayers

*God raised us up with Christ and seated us
with him in the heavenly realms.*
EPHESIANS 2:6

In Word

Salvation is more than forgiveness from sin and an escape from hell. God didn't just save us in His mercy from the wages of sin; He also saved us into a privileged position in His Kingdom. From before the foundation of the world, God planned creatures who could be intimate with Him forever. He has saved us so we can think His thoughts, understand His heart, and know His plan. More than that, He has seated us with Jesus in awesome authority. We will reign with Him forever.

That would be considered shamefully egocentric if it were not a solidly biblical theme, but it's true. As coheirs with Jesus of all God's Kingdom, we are brought into His reign specifically to administer His plan. That's why Jesus gave His disciples authority to bind and loose on earth what was bound and loosed in heaven. That's why He made such magnificent promises regarding our prayers. That's why He called us "friends" (John 15:15).

Think of what that means for your prayer life. If prayer is just a hit-or-miss attempt to discover God's will, it won't be very appealing. But if it's an opportunity to enforce His reign on earth and to declare His Kingdom's opposition to all evils and injustices, then it's a profoundly moving activity. Our prayers can bear eternal fruit and influence. It's the single most important activity we can do in the Kingdom of God.

In Deed

We need to learn to see ourselves as vital links between heaven and earth, following the calling and command of Jesus, our great High Priest. We have a critical role to play in the Kingdom of God, far more critical than we ever thought. Our relationships, our money, our time, our talents, and all of our work can be leveraged for the eternal Kingdom. And the vital activity that undergirds all our other investments is the kind of prayer that claims Kingdom ground in hostile places. Pray as though the Kingdom will be shaped by your prayers; Jesus promises that it will.

> You know the value of prayer; it is precious
> beyond all price. Never, never neglect it.
> —THOMAS BUXTON

Eternal Evidence

We are God's workmanship, created in
Christ Jesus to do good works.
EPHESIANS 2:10

In Word

Trophies of His grace. Testimonies of His goodness. Examples of His workmanship. These are the implications of Ephesians 2:10. We were created for good works, not simply for the sake of good works, but as evidence of God's master craftsmanship. Salvation reaches us in the depths of our hearts, but it has a very external result. We are to do God's work.

In a sense, those who believe in Jesus and are being transformed into His likeness are exhibit A in the case for His mercy. We are sent into the world to be like Him, to look like Him, and to think like Him. What makes that an astounding mission is the remembrance of where we came from: death, rebellion, wrath (vv. 1-3). We are the most unlikely ambassadors for this King, and as such, are best qualified to demonstrate His power. If He saved us, He can save anyone. If His mercy extended to the likes of dead rebels, it can extend anywhere. He displayed His workmanship in us because we were His greatest challenge. Saved from anarchy to the divine government, from the gutter to the throne, and from death to life makes us the ultimate rags-to-riches story. And good stories always say something profound about the main character.

In Deed

We often live as though our salvation were primarily about us, but we forget. First and foremost, our salvation is about Him. We are His workmanship because He wants to display His artistry in the galleries of heaven and earth. We have a holy calling: to walk in the works He has prepared for us.

Live with a sense of sacredness. The ultimate rags-to-riches story is being told in each of our lives every day that we live. It is a universal testimony for all who live, both seen and unseen. Salvation has an ultimate purpose that is much, much higher than our own welfare. It is a magnificent statement about the mercy, power, wisdom, and love of our God. Make that statement well as you walk in this world.

> Do all the good you can, by all the means you can, in all
> the ways you can, to all the people you can, in all the
> places you can, as long as you can.
> —JOHN WESLEY

Redemption's Promise

*Our present sufferings are not worth comparing
with the glory that will be revealed in us.*
ROMANS 8:18

In Word

The amazing turn of events in the New Testament—the re-creation with all its promises—authenticates a prominent biblical theme: The suffering of this age will give
way to the glory of the next. That was true for any Israelite held captive in Egypt, for
every Jew under judgment in Babylon, for each prophet martyred for God's word,
and for every Christian persecuted for the faith. The human story will not end in its
current tragic state. How do we know? Because God became human flesh and willingly suffered, affirming the promise of glory. He validated the pattern: futility now,
fullness and joy later.

His incarnation not only affirmed the pattern, it secured the promise. If Jesus
endured the Cross for the joy set before Him (Hebrews 12:2), we can endure our
crosses while maintaining the same hope. We can be content in this painful world
because we know the story doesn't end here. The Redeemer has a plan for our suffering: He will turn it to glory.

That's the overwhelming message of the Bible from beginning to end. Though
we live in a creation that groans for redemption, we know we will not live in futility
forever. The God who began it all, knowing ahead of time that sin would come and
pain would torment humanity, had a plan before the foundation of the world. For
those who trust His rescue plan, He would leverage every trial for good. And in the
process, suffering would shape the hearts of those who appreciate His glory and look
forward to His Kingdom. None of it is wasted. In other words, redemption is real.

In Deed

At a practical level, that means the hardships you endure today are pointing toward a
purpose. They will give Him occasion to demonstrate Himself, and they will give you
occasion to demonstrate your faith. Both occasions lead to a glory that far outweighs
the pain. In the end, it will all be worth it. The God who endured the Cross gives you
His guarantee.

> Anxiety, sickness, suffering, or danger . . . these
> are nothing when compared with the glory
> that will be revealed in, and for, us.
> —DAVID LIVINGSTONE

Redemption's Pain

*The creation was subjected to frustration . . . in hope
that [it] will be liberated from its bondage to decay.*
ROMANS 8:20-21

In Word

It's hard to imagine a God of love purposely frustrating His creation, but that's what He did. If He hadn't, sin would have seemed to have paid off. We would have continued in our rebellion, certain that the serpent was right: sin isn't a big deal. The wages of sin would have been life and peace and prosperity. Or at least not costly enough to hinder our life and peace and prosperity. So God subjected us to futility and frustration—in His mercy.

From God's point of view, the only way to bring a treasonous, hardened creation back to Himself was to ensure that the wages of sin were not worth the trouble. All of the pain the world has ever known exists to demonstrate a point: creation cannot exist apart from the Creator. We need His sustaining power, His forgiving love, and His expert wisdom. If God had not subjected us to futility, we would have found it quite easy to ignore Him. And since the whole purpose of creation was to love Him, not to ignore Him, we needed to know: a divide between God and His people is devastating.

In Deed

Have you ever thought of your troubles that way—as part of the fabric of this world because God loves you enough to let you suffer? That He cannot let you be content without Him, because then you would be . . . well, content without Him? Like it or not, your pain exists to drive you to the Healer, the Forgiver, the Redeemer. It has to be that way.

That means that when we read the headlines—those excruciating reports of the world's tragedies—we can be assured that God has willingly allowed them. We can't blame Him for evil, of course. He doesn't author it. He simply lets the world go its own way so that it will eventually have enough sense to come back to Him.

Remember that when you read of suffering or even when you experience it yourself. Let the futility of this world drive you toward a God who redeems all futility. There's glory in store for those who do.

> The strangest truth of the gospel is that
> redemption comes through suffering.
> —MILO CHAPMAN

Redemption's Inheritance

*We ourselves, who have the firstfruits of the Spirit, groan
inwardly as we wait eagerly for our adoption as sons.*
ROMANS 8:23

In Word

We groan within ourselves because we know—we have always known, from our earliest days—that something is dreadfully wrong. We have dreams of things working out, of peace in our hearts and favor in our circumstances, of that elusive condition known as the "shalom" of God—His peace. That kind of fullness and completeness is written on our hearts, something placed there by the God who made us in His image. From hard experience over the years, we know it isn't fulfilled in a world like this, but that doesn't keep us from dreaming about it. We groan because we have eager expectations. We always have.

The Christians of the first century slowly realized that this was what redemption was all about. The shalom of God was a coming reality, hinted at in miracles and in the unity of fellowship. The Spirit clearly pointed to a purpose for this seemingly futile creation. Those who believed in the Redeemer by faith would be adopted by Him as sons and daughters. The spiritual orphans of this world would be adopted by the most loving Father of all. Shalom was on its way.

In Deed

One of the marvels of the new creation is that God redeemed His people not only collectively—those who trusted the Messiah by faith, whether of ethnic Israel or not—but also individually. He isn't building an earthly kingdom of princes and governors, but a heavenly Kingdom of prophets and priests. The redemption secured by the Messiah gives everyone the opportunity to live in God's household, where shalom is room temperature and fulfillment is inescapable. For that kind of promise we groan.

Yes, life in this world is hard. But sons and daughters inherit a father's estate, and the estate of our Father is incomparably extravagant. The futility of your life is temporary. The glory of His is not. Always let the glory loom larger.

Earth has no sorrow that heaven cannot heal.
—THOMAS V. MOORE

Redemption's Hope

*If we hope for what we do not yet
have, we wait for it patiently.*
ROMANS 8:25

In Word

Hope seems so abstract. The English language is partly at fault for that. We use the word hope casually, from dreams about our future to long shots on our Christmas lists. We hope for rain or sunshine, for a raise, for good health, for good luck, or for anything our heart can set its fickle desires on. But biblical hope is not so abstract. It expresses future certainty. In the Bible, hope is placed in things that are guaranteed but simply have not happened yet. It's the reality that is to come.

Since that's the case, we don't persevere because we "hope" God might work things out for good one day in the future, if we're lucky. We persevere because He has made a promise, and His promises cannot be broken. If God has sacrificed His Son on a cross and then given us His Spirit as a pledge of future glory, the future glory is concrete reality. The only difference between God's past miracles and His future promises is timing, not truth. One is just as real as the other. The word of a gentleman is his honor; the Word of our God is the Word of the ultimate gentleman.

In Deed

Have you thought of hope working its way out in your life that way? It must. It can't be just an internal wish list, a dream that you entertain when you're feeling optimistic—not if it's biblical. The truth is that God has left you in this painful world for a time, but He has also given you future certainties to look forward to. The future certainties are everlasting, while the pain is temporary. This fact should shape your reaction to every trial you face.

The Bible urges you to persevere because God knows you will face trials and hardships in many areas of life. But He would not let you base your perseverance on an abstract optimism. He tells you to base it on the reality of His Kingdom. In light of that Kingdom, perseverance becomes a lot easier than you ever thought possible.

Waiting patiently in expectation is the
foundation of spiritual life.
—SIMONE WEIL

Redemption's Witnesses

*The creation waits in eager expectation for
the sons of God to be revealed.*
ROMANS 8:19

In Word

There's a split personality in this creation: people want to know truth, but they don't like the truth God has revealed. So philosophers speculate, people hunger for meaning, and the people of God wonder if the Lord will ever settle the issue for them. Romans 8:19 assures us that He will.

For now, we are reluctant to be displayed as His children. After all, the church has been persecuted throughout the ages for claiming a divine connection. The idea that God might be working in this world to upset the status quo is disarming to many, and they lash out when we proclaim His plan. So the church frequently steps out of the limelight and into the shadows. Human nature urges us to save our skins.

But God continually nudges His people back into the light. It hurts when He exposes His people to persecution, but it's a revelation with a purpose. Despite its anti-God agenda, a rebellious world deeply skeptical of faith still hungers to know if anyone has really found Him. When Christians endure the pain while maintaining the Father's character, God is honored. The revelation of His children has served a purpose.

In Deed

The current stage is not the final revelation. This exposure as God's children is a glimpse of future redemption, not its final demonstration. But one day, the revelation will be complete, irrefutable, and impossible to persecute. The children of God will be visible in His glory, and all the tongues newly confessing Jesus as Lord will have to recognize those who already have.

Meanwhile, we are to avoid our tendency to withdraw from the stage and let, instead, God reveal us as His children. The world may dread the implications of really knowing God, but we are still called to demonstrate Him. Until He reveals Himself completely, we of the new creation are the clearest revelation of Him that the world will be able to see.

> The world is far more ready to receive the gospel than Christians are to hand it out.
> —GEORGE W. PETERS

A Grateful Heart

Be thankful.

COLOSSIANS 3:15

In Word

The revelation of the new creation of grace, replete with the promise of a resurrection, prompted a huge question among early Christians: what is left to do? Perhaps there were several answers to that question, but there was one overriding response: be thankful.

That should be easy enough, but we amazingly miss both the pleasure and the purpose of gratitude. We get hung up on the details of life, on the worries and fears that plague us, and on the complications of relationships. We forget the main thing—in Jesus, God has saved us ultimately from everything, and it's all received by grace through faith. There's nothing we can do to earn it, no obligation to fulfill. It's a gift, and it's comprehensive. Thankfulness ought to be easy.

There's only one way to maintain a grateful heart, and that's to meditate on all the reasons we should be grateful. When we remind ourselves of the abundance of riches God has lavished on us, the incomprehensible measure of grace that covered all our sin, the excruciating price He paid to redeem us, and the extravagant promises of future glory, gratitude is a natural response from our hearts. The new covenant is radical in its mercies, mind-boggling in its wisdom, and overwhelming in its power. Thankfulness flows from awareness of such things.

In Deed

Measure the level of gratitude in your heart. It's easy to see; if bitterness and complaining are commonplace within you, gratitude isn't. It's time to cultivate a spirit of thankfulness.

If you need to cultivate an appreciation for what God has done—an appreciation that extends beyond the borders of your circumstances, no matter how difficult they are at the moment—spend some time contemplating your former lost condition. Then spend some time contemplating God's efforts to redeem you. Spend enough time trying to understand those two extremes, and you'll soon find yourself as grateful as someone who was just saved from certain death. All other concerns will pale in comparison. Gratitude will flow from your heart.

No duty is more urgent than that of returning thanks.

—AMBROSE

God's Peace

Let the peace of Christ rule in your hearts.
COLOSSIANS 3:15

In Word

No one likes to be taken for granted. That applies at all times to all people, but it especially applies to those who have made enormous sacrifices for others. So imagine how God feels when His people are restless in their hearts over their annoyances of the day or the mundane details of their lives. If peace is absent, a spirit of gratitude is lacking. And if a spirit of gratitude is lacking, so is an awareness of God's mercies. Understanding results in thankfulness, and thankfulness results in peace and rest. A disturbed heart has ignored the goodness of God.

God's desire for His children is for them to have peace in their hearts and fellowship with His Spirit. His mercies are to lead to sweet fellowship with the One from whom all mercy flows. He is not being egotistical when He commands us to be grateful; rather, He is calling us into His embrace for a time of intimate rest. The One who fashioned our hearts knows full well that when we are preoccupied with the troubles of life, we have magnified our troubles to be larger than He is. And He wants to set things right. He is larger than they are, and a heart that knows that can be at peace. It can rest in Him and give thanks. It can see life as it really is.

It's amazing that the self-sufficient God of the universe seeks love and gratitude from us, but it's true. Over and over again, the Bible pleads with us to love Him alone, serve Him alone, fellowship with Him above all others, seek His will above all others, and find our rest in Him. It calls our unsettled hearts to finally settle into His love.

In Deed

Peace in your heart is God's plan for you. Fear, worry, and discontent are not. One of the goals of the new creation, among many others, is to secure a calm, confident heart in you. Christ's command to let His peace rule within is one of the most enjoyable commands He has given. Don't disappoint Him—or shortchange yourself—by missing out on its benefits.

> Every furrow in the book of Psalms is sown
> with the seeds of thanksgiving.
>
> —JEREMY TAYLOR

The Word That Sings

Let the word of Christ dwell in you richly . . . as
you sing psalms, hymns and spiritual songs
with gratitude in your hearts to God.
COLOSSIANS 3:16

In Word

The redeemed heart of the new creation has a song in it. It doesn't matter if the possessor is naturally musical or not. The Spirit of the new birth puts a divine melody in the heart that is right with Him. The song is a song of gratitude and worship, and it always overflows. Always.

That sounds beautiful, but it's not the experience of many Christians. We get just as burdened as the unredeemed because we still live in the same world. We make the natural mistake of letting our circumstances and our fears dictate our contentment, and soon we are just as unsettled as those around us. We have forgotten a vital principle: joy comes from above and within, not outside and around.

That's why Colossians 3:16 says to let the word of Christ richly dwell within us—because within us is where joy and peace are to reside. If the Word of Christ rules within, circumstances remain without, where they can do no internal harm. If the Word of Christ does not dwell within, however, there's a vacuum in our hearts that circumstances will quickly fill. Fear and worry love seeing a void in our lives and will never leave it alone. The only way to live above them is to fill the void with something else: the Word of Christ.

In Deed

How do we let the Word of Christ dwell richly within us? We meditate on it, memorize it, sleep on it, refresh ourselves with it, crave it, and absorb it. We become consumed with truth because we're in love with the Spirit of truth. We recognize that the source of life is wisdom from above, and the Father who gives it always gives generously.

If you find yourself frequently disturbed or discontent, there's a solution. Don't let disturbances and discontent dwell within you. Replace them with something infinitely more worthwhile—and reliable. Replace them with the Word of Christ. It will put a song in your heart.

> Gratitude is born in hearts that take
> time to count up past mercies.
> —CHARLES JEFFERSON

Offering Thanks

Do it all in the name of the Lord Jesus, giving thanks.
COLOSSIANS 3:17

In Word

Hebrews 12:28 says that gratitude is an acceptable offering to God. Why? Because it acknowledges who He is better than any other attitude. It recognizes that He is a Blesser, a Giver, and a Redeemer of incomparable worth. Gratitude sees God as He is.

Gratitude especially sees God accurately when it sees Him through Jesus. After all, the Incarnation was God's plan to make Himself visible to human eyes. It was His aggressive strategy to make Himself accessible to sinners in need of salvation. Jesus is the ultimate act of God in this world.

For the early church, Jesus quickly became the identity of the believer. Paul, for example, saw himself to be crucified with Him, buried with Him, raised up with Him, exalted with Him, seated in heavenly places with Him, and united with Him forever. When someone is that identified with his Redeemer, the attitude of his heart becomes a clear statement of the Redeemer's worth. If gratitude isn't there, the Redeemer isn't worth much to that person. If we value Jesus as our identity, we will be exceedingly grateful for what He means to us.

In Deed

You may faithfully make offerings of money and time, but what are you offering God with your attitude? Is it an acceptable offering, declaring His worth accurately? Or does it underestimate His value in your life by neglecting the thankfulness due Him? Or were you even aware that the attitudes of your heart are, whether you mean it or not, a statement about Him and an offering to Him?

Watch your heart carefully. Whatever fills it will soon dominate your life and experience. With that in mind, let thankfulness flow from within as a sacrifice to God. Insist that your heart make statements of truth about your Redeemer, acknowledging the enormous sacrifice He made in order to offer you enormous glory. Recognize the salvation—the utterly complete, comprehensive salvation—that now defines your life. Whatever you do, do it in His name with thanks for who He is.

> The best way to show my gratitude to God is to accept everything, even my problems, with joy.
> —MOTHER TERESA

Against the Tide

Whatever you do, whether in word or deed,
do it all in the name of the Lord Jesus, giving
thanks to God the Father through him.
COLOSSIANS 3:17

In Word

We live in a culture of entitlement. Whenever something goes wrong, people point fingers. Lawsuits abound because our society can't get over the fact that this fallen world isn't just someone else's fault; it's our own. We expect things to work out, we complain when they don't, and if there's anyone at all we can possibly blame, we do.

This sense of entitlement comes naturally to fallen flesh. It was there when Cain killed Abel, and it lives on in the spirit of our age. It is our instinct to protect our own egos, so when we don't have our way, we want to look anywhere but inward. We feel as if we have to justify ourselves in our fallenness, and the only way to do that is to look toward the fallenness of others. We dread owning up to the frailties within.

So when a Christian comes along with a song in his heart and an attitude of thankfulness to God, regardless of the circumstances, the tide of the culture is challenged. A grateful heart is an open rebuke to the defensiveness our world uses to protect its own ego. A grateful heart has owned up to sinfulness and accepted abundant grace, and no further defense is necessary. It is a monumental, countercultural statement.

In Deed

That's why thankfulness is such a valued commodity in the Kingdom of God. It goes against the currents of the world in a noticeably winsome way. It stands out as an intriguing witness to the grace of God, and it's often a better witness than direct evangelism or good morals. The world doesn't understand deep gratitude to God, and when it sees it, it marvels.

If you want to impact your culture and be an effective witness for the Kingdom of God, be thankful. Let gratitude fill your heart and then overflow into your surroundings. People may wonder why, but eventually they will know: God has done something profound in your life. And they will want Him too.

> If the church is in Christ, its initial act is always the act of thanksgiving, of returning the world to God.
> —ALEXANDER SCHMEMANN

Faith, Then Obedience

To the man who does not work but trusts God who justifies the wicked, his faith is credited as righteousness.
ROMANS 4:5

In Word

For years, God's people had lived with the assumption that the work of obedience earns salvation. We can understand the assumption. After all, God spent a lot of time in Scripture explaining His laws and urging His people to obey Him. And by definition, sin is a failure to meet God's standards; that's usually a behavioral issue. The law was given to guide behavior; it only makes sense that obedience is important to God.

There's so much truth in scriptural appeals for obedience that we can scarcely criticize the obsession of first-century Pharisees. With a law-giving God, behavior matters. The Pharisees were not wrong about that. The problem with their idea of obedience was that it ignored the foundation. It forgot that underneath every command in the Old Testament was a prior command: love God and trust Him. In other words, faith comes first.

That's why Paul spends so much time in Romans, Galatians, and elsewhere explaining that we are justified by faith, not by law. It isn't that obedience isn't important. Obedience is hugely important, but only when it comes from a relationship of trust in God. It cannot be a means to get to God, because it places far too much stock in human effort and ignores the enormity both of sin and of God's grace. Obedience, in itself, cannot lead to God because it is based on our own capacities, and we don't have the capacity to obey perfectly. Faith, on the other hand, is based on the mercy and grace of an eternal Being.

In Deed

Never let your obedience become a means to appease or manipulate God; rather, let it flow from the gratitude in your heart and a sincere desire to do His will. Obedience as an outcome of faith is always pleasing to God. Obedience that grows out of a heart of faith is the Bible's emphasis—always. Let it be yours as well.

As the flower is before the fruit, so is faith before good works.
—RICHARD WHATELY

The Free Gift

*It was not through the law that Abraham and his
offspring received the promise . . . , but through
the righteousness that comes by faith.*
ROMANS 4:13

In Word

Use your imagination for a moment. If you were God, would you rather have a people who loved you insincerely or who loved you with all their hearts? Would you want people to obey out of compulsion or because they trusted you implicitly and knew you were working for them? Would you rather they obeyed because they thought they were good enough to do so or because they were humble enough to depend entirely on your goodness? From God's perspective, these are easy questions to answer, aren't they?

So we can begin to see why salvation is by grace through faith. That's not a new declaration, first made after the resurrection of Jesus. It's an Old Testament reality from Abel's sacrifice to Abraham's calling to David's throne to John the Baptist's sermons. Faith is the critical foundation to a relationship with God because faith says, "I love You and trust You," and rote obedience without faith says, "I'm afraid of You." No god would go to the trouble of creating a universe for the sake of relationship and then base the relationship on fear. And the heart of our God could certainly desire no such thing in the first place. No, God created us for love, and faith fits His plan.

In Deed

That's a strange sound to religious ears. The religions of this world are all about what we can do to get to God, or at least to get beyond the world. The gospel of Jesus is all about what God did to get to us. If He had given us a set of instructions for behavior that would make us acceptable to Him, then faith wouldn't be necessary. But since salvation is a matter of His initiative and His work, nothing but faith will do. There's nothing to add to God's saving work, and to imply otherwise is an insult. God's grace is to be accepted, not downplayed by our self-righteousness. When He offers such an amazing, free gift, there's only one thing to do: accept it freely.

Ultimately, faith is the only key to the universe.
—THOMAS MERTON

Intentional Rest

He did not waver through unbelief
regarding the promise of God.
ROMANS 4:20

In Word

On the surface, the grace life should be easy. All that's required is belief in God's mercy, His power to save, and His ability to sustain. But in fact the grace life is difficult, not because of the effort required, but because of our tendency to default back to what we can do for ourselves. We must intentionally set our minds to live by faith.

The Galatians, for example, had problems balancing grace and works, and they had lapsed back into their traditional form of legalism. They knew they had been accepted by God in His mercy, but forgot that mercy was to sustain them daily. They tried to live their life in the Spirit by the strength of their flesh. That's not God's plan.

We do that too. We well understand that the blood of Jesus was spilled as payment for our sin, a holy sacrifice for an unholy race. We also understand that obedience is required of us. But when it comes to relating to God daily, we neglect our dependence on grace and revert to the self-reliance of our best performance. All of our obedience may be good and pleasing to Him, but only as an outcome of our dependence on His mercy, never as a means to earn it. His grace put us in good standing with Him; our good deeds are to be done out of love.

In Deed

Regardless of how long you've been a Christian, your human nature will tempt you to revert to works. Saved by grace, you'll be tempted to live by your ability to be righteous by your own efforts. You'll do all sorts of gymnastics to get God's approval and keep it—unless, that is, you remind yourself frequently that Jesus won His approval and invited you into it by faith.

If you're burdened by the Christian life, remember that just as God has given you grace for salvation, He will give you grace for obedience through faith. Live in dependence on God—for everything—and rest. The grace walk is relaxing when we learn it. Keep your eyes fixed on Jesus, the author and perfecter of our faith (Hebrews 12:2), and be at peace.

Faith is reason at rest in God.
—CHARLES SPURGEON

Hope Against Hope

Against all hope, Abraham in hope believed.
ROMANS 4:18

In Word

Hope against hope. That's how Paul described the faith of Abraham, and by that faith, Abraham received God's promises. But he didn't see them with total clarity. Abraham had been promised a multitude of descendants, even while he was childless. As each year passed, the promise seemed more unlikely. Abraham questioned it at times, and he even tried to work it out in his own way (Genesis 16). But God had not promised Abraham descendants based on Abraham's own efforts. God promised according to His plan and His work. There's a huge difference.

That's the way it is with God's promises in our lives too. We are given many in His Word: eternal life, an inheritance with Jesus, answers to our prayers, fulfillment of our deepest desires, a godly character, fruitful work, and more. When years elapse between the promise and the fulfillment, we have questions. And like Abraham, we often try to work things out on our own. We forget the principle of hope against hope.

The death and resurrection of Jesus should be the final nail in the coffin of our doubts, but we often let the resurrection of our doubts loom larger than the resurrection of our Savior. The promises of God seem so far off that we despair, wondering if we've somehow misinterpreted them. We forget the truth of Hebrews 11:1, that faith is the assurance of things hoped for but not yet seen. We think if we haven't seen the promises fulfilled, they might not be true. Faith says otherwise.

In Deed

The life of faith—the pattern of relating to God from the beginning of time, but especially in the new creation—depends on seeing things that aren't seen. Faith is substance, our hope made real, the future promises made present. Our faith wages epic battles against our sight, and we must always let faith win. The principle that God honors is hope against hope, as long as it's based on His Word. Abraham was blessed by that principle; we will be too.

> Faith is to believe what you do not yet see; the reward for this faith is to see what you believe.
> —AUGUSTINE

Faith versus Sight

*God will credit righteousness—for us who believe in
him who raised Jesus our Lord from the dead.*
ROMANS 4:24

In Word

The world lives by sight; the body of Christ lives by faith. That, more than anything,
explains why there will always be enmity between the two.

Think about the world's dependence on sight—human reasoning as the key to
solving humanity's problems. The world thinks the scientific method will correctly
analyze social problems and find solutions for them, and that it will correctly diag-
nose biological and environmental pathology and find appropriate cures. The right
human leadership, endowed with enlightened political philosophies and compassionate intentions, will presumably take us where we need to go. And social capital—
the common efforts of a tolerant and hardworking society—will pull us together to
conquer any evil and establish peace. But for all its focus on sight, the world doesn't
understand sin. It overestimates our ability to succeed. The world doesn't get it; life
in this world, without God, is futile. And it always will be.

Christians, on the other hand, have nothing against the scientific method, human
leadership, and social capital. We just don't see them as the answers. Under the guidance of a God with a plan and infinite wisdom, they are useful tools. But the solution?
Never. Living by sight, on those terms, is blind.

In Deed

That's why faith is held in contempt by secular society. Christians approach life from a
different vantage point: the world strives for independence; we strive for dependence.
We know deep down inside that we are subject to a greater will.

It is the responsibility of the body of Christ to live by faith in this vision-impaired
world. We are the only ones who see—not by our own eyes, but through the eyes of
Scripture—the direction of history. We are the only ones who see—again, through
the Word—the will of the Father. We are the only ones who know the design of this
universe and the divine heart that designed it. Faith calls us to live boldly—hope
against hope—as citizens of the Kingdom of God.

God has made for us two kinds of eyes:
those of flesh and those of faith.
—JOHN CHRYSOSTOM

Holy Audacity

Taking him by the right hand, he helped him up.
ACTS 3:7

In Word

Peter was bold. Unreasonably bold, many of us would have thought if we'd witnessed him in action. After all, who in his right mind would walk up to a man who had never stood on his own two feet and tell him to get up—in a very public place, no less? And then have the nerve to seize the man by the hand and pull him up? What would have happened if the man had fallen back to the ground? The Christian faith would have suffered an enormously embarrassing blow. Peter and John would have been seen as apostles of foolishness rather than apostles of faith.

In fact, that's the very thin ledge we all walk on. When we're living by faith, we see on one side the power of God and the vindication of what we believe. But if faith doesn't turn out the way we expect? Embarrassment and futility. Faith causes us to put all our cards on the table; it's a position of risk. And that's why most of us are afraid to live as boldly as Peter did. The possibility of failure is huge.

God doesn't remove that possibility, that fear of the unknown, that mysterious "what if." No, if he did that, we'd be walking by sight and not by faith. If faith ruled out the possibility that things might not work out exactly as we expect, then it would cease to be faith. Faith, we're told in Hebrews 11:1, is the assurance of things we *don't* see. A certain blindness is necessarily part of how we're supposed to live. We're required to trust God.

In Deed

Christians are often tentative in the very area that's supposed to define us. There's a reason we're called *believers*. We're supposed to believe God—boldly. We need to avoid the tendency to fear the possibility that God won't vindicate us, that prayers won't get answered, that lame people won't get up and walk. We need to pray audacious prayers that would embarrass us if God didn't answer them. And we need to walk in the complete confidence that He will.

> Seeing is not believing. Seeing is seeing.
> Believing is being confident without seeing.
> —G. CAMPBELL MORGAN

A Personal Miracle

He jumped to his feet and began to walk. Then
he went with them into the temple courts,
walking and jumping, and praising God.
ACTS 3:8

In Word

The beggar had been sitting at the gate of the Temple for years. Not in the Temple—his infirmity ritually disqualified him, or made him unclean, as they called it (Leviticus 21:16-21). No, both literally and figuratively, he was outside the house of God. Even Jesus had passed by that gate during Jerusalem's feasts, but still the beggar sat, unable to do anything else.

Peter and John were on their way to the Temple to pray at the designated time for afternoon prayers—or, as they were commonly referred to, the "standing prayers," so called because everyone stood. Everyone who *could* stand, that is. Everyone who had healthy legs and was fit to enter the Temple in the first place. Everyone who wasn't, from all outward appearances, excluded from the Kingdom of God.

So Peter's challenge to the man's lameness was more than a bold statement of faith. It was a sign of God's desire to include, of God's veto of the things that marginalize people and keep them from His presence, of His intimate awareness of the personal needs of a human heart. At Peter's command, the man rose and walked. Where? *Into* the Temple he had been excluded from. Just in time for the standing prayers.

In Deed

That's just like God, isn't it? A tailor-made miracle that came at exactly the right time to let a poor man know that his needs were met and his heart had been known. No wonder there was exuberant leaping and praise. A man who couldn't walk met the God who had created him to be different, and his life was redeemed.

God's miracles in our lives are tailor-made too. We may, like someone disabled from birth, wonder for years what's taking our God so long to notice us. But when He shows us that He does, it hits us right where our hearts are. It meets our deepest needs. His works in our lives fit who we are—at exactly the right time. Hold out for that. Don't lose heart. The time for leaping and praising always comes.

With infinite love and compassion, our Lord
understood the human predicament.
—CHARLES L. ALLEN

In the Beginning . . .

The Scripture foresaw that God would justify the Gentiles by faith, and announced the gospel in advance to Abraham.
GALATIANS 3:8

In Word

God has always been the God of the gospel. That may not seem to be apparent in much of the Old Testament, filled with detailed rituals and obscure history, but if we look closely enough, the gospel is there. It was there when the prophets promised forgiveness and restoration to rebellious Israel; it was there when God delivered a nation of slaves into their own Promised Land; and it was there even earlier with Abraham, when God gave Him a promise impossible to fulfill, then fulfilled it with a son, then asked for the son as a sacrifice, and then gave back the son in life. The Scripture is clear: as long as there has been sin in the world, there has been the gospel.

When Jesus revealed the fullness of the gospel, it was a crisis for first-century Judaism. It wasn't at first apparent how He fit in with all of God's promises. But as early Christians wrestled with the questions, they found their answers deeply embedded in their history and spiritual identity. When we read the New Testament, we notice an interesting phenomenon: the gospel was not defended with newfangled ideas, but with ancient Scriptures. The key to this first-century crisis of faith was an appeal to biblical precedents.

In Deed

What does that mean for us? It means that God has always been a solution giver. He has not been silent, not even on day one of the Fall. He preached the gospel to Abraham, to Moses, to David, and to the prophets, and He still preaches it to us. He may make His promises real in ways we never expected, but we can count on this rock-solid principle: God is a God of answers. He has a solution both for our petty problems and for our deepest crises. How? Through His Word and by His Spirit. When? As we seek Him and His answers in His Word. Why? Because He has always been the God of the gospel.

The gospel is given in Genesis 3:21, when Moses tells us that God clothed them.
—JOHN MACARTHUR

God on Our Side

*Christ redeemed us from the curse of the
law by becoming a curse for us.*
GALATIANS 3:13

In Word

Paul and other new believers must have spent hours upon hours and even years upon years contemplating the heart of God. They knew, as did all Jews and God-fearing Gentiles, that He was righteous and loving. They had no idea, nor did anyone, that a sovereign God would be so sacrificial as to take human sin upon Himself.

That's hard for us to grasp too. The thought that a God who hates sin would let His Son become sin on our behalf, and then pour out His wrath on sin at that moment in time, is almost unthinkable. But this plan gives us a glimpse into the heart of God like nothing else could. What we see is a King who would fight epic battles and pay enormous costs for His desired bride. We see a Ruler whose promises and loyalties are not turned off by rejection and rebellion. We see a Warrior who will battle to the death to accomplish His plan. And we see a Mastermind who executed a perfect strategy across diverse millennia and cultures in order to defeat His enemy.

In Deed

When you read that Christ became the curse for us—that the God who hates curses clothed Himself in a curse in our place—what do you think of Him? Does this come across as an unfathomable mystery? Have you heard it so often that it seems commonplace? Does it thrill your soul or bore you? What goes on in your mind when you hear of this completely unexpected, cosmically astounding event?

The early Christians were utterly confounded by the mystery and took years to sort it out. And what eventually dawned on them, as reflected in Paul's letter to the Romans, is that if God did this for us, what would He not do? Do passionate lovers pay ultimate sacrifices and then walk away from their love? Never. The God who laid down His Son's life for us is the God who hears our prayers today, who carefully watches over us, and who is guiding us home. We can approach Him with confidence because He has already demonstrated, emphatically, that He is on our side.

> Justification takes place in the mind of God and
> not in the nervous system of the believer.
> —C. I. SCHOFIELD

Inseparable

All of you who were baptized into Christ
have clothed yourselves with Christ.
GALATIANS 3:27

In Word

When we accept Christ, our lives may change radically. Even so, we rarely realize just how radically different we are seen by God. While we were once seen as corrupt, depraved, and even dead, we are now seen as . . . well, as Jesus. It isn't that God now sees us alive and well; He sees us in Christ, covered and clothed by Him. When He died on the cross, we died with Him. When He was buried in the tomb, we were sealed up with Him. When He was raised, we were raised. And when He ascended and was seated at the right hand of the Father, so were we. By faith in Jesus, we have been inseparably bonded with Him in such a way that whatever is true of Him is true of us. That's bad news for our sinfulness; it's wonderful news for us.

That's the truth we need to dwell on daily. The Christian life is not so much a matter of doing right, thinking right, and feeling right. It's not a matter of reformation or even revival. It's a matter of being completely hidden in Jesus (Colossians 3:3-4). When God looks at us, He sees us through Jesus.

In Deed

The implications of that truth need first and foremost to be worked out in our own minds. We often see ourselves incorrectly: as individuals redeemed to a better life, a law-abiding life, a spiritually meaningful life. Those things are true, but they are not enough to change our thinking as much as God wants to change it. He would rather we see ourselves as dead to law, dead to sin, dead to the old nature, and dead to the ways of the world. Our new life is not just as followers of Christ, but as genetic heirs of His Spirit and as integrated members of His body. Dead branches have been grafted into a live stem. We are organically united to Him.

Meditate on this unity often. Let it shape what you think of your sin, your calling, your work, your relationships—everything. Your life is His, and His is yours.

> All God's love and the fruits of it come to us as
> we are in Christ, and are one with Him.
> —RICHARD SIBBES

Beloved Children

You are all sons of God through faith in Christ Jesus.
GALATIANS 3:26

In Word

Every step you take is sacred. Perhaps you didn't know that. After all, it's easy to go through the motions of our day, living humdrum lives as we fulfill our responsibilities. Life can easily turn into routine, and routine can seem far from sacred. But that isn't reality.

No, reality is that we are sons and daughters of the living God. We have His spiritual genetics within us. We haven't simply been taught a better way, we have the Spirit of the true way living within us. We have been reborn and remade with a heavy, holy price.

Think about what it means to live as a son or daughter of God. Children of earthly kings have enviable privileges, the best that money and position can buy. They get the best education, never lack for work opportunities, have enough influence to say what they want to say and live where they want to live, and they never go without anything they truly desire. While God does not spoil His children as earthly kings sometimes do, there are certainly parallels. We are given His Spirit as a guide; we are placed in exactly the right opportunities for ministry; we are promised fruitfulness as long as we are faithful to Him; and we are given everything related to life and godliness (2 Peter 1:3). That doesn't leave much to the imagination; according to the Word of God, we lack nothing.

In Deed

Yet we live as though we are the neediest of creatures. Is it that we have set our desires on the wrong things? Or that we simply haven't learned to apply the promises of God to our lives? Perhaps we have not distanced ourselves far enough from the ways of this world. Perhaps we have forgotten that every step is sacred.

Live with a sense of sacredness. You are a child of the highest King, a privileged member of the household who should never lack for anything that the Father wants you to have. Learn to live as a beloved child, and expect His abundance in your life.

In His love, He clothes us, enfolds and embraces us.
—JULIAN OF NORWICH

Law, Then Grace

The Scripture declares that the whole world is
a prisoner of sin, so that what was promised
. . . might be given to those who believe.
GALATIANS 3:22

In Word

There's no excuse and no way out. According to the Word of God, all are guilty. There are no exceptions. Even those who never knew the written, revealed law of God are condemned by their own failures. Everyone on the planet who is honest will have to admit that they have fallen far short of His glory.

That's what Paul means when he says Scripture declares all mankind imprisoned. God doesn't love condemnation, of course—not at all. But in His mercy, He confirmed our unrighteousness so we would have to seek truth outside of ourselves. He let us all establish our guilt and get stuck in it so we could experience His forgiveness.

The world doesn't like that message. It likes to entertain thoughts of the god within or the goodness of the self. It takes a biblical truth—that we are created in the image of God—and distorts it into self-idolatry. It thinks we can be righteous and justified with an honest effort and a sincere heart.

In Deed

Believers must challenge that assumption. We can't let it slide. The truth is that grace is given for those who know their guilt; but what about those who don't? When we encounter people who know they have fallen short of God's glory, we need to be ready with the message of salvation. But for those who think anything goes—that there is no such thing as spiritual guilt—we're right to emphasize God's holiness. What does grace mean for someone who believes there are no absolutes to fall short of? Nothing. The standard of holiness has to be established before the gospel of grace means anything.

Christians cannot be legalists, giving the impression that the way to God is through good works. But we cannot preach mercy to people who have no concept of sin. The answer is to live holy lives, declare the righteousness of God, and then explain our peace in terms of the gospel. The message we have been given is clear: there's no way to salvation except first to realize we need it, then to accept the Savior.

> The law reflects God's holiness; it is a plumb
> line that shows us that we are crooked.
> —ERWIN LUTZER

Surprised by the Spirit

*The circumcised believers who had come with
Peter were astonished that the gift of the Holy Spirit
had been poured out even on the Gentiles.*
ACTS 10:45

In Word

Peter had never even been inside a Gentile's house. Good Jews didn't risk defilement like that, and Peter had always been a good Jew. So the thought of entering the house of a Gentile, eating at his table, and fellowshiping with his friends and family never even entered his mind. Surely that would violate God's holiness.

But God was the one who sent Peter to Cornelius's house, though it took two dramatic visions to bring the two men together. Still, it was an awkward scene. It grated against everything Peter had thought to be true about God's chosen people remaining separate from the world. It grated on other people's nerves, too, as his fellowship with the Gentile would later invoke the wrath of good, honest Christians back in Jerusalem (Acts 11:1-3). It was shocking. Scandalous. And entirely God's doing.

That's often how God works: surprisingly. Even for those well-versed in Scripture—those of us who have studied God's ways and think we know the parameters of His character—His movements often blindside us. Why? Because God doesn't fit in a box. Our theologies can't contain Him. He defies expectations and refuses to abide by our cultural assumptions. He doesn't play by our rules.

No, God plays by His rules, many of which are known only to Him. His ways are high above our ways, and His thoughts extend far beyond what our minds can conceive. He often lets us in on His plans, but the formulas we develop from His past revelation can't always predict His heart's desires. He has plans that are still unfolding.

In Deed

Are you open to God's movements? Do your expectations for God rule out the improbable, the unlikely, or the impossible? If so, readjust them. Expect the unexpected. Revival in your life or your church may look different from what you thought it would. Your prayers may be answered from a different angle than you predicted. The Spirit will often astonish you because we serve a God who loves surprises.

I believe in the surprises of the Holy Spirit.

—LEON JOSEPH SUENENS

Tangible Evidence

The Holy Spirit came on all who heard the message.
ACTS 10:44

In Word

Repeatedly in Acts, the presence of the Holy Spirit is evident. He was tangible to the early church—believers praised God, spoke in tongues, were filled with joy and faith, uttered bold statements, and more. In fact, the primary argument that God approved of the mission to the Gentiles was the obvious endorsement of the Spirit. When He came upon people, observers knew it. They saw the evidence with their own eyes.

We don't always talk about the Spirit in those terms today. He's much more nebulous, much less tangible, much more subtle. And we're right to think that He works behind the scenes and discreetly. He often does. But according to Scripture, He also works very overtly and obviously. Somehow, many in the church have lost that understanding. It's rare that we look at another believer and instinctively and immediately know that he or she is filled with the Spirit. Over the course of church history, we've "spiritualized" the Spirit to the point of being almost unrecognizable.

Even more disconcerting is that many Christians are comfortable with this lack of evidence of the Spirit's work. We just assume that He's busy behind the scenes and don't press in to understand why. But if the overwhelming testimony in Scripture is that the Holy Spirit is tangible, and the overwhelming testimony in a person's life or a church's fellowship is that He isn't, we have a problem. It's called complacency.

In Deed

Learn to appreciate the fact that the Holy Spirit is at work in your life whether you see Him or not, but don't be content to leave it at that. Ask for concrete interaction with Him. Ask Him to manifest Himself in your heart, in your actions, and in your circumstances. Ask Him for the joy and faith and works that naturally flow from the river He has placed within you. And don't stop asking until you and discerning people around you can see that He is alive and active in you and in your church. His desire, according to Scripture, is to make a tangible impact. Invite Him to do so often.

> For Paul, the Spirit was an experienced reality.
> —HERMANN GUNKEL

A New Community

Every day they continued to meet together in the temple courts. They broke bread in their homes and ate together with glad and sincere hearts, praising God and enjoying the favor of all the people.
ACTS 2:46-47

In Word

The temple of God. The body of Christ. The beloved bride. The fellowship of the saints. All of these are biblical descriptions for the unique, organic entity known as the church. The world thinks of it simply as an institution, and unfortunately we have seen it resemble one far too often. But it is more than an institution, more than an organization, more than a movement. It is the Kingdom of God on earth and a spiritual companion of Jesus.

That's easy to forget, isn't it? We get into habits, we play roles and fulfill responsibilities, and we go through the motions. But the gathering of believers—whether on Sunday morning or any other time—is the visible expression of an invisible reality. Despite all of its flaws—and there are many—the church is where Jesus works in the world today. It is, at risk of using a familiar term, His body.

That's not a metaphor; it's literal. The fruit of the Spirit is expressed primarily in the body. The gifts of the Spirit are expressed primarily through and for the body. When Jesus ascended, He did not leave this world. His presence is still very visible and very real, and it can only be experienced in His fullness when believers unite in worship and ministry. Whether we can comprehend it or not, the Savior who walked the dusty roads of Israel two thousand years ago still walks in this world today—through us.

In Deed

Remind yourself of that often. The church is not an obligation; it's a holy presence. It may look and act awfully unholy sometimes, but regardless of its shortcomings, the Spirit of Jesus inhabits His people. For that alone, the church requires utmost respect, sincere devotion, and every ounce of passion we can give it. It isn't just a group of people we know; it's a group of people Jesus lives in.

> The church is in Christ as Eve was in Adam.
> —RICHARD HOOKER

A Welcoming Environment

The Lord added to their number daily
those who were being saved.
ACTS 2:47

In Word

Deep in ancient history is a tragic fall, a day when a catastrophic choice by humanity's first couple shattered the clear image of God in them. From that day on, the God who created this world has been an alien in it. Though He has intervened in earthly affairs often, He is generally not welcome. His people have always loved His blessings while holding Him at arm's length. The heart of God and the ways of this world are not compatible.

God has always preserved a remnant for Himself, a remnant that would love Him and serve Him in faith. But compared to the world's total population, it has historically been a rather small remnant. His design, especially since Jesus' first coming, has been for that remnant to grow. The early Christians understood that, and they sought growth with a passion. They knew they constituted the one movement in this rebellious world in which God is not an alien but a welcome Father.

If you really want to know the heart of your Father, you will begin to see the church not as an institution but as an enclave in the hostile environment of creation. We are the one community on this planet that can roll out the red carpet for God's presence. We are the one fellowship that is open to His correction and guidance. We are the one body that He inhabits and through which He expresses His love and mercy to a hurting world. No wonder He seeks to add to our numbers.

In Deed

For the church—or even an individual, for that matter—to fulfill its purpose, we need to hold our arms open to God. We might think that's an obvious tenet of our faith, but a quick survey of Christian fellowships will reveal that this posture is not universal. We are not always prepared for God to work in us and through us. We are not always open for Him to add to our number daily.

Pray today that God would add to your fellowship. Pray that your church would be all He intends it to be. And pray above all to be, both individually and corporately, a welcome environment for His presence in the midst of a hostile world.

The church has many tasks but only one mission.
—ARTHUR PRESTON

A Holy Focus

*They devoted themselves to the apostles' teaching and to
the fellowship, to the breaking of bread and to prayer.*
ACTS 2:42

In Word

We live in a consumer society that has shaped our attitude toward church. The fellowship, in our minds, is often only a place where we can get our needs met. If the fellowship ceases to meet our needs—as we perceive them—then we fall away from it or seek another. While there's nothing wrong with having our needs met, there's a problem when that's our primary focus. We end up as shoppers wanting the best deal we can get.

The kind of fellowship inspired by the Holy Spirit is different. It is others-centered, not self-centered. And the first "other" to which it directs our attention is God Himself. The first order of business for the church member is to diligently devote himself or herself to the teaching of the apostles (the New Testament), and then to the fellowship itself.

That requires a change of mind for many of us. And it isn't just a small adjustment; it's a radical change of mind. A God-centered, others-oriented attitude is not natural to us, and we don't even perceive it as possibly being fulfilling. But it is. At whatever level we are dissatisfied, a frame of mind that is absorbed with God and the needs of others is the cure. When our hearts are focused on Spirit-inspired teaching and Spirit-inspired fellowship, dissatisfaction doesn't stand a chance. The consumer has the best deal available.

In Deed

Pray today that God would work a transformation in your heart and mind. You may be close to His standard for fellowship already, but you can always grow closer to the model His Spirit gives in Acts 2. Ask Him to put within you an unbridled passion for Him and His people. Then delve into His Word, devote yourself to others in your fellowship, celebrate His sacrifice and resurrection often, and pray your heart out. You will find yourself strangely drawn to the community of believers in deeper ways than before. And there's no better deal than that.

> The church of Christ is not an institution, it is a new life
> with Christ and in Christ, guided by the Holy Spirit.
> —SERGEI BULGAKOV

A Deeper Generosity

All the believers were together and
had everything in common.
ACTS 2:44

In Word

When you've celebrated the sacrifice of Jesus with others in the fellowship sincerely and often enough, you begin to realize the natural outworking of that celebration. You become sacrificial yourself.

The ideal picture of the new community in Christ is deeply reflective of His generous sacrifice: it is a picture of people constantly laying down their lives for one another. Such sacrifices may show up in finances, as they did in the verse above; they may show up in the giving of time or talents, or the sharing of spiritual gifts; and they may show up in less tangible ways, such as counsel and encouragement and hospitality. Regardless of the means, the early church is a good model. It was overwhelmed with grace; it could not help but overwhelm others with similar grace.

This kind of fellowship is a taste of the Kingdom of God. This is what the rule of the Messiah will be like. Everyone will have enough because everyone will give enough. Not only will they give enough, they will give cheerfully and excitedly. It will not seem like a sacrifice because personal property won't seem so . . . well, personal. The guiding principle of life will be what's good for the fellowship, not what's good for the individual.

In Deed

That's an attitude to embrace now. It isn't just a heavenly reality that we'll never realize this side of death; it's a principle of God's Kingdom that has already been decreed. When the Holy Spirit fills His people, He fills them with a sense of fellowship and mutual generosity. If we don't have that, we aren't filled.

That's a far cry from much of Western Christianity, isn't it? Yes, we have our soup kitchens and crisis committees, and we'll offer up a prayer for anyone's need at any time. We'll even gather around people in need with extreme generosity from time to time. But it's a punctuated generosity, not a constant expression of availability. The way of the Spirit is to be consistent in our lives. Seek His generosity always.

A cheerful giver does not count the cost of what he gives.
His heart is set on pleasing him to whom the gift is given.
—JULIAN OF NORWICH

An Amazing Phenomenon

Everyone was filled with awe, and many wonders and miraculous signs were done by the apostles.
ACTS 2:43

In Word

We get the impression, when reading the accounts of the first Christians, that if we were fulfilling God's purpose in our fellowships, the world would be drawn to us. The truth of the matter is that only the Holy Spirit can draw people to God. But if the Holy Spirit is evident among believers, wouldn't people be drawn to believers?

That was certainly the case in Jerusalem at that first Pentecost festival after Jesus' ascension. The Holy Spirit filled believers, and amazing things happened. They had a sense of fellowship they had never had before, miracles abounded, and people marveled. The God of power and might made Himself known in undeniable ways. Everyone was filled with awe.

Few non-Christians today look at our churches and are filled with awe. Why is that? Did the Holy Spirit, after His grand entrance, withdraw from the stage and leave us to ourselves? Did He simply go undercover—present but unnoticeable? Or is the problem on our end? In short, are we missing something?

Whatever the answer to those questions may be for your particular fellowship, we can be certain of this: the world needs evidence of God as much as ever, perhaps more. Those who do not accept Christ need to see His power. In order for them to see, we need to demonstrate it; and in order for us to demonstrate it, we need to be as in tune and devoted to Him as we can be. Amazing fellowship among people begins with amazing fellowship with God.

In Deed

The world may not know this, but it is counting on your fellowship with God. It hungers for what is real and powerful and true. Those who don't know Jesus are blind, according to Paul (2 Corinthians 4:4). Those of us who do know Jesus must live in the power and awe of the light. It's the only way the world will ever know Him.

I would not be a Christian but for the miracles.
—AUGUSTINE

Freedom

Now the Lord is the Spirit, and where the
Spirit of the Lord is, there is freedom.
2 CORINTHIANS 3:17

In Word

Paul has been writing about the difference between the revelation that came through Moses and the new covenant. The first, he says, brought death. Though glorious and clearly from God, it was a ministry of condemnation. The new covenant, however, is full of life. It brings righteousness, not condemnation. It's the ministry of the Spirit. And where the Spirit of the Lord is, there's freedom.

What kind of freedom is Paul talking about? Not freedom from obedience to God—plenty of New Testament writers affirm the importance of obedience. Not freedom from moral obligations—lawlessness is harshly condemned in the new covenant just as it was in the old. So what is this freedom that the Spirit brings? How do we live without feeling burdened and constrained? That's a mystery to many Christians.

The primary difference between the old covenant and the new is the direction it works. A law that comes from outside of us and tries to conform what's inside of us brings death. It condemns. It can cause us to modify our behavior, but it can't change our hearts. The result is a constant struggle to go against our grain—to do what's right in spite of ourselves. That's ultimately ineffective. But a law that is planted deep inside of us and changes our hearts works its way outward. What we do is then the product of who we are, not the product of what we were told to do. Righteousness becomes natural, not imposed. That's a life-giving dynamic.

In Deed

If righteousness is a struggle and feels like a confining burden, there's an internal problem. God's solution for us is not a set of commandments to do the right thing. A life of uncomfortable obedience is not what He wants. No, his solution is a changed nature that works its way outward into our behavior—naturally. If that isn't happening in our lives, the answer is to ask for it, to seek the Spirit's fellowship more intensely, and to come face-to-face with the glory planted inside of us under the new covenant. That is neither law nor lawlessness. It's freedom.

> God works immediately by His Spirit in
> and on the wills of His saints.
> —JOHN OWEN

Glory

We, who with unveiled faces all reflect the Lord's glory, are being transformed into his likeness with ever-increasing glory, which comes from the Lord, who is the Spirit.
2 CORINTHIANS 3:18

In Word

The freedom that comes through Jesus comes not by raw obedience but by gazing at the right source. That's why Paul talks about the removal of a veil. Those who gaze at the law of Moses see the Lord through a thick veil. There's a covering over the heart that separates the believer from the glory. But when we come to Christ, the veil is removed (v. 16). There's no layer obscuring the view, no hindrance to pure fellowship with the Son. The light from His face shines directly on us, and we reflect His glory. And the result? We're transformed. We become like Him.

That's why Paul can mention righteousness and freedom in the same passage. A removed veil and a gaze into Jesus' face changes us to be like Him. He doesn't need commandments to tell Him how to live righteously. He does so because that's who He is. As we become like Him, we do too. If we have His nature, we'll find ourselves behaving less and less out of what we're instructed to do and more and more out of who we are. Our hearts will become righteous because we are like Him.

How does that happen? Paul makes it clear: it's from unveiled faces looking in the right direction. We gaze at the source. The more we look at the light—and by implication, the more we fellowship with Him—the more His glory increases in our lives. Those in search of a path to righteousness will find it here and nowhere else. No set of rules can change us like that.

In Deed

Many Christians live in a sad pattern of trying hard, then falling, then trying harder, then falling again, then . . . well, you know the rest. It involves a lot of genuine but short-lived repentance, as well as plenty of self-condemnation for the futility of trying. And while the New Testament tells us plenty about obedience, it never tells us simply to try harder to do it right. No, it sends us to the power source. It tells us to fill our gaze with the Righteous One. It emphasizes that the life of glory comes, by the Spirit's work, from within.

> Nature forms us, sin deforms us, school informs us, Christ transforms us.
> —ANONYMOUS

Born to Serve

*In Christ we who are many form one body, and
each member belongs to all the others.*
ROMANS 12:5

In Word

You belong to other church members. That may be hard to swallow in an individualistic society, but Scripture is clear. We are not our own, having been bought by the Lord; and in His gracious return, He not only gives our lives back to us, He also gives them to other Christians. Because Jesus has a claim on us, those in Christ also have a claim on us. In Him, we are literally one.

The bottom line for us is that we were born to serve not only God but others, and to the extent we don't, we miss our purpose. Service may take a wide variety of forms—high- or low-profile, heavily spiritual or intensely practical (or both)—but it must all boil down to an edifying role in the Christian community. More important than the form our service takes is the motive behind it. If we want to be Christians who fulfill the Word of God, we must focus our attentions, our time, our talents, and our work on others. That's what God did, and He designed us to do the same.

That attitude begins with a proper understanding of self: "Do not think of yourself more highly than you ought" (v. 3). That's where service begins—with an appropriate humility and a love for others. If we have that, the rest comes almost naturally.

In Deed

This passage, Romans 12:3-21, is perhaps the most comprehensive explanation in the New Testament of a Christian's relationships. It addresses our relationships to other Christians, the exercise of spiritual gifts for the common good, our relationships with outsiders, and our relationships with our enemies. It covers almost all the bases. It is foundational.

A good exercise would be to read the entire passage every day this week. It isn't very long, but it is full of power. As you read, stop and meditate on each of Paul's pithy, pointed statements. Measure your life against them, and ask God where He wants to work. The work of relationships begins deep inside. Trust Him to begin that work in you today.

Our lives will harmonize best with God's will
. . . when they serve other people best.
—JOHN CALVIN

Always Good

Do not be overcome by evil, but overcome evil with good.
ROMANS 12:21

In Word

When Moses stood in the cleft of the rock and God passed by in His glory, there was a twofold promise we often miss: not only would God show Moses His glory and goodness, He would also proclaim His name.

What did God say about Himself? "The LORD, the LORD, the compassionate and gracious God, slow to anger, abounding in love and faithfulness, maintaining love to thousands, and forgiving wickedness, rebellion and sin" (Exodus 34:6-7). The words God used to describe Himself are remarkably consistent with the words the New Testament uses to describe Christian character. There's a connection between the love of God and the love of the believer. That makes perfect sense for a people made in His image.

That's a high calling, and it's always a challenge for fallen flesh. We are utterly insufficient in ourselves to display the character of God. Yet we know that the Bible does not command impossibilities. Our insufficiency can be filled with God's sufficiency. Our weakness exists to display His strength. Our inabilities make room for His abilities. We are to be empowered by God Himself.

In Deed

That's the only way the verse above can be lived out. We can't overcome evil with good unless we are filled with the goodness of God. In fact, we can't even love sincerely, forgive fully, or do any of the things this passage tells us to do unless we are enabled by the Spirit of God. It's the only way.

But it's a way freely given. The lives of Christians are to be marked by constant goodness in our relationships. When everyone's nice to us, we are to be good. When people are rude and offensive, we are to be good. When we are slandered or threatened or stolen from, we are to be good. There is no loophole for us; we are always to be good. Why? Because we are made and remade into the image of a very good God.

> At the heart of the story stands the cross of Christ,
> where evil did its worst and met its match.
> —JOHN W. WENHAM

Beyond Apathy

Never be lacking in zeal, but keep your
spiritual fervor, serving the Lord.
ROMANS 12:11

In Word

Why, in the middle of a passage about relationships, does Paul tell us to keep up our zeal in serving the Lord? Because serving the Lord zealously is a key to our relationships. If we thought our relationship with God and with others fell in two different categories, we were wrong. The two are wrapped up together: how we serve God has a lot to do with how effectively we relate to others.

That's true at a number of levels: our motives for serving God and others are the same; our love for God is to translate into love for His people; and our means of serving God and others often overlap. Our feelings for God and our feelings for people must be integrated.

That's important to know, because the hard work of interpersonal relationships often saps our zeal. Conflict can drain us, personality differences can irritate us, and growth in depth and intimacy can require more energy than we think we have. Sometimes in the midst of our dealings with other people we can lose heart or give up. Paul tells us not to. Why? Because it's not a people issue; it's a God issue.

In Deed

Understand that God made you for service and ministry, and when you serve other people, you are serving Him. Don't let the disappointments of relationships drain you or distract you—those relationships are still His work. That is where God has called you and equipped you to serve. Under His guidance you will need to determine how much to invest in each of your relationships and how to manage the seasons that will inevitably transform them, but you can't be halfhearted about them. There are examples in Scripture of relationships being appropriately ended or suspended, but there is never an instruction to be apathetic about them.

Approach your relationships with zeal and faithfulness, as though they were issues between you and God rather than issues between you and others. In many ways, they are.

A zealous man feels that like a lamp he is made to burn.
Such a one will always find a sphere for his zeal.
—J. C. RYLE

Generous with Honor

Honor one another above yourselves.
ROMANS 12:10

In Word

Honoring one another is really the essence of Christian relationships. It grows from the conviction that every person, redeemed or not, was made in the image of God. That should give us a love for even the least lovable people in the world, but it goes even further with Christians. Every brother or sister in Christ is inhabited by the very Spirit of the living God. He may be hard to see sometimes, but He's there. Our relationships with other believers are holy ground.

We don't usually approach them that way. We treat people casually because we don't see the sacredness of their redemption. We don't recognize them as building blocks of the temple that houses the Almighty. We don't perceive them as the literal body of Christ. We don't understand the intricacies of their creation—how specially designed they are. We forget that every single redeemed person, in body and in Spirit, is an expression of some aspect of God's character.

Once those implications dawn on us, we can't ever treat people the same. We begin to realize that our conversations are sacred, our hospitality is sacred, and our mutual service is sacred. We start to understand that God has built into the fabric of our relationships a capacity to reflect Himself. Our friendships become visible expressions of His hidden nature, and our broken relationships become tragedies against the image of God.

In Deed

Honor is important. God bestows it on us (Psalm 84:11), and in turn we are to recognize it in others. It is the key to healed, whole relationships.

Think of ways to honor the other members of your fellowship. Could you stand to give more encouragement or compliments? Do you need to affirm the gifts of others in more visible ways? Has God been urging you to make deep sacrifices for the needs of others? The possibilities are limitless, and the implications are critical. Focus today on honor—not yours, not even God's, but that of your brothers and sisters. Then find a way to demonstrate it.

Love seeks one thing only: the good of the one loved.
—THOMAS MERTON

Committed to Peace

Be careful to do what is right in the eyes of everybody. . . .
As far as it depends on you, live at peace with everyone.
ROMANS 12:17-18

In Word

It's a vicious world. Gossip abounds, deception is rampant, and faithfulness is hard to find. People stab each other in the back, sometimes even literally. Relationships are often based on fragile conditions that eventually undo them. Truth is treated as a relative concept, and integrity is a rarity. We see pockets of commitment and honesty in the relationships around us, but mostly the landscape is littered with human failures. Relationships can hurt.

That's the context in which Christian community is supposed to shine. We are to be lights that point to the true nature of a relational God, or islands of refuge for those who are drowning in the violent seas of brokenness. Our relationships are to demonstrate God in such a way that people can clearly see ideals of peace, love, generosity, and all that is true. We are supposed to be a taste of heaven in the midst of whatever hell lonely and hurting people find themselves in. We are supposed to be safe.

That the church is sometimes indistinguishable from the culture around it is a hideous tragedy. We miss a golden opportunity to represent the Kingdom of God in a dying world whenever we forget to act like Kingdom citizens. And it often is just that: a matter of forgetting. We need to remind ourselves often not to contribute to the tragedy. We need to be godly.

In Deed

Above all else, make sure your relationships exemplify God. That's what the new community in Christ, the new creation we were redeemed to live in, is all about. That is the only thing that will convince a hurting world that the Kingdom of God is worth its time. Our words of evangelism and proclamation don't matter if the gospel hasn't proven radically effective in our lives. Whatever it takes, live at peace—real, meaningful peace—with everyone.

A peaceable man does more good than a learned one.
—THOMAS À KEMPIS

Holy Foolishness

The message of the cross is foolishness to those who are perishing, but to us who are being saved it is the power of God.
1 CORINTHIANS 1:18

In Word

Think of how ridiculous it sounds: The only reason we can know God and go to heaven is because a radical teacher was executed two thousand years ago. Does that make any sense at all? Not on the surface, especially when we consider what a cross meant. It was the ancient version of an electric chair or a gas chamber, only much slower and more painful in accomplishing its purpose. The idea that we can have life only because a long-ago troublemaker made enough trouble to get Himself killed simply doesn't compute. It seems absolutely absurd.

But God has frequently worked in seemingly absurd ways, hasn't He? He once told a man to build an enormous boat in the middle of dry, elevated land. He once ordered a very old father to sacrifice his long-awaited son, even though the sacrifice would wipe out every vestige of an ironclad promise. He picked an old exile to deliver a people from the world's most powerful nation, a young shepherd boy to defeat an enormous giant, and a small army to defeat a vast coalition using nothing more than praise songs. If we were looking for a conventional deity to impress us only with lightning bolts and a thundering voice, we picked the wrong God. Our Father usually prefers to demonstrate His power in unlikely ways.

That's because He has inside information that we don't have. We had no idea that we needed a holy sacrifice to die in our place. We didn't know the enormity of the transaction that went on behind the scenes of the Cross. We didn't know the dead Savior would rise again. We only learned by revelation that something so absurd as his death could result in something so amazing as our life.

In Deed

Never distance yourself from the foolishness of the Cross—or from the foolishness of the Christian faith in general. To the world it looks absurd, but to us it's the most powerful force in the universe. Unbelievers will one day be ashamed of the things they have laughed at, and we will one day be grateful for looking like fools. Always choose the foolishness of God over the wisdom of the world.

> The cross is a picture of violence, yet the key to peace; a picture of suffering, yet the key to healing; a picture of death, yet the key to life. —DAVID WATSON

Chosen Fools

God chose the foolish things of the world to shame the wise.
1 CORINTHIANS 1:27

In Word

Many Christians and many churches spend an awful lot of time and energy trying to look respectable. It's only natural—we want people to look up to us and to visit our fellowships. Dignity and sophistication are universally admired. And foolishness is hardly seeker friendly.

While Scripture never tells us to try to look like fools, certain aspects of our faith simply can't be covered up. We follow an unlikely Savior. We stick our necks out in faith, sometimes to absurd lengths. We urge righteous behavior even when it means less profit and fewer friends. And we appear very naive to praise a good God in the midst of evil circumstances. No amount of sophisticated theology can obscure the strange picture our faith sometimes creates.

The fact is that no matter how simple or naive or foolish we look, those who seek God will be drawn to His power seen in changed lives. Those who won't accept God unless He looks respectable, refined, and dignified aren't really after God in the first place. We see that clearly in the life of Jesus. A Galilean? A poor carpenter's son? The product of a questionable pregnancy? A teacher of strange and often offensive truths? There was nothing in the packaging that screamed "here is a deity." No, those who cared about appearances weren't hungry for God. But those who hungered for God didn't care about appearances.

In Deed

There are two ways this principle applies to our lives. First, we need to be able to see the character and power of God in unexpected ways. We have to be willing to look for Him in places like a dirty manger or in people as unlikely as the apostle who wrote this verse. Second, we need to let Jesus be whoever He wants to be in us. He doesn't want us to dress up our faith experiences or our personalities to make them palatable to a skeptical world. He wants to live freely within us and through us—however that appears.

I'd rather be a fool in the eyes of men
than a fool in the eyes of God.
—ANONYMOUS

Supernatural

God did extraordinary miracles through Paul.
ACTS 19:11

In Word

Paul was preaching boldly in a city where Satan had a massive stronghold: Ephesus, the center of the Roman Empire's worship of the great goddess Artemis. For two years he explained the gospel clearly and powerfully, and many believed. But it wasn't just proclamation of the Word; God backed up Paul's preaching with miracles. Even handkerchiefs that had touched Paul were taken to the sick, who were healed and delivered of demons by this indirect contact. If that wasn't a sign from heaven, nothing is.

But if we thought such signs and wonders were exceptional, the wording of the verse makes us think again. Luke tells us that God did "extraordinary" miracles through Paul, as though we needed a distinction between these miracles and the ordinary kind. The good doctor could have told us simply that Paul's ministry was accompanied by miracles, but apparently that wouldn't distinguish the apostle from all the other signs and wonders taking place in the church. No, miracles weren't all that unusual among early believers. In order to understand the impact of Paul's ministry, the extraordinary nature of the miracles must be specified.

In Deed

Christianity is supernatural, not just in the early days of the church, but always. In fact, it cannot be otherwise; we serve a risen Savior who is simultaneously seated at the right hand of God and inhabiting our very souls. It's impossible to be a Christian by natural means, and it's impossible to really live a Christian life without the benefit of supernatural power. Whether miracles are manifested visibly in the physical realm or in the secret recesses of our lives, they are miracles nonetheless. That's because Jesus is our life.

Is there evidence of the supernatural in your life? If not, ask God why. More than that, ask Him to provide some. He isn't interested in powerless faith any more than you are. Pray for supernatural power, and expect Him to miraculously work in all kinds of ways. Even extraordinarily.

I never have any difficulty believing in miracles since I experienced the miracle of a change in my own heart.
—AUGUSTINE

Victorious

*They were all seized with fear, and the name
of the Lord Jesus was held in high honor.*
ACTS 19:17

In Word

The New Testament is the story of a clash of kingdoms. The light stepped into the darkness (John 1:9), and the darkness has been trembling ever since. Throughout church history, citizens of darkness have been plucked out of that kingdom and placed in the Kingdom of light, which will never cease to increase (Isaiah 9:7). It's a perpetual victory that will never end.

We need to be reminded of that, mainly because we still see a lot of darkness in the world. Sometimes it even seems that evil has the upper hand. Life can feel like an uphill climb, and a lifestyle of victory seems like a distant hope. Strategically wedged where the clashing kingdoms meet, we can get awfully injured in the cross fire. Sometimes we just want relief.

That's why it's important to immerse ourselves in stories of darkness being humiliated by the light, as in Acts 19. The gospel demolished a stronghold of Satan in Ephesus. Paul, his coworkers, and the believers in general faced vicious opposition from a number of sides, yet Jesus won every power clash against the enemy. Extraordinary miracles were taking place, people were being healed and delivered, and counterfeit spirits were being roundly defeated. The result? "The name of the Lord Jesus was held in high honor."

In Deed

Stories like Acts 19 give us the knowledge and the tools we need to endure every kingdom clash we experience and to emerge victorious from them. Regardless of what side an attack comes from—relationships, health, work, matters of the heart and mind, or any other arena of life—we need to know that the power of Jesus is overwhelmingly able to defeat the enemy. If only we can persist in our faith, we eventually see an amazing phenomenon both within us and around us: darkness dissipating, unable to maintain its influence in the face of the Light.

Nothing that is attempted in opposition
to God can ever be successful.
—JOHN CALVIN

Unsettling

There arose a great disturbance about the Way.
ACTS 19:23

In Word

When the Christian faith hit Ephesus, it made waves. It undermined the major religion, which in turn undermined the backbone of the local economy, which in turn caused problems for governing leaders. In other words, the Way was bad for business, and the chamber of commerce wasn't happy.

So the local artisan guild provoked a riot, and the city rose into an uproar. Many rioters joined in the protests without even knowing what the protest was about, and confusion reigned for the better part of a day. When the dust finally settled, no Christians had been killed and the local temple cult was still waning in influence. But Paul decided to leave town—violence frequently seemed to prompt that result—and the faithful continued to be viewed with suspicion. Christianity was a wild card in the diverse deck of society, and it made a lot of people nervous.

Many Christians are afraid to play that role today. Most of us don't particularly want to make waves, and even those who do often make them for the wrong reasons. Society rarely gets nervous about the power of our lifestyle. Why? Maybe it's because we don't often live with power or because we desperately want to fit in to our culture. Whatever the reason, we blend in far too easily. There are not many disturbances about the Way in our cities.

In Deed

Some Christians make the wrong kind of waves, blustering their way into a bad reputation over issues that are only peripheral to the gospel. Others make no waves at all. But biblical Christianity makes the kind of impact that can change a culture. It doesn't shy away from crisis moments that set the stage for God to prove Himself and His Word.

Neither should we. God frequently puts His people in the middle of a storm in order to show the world who we are and who He is. To the degree we allow Him to do that in our lives, we can change our world.

> If we are intended for great ends, we are called to great hazards.
> —JOHN HENRY NEWMAN

Love First

These three remain: faith, hope and love.
But the greatest of these is love.
1 CORINTHIANS 13:13

In Word

The thirteenth chapter of 1 Corinthians is such a familiar passage of Scripture to most people that we hardly contemplate its meaning anymore. Rather than prompting deep contemplation, it evokes images of sentimental weddings and leads us to a superficial summary of the Christian faith. But this passage is neither sentimental nor superficial. It is as practical and substantial as New Testament teaching gets. It describes the heart of God.

The context, of course, is a church that was acting rather selfishly. Its members didn't get the implications of being the body of Christ and a witness to the world. They competed for attention and status, and they were careless with the grace of God, recklessly sinning under the assumption that grace would cover it all. In their meetings, they ate too much and spoke too often. They did a lot of godly things, but without much love. And without love, godly things aren't very godly.

That's Paul's assessment, anyway. One can display all sorts of spiritual gifts, but if love isn't in them, it doesn't matter very much. Would God really want the Corinthians to accomplish His works without His heart? Paul sets forth the absurdity of such an attitude. Of course God wouldn't want that. That's only a sanitized, Christian form of Pharisaical hypocrisy. God judges people for such things.

In Deed

We can hardly criticize the Corinthians for doing what we often do ourselves. We tend to strive to do the work of God without considering whether we are motivated by the heart of God. We focus on outcomes first and motivations second. Paul urges us to get the order right; if love isn't central to our Christian lives, our Christian lives aren't actually Christian.

Examine your motivations today. Is love behind them? Or is it something else— like a desire for significance or self-fulfillment? The well-being of the body of Christ depends on your answer.

He does much who loves much.
—THOMAS À KEMPIS

Where Love Begins

Love is patient . . . kind . . . does not envy . . . does not boast . . . is not proud . . . is not rude . . . is not self-seeking . . . is not easily angered . . . keeps no record of wrongs . . . does not delight in evil but rejoices with the truth . . . protects . . . trusts . . . hopes . . . perseveres.
1 CORINTHIANS 13:4-7

In Word

Is Paul describing the heart of God or an ideal for the believer? The answer is yes on both counts. One implies the other. It's inconceivable that God would redeem those whom He had made in His image and not ask for their hearts to be consistent with His character. A solid principle of biblical discipleship is that whatever is of God's character is to be of the believer's. We are to be like Him.

Jesus, the incarnate God who saves us, fits the description of this passage perfectly. He came to model the character of God for us, and then He sent His own Spirit to live within us. The goal of Christian discipleship is to be conformed to His image. And if we wanted a good summary of what His image entails, this is it. This kind of love, in a nutshell, is discipleship.

The new community in Christ—this new creation that was born out of His blood and resurrection—is to be marked by these distinctive characteristics. Real love—not the sentimental kind of love the world preaches, the kind that never confronts or challenges—is to be the hallmark of the Christian community. We are known as His disciples by whether we have His kind of love.

In Deed

Christian love doesn't begin with a focus on others. It begins with a focus on God. Meditating on His deep, sacrificial love to understand His heart is the key to being able to love others in the fellowship. Only His Spirit can give that kind of understanding and fill us with His kind of love.

Ask for that today. Ask for the Spirit to show you His love, fill you with it, and enable you to live it and show it to others. It's a prayer He's certain to answer—with all His heart.

For the love of God is broader than the measures of man's mind; and the heart of the Eternal is most wonderfully kind.
—FREDERICK WILLIAM FABER

Love Within

We see but a poor reflection as in a mirror;
then we shall see face to face.
1 CORINTHIANS 13:12

In Word

Yes, the love that flows out of your discipleship is not going to be perfect. It will come from the Spirit who lives within you, but the Spirit isn't all that lives within you. You and God are cooperating to dispel the confusion and the sin that once reigned in your flesh, and it's a process. In the meantime, love flows sporadically and sometimes impurely. That's just reality.

Even so, the believer is to be captivated by the love God has put within us. We are always to strain to see in the mirror more clearly. The God whose image we bear is revealing Himself more and more, but only in proportion to how intently we look. Paul says in his next letter to the Corinthians, "We, who with unveiled faces all reflect the Lord's glory, are being transformed into his likeness with ever-increasing glory" (2 Corinthians 3:18). Until that process is complete, we may strain to see clearly. But we are nevertheless to strain zealously and expectantly.

That's what needs to happen in the heart of the believer daily: a gaze at the Savior and a desire to put what is seen into practice. We have this twofold dynamic at the very core of our discipleship. We observe Him, and we conform to Him. When we get that dynamic working properly, we can't help but grow as His disciples. We will inevitably bear His fruit.

In Deed

Spend some time today gazing. That may not seem very practical, but it will have incredibly practical outcomes in your life eventually. If you earnestly desire to see Him—to consider His character and meditate on His love—and then consciously ask Him to help you live out what you've seen, you will grow by leaps and bounds. You will become conformed to your Savior in ever-increasing glory.

At the heart of your transformation will be love. Count on that. According to John, God is love, and we love because He first loved us. Get to know His love well—let it be part of your gaze—and you will find it much easier to love others. His Spirit within you yearns to cultivate your love.

He who is filled with love is filled with God Himself.
—AUGUSTINE

Love Always

We know in part and we prophesy in part, but when
perfection comes, the imperfect disappears.
1 CORINTHIANS 13:9-10

In Word

Knowing, prophesying, giving to the poor, moving mountains by faith, practicing ministry, and all the other good works we do as Christians will one day cease. Love won't. It's different. It is part of who we are, not what we do. When Jesus comes again and rewards us according to what we have done or not done, the good works of the kingdom on earth will essentially be over. But love? It's part of who we are, and it lasts. It's eternally in the character of God and, by design, in the character of His people.

That's why, as important as ministry and good works are, love is more important than all. Faith is about what is unseen, and what is unseen will eventually be completely revealed. Hope is about what will come, and what will come will also be revealed. But love is about who we are forever. There will never be a time, in this age or the next, in the kingdoms of this world or in the Kingdom of God, when love doesn't count.

That's why Paul tells us to make it count today. It's a "forever" principle, unlike almost everything else the New Testament urges us to practice. The fellowship of believers is going to last as long as the Kingdom of God lasts; that alone should convince us to major on the quality of the fellowship. And the quality of the fellowship depends almost exclusively on love. It's extremely important.

In Deed

Does your life reflect the importance of love? Or have you mistakenly made other aspects of your character a priority? Examine yourself well, and ask God to help you focus on love. Then practice it always.

Have faith and maintain hope. Increase your knowledge and aim to prophesy—to understand God's truth and put it into practice. Do good works of ministry and charity, telling others about Jesus and reconciling the world to God. But do it all in love. Without that, none of it is right.

> Our Lord does not care so much for the importance of
> our works as for the love with which they are done.
> —TERESA OF AVILA

Love's Witness

If I have a faith that can move mountains,
but have not love, I am nothing.
1 CORINTHIANS 13:2

In Word

Paul is emphatic that nothing he does—not exercising his spiritual gifts, not giving sacrificially, not ministering to others, nothing—means anything unless the love of Jesus is behind it. We could carry his statements to even further, more contemporary implications. If we provide for our families, for example—but out of obligation rather than love—we've missed the point. If we do our work faithfully, but not out of love, we've missed it again. If we give to charity and vote our conscience, but not out of love, we're off base. If we go to church and worship, but there's no real love in it, it's meaningless. If we win a hundred souls to Christ, but not because of love for those souls, we've done nothing praiseworthy. Love is the key that puts meaning into our discipleship and ministry.

Those are hard words, but they are biblical. In the Old Testament, God harshly judged people who worshiped and ministered without their hearts. Fasting, praying, singing, and sacrifice are meaningless without the substance of the heart behind them. It is clear from both the prophets of God and the apostles of Jesus that inner motivation matters more to God than outer behavior. He wants both, certainly—motivation with no result is appalling too—but it begins within. Whatever God wants us to do, He wants us to do it in love.

In Deed

That's the critical difference between the good works of the secular world and the good works of the disciple of Jesus. Anyone can do good things from learned behavior and social expectations. Anyone can even do good things from sentiment and a sense of purpose. But only a Christian can do good things because of the love of the Spirit working within. When we do, a lost world just might notice the difference.

Jesus said that the world would know us by our love. The question you must answer today is this: does it know you by your love?

> Love one another that it may at last be said of Christians
> as it was at first: "Behold how they love one another."
> —RALPH VENNING

Intense

So Peter was kept in prison, but the church
was earnestly praying to God for him.
ACTS 12:5

In Word

It was a crisis situation. James the disciple, brother of John and son of Zebedee, had been killed by Herod. This pleased certain influential people in Jerusalem, so Herod arrested Peter as an encore. This time he would make it a public spectacle while crowds were still in town for Passover. The tide of public opinion combined with the zeal of a people-pleasing politician made for an ominous threat. Peter's execution looked inevitable.

So what did believers do? They did what believers always do in a crisis—they prayed. They gathered in the home of John Mark's mother, Mary, and prayed their hearts out. And this was no ordinary kind of prayer. There was nothing casual about it. In writing the story, Luke uses the adverb *earnestly*, a word that occurs only rarely in Scripture, a word used also to describe the intensity with which Jesus prayed in the garden of Gethsemane. This was a desperate prayer—a gut-wrenching, sweat-inducing prayer accompanied by loud crying and tears. The kind of prayer that seems to reach God's heart better than any other.

That kind of prayer can come only in the intersection of two conditions: extreme need and an awareness of God's ability and willingness to meet it. Desperation alone won't drive us to that kind of prayer; without us knowing who God is, extreme need leads only to frustration. No, in order to have any hope in a crisis, we have to bank on the character of the One who is above it.

In Deed

What's your first inclination in a crisis? Is it to panic? to feel defeated? to carry on in spite of your losses because that's just how life goes? God's desire for us is to pray—not to halfheartedly ask for an intervention that we don't expect to come, but to earnestly, persistently, passionately cry out in our need. And it's a decision we need to make up front, at the very beginning of the crisis. We recognize that our desperation is God's opportunity, and we take it to Him.

Our extremities are God's opportunities.
—CHARLES SPURGEON

Unexpected

*Peter continued knocking; and when they had opened
the door, they saw him and were amazed.*
ACTS 12:16 (NASB)

In Word

Jesus emphasized the importance of praying in faith. He told His disciples, "Whatever you ask for in prayer, believe that you have received it" (Mark 11:24). The writer of Hebrews was even more emphatic: "Without faith it is impossible to please God" (11:6). The father of God's people, Abraham, was known primarily for his faith, and the Bible stresses the importance of believing God, from Genesis through Revelation. Nearly everything we receive from God comes through faith.

Still, we fall short in that area, don't we? We pray our hearts out and still are shocked sometimes when God answers. Such was the case with the believers in Jerusalem who were desperately crying out for God to deliver Peter. An angel came into his prison cell, broke his chains off him, and led him out into the streets. But when he knocked on the door of Mary's house and the servant reported his presence, the "believers" didn't exactly believe. "You're out of your mind," they told the girl. They might as well have said, "That can't be Peter at the door. He's in prison, and we're praying for him to get out!"

In His mercy, God answered their desperate prayers, even though they demonstrated they weren't exactly expecting an answer. He does that often—He has to because our faith is rarely completely pure. But surely we ought to expect greater things from God. When we cry out to God, it should never be a surprise when He responds.

In Deed

Perhaps we lower our expectations for God based on past disappointments, times when we prayed and got no discernible answer. But whatever the reasons for those disappointments were, past experiences are not an accurate statement of God's power and love today. He is able and willing to step into any situation at any moment when we ask Him to. The prayers that expect Him to do exactly that are the ones that honor Him most. Faith is always the appropriate attitude when we pray.

Prayer makes things possible for men that
they find otherwise impossible.
—SUNDAR SINGH

United

*Make every effort to keep the unity of the
Spirit through the bond of peace.*
EPHESIANS 4:3

In Word

The early Christians noticed that God was calling them to live distinctly from their culture. That wasn't a foreign concept to the Jewish mind, but to those Gentiles who had been called into the church, it was a radical idea. Here in isolated communities of believers in Jesus, the Kingdom of God could be seen. Sometimes it was a fuzzy picture, but it was still a picture. These "holy people"—or saints, as the New Testament writers called them—were a glimpse of the Kingdom to come.

That's why unity is such an emphasis in the New Testament. The Kingdom of God is governed by the triune King who, while having three distinct persons within Himself, has absolutely no discord. There is nothing incongruous in the character of the Creator, and there is to be nothing incongruous in the character of His redeemed people. So Jesus prayed for the unity of His disciples in John 17, and He bases the unity of the church on the unity of the Trinity (John 17:20-23). Regardless of the differences in believers' personalities, giftedness, and opinions, the church is to be one. The Spirit of Christ cannot be divided into segments.

In Deed

Paul urges Christians to "make every effort" to be united. That means that it's more than a high ideal, more than a noble cause, and more than a good suggestion. It's an imperative. The nature of the church is meant to reflect the nature of God. If we don't have unity, we have done nothing to show the world a God of peace.

Have you made every effort to have unity with other believers? Yes, there are principles worth dividing over, but only if they are principles that distinguish believers from nonbelievers. Anything less is insufficient cause to break fellowship with the saints. Your understanding of God's Spirit—or better yet, your experience with Him—will shape your sense of unity with other believers. If you know Him and let Him fill your heart, you will want your fellowship to reflect your King. Make every effort to reflect Him well.

If we focus on our differences, our focus is on
ourselves. If we focus on unity, our focus is on God.
—ANONYMOUS

Gifted

To each one of us grace has been given
as Christ apportioned it.
EPHESIANS 4:7

In Word

God has a purpose for your gifts. You probably know that intellectually, but few of us have let that truth really sink in. In Christ, we have been given grace in ways that are to be manifested in the body of believers. There is a role in the fellowship that only you can fill.

Think of God's purpose in giving His grace to individuals. He has redeemed billions of people throughout history in order for each person to reflect some unique aspect of His character. That might boggle our minds, but it makes sense for an infinite God. As immensely and diversely worthy as His attributes are, there is plenty of opportunity for each redeemed soul to worship Him uniquely. That is our calling.

At the same time, He has redeemed us in one Spirit. There is not a Spirit of grace, a Spirit of deliverance, *and* a Spirit of providence. There is only one Spirit, who gives all gifts from the same God. While grace is manifested in vastly different ways, it is all from the same source. And there is no internal contradiction within that source. The Father, the Son, and the Spirit are one, never diverging in purpose or character. The integrity of the Godhead is as pure as pure gets.

In Deed

Have you considered what conflict with other believers implies? It implies a God who can't keep His people together. It implies a multitude of spirits with a multitude of purposes. It implies a fragmented kingdom that may or may not be worth spending eternity in. In short, it slanders the integrity of God.

None of us mean to do that, of course. We're so used to seeing discord in this world that we've grown casual about it, accepting it as part of the human condition. But Christians are not called to reflect the human condition, not in its fallenness. We're called to reflect God. Unity does that. Discord doesn't. It is never a casual matter to the Father who fills us with one Spirit.

> The whole church which is throughout the whole
> world possesses one and the same God.
> —IRENAEUS

Worthy

I urge you to live a life worthy of the calling you have received.
EPHESIANS 4:1

In Word

We know that the unity of the church is an important issue, but it rarely takes priority over the issues deep in our hearts. We want to live and grow as disciples, serving the Lord and following His will. We want Him to change us within and answer our prayers. It is a very personal process.

But we forget how public a process it is supposed to be. Our personal issues are not, of course, always on display for others to see. God does deal with us privately. But to Him, the unity of His church is just as important as the deep desires in our lives. At the root of disunity is a heart issue. When God's people are not in harmony with each other, it is a certain sign that hearts are not in harmony with God.

We have little trouble agreeing with that, as long as we can point our finger at those whose hearts aren't right with God. But what about our own? Is there any contempt within us for others? any tendency to judge? any desire for self-promotion at the expense of others' gifts? any self-will at all?

In Deed

Of course there is. We know that. We are redeemed, but we have vestiges of fallen flesh that continue to pester us. And as much as we like to point, we know the first place to look for the seeds of discord is the mirror. We know, at some level, we have failed to live up to verse 3; we have not made every effort to live at peace with our brothers and sisters in Christ.

Meditate on that today. Think about the statement we make when we tell Jesus we want His Spirit in us but couldn't care less whether it's in others. Consider what He must think of those who pray for His blessing without seeking His unity. Understand how it must grieve Him to see His Spirit "fragmented," so to speak, among a multitude of individuals who want Him for themselves. Then think about what it means to live a life worthy of His calling. Has His calling drawn you into close fellowship with diverse believers? If not, let it. He is worthy of the calling He has given you.

The Bible knows nothing of solitary religion.
—JOHN WESLEY

Equipped

He . . . gave some to be apostles, some to be prophets,
some to be evangelists, and some to be pastors and
teachers, to prepare God's people for works of service.
EPHESIANS 4:11-12

In Word

The first purpose of unity is to reflect the God of peace who has no conflict within Himself. But there's a second purpose, and it's almost as important. We are to be united in the body of Christ in order to actually function as His body. We are to do the works He did while He was in the flesh, and we are to be coordinated about it. The Spirit has gifted the body in order for the body to fulfill the mission of Jesus. We are to reconcile the world to God.

How can a divided body do that? Only slowly and spastically. A fragmented church is like a palsied body that cannot coordinate its movements with its mind. But serving God is not supposed to be like that. Everyone has a gift, and God assigns individual roles. Those individuals acting in coordination—under the guidance of the head, who is Jesus—can do remarkable work in the power of His Spirit. The effectiveness of the mission depends on the unity of the body. No wonder Satan targets our fellowship.

If we're honest, we can see that the enemy has been highly effective in his mission. Nearly every church body has discord at some level. It is possible to deal with disagreements in ways that honor God and further the mission, but we often do not find them. We allow our disagreements to distract us from the mission, and the body suffers. Satan loves that. God is grieved.

In Deed

Contemplate your service in the Kingdom today. Have you been distracted? Is there any conflict in your fellowship that has hindered your service—or even your attitude toward your service? If so, resolve to return to your focus. Then do something about it. Seek unity, and serve with love in your heart toward your fellow believers.

> It's hard enough resisting the real enemy. If we start fighting other Christians, we're fighting two wars—and one of them is suicidal.
> —JOHN WIMBER

Mature

*Speaking the truth in love, we will in all things grow
up into him who is the Head, that is, Christ.*
EPHESIANS 4:15

In Word

As long as human beings have recorded their own history, stories of utopia have
been dreamed of and written down. World literature has ample specimens of utopian
visions, whether it takes the form of heaven, nirvana, paradise, or any other abstract
desire. In our hearts, we know something is wrong. Also in our hearts, we dream of
things being made right.

But for a lost world to *crave* the Kingdom of God specifically, it must once in a
while *see* the Kingdom of God specifically. Utopian speculations don't instill confidence in anyone. We know that the world groans for redemption (Romans 8:22), but
there are few specifics to its groaning. Those who are lost know only that something
is wrong; they don't have a clear picture of what is right.

That's the role of the church—to demonstrate what's right and to tell it truthfully.
We are to give the world snapshots of its desired destination: the Kingdom of God.
Our transparent, honest love for one another and the genuine unity it engenders are
to witness to a God of peace who has the power to reconcile diverse people to Himself
and to each other. We alone can replace the world's utopian speculations with a visible basis for faith. But in order to do so, we need to be people of truth and love. That
means complete honesty and unwavering compassion, both at the same time.

In Deed

That's a hard line to walk. We sometimes think honesty is too brutal to be loving, or
that love precludes the painful truth. But the Spirit of God has modeled the balance for
us: He painfully convicts us of sin while warmly welcoming us into His fellowship.

We are to follow the model. An integrity-starved world isn't used to that kind of
fellowship, but it's always appealing. So exemplify it. Let your fellowship be transparent, honest, and uncompromisingly loving. That kind of mature unity is one of the
clearest gospel witnesses the world can see.

Division has done more to hide Christ from the view of
men than all the infidelity that has ever been spoken.
—GEORGE MACDONALD

Stretch

God, who knows the heart, showed that he accepted them
by giving the Holy Spirit to them, just as he did to us.
ACTS 15:8

In Word

It seemed like an open-and-shut case. God had commanded in Holy Scripture—His eternal, unchanging Word—to circumcise baby boys (Genesis 17:10-14; Leviticus 12:3). He said it signified an everlasting covenant (Genesis 17:13), so no one could argue that it was temporary. He said it applied even to foreigners living with Israel (Exodus 12:49), so no one could argue that it was specific to one ethnic group. No, any competent Bible scholar could come to only one conclusion: God requires circumcision. Always.

So the competent Bible scholars who had become Christians preached this truth to new believers, even those who had come to faith without having been circumcised. If they really wanted to be right with God, if they really wanted to be obedient and to partake of this everlasting covenant, they would have to undergo full conversion into Judaism through this sacred, God-given rite. And it makes sense, doesn't it? The Word of God is unchanging. The Pharisee believers were simply preaching the Word.

But the experience of the Gentiles who had come to faith in Jesus contradicted this teaching. Peter and Paul had both received dramatic visions instructing them to preach the gospel to Gentiles. God didn't settle the circumcision issue in those visions, but His Holy Spirit readily fell on the uncircumcised. These non-Jews were filled with the Spirit independently of conversion rites. Could Peter explain that scripturally? No, and he didn't even try. His only defense was that "God, who knows the heart, showed that he accepted them."

In Deed

In trying to discern truth, we often look more to our own understanding of Scripture than to the heart of God behind it. Can we explain everything He does by pointing to chapter and verse? No, we can't. He fits in no boxes, not even in the ones we think are divinely inspired. Scripture is absolutely true, and it shows us who God is. But our understanding of Scripture can't contain Him. Let Him stretch your mind. Let Him drive you deeper into His Word. And let Him reveal His heart in surprising ways.

God cannot be grasped by the mind. If He
could be grasped, He would not be God.
—EVAGRIUS OF PONTUS

Listen

*It seemed good to the Holy Spirit and to us not to burden
you with anything beyond the following requirements*
ACTS 15:28

In Word

The book of Acts is full of clear, specific direction from the Holy Spirit. People spoke
words directly inspired by the Spirit. Agabus accurately predicted a famine and Paul's
sufferings (11:28 and 21:11); Paul exposed a sorcerer (13:9-11) and was led away
from two territories (16:6-7); Peter and Stephen defended themselves with the words
of the Spirit (4:8 and 6:10). Even common, everyday believers not known as apostles
or prophets could speak in the Spirit's voice (21:4). There seemed to be a free flow of
communication between the Spirit and His people.

Even so, there were times when opinions differed and decisions had to be made.
Not all issues were clear. Such was the case when James decided that circumcision
should not be required of Gentiles coming to Christ. What should they be told? What
ground rules should be established for fellowship between Jewish and Gentile believers? Since God didn't spell that out in His Word, how should it be spelled out now?
This was uncharted territory, and the right decisions—at least the minor details of
those decisions—weren't clear.

That's why James says, "It seemed good to the Holy Spirit and to us." The words
of the Spirit weren't obvious, but His presence seemed to validate the direction the
council was taking. They didn't have an exact road map, but the Spirit wasn't block-
ing their way. In fact, in their intimate fellowship with Him, He seemed to be pleased.
They could proceed as they thought best.

In Deed

There are times when it's wrong for us to move forward without clear and specific
direction from God. When the Spirit hasn't spoken and we still have reservations
about what to do, it's sinful to proceed without faith. But there are times when the
Spirit lets us go the direction that seems best. He's there to guide and will warn us
when we're getting off track. But in the details of life that aren't specifically covered
in His Word, sensing His presence and His pleasure is enough. When it seems good
to the Spirit and to us, we can be confident about where we're headed.

> Deep in your heart it is not guidance that
> you want as much as a guide.
> —JOHN WHITE

Conflict Resolution

Your attitude should be the same as that of Christ Jesus.
PHILIPPIANS 2:5

In Word

We call Him Lord. We worship Him as our Savior and King. We say we are disciples who follow Him. But if we're honest with ourselves, our words don't always reflect the truth. Though we say we are like Him, our attitude gives us away. Our attitude doesn't always resemble the attitude of Jesus.

What was His attitude like? The next few verses tell us: He exemplified humility, even to the point of death. He was obedient, emptying Himself of self-will and submitting to the will of the Father. He was everything our fallen human natures are not. He gave Himself up for others.

That's our calling. Though the church is called to a radical sort of unity that the world cannot understand, we don't have to be Christians long to realize that discord still strikes our fellowships. The redeemed have been made holy in God's eyes, but we do not always act holy in one another's eyes. So when conflict arises, the Bible points us to Jesus and says, as Paul proclaims in this verse: "Be like Him."

In Deed

It's a high calling, but it makes sense for those who call Him Lord. If we say we are followers of Jesus, it only seems right to follow His attitude. And His attitude was humble and self-sacrificing. He never made conflict without a holy purpose.

That doesn't mean that conflict is always a sign of sin, of course. Jesus pointedly rebuked the teachers of the law and Pharisees often. Paul and Barnabas once had such a sharp disagreement that they agreed to part ways. Conflict can be God's design to highlight different goals and agendas, to spread His ambassadors out in this world, or to express His Spirit's compassion for all sides of an issue. It isn't always bad.

But it can always be sorted out with humility. Conflict is one thing; prideful conflict is another. The Spirit allows the former, but never the latter. When you disagree with other believers, step one is to take a step back. Let humility reign.

> Humility is that holy place in which God bids us make the sacrifice of ourselves.
> —ANONYMOUS

Spiritual Affirmation

If you have any encouragement from being united with Christ, . . . then make my joy complete by being like-minded.
PHILIPPIANS 2:1-2

In Word

We are not left alone in this world to do as well as we can. We have been united to the Spirit of the Savior, to the extent that we are in Him and He is in us. This is no abstract union, but a concrete reality. Anything we need from Him, we can have.

That's why Paul appeals to the Philippian church to be like-minded. It isn't just a matter of getting the conflicting parties to compromise; there's a spiritual reality that can bring them together. If both Euodia and Syntyche (the two women in contention mentioned in chapter 4) would recognize that the humble Spirit of Jesus was living within them, perhaps they could unite on grounds of love and a common purpose. Whatever issue was at stake, it wasn't greater than Christ. He is the great uniter, because He is the ultimate purpose and passion of the church. When people agree in His Spirit, agreement on other issues comes much more easily.

In Deed

That's God's desire for His people. No, He doesn't expect us always to agree on everything. He does, however, plan for us to be united on the main issue: Jesus. If we are in His Spirit, then we are brought together in love and purpose. The Source of our life doesn't expect us to abandon Him for smaller issues. When we do, He is grieved.

A necessary step toward conflict resolution within the church is to realize the heart of God and comply with the power of His Spirit. As long as we hold our agendas tightly, He does not reign, even when we are convinced our agendas are His. But when we are consumed first and foremost with our greatest love, our Savior, we immediately are united with other believers in the issue that is by far most important. And if that issue is settled, well, the rest is secondary.

If your fellowship is in conflict, focus on God's heart. Help others to do the same. Ignore the divisive issue until you have in common a love for Jesus. Then watch His Spirit work.

> Sanctification is a life of Christ-centered choices,
> made evident in loving obedience to God.
> —MEL DE PEAL

Internal Revolution

Do nothing out of selfish ambition or vain conceit.
PHILIPPIANS 2:3

In Word

It's a heart issue. If we are to develop the kind of unity that God desires for His people and that avoids or resolves the kind of conflict that brings dishonor to His name, the process must begin in our hearts. And the instruction Paul gives for us is painful: we must "do nothing out of selfish ambition or vain conceit."

That may not seem painful on the surface. After all, most of us are not that selfish and vain. In fact, we are pretty magnanimous with our peers, giving generously when we can and getting along with everyone who is reasonable. The problem comes when we have to deal with unreasonable people or misguided agendas. Then we have to put our foot down.

But that's the problem. All churches run smoothly when they are narrowed down to the people who get along naturally anyway. In fact, that's true of all secular institutions as well. Any organization can function when the clique is purified and the undesirables run off. But the church is to be different. It's to be united even when the proverbial squeaky wheels aren't getting the grease they so desperately want. It is supposed to be able to manage conflict among even the most diverse opinions and personalities. It is supposed to reflect the Kingdom of God.

In Deed

That's what Jesus' twelve disciples exemplified. The Savior took twelve guys who ordinarily would butt heads with each other regularly and told them to be one as He and the Father were one. He taught them about servanthood and humility and crosses and sacrifice. He showed them a different way.

The church today is also to be the people of the different way. We are to find the seeds of this unity, this ability to resolve deep conflict through a deeper Spirit, by looking within and rooting out selfishness and vanity. Only then will the fellowship of Christ make an impact in this world. Only then will conflict be resolved.

> If I really love God, my innate and persistent selfishness will have received its death blow.
> —ALEXANDER SMELLIE

External Renovation

In humility consider others better than yourselves.
PHILIPPIANS 2:3

In Word

It's so unnatural. We don't consider others better than ourselves, because if we aren't looking out for ourselves, who will? At least that's what we've asked ourselves, certain that our "self" instincts are necessary. But God has an answer we didn't expect. Who will take care of ourselves if we don't? He will. That's a promise.

That is why a Christian can recklessly live for the interests of others. God will keep our interests for us, taking care of whatever we need. We don't need to obsess about them. That selfishness and vain conceit Paul mentions early in verse 3 can be abandoned. We don't need it. We have a God who looks out for us.

That frees us up to focus on others. We can serve, knowing God will give us everything we need and deserve. We can sacrifice, knowing that the blessing will always outweigh the cost. We can actually consider others better than ourselves, knowing that God loves us infinitely. We risk nothing in the exchange. We can lose our lives for His sake, and He guarantees that we will find them.

In Deed

Few people live this out, but imagine what our churches would look like if we did. How would conflict appear in your church if the majority of your members were wholeheartedly sacrificing for others? What unmet needs would people argue over? What areas of service would remain unattended? What grudges could reasonably be nurtured? What recognition or affirmation would your members miss out on?

The vision seems utopian, but it's startling, isn't it? And it's even more startling when we begin to realize that this is a possibility. Churches can actually function this way. All it takes is for a few people to abandon themselves to others and watch the ripple effects. Consider being one of those people today. And watch God use your life in remarkable ways.

> Christ regarded the self-loving, self-regarding, self-seeking spirit as the direct antithesis of real living.
>
> —J. B. PHILLIPS

Cultural Contradiction

*Each of you should look not only to your own
interests, but also to the interests of others.*
PHILIPPIANS 2:4

In Word

We live in a self-absorbed world. We like to think we came out of that culture when we accepted Christ, but the truth is that we can be just as self-absorbed as always. Self-centeredness once took the form of ambition and status; now that we are redeemed, it may take the form of our own spiritual growth and maturity. We've changed our expressions of self, but self resides within.

That's okay to a point. But Jesus would have us look out for the spiritual growth of others as much as we look out for our own. He wants us to be focused upward (toward God) and outward (toward others). He knows that we will grow best in His Spirit when we aren't always examining the Spirit's internal work.

The result of our outward focus ideally makes us a holy people who confront the ways of the world with a radical way of life. Selfishness rules the world; the Christian community's selflessness is to be an open rebuke to the prevailing culture. Fallen humanity will never recognize God in its midst until it recognizes the godly in its midst. And the best way for the godly to be recognized is for the godly to be selfless. Radically selfless. Passionately, conspicuously selfless.

In Deed

Is that how people describe you? Radically, conspicuously, passionately selfless? If not, why not? If you're like most Christians, it's because you default to your human nature far too often and you are influenced by the fallen culture you came from far too easily. To be selfless, you have to swim against a very strong current; sometimes that seems impossible.

When that's the case, turn your eyes back to Jesus. See how radically He cared for others, even to the point of His own death. You don't want to go that route? It's the way of the Cross, and it's your calling. Disciples of Jesus must go that route. It's what we were made for. And it's what God uses to open the eyes of a self-focused world.

We may easily be too big for God to use, but never too small.
—D. L. MOODY

Ministers of Grace

Just as the sufferings of Christ flow over into our lives,
so also through Christ our comfort overflows.
2 CORINTHIANS 1:5

In Word

The Christian life is painful. We may not like to acknowledge that fact—we prefer to focus on the joy and peace, not the pain—but it's true. Paul and Barnabas told the believers in Antioch that "we must go through many hardships to enter the kingdom of God" (Acts 14:22). In a promise that's rarely claimed by faith, Jesus even guaranteed His disciples that they would suffer in this world (John 16:33). If that doesn't fit today's concept of the Christian life, it's no fault of the Bible. No, the Bible is clear. We will have hardships and pain until the Kingdom comes in all its glory.

For that reason, the New Testament writers continually urge believers to bear one another's burdens and to be an encouragement to others in the faith. They understood well that the God of comfort would probably administer His grace not out of thin air but through His people. The grace of God in a trial is to be experienced through the mouths and hands of fellow believers. If they aren't there to express God's comfort, it often isn't expressed.

Paul used a lot of ink to encourage Christians himself, and he also urged them to encourage one another. It was more than a nice thought to add a smile to one's day; it was a valid and essential ministry. In a fallen world, where trials are frequent and pain is intense, encouragement matters.

In Deed

Think about the times another believer has encouraged you. You can probably recognize that a word or act of encouragement had the power to change your perspective on your situation or at least to help you make it through the day. If words of encouragement have that kind of power, is there any reason not to use them?

Think of someone in your life who needs encouragement. Then tell that person today that you are praying for him or her, or that God cares, or something that will convey the Father's blessing. You are doing more than prompting a smile. You are administering the grace of God.

Encouragement costs you nothing to
give, but it is priceless to receive.
—ANONYMOUS

A God of Comfort

Praise be to the God and Father of our Lord Jesus Christ,
the Father of compassion and the God of all comfort.
2 CORINTHIANS 1:3

In Word

Sometimes we think of Him as the Father of hardship or as the God of the difficult path. We sometimes wonder why, when we say "not my will but Thine," He seems so eager to take us up on the offer. We strive and we struggle and we get discouraged. We forget that He is called "the Father of compassion and the God of all comfort."

Why do we forget that so easily? Perhaps it's because the struggles are so easy to see and the encouragement isn't. Perhaps only the eyes of faith can see the ways He works to comfort us. Or perhaps the members of the body who should be giving us encouragement have missed their assignment. Regardless, we hurt sometimes, and all we want is for our Father to notice and to let us know He cares. When we feel like that, we need to refer back to this verse. Compassion and comfort are what He's all about.

It's true. God lets us suffer, but He also longs to embrace us. He wants us to see the end of the story and know that the glory He's promised will always outweigh the pain we've suffered. He wants His other children to gather around us and express His love. He knows life is hard. And He wants us to know He isn't.

In Deed

Romans 8:32 assures us that if God gave up His Son for us, we can count on the fact that He's on our side. Even when life seems to argue against that point, faith tells us that it's true. The God who made us, redeemed us, guides us, and loves us is the God of compassion and comfort.

Do you need compassion and comfort today? Seek it in your Father. He offers it, even when His people neglect to show it. Rest in His Word and imagine His loving arms holding you up in your trial. You'll never become a minister of His grace until you know how to receive it. So today, just receive it. Let God comfort you. He is never reluctant to do so.

In Christ the heart of the Father is revealed, and higher comfort there cannot be than to rest in the Father's heart.
—ANDREW MURRAY

Enduring Love

*If we are comforted, it is for your comfort, which produces
in you patient endurance of the same sufferings we suffer.*
2 CORINTHIANS 1:6

In Word

Perhaps you haven't come face-to-face with the fact of suffering yet. A lot of Christians haven't, assuming that if all is well in their relationship with the Lord, all will be well in their circumstances. But a quick survey of Jesus, Paul, Peter, James, John, Stephen, and practically any other follower of the Lord will convince us that pain is part of discipleship. After all, Jesus had told His disciples to count the cost. That means there is one. Always.

The question for the believer is what that cost is going to do to us. For some, it destroys faith, pointing them only to a God who doesn't care. For others, it's a mystery that should never be probed and that can never be explained. But the biblical testimony about our trials is this: sometimes God delivers us miraculously, sometimes He doesn't, but He always comforts us with His promises and His presence. Regardless, trials have their fruit in our hearts. They can produce an eternal perspective, an enduring character, and a stronger faith. If we let them, they can bring us closer to God.

In Deed

It's a mystery why some people let trials move them away from God while others let trials move them toward Him. The biblical ideal, however, is that they should always result in patient endurance. They are clear evidence that our world is still fallen and our race is still sinful, even though the Kingdom has been promised and has even begun to sprout up here and there. There is an "already" and a "not yet" in the gospel of redemption, and we live between them. Meanwhile, God works.

Let God work in your heart. Your trials aren't fun; everyone knows that, especially Him. But they are useful. They produce perseverance, and as James says, perseverance has a perfect result: our maturity (James 1:4). And while we are persevering, we can know this: God is there. He cares. And His comfort is always available.

Nothing great was ever done without much enduring.
—CATHERINE OF SIENA

Truth in Trials

[God] comforts us in all our troubles, so that we
can comfort those in any trouble with the comfort
we ourselves have received from God.
2 CORINTHIANS 1:4

In Word

Think of a time when you needed God's comfort. How did it come to you? Did a Bible verse jump off the page and speak to you? Did a timely sermon address your situation? Did a friend offer a word of encouragement? However it came, it was probably a reminder that God is who He says He is and your trials do nothing to change that fact. The thing that helps the most when you hurt the most is often simply a new glimpse of the truth of God.

We need that because we listen to the lies. When we suffer, we hear internal voices that tell us perhaps God isn't good, or He's good to everyone but us, or He's good but His goodness will always require us to walk the most difficult and distressing path, or some other such nonsense. In the midst of a crisis, we see God least clearly, and we begin to question His intentions. We're afraid He might let us down. We need someone to tell us the truth about God.

Having heard the truth—which always gives some degree of comfort and hope—we know how to help others who are going through similar trials. If God has comforted us in our crises, whether through a Scripture passage, a sermon, an encouraging friend, or any other means, we have some idea of how to comfort others in their crises. We may not know exactly what they are going through—all trials are different, after all, and so are the personalities dealing with them—but we know something about our Father. We know how to tell the truth about Him.

In Deed

That's what people need in the midst of trouble: the truth about God. They need to know that He can deliver, sustain, strengthen, comfort, heal, save, and provide. Having found Him in our need, we can offer Him to others. If we have learned the truth about God, we must tell it. There is no greater comfort.

More people fail for lack of encouragement
than for any other reason.
—ANONYMOUS

Sacrifice for the World

If we are distressed, it is for your comfort and salvation.
2 CORINTHIANS 1:6

In Word

Paul conducted his ministry with a sacrificial spirit. Whatever hardships he went through, whatever persecution and pain, he did it for the glory of Jesus and the benefit of believers. That's because Paul understood something that we often forget: the way of the Cross is a necessary part of discipleship.

It's true. No mission, no ministry, no personal growth can occur unless there is sacrifice involved. We don't know exactly why that is, but we can see it on nearly every page of Scripture. Abraham left home for an unknown land, and he also walked his son up a mountain to sacrifice him; and the people of God were founded on the faith of this father. David became king only after years in caves and exile from an insanely jealous Saul. And if the scriptural biographies aren't enough, we have the words of Jesus Himself: "Anyone who does not carry his cross and follow me cannot be my disciple" (Luke 14:27). For God's work to be done, for His fruit to grow, there is always a cost.

Think about it: if it costs us nothing to tell the world of Jesus and bring souls into His Kingdom, how will they see? If people do not see God comfort us in our trials, how will they trust Him in theirs? If no one sees how we are sustained in hardships, why would they seek His sustenance in their hardships? The way of the Cross is essential if anyone is to see the God of the Cross. The God of all comfort must be more than a topic of discussion; He must actually be demonstrated in our need.

In Deed

We wonder why so much of the world remains unconvinced of the gospel, but perhaps one reason is that it does not see the gospel functioning in our largely sacrifice-free lives. There is power in our distress, if we'll embrace it—that's where God shows up. If we are convinced that the world needs to see Him, we must be equally convinced that it needs to see Him in us. And the only way is to count the cost and make a sacrifice for the Kingdom.

Ministry that costs nothing accomplishes nothing.
—JOHN HENRY JOWETT

Still Beautiful

He had no beauty or majesty to attract us to him,
nothing in his appearance that we should desire him.
ISAIAH 53:2

In Word

"He will not judge by what he sees with his eyes, or decide by what he hears with his ears." That's what we are told about the Messiah back in Isaiah 11:3; His judgments on behalf of the poor and oppressed will not be swayed by how things look on the surface. Now in Isaiah 53, we're given the impression that we shouldn't be swayed by external appearances either. After all, the Messiah seemed to be a commoner from the poorer part of the country—no high position in society, no discernible pedigree, no bank account. Even more, He died a disgraceful death among criminals, clearly outside the favor of God. If we judged by what we saw with our eyes, we would reject Him—like most did. Then again, looks can be deceiving.

That's still the way it is. Jesus is rejected by many today because Christians and the church don't look all that impressive. We don't drive the culture like Hollywood does, we don't drive the economy like Wall Street does, and we don't drive policy like Washington does. We also make a lot of mistakes and blend in with the culture; non-Christians sometimes have a hard time recognizing us. Yes, if the world judges by appearances, Jesus will still be rejected often.

But Jesus is now resurrected and exalted. His Spirit can do the miracles He did and transform us just as His disciples were transformed. For those with eyes to see and ears to hear, there is beauty and majesty to be found in our Savior. He is what we truly desire.

In Deed

A constant temptation of the Christian life comes from the tension between the appeal of this world, with all its glamour and glitter, and the appeal of Jesus, with all His humility and grace. The irony is that choosing Jesus will dazzle us in every way over the course of eternity, and choosing the world will disappoint us quickly. When you're tempted between two worlds, choose Jesus. That's where beauty and majesty really are.

If you are looking for an example of
humility, look at the cross.
—THOMAS AQUINAS

Pleased to Suffer

It was the LORD's will to crush him and cause him to suffer.
ISAIAH 53:10

In Word

It was the Lord's will to crush the Messiah. Not only was it His will, the real sense of the Hebrew expression in verse 10 is that God took pleasure in the Messiah's suffering. We have a hard time with that concept because we don't think God has any pleasure in human pain, especially the pain of His own Son. While God didn't enjoy Jesus' suffering—or ours either, for that matter—He was pleased to ordain it. The benefits exceeded the cost. They were well worth it to Him. It wasn't a hard decision.

We see that attitude reflected in Jesus too. He endured the cross "for the joy set before him" (Hebrews 12:2). We know He didn't enjoy it; a dreadful night in the garden of Gethsemane made that clear, as did His cries of anguish as He died. But He willingly made the sacrifice because of the joy it would bring. He would have intimate fellowship with all who come to Him in faith. That was well worth the brutality of the torture He endured.

That thought is a dramatic picture of the heart of God. He experiences tremendous joy over those who love Him. The painful cost of redemption was not paid grudgingly, a reluctant last-ditch effort to salvage what He could of His broken creation. It was planned from before the foundation of the world—with pleasure. His love for His people is great enough to drive Him to extraordinary lengths that will cause angels and humans to marvel forever and ever. That's a zealous, relentless love.

In Deed

Do you see yourself as the object of God's zealous, relentless love? Do you realize that His love for you prompted Him to pay extraordinary costs to bring you into His fellowship and that He did it gladly? Most Christians know that intellectually but don't believe it deep in their hearts. They see God as a reluctant, obligated lover. But that's not how He portrays Himself. He's delighted to sacrifice for your love. Make it even more worthwhile by loving Him deeply in return.

> For the sake of each of us, He laid down His life—worth no less than the universe.
> —CLEMENT OF ALEXANDRIA

Gratitude and Love

We all, like sheep, have gone astray, each
of us has turned to his own way.
ISAIAH 53:6

In Word

Long, long ago in a distant garden, God and humanity had perfect fellowship. We can only imagine what that was like, being so far removed from it today, but we can be sure that it was an incredible experience. God's will was clearly known, His voice clearly heard, His presence clearly sensed. There was no need to diverge from His perfect path. There was enormous freedom to be completely, authentically human in His presence, with no shame involved. There were no unfulfilled desires and no disappointment. Humanity was in perfect harmony with the heart of God.

That all changed, of course, when a slithering liar created the illusion of unfulfilled desire and tricked humans into developing a will independent of their Creator's. The results, as we know, were tragic, and we still feel the consequences of them today. Each of us has followed the path of our first parents; we all, like sheep, have gone astray and turned to our own way. We became ruled by self-will and grew more blind and more deaf to the voice and the presence of God. Our senses dulled to the point where many of us have even wondered whether He exists. We became like patients in intensive care whose nutritional supply has been cut off, and we were slowly slipping away.

That's why the Messiah came, suffered, and died. We needed a life transfusion, and the only way to get it was for life to be drained from the Living One and given to us. Our death was reversed because a human not worthy of death came to us and died. His Resurrection overcame the disaster of our self-will. We no longer need to go our own way.

In Deed

The Shepherd could have cut His losses and let His sheep wander into oblivion, but He didn't. He came after His straying flock and brought us back into His pasture. When we understand what really happened in our fall and redemption, we can't help but marvel. Our fate was worse than we thought, and our salvation is greater than we think. All that's left is gratitude and love.

> A true Christian is a man who never for a moment forgets what God has done for him in Christ.
> —JOHN BAILLIE

Heaven on Earth

The punishment that brought us peace was upon him, and by his wounds we are healed.
ISAIAH 53:5

In Word

We celebrate the gift of salvation. Most of us celebrate because of the eternal life we know we'll have in heaven. Though we suffer pains and trials today, we know it won't be this way forever—that in heaven there will be no more sorrow and no more tears. We look across the Jordan and into the Promised Land, wondering when we'll cross over and leave this wilderness behind. We love the prospects of our future.

But the Messiah's ministry is much more than a ticket to future glory. It has present implications that, if we had faith to believe, would allow us to taste glory right now. Many of God's promises included in redemption are for "the land of the living" (Psalm 27:13). His benefits are more than a distant hope (Psalm 103:2-5). The punishment that Jesus suffered on our behalf brought us peace—notice the fullness of life experienced by His followers in Acts—and by His wounds we are healed. The blessings of salvation began the day Jesus blew the doors off of a tomb. If we place all of our hopes in the future, we're missing an awfully large part of salvation.

In Deed

Does your life revolve around a future hope or a present reality? The truth is that both should shape the decisions of each day. But when the life we live doesn't measure up to the life we're promised, we're often content to shrug our shoulders and assume the promises of God are all for our life beyond the grave.

God disagrees. He gave His disciples the gift of faith—an unnecessary gift in the clear vision of heaven, by the way—in order to bring heaven into the now. Jesus even commanded His disciples to pray that God's will be done on earth as it is being done in heaven. The truth of salvation is not just that we will go to heaven, but that heaven will come to us in the here and now—if we believe. Live in that truth, praying and acting as though the Kingdom is invading your life. The punishment that brought us peace and healed our wounds means that it truly is.

> It is certain that all that will go to heaven
> hereafter begin their heaven now.
> —MATTHEW HENRY

World Changers

I will give him a portion among the great,
and he will divide the spoils with the strong,
because he poured out his life unto death.
ISAIAH 53:12

In Word

Imagine what the inheritance of the Son of God is. Psalm 2 says the whole earth and all the nations are included in His inheritance. Paul referred to heavenly riches, and Peter spoke of an inheritance that will not fade away. What's really incredible is what else the New Testament writers say about the inheritance of the Son: it is shared with us.

That's what Isaiah's prophecy is pointing to. God looks at the obedience of His Son with delight and turns all creation over to Him. Jesus is the heir of the King's estate, and with an infinite King, the estate is greater than any mind can imagine. The extravagant God is ridiculously wealthy with all kinds of riches, and He wills them all to His Son. His Son, in turn, shares His inheritance with His bride—all who believe in Him. It's the best deal we ever got.

Did you realize that? The Bible gives us two pictures of eternal inheritance: the Father gives everything to the Son, who shares with His brothers; and the Father endows everything to the Bridegroom, who allows His bride to marry into His wealth. That means that God bestows on us what Jesus deserves from His obedience. And if we think about what Jesus really deserves . . . well, that's a staggering thought. And the truth is that it's ours as well as His.

In Deed

Too many Christians walk through this world convinced that God answers only their small prayers, that His arm has to be twisted to give us what we need, that He's reluctant to use us to change lives. But God and Scripture shout "No!" When He promises His Son the nations, He promises us the nations. When He promises His Son the extravagantly life-giving, fruit-bearing Spirit, He promises us the extravagantly life-giving, fruit-bearing Spirit. Faith takes hold of those promises and won't let go. And those with that kind of faith become history makers and world changers. To Him—and to us—are given the spoils of His victory.

> God is more anxious to bestow His blessings
> on us than we are to receive them.
> —AUGUSTINE

A Prayer Agenda

I urge, then, first of all, that requests, prayers,
intercession and thanksgiving be made for everyone.
1 TIMOTHY 2:1

In Word

If you're like most people, your prayer requests begin with your biggest and most pressing needs and, if they go beyond that at all, extend outward to people further away from you and issues less urgent. God understands that, and He responds to the issues close to our hearts. But He responds even more readily to people who have a larger view, who lift up their eyes to see not only their own problems and desires but also the big picture of His Kingdom. Those whose view is expansive find that He answers more expansively—*and* that He addresses those personal concerns as well. When we take up His highest agenda, He more readily takes up ours.

So Paul instructs Timothy and the people under his charge to pray. A lot. For everyone. There are no limits here. We aren't to pray just for Christians or just for the lost but for both. We aren't to pray just for people we know but also for those we simply hear about. We pray for individuals and groups, people in authority and "nobodies," those in deep need and those who can provide. Everyone is fair game.

And we don't just pray one type of prayer either. Paul uses four different words: requests, prayers, intercession, and thanksgiving. Some of those are rather expected and self-explanatory, but some are startling. In addition to our prayers for personal need and of intervention on someone's behalf, we also give thanks. For everyone— those we've never met, those inside and outside the Kingdom, those who rub us the wrong way, government leaders we don't like, and more. Somehow our prayers need to recognize the preciousness of every person God has made and His desire to use them either directly or indirectly in our lives and the lives of others. Everyone is a cause for gratitude. That's what the verse says.

In Deed

That requires a radical readjustment for most of us, but it's what Scripture tells us to do. Pray. How? In every way, at all times, for everyone. If you aren't accustomed to doing that, today would be a good time to start.

Whether we like it or not, asking is the rule of the kingdom.
—CHARLES SPURGEON

A Peaceful Purpose

... that we may live peaceful and quiet
lives in all godliness and holiness.
1 TIMOTHY 2:2

In Word

Many Christians pray for God's judgment on corrupt leaders and for the downfall of those whose policies they disagree with. And while God certainly hears our requests for righteous leadership and godly policies, the spirit in which we pray is often far from His heart. Perhaps He wants to hear prayers that leaders, even godless ones, would finally turn to Him for wisdom and seek His favor. Perhaps He even allows unholy but otherwise effective kings and prime ministers and presidents to govern well so that His people can exercise their faith in peaceful times. The relationship between God, governments, and the societies and cultures of this world is hard to understand, but that's not the point. Regardless of whether we understand, we are told to pray for everyone, including those in authority. Why? So that we might "live peaceful and quiet lives in all godliness and holiness."

Tranquility is a valuable condition, whether we're referring to the peace in society at large or the peace in our hearts. And the peace that Paul refers to here is more than the absence of turmoil; it's an ability to live without fear of punishment, without unreasonable restraints and pressure, without alarm about what might happen next. In an uncertain world, this kind of peace is a very precious commodity.

In Deed

That's what our prayers are meant to provide—or, rather, what God provides for us in response to our prayers. We lift up our requests in order to create a protective hedge around our ability to exercise our faith. We petition God, not only to help us be godly and holy, but also to give us an open arena in which to exercise our godliness and holiness freely. Whether that applies to your government's policies or your hectic schedule today—or anything in between—it's available. We are urged to pray for the opportunity to live in open devotion to our Lord.

Give peace in our time, O Lord.
—BOOK OF COMMON PRAYER

Crossing Barriers

Don't show favoritism.
JAMES 2:1

In Word

One of the distinguishing characteristics of the new community in Christ was its acceptance of all kinds of people. Paul wrote that there was no longer Jew nor Greek, male nor female, but all were one in Jesus. Historians and sociologists who have studied the first century note that one reason for the early church's growth was its ability to reach across social barriers and make its invitation to all segments of society. That's because when people realized that Jesus had bridged heaven and earth for their salvation, other divides between people seemed less significant.

That makes sense. If your Savior left the glories of heaven for the difficulties of earth, it would be hard to begrudge a neighbor the love of that Savior. There is no greater cultural or economic barrier to overcome than that. For a disciple intent on following in the footsteps of his Teacher, the logical thing to do is to cross barriers for the sake of the gospel.

The point of James's teaching is that the church cannot afford to show favoritism if it still wants to represent its Savior. God led the way by sending Jesus directly to the poor of the world first, having Him born in a stable and into a carpenter's family. And the New Testament's emphasis on hospitality is nothing new; compassion for the stranger and the poor is a consistent theme in Old Testament law and prophecy. If the church reflects the heart of God—as it is revealed in ancient Scripture and the life of Jesus—it simply must be hospitable and generous with those on society's fringes.

In Deed

The church in Jerusalem, from which James was writing, forgot that. So do we sometimes. We can be awfully homogeneous, associating with only those who look like us, act like us, live like us, and spend like us. When we do, we are misrepresenting God's Good News.

James urges us to get back to the gospel. It's about the hospitality of God, and it should translate into the hospitality of the believer. Ask Him to show you today how to reflect God's heart.

Hospitality is one form of worship.
—ANONYMOUS

Understanding God

Has not God chosen those who are poor in the eyes
of the world to be rich in faith and to inherit the
kingdom he promised those who love him?
JAMES 2:5

In Word

Why did God do this? Doesn't He love everyone, including the privileged? Yes, but the wealthy often won't receive His love. There's a tendency among the well-off in this world to feel satisfied and comfortable—two very dangerous assumptions that don't reflect spiritual reality. So God began with the poor, the disenfranchised, and the marginalized. Their physical need would parallel their spiritual need. They would have a heart for Him.

There's a lesson in that for us. God chooses those whose hearts are not deceived by the trappings of this world. When He first told His disciples, "Blessed are the poor in spirit" (Matthew 5:3), He indicated that a sense of need in a person's life would open the door for God. And we can observe the same thing today. Those who think they "have it made" by the world's definitions of success are much more resistant to the gospel than those who see their need daily. Material insufficiency points to the deeper need we all have. It prepares us to ask God for His mercy.

In Deed

Do you see your deeper need? Your relationship with God will depend on how insufficient you feel at any given time. That's not a comfortable position, but it leads us to God. When we know our weaknesses, we can know His strength. Our inner sense of poverty is almost always what opens the door for God.

Take note of that when you interact with your world. There are people you come into contact with who know their need for God right now. Others won't hear the gospel, no matter how clearly it's explained, because they are satisfied with their lives. It's a false satisfaction, but it closes ears. Like God, reach out to the "poor"—those who know their need because the circumstances of their lives have made them sensitive to His voice.

He who wants anything from God must
approach Him with empty hands.
—ROBERT C. CUNNINGHAM

Fulfilling Law

*If you really keep the royal law found in Scripture, "Love
your neighbor as yourself," you are doing right.*
JAMES 2:8

In Word

If God's law is going to be fulfilled in our lives, it has to begin deep within our hearts.
Superficial obedience alone has never been pleasing to God. From the testimony of
the Old Testament prophets to the testimony of the Spirit who came at Pentecost, the
rule of God is intended to be deeply internal. God desires transformed hearts, and the
transformation He seeks most is a transformation of love.

We know that. It's a basic truth of the gospel that we learn when we first become
Christians, if not before. But in spite of our familiarity with the law of love, we don't
quite fulfill it as we should. We may take a lifetime trying, but we have to admit that
our natural tendency is to love ourselves, our families, and our friends first, and then
to get to our neighbors as we're able. We don't easily turn our focus outward.

But it's the law. More than that, it's the heart of God. This is what Jesus demonstrated for us and what God did in redeeming us. He took our concerns upon Himself
and bore our burdens. Then He put His nature within us through His Spirit. If we live
by His Spirit, we will fulfill this law. We will love as He loves.

In Deed

That kind of love, of course, is one of the defining characteristics of the new community of the redeemed. The early believers loved like no one else in their culture loved.
They reached out with extravagant hospitality to those who were sick, those who were
persecuted, and those who were needy. In doing so, they demonstrated the heart of
God. The church grew because people were able to see God in its members.

Do people see God in you? Does your hospitality, your urge to reach out, demonstrate the Father's heart? If not, realize where it needs to begin—deep within, where
all true law is fulfilled. Let God's Spirit do His work inside you, and then let Him reach
out through you.

Love of man necessarily arises out of love of God.
—JOHN HOOPER

Reaching Out

*If you show favoritism, you sin and are
convicted by the law as lawbreakers.*
JAMES 2:9

In Word

Many have remarked that Sunday morning from eleven to noon is the most segregated hour in America. Perhaps that's true. If so, it's a tragic distortion of the Kingdom of God. And this statement is not just about race relations; it's about economic status, educational levels, labor sectors, and cultural preferences. We tend to worship with those who are as much like us as possible. We may find it hard to worship if we aren't comfortable with the people around us.

But God never called us to comfort. The early church's ministries took Philip to an Ethiopian, Peter to a Roman, and Paul to Greeks. Many of the Jerusalem Christians, mostly from Jewish backgrounds, were deeply unsettled by this trend. That didn't bother God. He put His Holy Spirit in all kinds of people and then brought them together into one church. He intended His Kingdom to reflect the diversity of His creation.

A major strength of the church is its openness to those who need its healing, comforting, and sustaining ministries. That applies to those within the church—many New Testament passages laud hospitality given to traveling ministers and evangelists—and to those beyond the church's membership, as New Testament missions exemplify. Historians say that the early church was remarkable in its ability to cross economic, cultural, linguistic, professional, racial, and gender barriers. Members often even reached out to those who were persecuting them. They were noticeable in their hospitality. It made an impression.

In Deed

You individually, as well as your church corporately, are given a sacred responsibility: to openly embrace whomever God puts in your path as a potential member of your fellowship. There is no one—no one!—who doesn't fit in God's Kingdom by faith. Be sensitive to favoritism in your fellowship, and then do radical, barrier-breaking things to undo the favoritism. The Kingdom of God is not confined by your culture. Don't let yourself be either.

> The Christian should offer his brethren
> simple and unpretentious hospitality.
> —BASIL THE GREAT

Demonstrating Mercy

*Judgment without mercy will be shown to
anyone who has not been merciful.*
JAMES 2:13

In Word

These are harsh words, and we don't like to hear them. God is merciful to all who have faith in Him, whether they have been merciful to others or not, right? That is perhaps true technically, but there's a profound observation in this verse. This isn't placing on us a behavioral condition for God's mercy; it's making a statement about those who have understood His mercy. If we do not demonstrate His grace, we don't understand it and probably haven't even believed in it. If we know Him and love Him, we will not live contrary to His heart.

When people come to church for the first time, they almost always attribute their attendance to one reason: they were invited. Neighbors won't show up at church simply because they know it's there, or because we've been a powerful example simply by pulling out of the driveway on Sunday morning. No, if they come, it's almost always because someone asked them to.

That's because God has built hospitality into His plan. He means for His character to be demonstrated in His people. Overwhelmingly, the reason people come to faith in Christ is because someone they know demonstrated Christ. In most cases, that means they demonstrated love and mercy. They were hospitable, just as God is.

In Deed

This is so important that God tests us on it. He puts people who need to know Him in our path to see whether we will care enough to exemplify Him. Sometimes, according to Scripture, He even tests us with His own messengers (Hebrews 13:2), just so we'll know whether our hearts are obedient to His Spirit within us. Why is this so important to God? Because (1) God loves the world; (2) the world needs Him; and (3) we are the evidence that can bridge the distance between the two. So live as evidence. Demonstrate mercy. Display the hospitality of your God.

Whoever practices hospitality entertains God Himself.
—ANONYMOUS

Undeterred

*They stoned Paul and dragged him outside the city,
thinking he was dead. But after the disciples had gathered
around him, he got up and went back into the city.*
ACTS 14:19-20

In Word

Paul's message received a good response from the synagogue leaders in Antioch initially, but when the city's Gentiles filled the building the next week, the message looked a lot more dangerous. So they chased him from the city, and when they heard about him preaching the same message in another town, they showed up to protest. And this was no peaceful protest—it got really messy. So messy that Paul ended up looking very much dead to people who knew what death looked like.

That's why this incident in Paul's life is more likely a resurrection than a resuscitation. Regardless, he was in no shape to get up and walk around. But he did, and in a surprising direction: right back into the city from which he had been dragged. It's true that he left the next day, but even showing his face among people who had just stoned him was a bold move. Paul was clearly not intimidated. That's because he was singularly focused on his mission, and someone so single-minded learns the meaning of perseverance very quickly.

It's natural to persevere when you have only one hope. When only one prize will do, there's nothing else to turn to when you face a setback. Paul wasn't just motivating his readers rhetorically when he wrote that he ran in such a way as to win the prize. He was tapping into his own experience. He endured beatings, shipwrecks, legal trouble—and, apparently, death. He didn't take such experiences as signs that God wasn't supporting him or as indications that he was preaching the wrong gospel. He knew his calling, and nothing would deter him. Not even his own mangled and bleeding body.

In Deed

Those who would follow Jesus fully can't be spiritually soft. We need to endure. Times are hard, circumstances get difficult, and some days everything seems to conspire against us. So what? God is for us, and He calls us forward. We must let no obstacle get in the way of our hope and our calling.

> He that perseveres makes every difficulty an
> advancement and every contest a victory.
> —CHARLES CALEB COLTON

The Harder Way

*Then they returned to Lystra, Iconium and Antioch,
strengthening the disciples and encouraging
them to remain true to the faith.*
ACTS 14:21-22

In Word

Paul and Barnabas could have gone straight on to their home base—the *other* Antioch—after starting a string of churches in those cities of southern Asia Minor, but they didn't. No, they turned in the opposite direction and went back through those same cities where they had been mistreated and threatened. Why? Because it was the right thing to do. Because nascent communities of new believers needed to be strengthened in order to survive the challenges they would soon face. Because a little baptism in truth isn't enough to grow disciples in the long run. They had to tend to what they had started.

That's what endurance is like. Sometimes we want to get back to where life is comfortable or where we have a lot of support from the people around us. And God is gracious to provide such seasons when we need them. But there are times when the calling He has placed on us dictates the hard path, the painful endurance, the pouring out instead of the drinking in. It isn't easy, but it's right.

That's why one of Paul and Barnabas's primary messages to the new believers in these cities was that "we must go through many hardships to enter the kingdom of God" (v. 22). That's a hard message for all believers, especially new ones. But they needed to hear it; they had witnessed the recent uproar over Paul, and many of them would face the same opposition. And as easily as we grow complacent, we all need the reminder: the Kingdom of God brings extravagant blessings, but believing it often involves enormous costs.

In Deed

Remember both the example and the message delivered by Paul and Barnabas. The city of God is paved with streets of gold, but the journey to the city can be arduous. Jesus gave us a free salvation, but He doesn't often give us a smooth, downhill road this side of heaven. Sure, God provides times of rest and refreshment, but the path between those times calls for endurance. When life gets difficult, persevere.

> Great works are performed not by strength but by perseverance.
> —SAMUEL JOHNSON

The Spirit's Gifts

To each one the manifestation of the Spirit
is given for the common good.
1 CORINTHIANS 12:7

In Word

Every believer has a manifestation of the Spirit. It isn't the same as a natural talent or a personality trait; it's an aspect of our ministry that is either birthed or amplified by the presence of God Himself. While we watch for God to show up in our circumstances, He is first and foremost working within us. His ministry on this planet comes through the filter of His people. Every one of us.

There's a reason we have spiritual gifts. It isn't to show off in front of other people or to elevate our status within the church. It isn't for self-esteem or for the sake of busyness. It's because the ministry of God to His people is so multifaceted, so vast and infinite, that it takes multitudes to express it. A God so large won't do His work in only one person.

There's another reason we each have gifts. It's because the God who has always lived in the fellowship of the Trinity requires us to live in fellowship with each other. As much as we want to experience God fully out in the woods or on a mountaintop, we can't. We can certainly pray to Him and know His presence there, but we can't receive the ministry He has designed to come to us through other people. We can't hear the exhortation of the Spirit, the encouragement of the body, a chorus of united prayers, or any other essential ministry except in fellowship with others. We are mutually interdependent.

In Deed

That goes against the natural understanding of those of us who were raised in an individualistic culture. Our society admires independence and trains us for self-sufficiency; God rejects such concepts entirely. We cannot know Him by ourselves.

If your relationship with God is a private matter, God has more planned for you. He wants to cultivate it in the context of the fellowship. That's the only place you can be blessed by the gifts of others. And it's the only place where you can bless others with yours.

Take note of what God gives you. Then you
will also know the task He gives you.
—HEINRICH EMIL BRUNNER

Varied

All these are the work of one and the same Spirit, and he gives them to each one, just as he determines.
1 CORINTHIANS 12:11

In Word

If an infinite God wanted to work through finite people to accomplish His goals, how would He do it? After all, finite people are by definition limited in what they can do. They don't have perspectives wide enough to consider every angle of a problem; their wisdom can't be complete. They don't have experience deep enough to meet every situation; their expertise can't be comprehensive. They don't have resources plentiful enough to address every need; their help can't be enough. Finite people aren't equipped to fully express an infinite God.

So what would God do? He would use many people. Lots of them. He would put them together in communities of faith in order to contribute finite portions to His infinite work. He would have them compile their gifts and resources in order to benefit the good of all. He would do amazing things through gathered multitudes because that's the only way a large God could reach into tiny corners of this world.

In Deed

Knowing God's purpose in giving gifts to His people, how do you feel about yours? You know, of course, that your gifts weren't given for your private use, but have you been diligent about blessing others with them? If not, remember that they are a vital expression of the ministry of God. If you don't use your gifts, something is missing from your fellowship. God's work is less diverse, less intense than it ought to be. His team is playing, in a sense, shorthanded.

Be diligent about using your gifts. You may feel that yours are nothing special, that other people can fill the needs better than you can. But if that were the case, God would have been shortsighted or superfluous in giving those gifts to you. And since God is neither of those things, you can know you are a vital part of His plan. He has eternal purposes for the gifts He has given you. His ministry includes you for a reason.

God doesn't call the equipped, He equips the called.
—ANONYMOUS

United

We were all baptized by one Spirit into one body.
1 CORINTHIANS 12:13

In Word

For centuries, the church has found varied and innovative ways to divide. We have split into factions, sects, movements, organizations, and denominations. We've argued about theology—some of it essential, some of it not—and about methodology for how we practice ministry and conduct worship. We have rightly divided from those who teach unbiblical doctrines of God and salvation. But we have also had churches split over the color of the new carpet and the style of the choir robes. We have far too often decided that others who were baptized into the same Spirit as we were are no longer important to us.

That's sin. There's no other way around it. God never urges us to compromise our beliefs or to abandon His truth, but He also never urges us to separate ourselves from those who are truly born of the same Spirit. The line often spoken at weddings—"what God has joined together, let no man tear asunder"—should apply not only to couples but to church bodies. It's a tragic event when the body of Christ is torn asunder.

In Deed

Jesus prayed for His disciples that they would be united just as He and the Father are united. That's close. That's inseparable, in fact. Whether we like it or not, divided fellowships are still born of the same Spirit. Though God can use our mistakes to spread His ministry outward—and He has done so often throughout history—He prefers to spread His ministry through missions, not schisms. He hates contentiousness and divisions.

Learn to grieve over the disunity of the church. The Spirit cannot be divided, but fellowships can be. In fact, that's one of Satan's highest goals. If he can disrupt the harmony of the church, he can obscure the unity and fellowship of God in this world. The peace of God and the bonds of the Trinity are not visible in fragmented communities of faith. Pray—diligently, persistently, and intensely—for the unity of your fellowship today.

> Church unity is like peace. We are all for it,
> but we are not willing to pay the price.
> —WILLEM ADOLF VISSER'T HOOFT

Important

The eye cannot say to the hand, "I don't need you!"
1 CORINTHIANS 12:21

In Word

Some spiritual gifts are highly visible. Those who preach, teach, and lead worship are in front of the people, displaying their gifts for all to see. Others—those who are hospitable, who encourage, and who serve—are often obscure. They support others, and sometimes their contributions are not even noticed. But according to the Word, they are all essential.

Paul used a powerful illustration to convey this truth. He reminded his readers that the "weaker" and "less honorable" parts of the human body are often indispensable (vv. 22-23). Just ask anyone with a sore toe or an ingrown fingernail if the minor parts of his or her body are important. We notice when everything isn't working right—even if the nonfunctioning part is one we've never noticed before.

That's the way it is in the church. The "minor" parts of the body are often not noticed until they are missing. Only when they are absent does everyone figure out that something is wrong. Those with visible gifts don't function as well when not supported by those with invisible gifts. The cohesiveness of the fellowship falls apart. The "unimportant" gifts prove to be rather important.

In Deed

Let that reality prompt two reactions from you. First, if you think your gifts are not very important, repent for underestimating what God has called you to do. God hasn't trifled with you, and He hasn't been inefficient. He knew exactly what He was doing when He gifted you. He knew the fellowship needed what you have to offer. The body can't function well unless you utilize your gift. Don't play it down.

Second, notice those among you who seem to be underappreciated. Then take matters into your own hands to correct the problem. Show your appreciation to those who serve in obscurity. Do something to demonstrate that you value their contribution to your fellowship. The God who sometimes gives small but essential gifts will be very, very pleased.

One of God's specialties is to make
somebodies out of nobodies.
—HENRIETTA MEARS

Coordinated

There should be no division in the body.
1 CORINTHIANS 12:25

In Word

The world has plenty of social organizations. It knows all about country clubs, political parties, athletic leagues, and civic associations. Secular culture sees organizations as nothing more than individuals uniting for a common purpose. It doesn't go any deeper than that.

The church, however, can be a profound witness to the world. The church is more than a collection of individuals. It is a single organism. We are the only example on this planet of one Spirit moving through many parts in a coordinated way to accomplish one goal. We are the only segment of society that is knit together by a life that is higher than our own. We are connected in ways the world only dreams about.

For our world ever to be convinced that God inhabits the church, it has to see something supernatural in us. At times in church history, or even in places today, miracles and signs are clear evidence of God's working. Changed hearts are also irrefutable pieces of evidence for the watching world, but they are subjective enough to be explained away by determined skeptics. But when churches function without division—especially when those churches are composed of diverse people with little in common other than a love for God—the world has no explanation. It just can't relate.

In Deed

Examine your gifts and use them to the fullest. Also examine the gifts of those around you and encourage them to use them to the fullest. There is no competition where God's gifts are given; when exercised properly, each one will result in the exact level of fruitfulness He desires—no more, no less. There is nothing to fear by zealously promoting the spiritual gifts of God in yourself and your fellow believers, and there is much to gain.

When secular observers see a diverse body acting in a coordinated fashion to produce arguably supernatural results, they will know there is an unseen Head. Our gifts will point to a higher source, and they will display His love and His power for a world that needs Him.

The church is the only society on earth that exists for the benefit of non-members.
—WILLIAM TEMPLE

Extravagance

Whoever sows sparingly will also reap sparingly, and whoever sows generously will also reap generously.
2 CORINTHIANS 9:6

In Word

From day one, generosity marked the church. Travelers were in town for Pentecost, and when the Spirit fell on a gathering of Jesus followers, no one could leave. Why? You don't just walk away from an unprecedented outpouring. So the community of Spirit-endowed people pooled their resources without restraint in order to support those who had no means of support. It was radical giving for radical times.

That sense of immediacy faded as time went on, and it had never been known by the churches outside of Jerusalem anyway. But when a famine hit Judea and Samaria, outside support for Jerusalem's Christians was needed. And who better to send it than the Gentiles, the legitimacy of whom many Jewish believers still questioned? So Paul taught them an inviolable Kingdom principle. Like farmers who plant crops, we reap according to what we've sown.

Jesus had taught this principle to His disciples too: "Give, and it will be given to you. A good measure, pressed down, shaken together and running over, will be poured into your lap. For with the measure you use, it will be measured to you" (Luke 6:38). If we sow love, we receive love. If we sow strife, we reap strife. And if we give generously to others, we receive generously—perhaps from others, and certainly from God. And we receive proportionally to our willingness to give.

In Deed

No one ever lost out by being too generous in Kingdom things. God's desire is for His people to pour out their lives—every aspect of them—sacrificially according to His purpose. And He never leaves them on the short end of the exchange; His giving always overmatches ours.

When you find your heart leaning toward a worthy Kingdom purpose, it's an invitation from the Spirit to invest in that purpose. Even when our means are limited, there's always something to give—time, talent, money, or whatever else we have. That's how we reflect the character of the God who poured Himself out for us. And that's how the Kingdom bears fruit.

> The world says the more you take, the more you have.
> Christ says the more you give, the more you are.
> —FREDERICK BUECHNER

Joyful Generosity

God loves a cheerful giver.
2 CORINTHIANS 9:7

In Word

In the Kingdom, it isn't enough just to give. A life of sacrifice given grudgingly isn't nearly the precious offering that a willing sacrifice is. No, God cares deeply about our motive for giving and serving. It must cost us something, but the desire needs to outweigh the cost. Our gifts can't be meant as a payoff to ensure God's blessing or as a burdensome obligation that we wish we didn't have to fulfill. God wants us to give like He does: cheerfully.

We certainly see this principle in the garden of Gethsemane, as Jesus wept and prayed desperately for another way. Why did He finally accept His Father's will? "For the joy set before him" (Hebrews 12:2). It was a difficult sacrifice, but ultimately not a reluctant one. There was joy in it. Jesus gave us the perfect example of what it means to give gladly.

There are at least two vital truths to learn from God's example. One is that He doesn't pour out His blessings on us hesitantly. We don't have to twist His arm to answer the prayers of miserable sinners like us. He really does enjoy giving out of His abundance; He takes pleasure in His own goodness. The other vital truth is that if we are being conformed to His image, this is how we will give too. Our generosity will look extravagant just as His does. We will be cheerful givers because He is a cheerful giver.

In Deed

Real giving in God's Kingdom isn't done under compulsion. It's motivated by love—love for God, for His purposes, and for His people. That's a noble generosity, perfectly befitting the character of the King we serve. He gave to us out of love, we give to others out of love. The principle of sowing and reaping bears the purest and best fruit when love and joy are its sources.

Whatever you give, give it gladly. However you serve, do it joyfully. Be motivated by nothing but gratitude to the one who gave Himself to you first.

> You can give without loving, but you
> cannot love without giving.
> —AMY CARMICHAEL

The Holy Ones

*You are a chosen people, a royal priesthood, a
holy nation, a people belonging to God.*
1 PETER 2:9

In Word

The new community in Christ has a new identity. We aren't just people who have
made a religious decision or aligned ourselves with a social movement. We aren't
an organization or an institution. We are a people hand-selected by God to be like
Him—to be different, to be set apart, to be holy.

That's how the early believers saw themselves, and apostles like Peter helped
cultivate this sense of identity. It was important to understand that this community
was not just a religious movement but a new kind of humanity. There was no room
for a sense of superiority—anyone who believed could join this new creation. No, it
was a humbling calling and a sacred identity. The children of God had been born. The
world had never seen anything like this.

That's our identity too. We forget it often, seeing ourselves simply as believers, or
churchgoers, or evangelicals. We are characterized by our society as a subculture or
a social sector. We have been explained in psychological, sociological, and historical
terms as one religious movement among the many that the world has known. But in
our hearts, we have to go beyond those designations. We have to understand that the
life we live is humanity fulfilled, a completion of what was lacking, and a restoration
of what was lost with the first sin. We are unlike any other human being. We are born
of God's Spirit.

In Deed

Do you believe that? Let it sink in. It's important because the lives we live will reflect
the sense of identity at our core. If we see ourselves as sinners who have made a religious decision, that's how we will act. But if we see ourselves as holy ones, set apart for
God's special use, a priesthood to stand between God and a lost world, that's how we
will act. It all depends on what we know, deep inside, about ourselves. And according
to God, we are chosen to be holy.

Holiness is the visible side of salvation.
—CHARLES SPURGEON

The Grateful Ones

. . . that you may declare the praises of him who called
you out of darkness into his wonderful light.
1 PETER 2:9

In Word

God had a purpose in the plan of salvation, and it wasn't just about meeting our needs. He loves us, of course, and He did save us for our benefit. But there's more to it than that. In this divine drama of human brokenness, God has used our fallen condition to demonstrate something about Himself. This sinful world has given Him the occasion to reveal what could not have been seen in a perfect heaven: His mercy, His unconditional love, and His power to deliver and save. We weren't the only ones with a stake in our salvation; it was designed to display God.

That's the meaning of 1 Peter 2:9. We are a chosen people, a royal priesthood, a holy nation, and a people belonging to God so that we might declare His praises. We can enjoy and celebrate the fact that we have gone from darkness to light all we want; but our celebration needs to end in gratitude and praise for the one who accomplished our salvation. This drama has never been entirely about us. It is ultimately about God's glory.

In Deed

Is God's ultimate purpose being accomplished in you? There are two sides to your salvation. First, you receive it and enjoy the grace He has given. Second, you give Him glory for it, praising Him for His extravagant mercy. Many Christians have excelled at the first side of salvation without ever arriving at the other side. But God has called us for this purpose. Accepting salvation benefits us, but it takes us only halfway to His ultimate goal. Until we have praised Him thoroughly and zealously for His work, we have unfinished business.

Take a step today toward finishing your business. Let your salvation have its result; let it glorify God. Spend some time reflecting on your chosenness and your holy calling, and then consider the amazing condescension of God to accomplish such things. Praise Him in your prayers today.

> Be not afraid of saying too much in the praises of God; all the danger is of saying too little.
>
> —MATTHEW HENRY

The Merciful Ones

Once you had not received mercy, but
now you have received mercy.
1 PETER 2:10

In Word

The holy ones are exhibit A for the mercy of God. We were lost, confused, living in darkness, needy, and often unaware of our need. More than that, the Bible tells us we were hostile to God, opposed to His rule, and determined to live by our own standards and for our own purposes. But God, because of His mercy, sent His Son to die for us before we had even shown any inclination to love or accept Him. He made a way before we wanted one. The church—the chosen people and royal priesthood—is evidence for how deep His mercy extends.

The best way to display that evidence is to be merciful. We can thank God for His mercy to us and praise Him for His goodness, but there's a hands-on way to demonstrate our gratitude and praise. If we go out and show His mercy to others—even before they indicate they might want it—we are being like Him. If imitation is the sincerest form of flattery, showing God's mercy is the sincerest way to praise Him. And if we are to show it, we have to know it. It has to have transformed our hearts.

Let mercy do its deep work in you. We don't like to think of the depths and darkness we used to live in, but we need to remind ourselves often what our former life was like. It's the only way we can continue to remember how great His grace is.

In Deed

The holy ones are to be people of mercy. We are to embrace it as God's gift, let ourselves enjoy it, thank Him for it regularly, demonstrate it to others, and tell of it often. When people think of the church, they should immediately think of mercy. If they don't, we need to get back to basics—immediately. Mercy is to permeate everything we do.

Nothing graces the Christian soul as much as mercy.
—AMBROSE

The Different Ones

I urge you, as aliens and strangers in the
world, to abstain from sinful desires.
1 PETER 2:11

In Word

The new community is in the world but not of it. Jesus made that clear when praying for His disciples (John 17:15-16). While we are living in this world, in the midst of its economic and social systems, we are not to be completely integrated into it. There is a sense in which we will always be separate because we are born of a Spirit alien to fallen humanity. We will never really fit in here anymore.

That bothers many Christians. Many of us want to feel comfortable both in the mainstream of fallen humanity and in the new community of Christ at the same time. But just as oil and water do not mix, neither do the Spirit and fallen flesh mix. Though we still live in this world, we are in territory that is hostile to God (1 John 5:19; James 4:4). If we are under the influence of God's Spirit, we can never be at ease in the midst of such hostility.

Our appropriate response is to love the world; after all, God does (John 3:16). Then we are to minister to the world; after all, that's our role according to Paul (2 Corinthians 5:18-20). But we are never to grow roots in the world. We cannot live as though the Kingdom of God is an afterthought, something to be considered after we've accomplished everything we want to do in the here and now. We are citizens of heaven (Philippians 3:20). We have to live like it.

In Deed

That's a twofold process. First, we abstain from sinful desires, as Peter urges. We refuse to trust the cravings of our flesh and deny them for the sake of a greater Kingdom and a holier Spirit. Second, we learn to be like God. We live according to His mercy, His purity, and His love. That kind of life will distinguish us from our world. And that's as it should be.

> The essence of true holiness consists in
> conformity to the nature and will of God.
> —SAMUEL LUCAS

The Visible Ones

Live such good lives among the pagans that, though they accuse you of doing wrong, they may see your good deeds and glorify God on the day he visits us.
1 PETER 2:12

In Word

This calling to live supernatural lives is daunting. We know we can't live up to it. We are commanded to have a kind of righteousness that exceeds human expectations. We are to be clearly distinguishable from the world we live in, yet we are not taken out of it; we have no choice but to live right in the middle of it, where customs and cultures pressure us and temptations wage war against us. This identity as the holy ones of God seems awfully far-fetched sometimes. It is assaulted daily.

Nevertheless, this is what God expects of us. This is how He told us to live. Jesus emphasized to His disciples that they were to be salt and light in this world, letting their good deeds be seen. Peter reiterates the teaching here. It is possible to live the kind of life that will prompt unbelievers to glorify God when they see Him.

There is only one way to do that. It is to be decisive and adamant in our resistance to the currents of this world. If we isolate ourselves from sinful neighborhoods and difficult situations, we have failed this command. And if we live in the midst of corrupt cultures and let them rub off on us, we have also failed this command. There is only one option for us: we have to live in hostile territory, and we have to live contrary to it.

In Deed

How are you doing with that? Do you tend to isolate yourself from secular influences or ungodly people? Then you can't be the witness God wants you to be. On the other hand, do you let the world influence you to the point that there is no distinction between you and your surroundings? Then you aren't the witness God wants you to be. Seek a balance. Don't avoid your world, and don't succumb to it. Live for His glory where you are.

A holy life will produce the deepest impression.
Lighthouses blow no horns; they only shine.
—D. L. MOODY

New Life

In his great mercy he has given us new birth.
1 PETER 1:3

In Word

It was in the 1970s during a presidential campaign that the term *born again* was first discovered by secular American media. The concept has been in the New Testament for two millennia, but most non-Christians were surprised to hear of it. It was a novelty, a strange description of the state of a believer. To many, it seemed like a fringe, cultish concept.

Those of us who are born again, however, may have the opposite reaction. It easily becomes just a symbolic description of what it means to start over when we've failed. We forget that when Jesus and the New Testament writers spoke of the new birth, it was not just a concept in the mind of the early church. It was an earth-shattering phenomenon. People could actually be born of a different nature than the one they had carried around all their lives. Their hearts and their souls could be fundamentally different. They could actually be—organically and genetically—children of God.

It's a shame that the idea is so strangely novel, even ridiculous, to secular culture, and it's a shame that it can be so mundane to us. The early believers thought they were witnessing a new kind of creation, just as radical and monumental as the first days of Genesis. And they were right. It is radical and monumental. The Spirit's advent into human hearts is amazing. We can't let our familiarity with the term *born again* obscure for us how phenomenal the regenesis actually is.

In Deed

Contemplate the new birth today. What does it mean to you? Do you really live as someone whose old self died and who now has a new, fundamentally different nature—complete with a clean slate with no past errors on it? If not, why not? Is it because you have been shaped more by the world's ideas of transformation than by Scripture's?

If so, let your mind repent of its casual approach to the new life. We all need to do that daily. Let it sink in that you are not what you once were—and enjoy the change.

> I remember this, that everything looked new to me . . . the fields, the cattle, the trees. I was like a new man in the world.
>
> —BILLY BRAY

God's Resources

Through faith [you] are shielded by God's
power until the coming of the salvation that
is ready to be revealed in the last time.
1 PETER 1:5

In Word

You have a lot at stake in your salvation. It's not only your well-being in this world, it's your eternal destiny. How you handle your salvation issues will determine what life will be like for you now as well as how you will live forever. Yes, you have an awful lot at stake.

Have you considered that God has a lot at stake too? He did not work out His salvation plan over centuries upon centuries, coming in the flesh to die on a cross for your sins, only to watch you passively from heaven and see how you'll respond. He is intensely interested in your response, of course, but your salvation is not entirely about you. He has a stake in anything that can glorify Him, and your salvation certainly can. Or not. And He wants to make sure that it does.

That's why, while we cannot live irresponsibly and unaware of the implications of our beliefs, we can be confident that the power of God will be with us throughout the whole endeavor. We don't walk through this world alone. There is a very interested, very passionate Helper who is deeply involved in the outcome. He wants us to do well. He wants us to glorify Him.

In Deed

Live with confidence. Your salvation is about you, but long before you were made, salvation was about God. You exist to display His mercy, His goodness, His love, His compassion, His power, and everything else that is good about Him. In fact, you were born as a poor, lost sinner for just such a reason: to be saved—and not only to be saved, but to be saved in a way that shows who He is and what He is like. God designed your salvation for Himself.

It doesn't seem like it sometimes, does it? Life is hard, and though you've probably met God from time to time, you may have asked where He is today. Fear not. He is here, with you, right now. Your walk with Him is shielded by His power until one glorious day when all becomes clear. Live in light of that day every day.

All the resources of the Godhead are at our disposal!

—JONATHAN GOFORTH

Real Faith

Though you have not seen him, you love him.
1 PETER 1:8

In Word

That's what faith is all about, isn't it? Loving without seeing. Believing before observing. Hearing the voice of God with your heart rather than your ears. Faith is the currency of the Kingdom of God, but it doesn't spend like cash. It's more like an electronic transaction—we don't see the currency change hands, and we have to trust the one with whom we transact. We love a very real, but invisible, God.

Peter, of course, was writing as one who had seen. He was with Jesus for at least three years, witnessing miracles and gawking at the holes in the hands of a risen Savior. But the Christians to whom he wrote, for the most part, had not been there. They weren't eyewitnesses of the Incarnation. They knew what they had been told, what the Spirit had done in their hearts, and the miracles of transformation that were taking place in their community. But the visible Jesus? No, He wasn't making many appearances.

But if human hearts have truly been reborn, His physical appearance isn't necessary, is it? Peter's readers had all the proof they needed. "You believe in him and are filled with an inexpressible and glorious joy," verse 8 goes on to say. Which leads us to a startling observation, but one that the New Testament affirms over and over again: belief and joy go hand in hand. Faith results in fulfillment. It is never blind and empty. Or joyless.

In Deed

If we have a problem with love and joy—and many Christians do—then we probably have a problem with belief. Think about it: If we really embraced the promises that the New Testament gives us—of which Jesus Himself assured His disciples—then discouragement and apathy would be rare exceptions, not common conditions.

Do you struggle with love and joy? Then check your faith. Do you really believe what He tells you? Then let your heart feel what He tells you. Faith is meant to work its way out into our works, our perspectives, and our attitudes. Let it.

> A little faith will bring your soul to heaven, but a lot of faith will bring heaven to your soul.
> —D. L. MOODY

Hard Trials

*In this you greatly rejoice, though now for a little while
you may have had to suffer grief in all kinds of trials.*
1 PETER 1:6

In Word

Not only does faith lead to love and joy, as 1 Peter 1:8 indicates, it also leads to grief. It's one of the mysterious paradoxes of the Christian faith: the believer can experience unspeakable joy and severe hardship, both at the same time. In fact, it's almost guaranteed that he or she will.

We don't like that aspect of our faith, but it's nonnegotiable. To understand the mercy of the Savior is to painfully understand the brokenness of this world. And as those who embrace the one who is at odds with the fallenness of this world, we set ourselves up for conflict. Those who reject God will reject us. Those who love sin will hate our definitions of it. Those who are passionate about another religion will see us as enemies. If we believe, we will in some way suffer.

In fact, Peter elaborates on this theme later in his letter. He tells his readers not to be surprised at their ordeal—after all, it's not strange that followers of a crucified man should suffer. More than that, he tells them to rejoice. It's a good thing. Hardship for the faith means that the Spirit is there. The trials are a blessing.

In Deed

Remember that if you're going through a hard time. "We must go through many hardships to enter the kingdom of God," Paul and Barnabas told the believers in Asia Minor (Acts 14:22). It wasn't considered an abnormality. Pain is part of discipleship.

Has that sunk in? As believers, we often assume that if all is right with God, all is right for us in the world. If we really believe that, we haven't read enough about Jesus, His disciples, or Paul. None of them had an easy time, yet all of them were obedient servants of God. If you're praying for God to get you out of a trial, don't give up the possibility that He will. But get more to the point: ask Him to strengthen you in the trial. And rejoice in what the trial will bring.

> While I continue on this side of eternity, I never
> expect to be free from trials, only to change them.
> —GEORGE WHITEFIELD

Revealed Glory

[Trials] have come so that your faith . . . may be
proved genuine and may result in praise, glory
and honor when Jesus Christ is revealed.
1 PETER 1:7

In Word

We can become awfully self-absorbed in the midst of our trials. We focus on what we did to get into the mess, what we can do to get out of it, how pitiful we are for being in it, and how odd of God not to care enough to get us out of it. We ask all sorts of questions like "why me?" and "how long?" Our capacity for self-pity is enormous.

Think about God's purposes though. Does He have something at stake in our trials? Like perhaps His glory? That's how it worked with Job, you know. Satan pointed Job out as a potential false worshiper, someone who only loved God when all was well. God let Satan put Job to the test, and eventually God received glory from Job's patience. There is a very real possibility—a biblical and experiential probability, in fact—that God will do the same with us. When we suffer, it may not be about us. It may be for His purposes, so that in the end people will praise and honor Him for His ability to sustain His servants in very difficult times. When people see patience, mercy, endurance, humility, and all those godly characteristics in our lives, they see a witness of God.

They need that. The world needs to know that when life crashes, there's a God who doesn't. When they wonder if this broken existence is all there is, they need to see eternity in the eyes of God's people. When you suffer, that may be exactly the purpose in it.

In Deed

Never forget that our sufferings are not just hardships for us, but opportunities for God. Focus on Him and His purposes. Trials are occasions for Him to show something about Himself, both to us and to those who observe. They are a platform on which He can display His glory, either right now (which we'd prefer) or in the end (which we'll just have to be patient for). Either way, God is honored. Any trial—any pain at all—is worth that.

Calvary is God's great proof that suffering in
the will of God always leads to glory.
—WARREN WIERSBE

Sufficiency and Strength

My grace is sufficient for you, for my power
is made perfect in weakness.
2 CORINTHIANS 12:9

In Word

We hate our weaknesses. We see them as our downfall, not as assets, so we put a lot of time and effort into eliminating them. That's why self-help and personal growth sections of bookstores and Web sites are often the most frequently visited. That's why we invest thousands of dollars in things that make us look better and live better. And that's why we put on a different face in public than we do in private. If our weaknesses can't be overcome, at least they can be hidden from view.

God instructs us, through Paul, to take a different approach. Instead of covering up our weaknesses or trying to discipline ourselves out of them, we can open them up for God to use. We can invite Him to fill the cavities in our soul with Himself—a better substance than anything we could put in those holes. His presence wherever we have wounds, emptiness, and brokenness turns those weaknesses into strengths.

We don't know what Paul's "thorn" was—some say a physical infirmity, though the word is used elsewhere in Scripture to mean persistent opposition—but we do know that he wanted it to go away. God said no. Why? For one thing, it kept Paul humble. Those who have been filled with the Spirit of the eternal King and who have received eternal truth can become complacent or proud. But it also led Paul to realize that a God-filled weakness in a person is a better solution than a new-and-improved person. That's a truth that can completely change the way we live.

In Deed

When you come face-to-face with one of your weaknesses, realize that the normal human way of overcoming such things is not the best solution. The better way, though it goes against every impulse we have, is to embrace the weakness and invite God into it. His grace will sustain us. When we exchange our weakness for His strength, His presence will make us stronger than we could ever otherwise be.

> We should keep up in our hearts a constant
> sense of our own weakness . . . to drive us out
> of ourselves in search of divine assistance.
> —HANNAH MORE

Strange Joy

*That is why, for Christ's sake, I delight in weaknesses, in
insults, in hardships, in persecutions, in difficulties.*
2 CORINTHIANS 12:10

In Word

We usually focus on the second half of this verse: "For when I am weak, then I am strong." That's encouraging because it reminds us that whatever weakness we have, whatever hardships we go through, God's strength is available to us. But for us to consider these things a matter of delight is another issue altogether. Most of us don't rejoice in our trials. We don't jump up and down with excitement and say, "Oh, how wonderful! Now God's strength can show up in my life in a new way!" No, we lament the trial, ask God to remove it—as Paul did with his—and console ourselves with the hope that somehow, imperceptible as it might be, God's strength will help us endure. We press ahead in spite of our circumstances.

God has something more in mind for us than simply enduring. There are times when endurance is our main lesson or foremost duty, but it isn't God's primary purpose for us. No, His primary purpose is to use our lives as a platform for His power and grace. We are the stage He performs on. When we have some semblance of self-sufficiency, God is a backstage character without any lines. But when we have deep needs and hard trials, He has an opportunity to come into the spotlight. He steps into the drama of our lives as the main character, and whatever He does—assuming that we let Him—is better than what would have happened if we had never had trouble in the first place.

In Deed

That's why your attitude in trouble can be one of delight and joy. It seems absurd, doesn't it? To celebrate insults, persecutions, and hardships is not a natural reaction. But Jesus told His disciples that they were blessed if they were violently opposed, that adverse circumstances and spiritual attacks were a cause of great joy (Matthew 5:11). When trials come, take them to God in prayer. But don't linger in your lament. Celebrate the opportunity your trials give Him to do something great.

> All God's giants have been weak men who did great things
> for God because they reckoned on His being with them.
> —HUDSON TAYLOR

The Coming Prophet

*The LORD your God will raise up for you a prophet
like me from among your own brothers.*
DEUTERONOMY 18:15

In Word

The prophet Moses delivered several lengthy sermons to the second-generation wanderers before they entered the Promised Land. In one of them, he gave an enigmatic prediction: there would one day be a prophet like him who would come from among them and speak the words of God to them.

That must have sounded strange to Moses' listeners. They already had a prophet like Moses: Moses himself. He had already spoken to them the words of God, words that many of the Israelites came to study diligently and treasure in their hearts for centuries. These words, the law of God, could not be expanded or diminished. It could be commented on—there has rarely in history been a shortage of commentary by sages and scribes—but it could not be changed. So why would the Jews need another prophet like Moses? What was left to say?

Regardless of their reverence for Moses as the greatest of prophets, Jews still looked for the prophet like Moses to come. He would save them, just as Moses delivered them from Egypt. He would teach them, just as Moses taught them from Sinai. He would lead them, just as Moses led them through the wilderness. And He would do miracles on their behalf, just as Moses had done.

In Deed

Centuries later, people asked John the Baptist if he was "the Prophet." John said no (John 1:21). Then they speculated about Jesus being "the Prophet" (John 6:14; 7:40). And, as we know, they were right. Jesus came speaking the words of God, delivering, teaching, leading, and doing great miracles. Moses even validated Him as the prophet on the Mount of Transfiguration (Matthew 17:3). Jesus came because Moses' words weren't the final revelation of God's will to His people. Jesus fulfilled the law Moses gave. And He shows us how we can too.

All lines of messianic prophecy meet in Jesus.

—FRED JOHN MELDAU

Hear Him

You must listen to him.
DEUTERONOMY 18:15

In Word

Two verses earlier, Moses told the Israelites that they must be blameless before God. The practices of the Canaanites around them could never be allowed to rub off on God's people. The law God had given through Moses had to be fully integrated into the lives of those who believed it. The righteousness taught by God had to be passed down from generation to generation. These people were to be blameless.

As we know from Scripture, the practices of the Canaanites did eventually rub off on God's people. The law was never fully integrated into the national life of Israel—only periodically and through a few good kings and priests. The righteousness of God often skipped several generations, as fathers and mothers neglected to teach it to their sons and daughters. The people weren't blameless at all.

That's why another prophet was needed. The laws and the prophecies of Moses pointed to Jesus, who would implant life and righteousness into the hearts of those who believed in Him. The fulfillment never came from external rules but from an internal Spirit. That's why God spoke to the Israelites through Moses and said: "You must listen to him." There would be no other way to fulfill God's requirements. Jesus is the only means by which human beings can become holy.

In Deed

Many Christians, however, believe in Jesus without ever really listening to Him. We read His words and try to follow them—a futile attempt unless His own Spirit is given free rein within us by faith. We become religious followers of Jesus without spiritually fellowshiping with Him. We listen to God's words and miss His heart.

Moses emphasized to Israel how important it was to listen to the prophet/Messiah who was to come. In Him, all humanity would see its true Savior, a teacher/deliverer/miracle worker who would show us the way to the Father. He would not dismiss God's rules, but fulfill them within us. Our spirits would be made alive together with Him, and our character would be changed. But only if we listen—obediently listen—to Him.

How many observe Christ's birthday, how few His precepts!
—BENJAMIN FRANKLIN

Receive Him

This is what you asked of the Lord your God.
DEUTERONOMY 18:16

In Word

After God thundered from Mount Sinai as He gave Israel the Ten Commandments, the people of God—His beloved, treasured people—asked not to hear His voice or see His fire anymore (v. 16). The intimacy was too overwhelming, His holiness too heavy. His presence got to be too much for them, and they thought they were going to die.

God agreed with them (v. 17). It probably wasn't because He needed a little more space—in fact, He likely desired even greater intimacy—but because they weren't ready for the weight of glory. They actually might have died. They were not the holy, separate people God had called them to be, and His presence was more uncomfortable than it should have been. They were wilderness wanderers whose parents had complained about God's works and disbelieved His promises, and though the second generation was not guilty of such crimes, they were raised by people of weak faith. The manifest presence of God would blow their circuits. Yes, this was a good request.

So God promised to send His presence in a different format. The Incarnation didn't come for many centuries, but it put the voice and fire of God into the midst of God's people. They couldn't handle it in the wilderness, and many of them couldn't handle it when Jesus came. But God, in His mercy, at least gave them an option that wouldn't kill them immediately. He sent His presence in the form of a Person.

In Deed

The question we must all consider is how much intensity we will accept in our relationship with God. He sent Jesus to us, and Jesus sent His Spirit into us. Many of us have mountaintop experiences with Him, only to distance ourselves a few days later. Why? Maybe because the presence of God is too much to take. We want a certain level of intimacy, but when it's too intense, we get uncomfortable.

What are you asking of the Lord? God will draw you as close as you want to get. If you ask Him to back off, sadly He will—for a time. If you ask for a deeper, closer relationship, you'll find that He wants it as much as you do.

> Oh, the fullness, pleasure, sheer excitement
> of knowing God on earth!
> —JIM ELLIOT

Embrace Him

*I will put my words in his mouth, and he will
tell them everything I command him.*
DEUTERONOMY 18:18

In Word

The Prophet who was to come, who would deliver like Moses and forever alter the history of God's people, would carry the authority of God in His voice. His words would come straight from the throne and would accomplish all that the Word of God can accomplish: they would refresh, restore, command, correct, heal, reveal, forgive, and breathe life into places where death once reigned. The Prophet would speak absolute truth.

Jesus did that, of course. He fulfilled Moses' prophecy so thoroughly that people marveled. They saw a miracle and said, "Surely this is the Prophet who is to come into the world" (John 6:14). They heard His words and said, "Surely this man is the Prophet" (John 7:40). Both His voice and His miracles reminded them of Moses. Many of them—those with ears to truly hear and eyes to truly see—became convinced that the presence of God was among them. They knew that these were words of eternal life (John 6:68).

The issue with words of eternal life is that people have to decide what to do with them. They aren't like a news report that can be selectively ignored. They don't go in a file to deal with later or come up at dinner only as a casual conversation piece—at least not without serious consequences. The kind of words that Jesus spoke—full of authority, straight from the throne, laden with power and purpose—are words that call for a decision.

In Deed

Many Christians, however, treat the words of Jesus casually. We debate about them, use them wherever and whenever useful in an argument, and put them in songs to sing or frames to hang on a wall. But the kind of words Jesus spoke requires something more: diligent application. Extremely diligent application, in fact. They are food and water, life and death, bread and blood to us. The voice of God insists on a life-altering response.

> Jesus was God spelling Himself out in
> language humanity could understand.
> —S. D. GORDON

Cling to Him

If anyone does not listen to my words that the prophet speaks in my name, I myself will call him to account.
DEUTERONOMY 18:19

In Word

The world does not understand that Jesus is a dividing line, the apex of history over which everyone must fall either to one side or the other. There are no in-betweens when it comes to the voice of God. Either it is heard or not. Either it is heeded or not. Yet we live in a salad-bar, fashion-trend kind of world that picks and chooses its truth, as though truth could change with the times. But the Ancient of Days doesn't tell us to anchor ourselves in seasonal truth. He grafts us into the eternal Son.

We live in a culture that embraces multiple "realities." The underlying philosophy of our age says that what's true for one may not be true for another. It lauds those who are open-minded and disdains those who think they are right. It believes that absolutist thinking is incompatible with love and kindness. It treats the words of Jesus as nice and helpful, not the dividing line of history.

According to Moses (and many others in Scripture), God will hold everyone accountable for the words of His Son—including us. The world dresses itself in trendy "truth" out of ignorance; when we do that, it's out of reckless neglect. Though God guides us through seasons of our lives, His character never changes. Neither does the foundation He laid for us. His words speak of eternal realities in heavenly realms, where shadows don't shift and night never falls. In heaven, truth is truth. When the King of heaven speaks, His words are truth. There are no other options.

In Deed

When you relate to your world, relate in love and kindness, in generosity and respect. But when you claim truth, don't compromise it. A firm stance on the words of Jesus is not narrow-minded, unloving, or intolerant, as we are often told. It's a compassionate embrace of what's really real. The words of Jesus are the only anchor for a reeling world. The most loving thing we can do is refuse to compromise them.

Truth carries with it confrontation.
—FRANCIS SCHAEFFER

The Beloved Servant

"Here is my servant, whom I uphold, my
chosen one in whom I delight."
ISAIAH 42:1

In Word

Jesus came as a servant, as He so frequently emphasized to His disciples. Not only did He serve God, He served people. He washed the feet of His followers and told them the way to become great was to become low. He was the ultimate servant, sacrificing His life out of love. And God truly did uphold His servant.

He still does. Jesus, the ultimate servant, is ultimately exalted. Those who follow Him in servanthood are upheld by the same hand that God used to support and exalt Him. In fact, the whole identity of the Messiah covers those who believe in Him. We are in Him and He is in us. We take on His name as a bride takes the name of her husband. We are filled with God's Spirit in the same way Jesus was filled with His Spirit. As with the mystery of marriage, two become one. We and Jesus are inseparable.

That means that not only are we upheld by the hand of God like Jesus was, but that God delights in us as He delighted in His servant. That's hard for many of us to believe, but it's true. When God looks at a person who is "in Christ," He sees Christ. And that brings Him tremendous pleasure.

In Deed

Above all else, find your identity in this servant sent to us by God. The Messiah came for this reason. He didn't free captives and heal sick people reluctantly; He did it with joy and delight. We have become one with Him, and God loves it. The Father can't love Jesus without loving us just the same. If that love doesn't shape our identity, we don't understand redemption.

If you want to be upheld by someone who delights in you, see yourself as one with Jesus by faith. Take on His identity. Be a servant, rest in His love, and rejoice in His will. God already sees you through the lens of His beloved Son; learn to see yourself through the same lens.

> God loves you as though you are the only person in the world, and He loves everyone the way He loves you.
> —AUGUSTINE

Shared Glory

*I am the LORD; that is my name! I will not give
my glory to another or my praise to idols.*
ISAIAH 42:8

In Word

God's glory has no true rivals. Sinful human beings have developed rivals in our own hearts, but none of them are legitimate threats to His glory. As Isaiah prophesied the coming of the Messiah across a landscape of idolatry, he voiced God's extreme hatred of false worship and His utter insistence of His own glory. Isaiah's picture tells us that as Jesus' reign spreads, idols are exposed as futile. In other words, God's glory comes out very clearly visible. As John said when Jesus came, "We have seen his glory" (John 1:14).

But that's not the end of the glory story. When Jesus prayed at the end of His earthly ministry, He made an amazing request of His Father: "I have given them the glory that you gave me, that they may be one as we are one" (John 17:22). When we become one with Jesus, we are no longer rivals to God's glory. We are participants in it. He shares it with us as a husband shares everything with his wife. God gives His glory to no rival; He does, however, give it freely to members of His own family.

We once worshiped the idols in our own hearts. In Jesus, we repented and our eyes were opened to the true worship of God. Having become one with Him, we are as closely united to the Trinity as we can get without infringing upon it. The result is that we are on the side of glory. The generosity of God has given us a privilege beyond all comprehension.

In Deed

What does that mean for us? It means that every blessing God has in His heart is available to those who love Him. It means that His generosity is no longer limited by the gap between sinful humanity and a holy God. It means that every prayer you utter is well received by the head of the family. And it means that God has irrevocably bound Himself to you.

> Our great honor lies in being just what Jesus was and is. . . . What greater glory could come to any man?
> —A. W. TOZER

The Road to Wholeness

I, the LORD, have called you in righteousness;
I will take hold of your hand.
ISAIAH 42:6

In Word

Deep in the heart of every person is a desire for wholeness—for things to work out, for fulfillment to come, for life to be filled with things that are right and good. In some hearts, that desire is deeply suppressed and obscured, probably from years of bitter disappointment. But it's there. It's always there.

The promise of the Messiah addresses that desire. Isaiah prophesied to a people in rebellion and headed to captivity, and he gave them a picture of deliverance, justice, restoration, and life (vv. 3-7). He would shine light in darkness and bring hope to every remote island. He would release captives and open eyes to see truth. He would give the human heart everything that long-buried desire was afraid to hope for. And He would bring it about by taking us by the hand and leading us into His righteousness and blessing.

Too many Christians approach the life of faith as an obligation, seeing obedience as a "have to" rather than a "get to." But according to God's Word, righteousness that comes from God is a privilege that leads to wholeness. It has the power to reach down into the soul, stoke the embers of that dying desire, and blow it into a living flame. His righteousness brings life and fulfillment—the kind we always hoped for.

The irony is that we think we can find life and fulfillment in other things and that righteousness will depress us with a long, painful to-do list. But the whisper that told us that didn't come from God. It came from a thief who steals, kills, and destroys, a liar who hates God and anyone He loves. The truth is that when God takes us by His hand and leads us in His righteousness, all of life comes into focus.

In Deed

Don't be afraid to be led by God, even at the expense of those things you thought might bring you life. Only His truth, His Messiah, His righteousness can make you whole. Walk in them. Run in them. Never let go of the hand that leads you.

The righteousness of God is not acquired by acts
frequently repeated . . . but is imparted by faith.
—MARTIN LUTHER

Under Grace

*Sin shall not be your master, because you
are not under law, but under grace.*
ROMANS 6:14

In Word

It's a nice theory. In principle, we died with Jesus, the law is no longer our master; therefore, sin is no longer an issue and grace rules. There's only one problem with it: we still sin. And though we try not to, it happens a lot. While Paul assures us that sin is no longer our master, it often seems so . . . well, masterful.

Why is that? Is this passage of the Bible wrong? Of course not. Or as Paul is fond of saying, "By no means!" When the Bible declares us free from sin, it means that we are free from sin. It isn't just a removal of the label from the same old disobedient acts. It isn't just an imputed righteousness that means we are clean in God's eyes but still filthy in our own. It means that sin has lost its power. Really.

That means, of course, that any time we say we couldn't help this or that sin, we really could have. It doesn't mean that the temptation wasn't real and powerful, or that the flesh wasn't really weak, or that the enemy wasn't incredibly deceptive and persuasive. But we can't get away with implying to God that our sin was unavoidable. He won't buy it. A Savior died to free us from it.

How can we tap into that freedom? We'll explore that in the next few days, but it begins with grace. When God freed us from the law by fulfilling it for us, He freed us to something else. Instead of being preoccupied with legalities, we can be preoccupied with Him. And the holiness of His very present Spirit will fill us with everything we need to follow Him well.

In Deed

Many Christians have given up this battle, assuming that victory over sin is theoretical rather than practical. Avoid that temptation. Somehow in our unity with Jesus' death and resurrection, we really are free. We may struggle with how to appropriate that victory, but we should never assume it isn't available. It is. Believe it. We have a much greater Master than sin.

> Let grace be the beginning, grace the
> consummation, grace the crown.
> —THE VENERABLE BEDE

With God

Offer yourselves to God.
ROMANS 6:13

In Word

If we're honest, we'll confess that this is often where our battle with sin is lost. We offer ourselves to the entertainments of our culture, the philosophies of our generation, the passions of our flesh, the interests of our intellect, and the amusements of our hearts, and then, when they've led us to natural conclusions, we ask God what went wrong. His answer, from the very beginning, is that we were to have offered ourselves to Him. He will never lead us into sin.

We might think that such an offering would completely isolate us from our family, friends, and society. Not true. God won't take us out of the world—not yet—but He will loosen the grip it has on our hearts. If He is first in our affections, everything else will be secondary. And if He has our affections, sin has met its match. A true, deep love for God is the ultimate armor against the evil one and his forbidden fruits.

So it begins with an offering—a "living sacrifice," as Romans 12:1 tells us. What does that mean? It means getting out of bed every morning with an awareness that you don't belong to yourself. You aren't your own. You have been bought and paid for. Your heart is God's possession, your body is His temple, your affections are subject to His guidance, and your ambitions are singularly focused on His will. You don't have plans, you don't have goals, you don't have any intentions at all—not until you've given Him the time and opportunity to inspire them.

In Deed

We all know that's an ideal and that we rarely live up to it. But a daily reminder to ourselves won't hurt. God never intends for us to be void of all feelings; He just means to be the inspiration behind them. In order for that to happen, we have to disavow our own will. Then we have to offer ourselves to Him. Sin has power over us only to the extent we offer ourselves to it. When we offer ourselves to God—really and truly—sin always loses.

> Sin is a power in our life. Let us fairly understand
> that it can only be met by another power.
> —HENRY DRUMMOND

Over Sin

Count yourselves dead to sin but alive to God in Christ Jesus.
ROMANS 6:11

In Word

How does a passage about grace, like Romans 6, turn into a passage about overcoming sin? Because grace isn't just about forgiveness; it's about change. God has taken losers in the battle against sin and given them the keys to victory. Grace that forgave us but left us in our sinful condition would be pitiful grace indeed. And there's nothing pitiful about God's grace.

In verse 11, Paul tells us the key. After God has done His part with the grace of forgiveness and the life of resurrection, our part begins in the mind. We are to "count," as this translation says. Others say "consider" or "reckon." What we think in our minds about the power of sin has a lot to do with whether we will be subject to it. What we understand about our new life determines to what extent we will experience it. If we consider sin an overwhelming battle, it will be. If we count ourselves dead to sin but alive to God, we will live for Him. It's that simple.

That doesn't mean it's easy. This is no psychological trick we play on ourselves, convincing our own minds that the battle is really won when it isn't. No, this is a matter of accepting what the Bible says about the death and resurrection of Jesus. Did His death defeat Satan? Is His resurrection eternal and invincible? Are we participants in both? If the Bible is true about these things, "counting" ourselves dead to sin isn't a psychological ploy, it's an effort to deny a lie and embrace the truth. It is believing what God says.

In Deed

Think about it. If we are really dead to sin—and believe it—then it has nothing to say to us. It isn't part of our lives anymore. Just as the temptation of a foreigner to rely entirely on his former language in his new country fades by necessity, so does our temptation to speak "sin" when we are firmly planted in the Kingdom of God. We don't fit the old culture anymore because we have mentally left it behind for a better one. If we do that with sin, we have fulfilled this verse. And victory will be much easier to see.

> When you attack the roots of sin, fix your thought more upon the God whom you desire than upon the sin which you abhor.
> —WALTER HILTON

After Cleansing

Shall we go on sinning so that grace
may increase? By no means!
ROMANS 6:1-2

In Word

The message that everything the law called sin is now forgiven by grace is a radical message. We might even challenge it, asserting that God still defines our sins by the standards of the law. But Paul's argument in chapters 5 and 6 of Romans is that Jesus fulfilled the law and we died with Him. The law has no more claim on us than a marriage certificate has on a deceased spouse. The bond has ended.

That's a radical message, and we might even be inclined to dispute it: "If law doesn't govern us anymore, what's to keep us from sin?" But we know this is exactly what Paul means, because he raises the rebuttal himself. "Yes, that's the logical question," he writes in essence. "And that would be the danger of grace except for one thing: we're dead to it" (Romans 7:4).

We have to admit that grace is dangerous in our lives too. If God has forgiven us freely, we think to ourselves, His grace has given us quite a bit of latitude. And what's a little sin with so much latitude? We begin to take grace for granted, which leads to taking sin casually, and then we grow careless. That's why Paul writes this chapter. He knows human tendencies well. The truth of grace is amazing, the distortions alarming. Sin is disastrous, and grace is precious. Neither should ever be taken casually.

In Deed

Unfortunately, history is filled with Christians who have taken grace casually. We have seen it abundantly and concluded that with so much of it to go around, we might as well spend it recklessly. Casual grace has led us to conclude that sin is not that big of a deal, that we weren't that bad off to begin with, and that God's not really as uptight and holy as we once made Him out to be.

But while that's the prevailing view of casual Christianity, it isn't biblical. To Paul, it was absurd. Grace was given to free us from sin, not to free us up for more of it. Make sure you understand the difference. God is still holy, and grace is still precious. Always live in a way that shows that both are sacred to you.

> Repentance is a thorough change of a man's
> natural heart on the subject of sin.
> —J. C. RYLE

Always Overcoming

We know that since Christ was raised from the dead, he cannot die again; death no longer has mastery over him.
ROMANS 6:9

In Word

The good news of our burial and resurrection with Jesus isn't just that sin is overcome. So is death. Our war with sin rages for now, even though we have the keys to victory and never need to lose a single battle. But it is a very temporary war in which the outcome is certain. And the outcome isn't just about sin; it's about life. The fact that Jesus is raised and we are in Him by faith means that we are raised. And if He is never to die, neither are we.

That's a glorious truth that we celebrate every Easter. It was radical to the early Christians, a reversal of an inescapable trend since the dawn of time. We forget how radical this concept is, but death was overcome at the Cross. Anything that once could have harmed us can't.

The problem is that we still live in a world that doesn't know this amazing truth. Oh, it knows that many of us believe it, but its citizens still grieve at what they see as the finality of death. This world allows us what it believes to be a fantasy—resurrection of the dead. It thinks we need that crutch. What unbelievers don't realize is that they need that crutch as much as we do. In fact, none of us can live without it.

In Deed

This really is the heart of the gospel, and it's the primary duty of every Christian to live a resurrected, victorious life. Does that mean we should live as though we have no problems? No, obviously not. That wouldn't be genuine. But we can live as though the Scripture is true, as though there is victory over sin, triumph over death, and a resurrected life.

The best way to be a witness for Jesus is not to argue with unbelievers about His lordship—although words are often very useful—but to live above the corruption and death of this world. Let others see eternity in your perspective on events. Let them see your confidence in the midst of your trials. Let them see a Lord over your sin. Let them see Jesus.

> The Christian's task is to make the Lord Jesus visible, intelligible, and desirable.
> —LEON JONES

All Things

*The mystery of his will . . . to bring all things in heaven
and on earth together under one head, even Christ.*
EPHESIANS 1:9-10

In Word

The story of God's people is a long one, stretching back thousands of years to the beginning of creation. What purpose did the Lord have in mind in this strange and beautiful world? What was He aiming for when He began the redemption story with a chosen family? What were all those Hebrew biographies and chronicles about? What ultimate purpose was it all pointing to?

God's ultimate aim was and is to bring everything in heaven and earth under Jesus. That goal was present in the Hebrew Scriptures, but it's only unveiled in completeness in the New Testament. This purpose is why we take every thought captive to Christ (2 Corinthians 10:5) and rejoice in the fact that every knee will bow to Him (Philippians 2:10). The fall of humanity scattered elements of creation out from under God's good dominion, and in Christ they are brought back into His hand. Jesus, as other translations of this passage say, is the "sum" of all things.

We often miss the significance of "all things." We think Jesus reigns over compartments of our lives, especially the spiritual things. But His reign is comprehensive; the whole earth, and in fact the whole universe, is coming into His dominion. The world doesn't always look that way, but that's the direction we're headed. Every knee *will* bow—it's inevitable. And *all* things, even the physical creation, will be restored.

In Deed

That's why the New Testament is so insistent on a *bodily* resurrection. Jesus is Lord of every atom in the universe. And that's why our tendency to confine His lordship to the purely "spiritual" aspects of our lives often leaves us with a sense of defeat and discouragement. But there's no need to limit our expectations of what we can bring to Him or what He might do. We can be encouraged that He is interested in every detail of our lives because every detail is ultimately His. Our whole life—including whatever we might be facing today—belongs to Him.

There is not a thumb's breadth of this universe about
which Jesus Christ does not say, "It is mine."
—ABRAHAM KUYPER

Heirs

You were marked in him with a seal, the promised Holy
Spirit, who is a deposit guaranteeing our inheritance.
EPHESIANS 1:13-14

In Word

What comes to mind when we think of the Holy Spirit? Comforter. Counselor. Guide. And so much more. But a security deposit? Tangible evidence of a future promise? That's a different picture than we're used to.

Think about what this portrayal of the Spirit means. First, it's clear that He's a substantial enough presence to be seen as evidence. A guarantee that can't be seen, heard, or sensed in any way is not much of a guarantee; that's not what Scripture offers us. The Spirit should be real enough in our lives to reassure us that something greater is in our future. He's a taste of what's to come.

Second, His presence makes it clear that we have an inheritance. The fact that we are portrayed in Scripture as heirs is startling, especially considering the position that makes us so. Paul explains it in Romans 8:17: "Now if we are children, then we are heirs—heirs of God and co-heirs with Christ." In other words, whatever inheritance Jesus receives is the inheritance we receive. He and we are in it together. As part of Him—members of His body and adopted sons and daughters into His family—we get what He gets.

That's incomprehensible. What does Jesus inherit? Everything. The universe. Every spiritual blessing in heavenly places. And that's exactly what He shares with us. In a creation in which every knee will bow to Him and everything will be brought under His lordship, we get the spoils of His absolute and unwavering victory.

In Deed

While the guarantee of our inheritance points to the future, the message of the New Testament is that the future begins now. We get plenty of foretastes of future blessings in every area of life. In fact, that's what faith is all about: bringing future promises into present reality. We can experience much of the inheritance now. Be encouraged by that. Ask for it and expect it. The Spirit of Jesus within you guarantees His presence and His Kingdom.

The future is as bright as the promises of God.
—ADONIRAM JUDSON

More Than Anything

*I consider everything a loss compared to the
surpassing greatness of knowing Christ Jesus my
Lord, for whose sake I have lost all things.*
PHILIPPIANS 3:8

In Word

The most striking, life-changing feature of the newly created individual is his or her love for Jesus. Some believers have this feature immediately, while others take a lifetime to cultivate it. But it's there. It has to be. It's the only thing that can make someone new.

Some people might think that the core of discipleship is training oneself to be like Jesus. Others might think their discipleship is a matter of submitting to His lordship. Still more might think it's simply a matter of believing the right things and being taught to understand the truth. And all of these are important; they are even vital elements of discipleship. But they aren't its core. No, deep down inside, the believer must learn to love Jesus more than all else. If that love is not there, the rest will be an impossible task. Love has to come first.

The essence of that love is captured well by Paul in this passage. Paul had lost a lot in his new belief in Jesus. He lost his career as a rising star in Jewish religious leadership circles. He lost friends and perhaps the love of family members. He lost a steady income and a place he could truly call home. Most of all, he lost his identity—his old one, that is. He could no longer take pride in his heritage and his pedigree. He could not define himself by his tribe or his nationality. His only identity now was Jesus. He lost everything in order to gain this Savior. And according to this passage, the trade-off was well worth it.

In Deed

That must be the mentality of the believer. Our hearts must get to the point where nothing matters but Jesus. Oh, we'll have our affections and goals, but they will sit unpretentiously below our greater love. When the choice between Jesus and any rival is presented, we won't need to hesitate for a second. The surpassing greatness of knowing Jesus—just knowing Him—will fill our hearts more than anything else.

Jesus Christ is God's everything for man's total needs.
—RICHARD HALVERSON

Fellowship of Suffering

*I want to know Christ and the power of his resurrection
and the fellowship of sharing in his sufferings.*
PHILIPPIANS 3:10

In Word

This is a strange desire to our ears. Sure, we can long for the power of Jesus' resurrection right along with Paul. But when it comes to the fellowship of His sufferings—"becoming like him in his death," as Paul goes on to say—we're not sure we want that. It's a high price to pay, even for a priceless Savior.

This is God's desire for us, though. Paul was only expressing what God had put within him. The desire of our Creator is that we be re-created, and the only way for that to happen is for the old self to die and a new self to be born. For the life of the new Adam (1 Corinthians 15:22) to reign within us, the life of the old Adam has to be abandoned. We can't hang on to the old order of creation and still embrace the new. We have to choose.

Paul made his choice, and it was a no-brainer, according to the rest of this passage. Everything in his life—everything!—was a pile of garbage compared to knowing Jesus. Even health and comfort. These are expendable commodities for someone who wants only Jesus. Following the risen Savior means first following the crucified Savior. It's a package deal, and it's worth it.

In Deed

This is a mark of Christian maturity, if we will accept it. The believer who loves Jesus will be brought by the very plan and design of God to a point of loss for His sake. We don't like that dynamic, and we often complain to God when He brings us there. But if we have loves that rival our Lord, He must bring us there. We can't fulfill His purpose for our lives—His wonderful, perfect purpose—while hanging on to lesser treasures.

Has God put hard choices in front of you? You may even be faced with such a choice today. Choose Jesus—nothing more, nothing less, nothing else. It will involve pain and sacrifice, but also surpassing greatness and joy. Forsaking all other loves for Him is always worth the price.

> They that deny themselves for Christ
> shall enjoy themselves in Christ.
> —JOHN MASON

Only Jesus

*. . . that I may gain Christ and be found in him, not
having a righteousness of my own that comes from
the law, but that which is through faith in Christ.*
PHILIPPIANS 3:8-9

In Word

Deep down in your heart of hearts, what drives you? What is your reason for being?
What kinds of passions keep you going and keep you from losing hope? These are
hard questions for some; it may be difficult to put your finger on your true motives
and desires.

But believers in Jesus know what is supposed to fill the center of their hearts.
Our human nature fills us with image-consciousness, self-justification, and all sorts
of shortsighted drives and passions, but we need none of that. At least theoretically.
Deep down inside, Jesus is our true image, He's our accomplishment, and He's our
justification. We have no need to rationalize or to impress. We are all about Him.

Does the ideal hold true for you? If you're like most people, you retained elements of the old human nature long after you believed in Jesus. You feel the need to
appear righteous on the outside, to be esteemed by others, and to rationalize your
shortcomings. Every time you do that, you are forgetting the purity and perfection of
the Jesus who has justified you and given you His righteousness. Once again you've
taken up the tendency to make a name for yourself. You've lost sight of the fact that
your identity is no longer in you; it's in Him.

In Deed

This is one of the hardest tendencies for a Christian to break, but it's essential to do
so. We can be either self-made or Christ-made, but not both. We can seek our own
identity or forsake our own for His, but not both. We can love our selves or lose them,
but not both. It's a constant choice.

Look into your heart. Ask yourself those hard questions. Then drop the pose,
admit your faults, and embrace Jesus—alone.

> If there be ground for you to trust your own righteousness,
> then all that Christ did to purchase salvation . . . is vain.
> —JONATHAN EDWARDS

No Confidence

It is we who are the circumcision, we who worship
by the Spirit of God, who glory in Christ Jesus,
and who put no confidence in the flesh.
PHILIPPIANS 3:3

In Word

The sense of identity we have inside us—whether it's based on self, circumstances, position, status, heritage, or Christ—will to a large degree determine how we live. We will fill ourselves up with whatever reinforces our self-image, and if that is something other than Jesus . . . well, we've seen the results of that. We live in a world of personal agendas and self-actualization. And it isn't very pretty.

Story after story is told of someone who went out into the world to "find" himself. But the gospel gives us a different strategy. Jesus said that whoever loses his life will find it (Matthew 10:39). In other words, whoever abandons the search for self-fulfillment will ultimately be fulfilled. It's a paradox, but it works. Jesus promised it would.

In daily life, this has powerful implications. Instead of building ourselves up, we are free to build others up. Instead of worrying about what will make us happy, we are free to consider the happiness of others. Instead of asking God to serve us—that's what many of our prayers are about, you know—we can ask Him how to serve both His Kingdom and the people around us. We can recklessly abandon the self-life and live a radical God-oriented, others-centered life. And in the end—and perhaps even in the meantime—God will amply reward us with fulfillment beyond our wildest dreams.

In Deed

That seems to be what Paul means about worshiping by the Spirit of God, glorying in Christ Jesus, and putting no confidence in the flesh. We become filled up with Jesus and lose all concern for ourselves. Or as Jesus put it, true life in Him is found in death to ourselves.

It feels like an enormous risk to live that way, doesn't it? It would be, if God were not utterly trustworthy. But He is, of course. Trust Him. Live for Him. Worship by the Spirit and glory in Jesus. Let your heart be consumed with Him. Your life will never be the same.

The more a man denies himself, the
more he will obtain from God.
—HORACE BUSHNELL

Contentment as a Witness

*Whatever was to my profit I now consider
loss for the sake of Christ.*
PHILIPPIANS 3:7

In Word

The world is wondering if anything is truly valuable. Have you noticed? People engage in the lifelong pursuit of treasure, prestige, comfort, and all sorts of other desirable goals, only to get to the end and ask themselves if there isn't anything more. People who have priceless possessions and make millions of dollars believe just a little bit more will make them happy. People who earn honor after honor feel like failures if the latest one doesn't come through. While the world is chasing after its treasures, its citizens eventually find out that nothing offered there will truly satisfy. And they want to know: Is anything really worthwhile?

We have the answer, you know. Paul expresses it here. "Whatever was to my profit I now consider loss for the sake of Christ." Only what is both good and eternal matters, and only He is truly good and eternal. If the world wants to know what is worth pursuing, our contentment can show them exactly where to look. Unless, of course, we aren't content.

We have to be honest: Discontentment is a problem, even among Christians. We've forgotten the art of finding ourselves in Christ alone and have begun searching for the kind of contentment the world craves but will never find. We hope for the eternal blessings of Jesus, but in the meantime we want the temporal blessings of the passing world. And while God often lets us have them—He's a blesser, after all—He never wants us to embrace them. All our love is to be invested first in Him. Everything else is secondary.

In Deed

Have you ever considered that your contentment honors God and witnesses to the world? When we strive after self-fulfillment and find that it always eludes our grasp, we are indicating that Jesus wasn't quite sufficient. If, on the other hand, we forsake all else and embrace Jesus, as Paul did, we are a shining witness to a world in futile pursuit of worthless things. We have found treasures others have never considered. We have pointed them to the Savior.

God is most glorified in us when we are most satisfied in Him.
—JOHN PIPER

Wisdom and Revelation

I pray also that the eyes of your heart may be enlightened.
EPHESIANS 1:18

In Word

We live in a world of darkness, and we get lost in it often. Plenty of voices offer to help us out too—there's no shortage of people who will offer advice and speculate on the right things to think and the right decisions to make. Navigating a landscape of diverse philosophies and beliefs can be very confusing.

That's why one of the greatest requests we can pray for each other, as Paul did for the Ephesians, is for a spirit of wisdom and revelation (v. 17). Or as he so colorfully puts it, "that the eyes of your heart may be enlightened." And Paul seems to have some pretty specific ideas about what our hearts need to be enlightened with. We need to know the hope of our calling, the riches of our inheritance, and the power that is available to those who believe. If those things are firmly embedded in our hearts, we won't find ourselves lost in the darkness very often.

Think about it: if we are certain of our hope and know what God has called us to do; if we understand what we have already begun to inherit; and if we realize the amazing power of God working on our behalf; then discouragement and confusion become a lot less prevalent in our lives. We may have moments when we need specific guidance or encouragement, but the overall picture is remarkably bright. None of the setbacks and opposition we face can even begin to undermine God's foundational promises. The hope, the inheritance, and the power are greater than anything that comes against us.

In Deed

This is a perspective-altering prayer. When the trials of our lives loom large in our vision, we become fearful and depressed. But when we lift our sights to the truths that are greater and even more real than our circumstances, we can overcome anything.

If any situation oppresses you today, lift your eyes higher. Get a clear picture of the hope, the inheritance, and the power of God, and live and pray as though they are more real than anything else in your life.

> Hope can see heaven through the thickest clouds.
> —THOMAS BENTON BROOKS

Unimaginable Power

*That power is like the working of his mighty strength, which
he exerted in Christ when he raised him from the dead
and seated him at his right hand in the heavenly realms.*
EPHESIANS 1:19-20

In Word

The power of God is at work in our lives. We know that because it's written so clearly in our Bible and has been preached and taught so often. But life has a way of beating us down as though someone or something—some archenemy or some elemental principle of a fallen world—is trying to convince us that the power of God doesn't apply to us, or that it isn't all that powerful in the first place. That's why many Christians feel defeated. The awesome power of God doesn't seem all that accessible in real life.

That has produced a curious dynamic. The Bible raises our expectations with miracles and the majesty of God, and then many well-meaning teachers try to lower our expectations again so we won't be disappointed. This dynamic sets up a choice for us: we can fix our hearts on what Scripture says, or we can accept the words of those who tell us to just be realistic. In other words, we have to choose whether we're going to have faith or not.

We know the right choice. Still, the promise seems too good to be true. The power at work in and through us is the same power that raised Jesus from the dead and exalted Him in heaven. That's what God offers us. That's the power we're called to place our faith in. And that's why our expectations get raised so high when we read Scripture. God gives us no ordinary promises. We're offered the greatest power in the universe.

In Deed

What will you believe today? In the trials you face, in the obstacles you come up against, in the discouragement that hounds you relentlessly, will you cast your confidence toward the power of God or the hard facts of "reality"? That's the question that confronts you moment by moment in the life of faith. You either believe in God's unimaginable power or you don't. Decide today that you will.

If you can't believe in God, chances are your God is too small.
—J. B. PHILLIPS

New Clothes

*Put on the new self, created to be like God
in true righteousness and holiness.*
EPHESIANS 4:24

In Word

Imagine having a set of new clothes that would make you look continually better day after day. These clothes would never go out of fashion, they would never fade in the wash, and they would never get tiresome. People would see you as different, elegant, and always prepared for any occasion. They might not always agree with your sense of style, but they would not be able to say you don't have one.

We do have new clothes, the New Testament tells us. Paul uses the metaphor here in Ephesians, but the garments of Jesus are referred to elsewhere as well. These aren't the clothes of first-century Israel; they are the character of those who love Jesus and are being conformed to His image. They have the power to change how we look and how we feel. They are the ultimate fashion statement.

Paul uses this metaphor to tell us to change. We are to take off the old self and cast it aside. The new self that will make us look like God Himself is ready to be tried on. We must shed the garments that made us comfortable in the culture of this world and begin dressing like those who live in the Kingdom of God. After all, we want to fit in.

In Deed

What fashion statement are you making with your character? Does your attire fit better with the culture of the world or with the culture of the Kingdom? It can't be both. The two cultures are too different. You have to decide which crowd you want to fit in with and then dress appropriately.

As you decide, remember this: The clothes of the Kingdom will never fade, will never go out of style, and will never look inappropriate. They are, after all, the same clothes worn by the King Himself. He gives them out freely, but He accepts no excuses for not wearing them. They are available to all who will put them on. Be aware of how you dress today. When it comes to character, your sense of fashion matters.

> We cannot help conforming ourselves to what we love.
> —FRANCIS DE SALES

New Character

*Surely you heard of him and were taught in him
in accordance with the truth that is in Jesus.*
EPHESIANS 4:21

In Word

There are all kinds of Christians in the world. There are nominal Christians, who inherited the faith from ancestors but give no attention to its meaning. There are cultural Christians, who practice the faith as a condition of the environment they live in. There are casual Christians, who have accepted Christ for His salvation but not in order to love Him or to follow Him as Lord. And there are zealous disciples, who want to love Him and be like Him.

Sometimes these differences are hard to distinguish, but they are there. Paul knew that when he wrote to the Ephesians, so he encourages them to live as children of the light, not as children of darkness. The difference is not so much in what they say they believe or even what they actually believe. The difference is in how they live. God's children, true disciples, don't live like they used to.

That was God's purpose in sending His Son—the truth incarnate—into this world. If truth as doctrine changed lives, the Israelites would have had salvation down pat centuries before. If truth as head knowledge changed lives, the Pharisees and Sadducees wouldn't have been far off the mark. But God's desire is not for us simply to know and understand truth. His desire is for us to live it.

In Deed

What is God's motive for our living the truth? Is it simply because He's a stickler for behavior? No, there's a lot at stake for Him and His glory. His character is displayed in the way His people live. If you ever wanted a high calling for your life, this is it. We who believe have the potential to demonstrate what God is like. Or not.

The world has seen plenty of Christians who do not demonstrate what God is like. It needs more examples of what He is like. He has redeemed us for just such a purpose—to display His glory. Do what you can to display it today.

It is time that Christians were judged more by their
likeness to Christ than by their notions of Christ.
—LUCRETIA MOTT

New Minds

*You were taught . . . to be made new
in the attitude of your minds.*
EPHESIANS 4:22-23

In Word

"You were taught . . ." In other words, this is something we should know. The renewal of the mind is a prominent New Testament teaching. When we become Christians, we are to think differently.

"To be made new . . ." We can take comfort in the fact that this is a passive command. We don't do the renewing; we simply subject ourselves to it. We submit our minds to God and let Him fill them with His truth. He is the guardian of our makeovers.

"In the attitude of your minds." Our thought life is a battleground. You've probably noticed that. There is a war going on for the ideas and affections of men and women in this world, and it's brutal. We are assaulted with falsehoods constantly, and sometimes they seem so close to truth that we fall for them. But the enemy is devious, we are gullible, and the war rages on. Satan wants our minds. Jesus wants them even more.

How can we win this war? Our culture doesn't help us out—not at all. Our entertainment is so filled with misperceptions—and so accessible to us, especially at the end of a long day—that we find ourselves soaking in falsehood regularly. What is a few minutes of Bible study and prayer each day compared to the several hours of TV most Americans average? How can our Bible's old news compete with our newspapers' new news? How can our minds be taken for Jesus when our culture and our adversary are so united and relentless in their assault?

In Deed

It's hard. There's no easy way. But the command remains: We are to fill our minds with truth and let God's Spirit renew them. As we immerse ourselves in His Word and let His teachings sink into our hearts, eventually our minds will learn to decipher truth from error. We will learn to see things from a Kingdom perspective rather than a worldly one. In effect, we will be made new.

The message of the Bible is addressed primarily
to the mind, to the understanding.
—MARTYN LLOYD-JONES

New Selves

You were taught . . . to put off your old self, which
is being corrupted by its deceitful desires.
EPHESIANS 4:22

In Word

Surely the old self isn't quite so corrupt as Paul makes it out to be, is it? God actually gave us the capacity for desire to begin with, didn't He? He gave Adam and Eve the desire for fellowship, food, intimacy, accomplishment, and more. So why is the Bible so hard on our desires? Why is it wrong for us to want these things too?

It isn't. The Bible has been misrepresented for centuries as a book of "don'ts" and "shalt nots." People have misread it to say that God is a spoilsport and doesn't want us having any fun at all—and certainly not having our desires fulfilled. But the Bible never says such a horrible thing. It affirms the desires of the human heart—as God gave them.

But there's the problem. Our natural, sinful tendencies and the enemy of our souls have conspired to corrupt our desires. They've infected them with all sorts of distortions and lies, making us actually think we know what we want better than God does. So we strive after this pleasure or that goal, certain that a good God would want us to have such things. All the while, our good God has a much better plan for us—if only we could get past the corruptions of our own misplaced desires.

In Deed

That's your job today. In fact, that's your job every day. Get past your misplaced desires by putting off the old self—take it off like an old, worn-out suit that's no longer in style—and let its corruptions go with it. The old self, in spite of its arrogance and assumptions, never knew what was best for you. It told you that God's plan was boring and confining, and its lies were effective.

Now you know the truth. Live with an awareness that God has replaced your corrupt, sinful nature with the Spirit of His own Son. Let Him have His way in your life today, and you'll be surprised at the results. You'll find that deep down, it was all you ever really desired.

> Our old nature is no more extinct than the devil; but God's
> will is that the dominion of both should be broken.
> —JOHN STOTT

New Lifestyles

You must no longer live as the Gentiles
do, in the futility of their thinking.
EPHESIANS 4:17

In Word

One of the most alarming findings of recent polls is that there is very little difference between the lifestyle decisions of Christians and non-Christians. With some exceptions—but not enough—we spend money in the same way, we divorce just as often, we have comparable moral behaviors, and we participate in our culture in remarkably similar ways. When it comes to average lifestyle, Western Christianity in the twenty-first century isn't very distinguishable from Western society as a whole.

That's tragic because it doesn't give the nonbeliever any options. If a non-Christian isn't satisfied with his current lifestyle, he's not going to find much appeal in the similar lifestyle among church members. Oh, if he looks hard enough, he'll find a few of us who have chosen to live more clearly redeemed lives—if we haven't completely isolated ourselves from society, that is. But on the whole, in the big picture, he won't find too many choices. He'll see that beneath an onion layer of difference between himself and church members, there's a similarly broken, compromising heart.

Is that too harsh? Perhaps so, for we know that not all Christians are alike. There are those who are radically renewed and conformed to the image of Christ, as well as those who blend right in to their cultural surroundings. Even so, we have much to mourn over the big picture of demographic segments. As a whole, we haven't followed New Testament teaching.

In Deed

The teaching we must embrace is that the Christian lifestyle is radically different from its surroundings. It isn't an isolated lifestyle, just a distinct one. To think that followers of Jesus might fit into this world is a contradiction. Jesus didn't fit in; neither do those who are like Him. If we fit in, we aren't like Him. And if we aren't like Him, we've got nothing to offer this world.

Cast off the futility of a misguided culture and demonstrate redemption. We were made to be like God.

The evidence of knowing God is obeying God.

—ERIC ALEXANDER

Single-Minded

*Now I want you to know, brothers, that what has happened
to me has really served to advance the gospel.*
PHILIPPIANS 1:12

In Word

Paul was under house arrest in Rome. It wasn't the worst of conditions—he could
have multiple visitors coming to tend to his needs, deliver his letters, and so on. But
he was still confined, guarded at all times. He couldn't travel to visit the churches he
had started, and he couldn't preach and teach around Rome. For a habitually active
apostle, he was very limited.

It's easy to imagine Paul being frustrated by his situation, perhaps even wondering whether his two years under arrest in Rome were wasted time. But there's no hint
of complaint, no indication that he questioned God's sovereignty over his situation.
Just the opposite, in fact. He seems to have relished the opportunity to minister wherever God placed him, whether it was in a Philippian prison (much less pleasant than
house arrest in Rome), aboard ship in a storm, at a contentious trial in Jerusalem, or
anywhere else. And in Rome, Paul clearly saw the rhyme and reason for his predicament. He was awaiting his trial, an opportunity to explain the Good News to Caesar;
and in the meantime, his guards, the palace community, and perhaps many families
associated with the government were hearing his testimony. Despite imprisonment,
Paul was in his element.

In Deed

That's an uncommon perspective for most Christians. We first question whether
we're in the right place and under the right circumstances, as though God somehow
lost track of us while we drifted into our predicament. Then we expend a lot of time
and energy praying to get out of our situation, rarely stopping to wonder how God
might use us in the midst of it. But a single-minded focus on being a Kingdom citizen
will cause us to see nearly every situation as an occasion in which to be Jesus-like. If
we're concerned only with displaying the heart of God to those around us, then what
"obstacle" in life is actually an obstacle? Every problem is an opportunity.

Who keeps one end in view makes all things serve.
—ROBERT BROWNING

Greater Gain

For to me, to live is Christ and to die is gain.
PHILIPPIANS 1:21

In Word

Paul was torn between two possibilities. On one hand, he could die and be with Jesus—the far better option, in terms of personal benefit. On the other hand, he could remain and continue to serve those who needed him. Though the "choice" was more a matter of God's sovereignty, he seemed to imply that his prayers had quite a bit of pull. He faced a decision: pray for his departure and, as he put it elsewhere, be absent from the body but present with the Lord; or pray for continuing fruitfulness in ministry. He seems to have settled on the latter—for the time being.

We generally don't consider death to be "far better" unless we're in extreme pain or hardship. Human beings don't instinctively desire to depart into a frighteningly unknowable afterlife. But Paul didn't consider the next step of his existence to be unknown. He had seen Jesus on a road decades earlier, and he had gazed at his Savior with his spiritual senses ever since. He had had too many heavenly experiences (2 Corinthians 12:2-7), too many directly answered prayers, too much verbal direction from the Spirit to consider the afterlife questionable. Heaven was to be desired, to be longed for, to be embraced as soon as his testimony was complete. According to Paul, a Christian's death is "gain."

In Deed

How would it change the way we live to have Paul's perspective? More ways than we might think. We would be more focused and less fearful, bolder in our faith and quieter in our complaints. We would live with an eye on the prize rather than an eye on the next business deal or the next item on our to-do list. Instead of desperately trying to find our heaven on earth, we would try to bring more of earth into heaven. We would run in such a way as to win the prize.

Fill your mind with a picture of the glory to come, and life will begin to look quite different. You will see your days as opportunities to represent Jesus, but your eternity as an opportunity to be with Him. And that is a greater gain than any of us can imagine.

Heaven is a prepared place for a prepared people.
—LEWIS SPERRY CHAFER

Faith in Real Life

*What good is it, my brothers, if a man claims
to have faith but has no deeds?*
JAMES 2:14

In Word

When we say we believe in Jesus, what exactly do we mean? On one hand, we could simply mean that we believe He is who He says He is and that He will do what He says He will do—mainly, save us. That's belief at an intellectual level. On the other hand, however, if we think this through, we can't stop there. If Jesus really is who He says He is, that means He is Lord of the universe and the reason for our own existence. God created us through Him. We belonged to Him at creation, and though we were lost in sin, we were ransomed back by His own death. If we believe in Jesus—at whatever level—we have to believe what He says.

Many Christians say they believe in Jesus, but they don't really apply His words to their lives—or even care to learn them thoroughly. Jesus asked a pointed question of His disciples: "Why do you call me, 'Lord, Lord,' and do not do what I say?" (Luke 6:46). In other words, if they really believed He was Lord, they would have followed His instructions precisely. But they didn't. They must not really have believed He was Lord.

We probably won't ever follow Jesus perfectly in this life, but if we really believe He is Lord, we will make an extraordinary effort to do what He says. James is pointing out to his readers in this verse that they are perhaps inconsistent in their understanding of who Jesus is. Their minds say He is Lord. Their actions do not.

In Deed

What do your actions say about Jesus? Ignore your mental beliefs, your intellectual understanding, and even your words for a moment. What do your actions say about Him? Do they declare who He is? Or is there an inconsistency between the beliefs of your heart and the beliefs of your deeds?

Be careful to make your faith real, not just in how it affects your thoughts and feelings, but also in how it affects your neighbors. Faith is not a sentiment; it is a lifestyle. Examine your lifestyle well.

He does not believe that does not live according to his belief.
—THOMAS FULLER

The Aroma of Faith

*You see that a person is justified by what
he does and not by faith alone.*
JAMES 2:24

In Word

Imagine a freshly baked apple pie coming out of the oven. Imagine the aroma filling the room and stimulating your senses. Imagine inhaling deeply and letting that wonderful smell create in you an acute anticipation of the enjoyment to come. Now after all that, can you comprehend such a delicacy coming out of the oven with no aroma at all?

Of course you can't. It doesn't happen. You can have the aroma without the pie—after all, there are some pretty close counterfeit smells in candles, air fresheners, and all sorts of products that simulate the real thing—but you can't have the pie without the aroma. The substance can't exist without some accompanying signs.

So it is with faith and works. Paul is clear in Romans and Galatians that we are justified by faith. But he never indicates that we can have faith without accompanying signs. If it's the real pie, so to speak, there will be some evidence. There will be an aroma of works that results from genuine belief.

A lot of Christians throughout history have thought that Paul and James contradict one another on this point, but those of us who are convinced that the whole Bible is inspired by God's Spirit know that there are no true contradictions within it. However, there are different emphases, and while Paul emphasizes the faith that saves, James emphasizes the fallacy of the faith that does nothing. It's ludicrous, he says in effect, to think that someone can believe God for who He really is and not act accordingly. He focuses on good works as evidence of the real thing.

In Deed

Don't fall into the trap of a works-less faith. We do well to avoid the trap of the Pharisees—good works without faith in the Savior—but we make a mistake when we think God isn't interested in good works. According to Ephesians 2:10, we were created for just such a purpose. God's design for us isn't strictly internal. Let your faith prompt you to outward action—today and every day.

It is faith alone that justifies, but the
faith that justifies is not alone.
—JOHN CALVIN

True Righteousness

The scripture was fulfilled that says, "Abraham believed God, and it was credited to him as righteousness."
JAMES 2:23

In Word

Think about what it really means to believe in Jesus. If we really believed—not just agreed with Him in principle, but really bought in to whatever He said—it would radically transform our lives, wouldn't it? When He said something like, "Give to the one who asks you, and do not turn away from the one who wants to borrow from you" (Matthew 5:42), or "Love your enemies and pray for those who persecute you" (Matthew 5:44), we would struggle and strain over exactly how to fulfill those commands. We would not take them as good suggestions or as optional add-ons for really serious disciples. We would take them to heart and consider them imperative. After all, if the Lord of the universe tells us to do something . . . well, how could we not?

We may not realize it, but what we really believe about God, and especially about His work through His Son, will find its way into our thoughts, our words, and our actions. Every attitude will be shaped by what we think of Him. If we think of Him as a taskmaster, we will be afraid of Him, even when we're obeying Him. If we think of Him as a sentimental Father of love who would never make us feel bad by telling us to repent of something, we will be awfully casual about our relationship with Him. If our thoughts are out of balance with regard to His holiness and His grace, leaning to one side or the other, our lives will reflect the imbalance.

In Deed

That's why God looks at what we really believe, as He did with Abraham. James says that Abraham believed God and was therefore considered righteous—he quotes the same verse as Paul on this point—but he points out that Abraham's beliefs had real results, like obedience and sacrifice. There was nothing theoretical about Abraham's faith, and there's to be nothing theoretical about ours. Righteousness begins within, but it works its way out. That's how our faith can fulfill the Scripture just as surely as Abraham's did.

> What I believe about God is the most important thing about me.
> —A. W. TOZER

Practical Help

If one of you says to him, "Go, I wish you well;
keep warm and well fed," but does nothing
about his physical needs, what good is it?
JAMES 2:16

In Word

What does a disciple of Jesus look like? If we are truly His disciples—in other words, if we actually try to live like Him—then we're going to do some of the things He did while He walked on this planet. We're going to do what we can to heal people, to comfort them, to teach them, to feed them, and even to take a firm stand in the face of falsehood. We're going to resist the forces of darkness and live in the light. We're going to love people however we can, whether that comes in the form of a compassionate embrace of a leper or a stern rebuke of a Pharisee. Above all, we are not going to be passive observers of those around us.

That goes against our human nature. Both selfish tendencies and our culture at large urge us not to involve ourselves in things that don't concern us—and it's true that the Bible never tells us to be busybodies in other people's affairs. But when we encounter people with needs, people whom God has put into our lives for a reason, we are compelled to do what Jesus Himself would do. Offer a miracle, or a prayer for a miracle, or a loaf of bread, or a compassionate word. We cannot simply wish people well. We often have to be the means by which they get well.

In Deed

How much of your life is spent meeting the needs of others? Do your resources, your time, and your efforts go toward practical help? If you take care of children or an aging parent, you may feel stretched in that area already. Still, there are others who come to your doorstep—literally or figuratively—who have desperate needs, and with a little bit of effort, you can find out what the needs are and how to meet them.

Don't follow the trend of our society to draw firm lines around family and friends, never reaching beyond them. The gospel isn't about isolation, it's about infiltrating the world with mercy. Demonstrate mercy in practical ways.

Faith is the root of works. A root that
produces nothing is dead.
—THOMAS WILSON

Powerful Witness

You believe that there is one God. Good! Even
the demons believe that—and shudder.
JAMES 2:19

In Word

Fallen human beings—even redeemed ones—have an enormous capacity for self-deception. We have the ability to listen to a sermon or read a book, nod our heads in agreement with whatever we've heard or read, and then go out and ignore our new knowledge. We often equate hearing the truth with believing it, and that's just where the enemy of our souls wants us.

James wrote about that phenomenon back in chapter one of his letter. "Do not merely listen to the word, and so deceive yourselves," he says (1:22). Then he urges his readers to do what they've heard. It's in the practice of faith that faith becomes real, not in the nodding of the head. Agreement does not equal belief anywhere in the Bible.

If we can let that sink in and make a difference in our lives, we can impact the world in powerful ways. First-century society was powerfully affected by the Christians who knew, when the lions were closing in on them in the arena, that it mattered whether they recanted their faith or not. Christians who refused to eat food sacrificed to idols or to visit the old pagan temple—even for purely social reasons—made a statement about the reality of their faith. More than that, the Christians who cared for their neighbors—their pagan, often hostile neighbors—when an epidemic struck were world changers. They gave their contemporaries a clear alternative lifestyle, a lifestyle that fit with an unearthly kingdom. Their faith was genuine.

In Deed

No matter how genuine you feel your faith is, the world won't know it until you live it. And oh, how it needs such a witness. If ever there was an age hungry for authenticity and a winsome kind of purity, ours is. We live in a time when people don't believe there's anything better out there. It's our job to show them that there is. Real faith will do that. When it's visible, it's powerful.

> Belief is truth held in the mind; faith is fire in the heart.
> —JOHN HENRY NEWMAN

First Love

Yet I hold this against you: You have forsaken your first love.
REVELATION 2:4

In Word

It was a commendation most churches would be proud of. Jesus affirmed the Ephesian church for its good deeds, hard work, and perseverance. He complimented their sense of discernment and ability to deal with false teachers. They knew the truth, and they lived it. What more is a church supposed to do?

But the church lacked one thing, one characteristic that would, if they couldn't regain it, result in His removing them from the scene. These believers knew the right things and did the right things, but their fellowship was still in danger of being snuffed out by the Lord Himself. Why? Because they lacked the zeal that is supposed to characterize Christians. The devotion they had for Him at first had weakened. They were deficient in the one attribute that Jesus said His disciples would be known for (John 13:35). They lacked love.

We don't know exactly what "first love" is supposed to mean—love for God or for each other or both?—but it's clear that this missing ingredient can begin with zeal and then grow stale. And the fact that this church was still doing the right things makes it clear that this love isn't simply an outward behavior. No, there seems to have been an emotional aspect of their attitude that had grown cold. Christ is focused not on the actions that result from love but on the heart behind it.

In Deed

Jesus' warning that He would remove this church's lampstand if its people didn't repent seems harsh, but it is a startling statement on how much God cares about our motives for serving Him. It isn't enough to have sharp, Spirit-honed discernment and to put feet to our faith in good works and acts of service. It isn't even enough to persevere in spite of opposition. We can do everything right, but if we lack love for Him and for others, we are not in His will. If you've lost your first love, do whatever it takes to get it back. Drop everything, seek His heart, and ask Him to help you find yours.

My spirit has become dry because it forgets to feed on you.
—JOHN OF THE CROSS

No Fear

Do not be afraid of what you are about to suffer.
REVELATION 2:10

In Word

When Jesus revealed His messages for the seven churches to John, He usually issued a few affirmations, then a rebuke or correction, and then encouragement. Not with the church at Smyrna. There was no rebuke for these believers who had been afflicted. They had suffered already, and they were poor—materially, not spiritually. After the Lord affirmed them for enduring slander and attacks, He gave them a warning of what is to come. They would suffer. Some would be put in prison. But if they were faithful even to the point of death, they would receive the crown of life.

Most of us don't receive such dire warnings from the Lord, and we would probably become unraveled if we did. But suffering has always been part of following Jesus. Martyrs still die at the hands of those who oppose God. Every day in many parts of the world, faithful believers lay down their lives for their Lord.

That puts some things in perspective for those of us trying to survive the daily grind and to persevere in the midst of difficult circumstances. We experience heartache in this world, and our faith gets stretched. Some of us ask God lots of "why" questions when things don't go our way, and some of us simply wonder where the excitement of following Jesus has gone. Underlying the faith of many is a deep disappointment that the faith adventure is harder than we thought it would be. The constant victory we long for is an increasingly distant ideal.

In Deed

The unspoken assumption of many Christians is that following Jesus should make life easier. And if by "easier" we mean more fruitful or ultimately more satisfying, we're right. But Jesus never promised a smooth road. Why would we become undone when we encounter a tragic accident or illness, suffer an injustice, or even simply get bored with routines and obligations? What did we expect?

Live in the victory promised by Jesus—He encouraged the Smyrnans by telling them that their suffering was temporary—but realize that no one can have victory without first having opposition. Face it by clinging to His promises for those who overcome.

> Afflictions are but the shadow of God's wings.
> —GEORGE MACDONALD

No Compromise

I know where you live—where Satan has his throne.
REVELATION 2:13

In Word

Jesus' words to the church at Pergamum could have been spoken to any of us. We may not live where Satan's "throne" is, but we live in territory that is heavily under his influence. No matter how many churches we have on the street corners of our communities, our culture is saturated with the philosophies of this world and the deceptions of our enemy. Until we are in heaven, we are living in a war zone.

It's comforting to know that Jesus is aware of where we are and that He will affirm us for remaining true to His name, as He did with the believers of Pergamum. It isn't easy to stubbornly insist on our identity in Him when the culture is trying to pull us in every other direction. We find pretty quickly that we can't live the Christian life on cruise control; it's a constant choice and requires consistent focus on who we are in Him. It requires a certain degree of stubbornness to swim upstream.

The church of Pergamum did that to a degree, but they were also rebuked for compromises they had made (vv. 14-15). They lived in a pagan atmosphere in which believers could easily be tempted to twist truth and indulge in sin. Jesus warned them that their lack of diligence could prompt Him to step into their midst to divide the faithful from the unfaithful with sharp words of truth. We aren't sure what that would look like, but the point is clear. If we don't defend the truth of God, there will be consequences.

In Deed

Some Christians take Jesus' warning as license to use the Bible as a weapon and attack everyone who doesn't agree with us. That spirit isn't found anywhere in Scripture; in fact, it would probably draw the same rebuke Jesus gave the Ephesians about losing their love (2:4). Our real calling is to be stubborn about who Jesus is and what His character is like. We are to refuse to compromise the integrity of who we are in Christ. Jesus knows where we live, and He wants to live in us unwaveringly right where we are.

> Never let us be guilty of sacrificing any
> portion of truth on the altar of peace.
> —J. C. RYLE

One Purpose

Whatever you do, do it all for the glory of God.
1 CORINTHIANS 10:31

In Word

Athletes train for one purpose: to win. Businesses exist with one goal: to earn a profit. Hedonists live for one passion: to have a good time. Misers hoard for one reason: to accumulate. Some of these ambitions are admirable, others misguided. But there's one key to seeing them come to pass: if we are single-minded about our pursuits, we are more likely to accomplish them.

Paul was single-minded about the glory of God. That's why being beaten nearly to death or imprisoned didn't seem to faze him. That's why no insult was harsh enough to get him off track, no philosophical argument strong enough to sway him. He was focused on the glory of God, and everything else took a backseat.

That's the attitude Paul urged his fellow believers to have. The Corinthians had gotten off track with a number of distractions—immorality, division, idolatry, and more. And in the middle of Paul's lengthy instructions about these and other issues, he summed up the remedy to them all with this one command: "Whatever you do, do it all for the glory of God."

Following this mandate would solve a lot of the problems we have in our discipleship. Instead of figuring out which freedoms we can get away with and which are actually sinful; instead of arguing with God over His will for our lives; instead of picking and choosing whom we will exhibit grace toward; we can always be guided by this one principle: If it gives God glory, it's probably worthwhile. If it doesn't, it certainly isn't.

In Deed

If you need a simple guiding principle for your life, consider this one. God's glory is the answer to many of the issues you struggle with. Let yourself be consumed with this one purpose, and let it become your driving passion. You'll be amazed at how insignificant many of your problems become. Your life will be defined by what you set your heart on. If you set it on the glory of God, you can never go wrong.

> My goal is God Himself, not joy nor peace, nor even blessing, but Himself, my God.
> —FREDERICK BROOK

Two Extremes

*God is faithful; he will not let you be
tempted beyond what you can bear.*
1 CORINTHIANS 10:13

In Word

There were two pressing issues for the Corinthians: that fragile balance between law and grace, and that ever-present temptation to love an idol. There were Corinthian Christians who said that grace was the rule and the law was no more, that all things were permissible. And there were also those who said that because the law was no more, idolatry was no longer an issue. Paul gave them all strong warnings.

Christians always struggle with law and grace because we know that while God's standards remain perfect, all righteousness was fulfilled and all sin paid for in Jesus. If God is still holy, but all righteousness has been fulfilled, what's left for the Christian? A way of life based not on the law but on God's character, according to Paul. Idolatry is still an issue because it deals with our love for God; and holiness is still an issue because we are born of His Spirit.

That's why Paul discusses temptation. It's still an issue. "Falling" remains a possibility. The gospel of grace is not a ticket to an "anything goes" lifestyle. Grace is sacred; though plentiful, it should never be taken for granted. So Paul urges faithfulness with this exhortation: there is always a way out of temptation. The faithful God will help you be faithful.

In Deed

That's both an enormous comfort, because God is providing for our spiritual needs at all times, and an enormous burden, because we have no excuse for our sin. We can be grateful for His care and His provision, but we also can never tell Him a temptation was just too much for us. He has forgiven us completely and dealt with our sin problem, but His work is thorough. He does not forgive us for sin while letting us remain slaves to it.

Have you felt like a slave to sin? By the promise of God's Word, you aren't. If you need a way out, look for it. The faithful God will point you to it every time.

To realize God's presence is the one sovereign
remedy against temptation.
—FRANÇOIS FÉNELON

An Intense Battleground

These things occurred as examples to keep us
from setting our hearts on evil things.
1 CORINTHIANS 10:6

In Word

Many Christians are surprised in their first few weeks of believing. The new birth was supposed to make us practically immune from sin, wasn't it? We have a new nature now, we're told, and that new nature comes from God Himself. What could be holier than that?

But we find out soon that having a new nature doesn't put an end to the old one. As far as God is concerned, the old nature is dead; that's how He sees us. Our sinful flesh and the enemy of our souls, however, want to argue the point. We find quickly that the struggle with sin is just beginning. Before the new birth, sin was clearly our master. Now there's a vastly more powerful rival in the Spirit of God. We have entered a war zone.

The front lines of the war zone are located in our hearts, and the battle there is intense. We will find it raging often, and we will frequently feel like giving up. But God has given us warnings throughout His Word and throughout history of what happens to those who stop fighting. Those who set their hearts on evil things—as the wandering Israelites did in this passage—find the costs far greater than the benefits. Worthless idols never deliver on their promises. God always does. It should be obvious where to set our hearts.

In Deed

The Bible frequently speaks of the human heart as a battleground. Psalms tells us to hide God's Word there; Proverbs tells us to guard it zealously; both the Old Testament and the New point to it as the center of the greatest commandments—to love God and others; and Jesus says the living waters of His Spirit will flow from it. In God's opinion, the human heart is a critical place.

In your daily war against the sin that so easily infects your life, remember to guard your heart. Watch where you set it. Be extremely careful not to let it dwell on impure or unworthy things. Let it be filled with God alone.

The capital of Heaven is the heart in which
Jesus Christ is enthroned as King.
—SUNDAR SINGH

A Firm Stand

"Everything is permissible"—but not everything
is constructive. Nobody should seek his
own good, but the good of others.
1 CORINTHIANS 10:23-24

In Word

What do you do with a law that (1) perfectly reflected the heart and character of God, and (2) was completely fulfilled by the only one who could do so? You can't reject it; that would violate point one. And you can't try to fulfill it without also claiming that the Savior's work wasn't sufficient. How do you live righteously in an economy of grace?

Many Corinthians said righteousness wasn't necessary anymore. All things were permissible, they said, because grace would cover it all anyway. And Paul never disagrees with them in his letter to that church. But he does qualify it; he redefines "permissible" for them. The guideline for righteous Christian living is whether our behavior is beneficial to ourselves—in God's eyes—or beneficial to others—also in God's eyes. And if we look to God for the definition of what's beneficial, we get something that looks a lot like the law.

Many of today's Christians view sin as the Corinthians did, seeing it as irrelevant. Our culture has told us that all things, even morality, are relative, and we've been influenced by the idea. We've also mistaken Jesus' warnings against judging others as an excuse for not saying anything specific about sin at all. In the process, we've grown awfully casual about what's right and wrong.

In Deed

The Bible is never casual about such things, not in the Old Testament or in the New. If we think grace means that sin no longer matters, we are as mistaken as the Corinthians were. It matters. A lot.

What principles guide your life? Are you aware of them? You probably don't slavishly follow the Old Testament law, but are you rigorous in your pursuit of God's character? When we ask what is permissible, we are usually asking the wrong question. It's better to ask what lines up with God's heart and what is beneficial in His eyes. Pursue those answers zealously.

It is the great moment in our lives when we
decide that sin must die right out.

—OSWALD CHAMBERS

A Way Out

Do not cause anyone to stumble, whether Jews, Greeks
or the church of God. . . . For I am not seeking my own
good but the good of many, so that they may be saved.
1 CORINTHIANS 10:32-33

In Word

If you had a terrible disease, it would matter to you a lot. You would do everything you could to defeat it. You would seek cures and follow medical regimens in order to be healed. You'd run from it . . . well, like the plague.

But your disease would also matter to the people around you. And if they happened to suffer from a similar condition, they would carefully observe your remedies. If you overcame your sickness, they would do exactly as you had done.

In a sense, that's what the world is watching us for. If we treat sin casually, it's public affirmation that the ways of the world are the ways of everyone, even the redeemed. But if we take a stand against sin, calling it what it is and doing everything we can to overcome it, we make a powerful statement. There will be those who disagree with us vehemently and those who think we're just strange. And some people will want the power to overcome for themselves. Regardless, everyone will know that we aren't content with the disease.

In Deed

We live in a world that knows it is sick but isn't sure from what. Many see human nature as faulty, or psychologically messed up, or love impaired. But in a culture that calls its problems "issues" and sees its goal as "self-actualization," making a statement about what God calls sin is important. In fact, making such a statement is a prerequisite to the cure. We can't tell people about our Savior until we tell them we need to be saved and why.

Paul says our behavior has the power to make other people stumble, so we have to be extremely careful. But he also says our behavior has the power to point to salvation, so we have to be extremely zealous. Sin matters. So does righteousness. Always point in the right direction.

God wills that you sanctify the world and your everyday life.
—VINCENT PALLOTTI

Out of the Darkness

We do not belong to the night or to the darkness.
1 THESSALONIANS 5:5

In Word

Creatures of the night have a culture of their own. They can get away with all sorts of things because no one is awake to see them. It is the hidden life, the life that is shrouded in darkness, and they love it that way. The best way to be one's own lord is to live in secret.

Those who have been born of God, however, do not live that way. Our sins have been brought into the light—they had to be in order to be dealt with. Our hearts have been made new in order to live before the all-seeing God and to share with others. We have no need for pretense—we've already declared ourselves corrupt and needy, so what's to hide? We can live in the light because the light has already exposed us. We need no secrets now.

The metaphor of darkness and light is one of the New Testament's most descriptive and persistent themes. According to the Gospel of John and that disciple's letters, Jesus is the light that came into the world. And according to Paul here in his first letter to the Thessalonians, the light is now our natural environment. We are no longer creatures of the night, but creatures of the day.

In Deed

That's important to remember, because the sinful nature still clings to darkness and will drive us there frequently if we allow it. Every Christian has felt that tendency to creep back into the shadows every once in a while, only to crave the light again afterward. Whether we live in light or darkness is a daily choice, and the fact that God's Spirit is within us makes us truly comfortable only in the light.

Remember that. There are times when the light is scary; after all, it exposes us. But like lifelong cave dwellers, our eyes will adjust to the sunlight over time. That's what our discipleship is about, and that's the instruction of the apostle. Live in the light. Get used to it and stop hiding. Let your eyes adjust. According to the Word, we will be here for a very long time.

> Darkness is my point of view, my right to myself; light is God's point of view.
> —OSWALD CHAMBERS

Into the Light

God did not appoint us to suffer wrath
but to receive salvation.
1 THESSALONIANS 5:9

In Word

In the beginning, the Bible tells us, the world was formless and void. And it was completely dark until God spoke light into being. That creation fell hard into rebellion,
so millennia later, God spoke light into the world again. This time, it wasn't the sun
or the stars; it was Jesus, the light of the world. The re-creation was as much about
turning darkness into light as the original creation was.

When that second great light came into the world, He explained His purpose
clearly: "God did not send his Son into the world to condemn the world, but to save
the world through him" (John 3:17). But the tragedy is spelled out two verses later:
"Light has come into the world, but men loved darkness instead of light because their
deeds were evil."

That's a great verse for evangelism, but how does it apply to Christians? Sadly,
this is where many of us live, at least occasionally. We want Jesus in our lives theoretically, but we don't necessarily want the light He brings. We want the faith that saves
but not the faith that changes us from who we are. We want the benefits of heaven
without preparing ourselves to fit in. We want the God of holiness, yet we're still
attracted to sin.

In Deed

If this were not true of Christians, Paul would have felt no need to write about it to
the Thessalonians—a church, and one of the better ones. Like them, we need to
be reminded: a day is coming when God will bless those who lived in the light and
rebuke those who didn't. The costs of clinging to sin are never worthwhile.

God's desire, expressed by Jesus and by Paul's statement in verse 9, is that we
experience His salvation fully. That means now. We are to let the salvation of the final
day shape our lives today. A Christian who does not set his heart on eternity and live
for eternity now is a Christian who is strangely deluded. But such is the seduction of
this world, and we've all given in. Paul says to snap out of it. Live the saved life today.
It's what children of the light do.

> To follow the Savior is to participate in salvation;
> to follow the light is to perceive the light.
> —IRENAEUS

Always Aware

Let us be alert and self-controlled.
1 THESSALONIANS 5:6

In Word

Imagine soldiers at the front lines sitting around playing cards and laughing. Is it appropriate? It depends, doesn't it? If there is no engagement with the enemy at the moment and if guards are posted, it might not be an inappropriate scene. If, however, the bullets are flying, the shells are exploding, and the injured are being brought in constantly, a friendly card game would be the last thing you'd see.

But that's how many Christians live. The darkness of this world isn't a silent shroud; it's chaos. The bullets are flying, and the shells are exploding. There's a war on, and while there are times when we can take a break and disengage from the action— God doesn't want us constantly stressed, after all—we must always be alert. A soldier who isn't alert is a soldier who is endangering his life and the lives of others.

If that's true, we can be awfully cavalier about the dangers we face. We forget the life-and-death nature of the spiritual battles we face. We have a hard time remembering that a little lack of self-control isn't just a character flaw, it's an opportunity for the enemy to cash in on our weakness. We need to be reminded, as Paul reminds the Thessalonians, that lifestyle matters to the Kingdom of God and to its citizens. Our prayers, our work, the condition of our hearts, and the degree to which we live in the Spirit are critical. Eternally critical.

In Deed

God never tells us in His Word to live with anxiety and stress about the intensity of the battle. He repeatedly tells us, however, to be sober minded. In other words, be alert. We are to know who we are, know who the enemy is, know who God is, and know where we stand on the battlefield. Not to know these things is to beg for disaster.

The only way to know these things is to immerse oneself in the Word and to pray for guidance and protection daily. Paul wasn't kidding when he talked about the armor of God. The Christian who is alert and self-controlled stands in safety.

The Christian life is not a playground; it is a battleground.
—WARREN WIERSBE

Living Right

Since we belong to the day, let us be self-controlled,
putting on faith and love as a breastplate,
and the hope of salvation as a helmet.
1 THESSALONIANS 5:8

In Word

Our battle is an open affair. We are not hiding from the enemy, we are not lurking in the shadows of this world, and we are not wandering around in the darkness without a clue as to where we're going. Things have been revealed to us that the rest of the world does not yet know—or has chosen not to believe. When we walk through this world, we have direction and purpose. And we fight in the daylight.

And we have to, don't we? This Christian life, regardless of what we thought at first, is not a passive life. We are assaulted constantly by the ways of the world and the strategies of the enemy. He hates us because God loves us, and he is determined to keep this world in darkness. We are a threat not because we are good and righteous or because we are powerful in ourselves—we aren't. Authority has been handed down to us from Jesus through the disciples, and we have been clothed in the white garments of Christ. No weapon, no accusation, no ridicule of our weakness can affect us. With Christ living within and giving us permission to use His authority, we are like beggars dressed in noble attire. And there's nothing in our attire that the enemy can exploit.

In Deed

You, as a soldier of God, have powerful weapons. They appear foolish and impotent to the experts of secular society, but we can't fault them for that. They don't know any better. We, however, do. We can do things with faith and love and hope that have eternal importance. And if self-control has been established first, we can go into battle with our protection firmly in place. Our armor and weapons are our answer to the assaults we face daily.

Have you considered the importance of self-control in your daily life? It's a powerful weapon. What about faith, love, and hope? They are impenetrable armor. Carry these things into your battles each day, and your days will never defeat you.

> Almighty God, give us grace that we may cast away the works of darkness, and put upon us the armor of light.
> —BOOK OF COMMON PRAYER

Strength for Today

Encourage one another and build each other up.
1 THESSALONIANS 5:11

In Word

Paul, in this passage and many others, has given us a clear contrast. We can choose which culture we will live in: the culture of darkness or the culture of light. We can lurk in the shadows of the world, or we can bask in the sunlight of heaven. But the clear calling for every believer is to be as different from the world as possible.

That means that we cannot indulge in the excesses of those who have no hope. Those who do not have their eye on the day of His appearing will live differently than those of us who do, and we are not to confuse the two cultures. The Christian gospel doesn't take us out of the world, but it makes us radically countercultural. We are different, whether we want to be or not. If we don't act differently, we're just denying who we are.

It's hard to live a countercultural lifestyle. It's virtually impossible without the support of a like-minded community. That's why there are still, to this day, neighborhoods of immigrants in our largest cities that speak the same language and eat the same foods. In an unfamiliar culture, community matters. We need that support.

As immigrants out of the kingdom of darkness and into the Kingdom of God, we need the support of other immigrants who have made the same transition. But our "neighborhoods"—our churches and Bible studies—are often less than supportive. We don't always know how to take care of our own.

In Deed

Paul tells the Thessalonians to take care of their own. They need each other's support. There is no way to remain in the light consistently and to fight the battles of day and night if we don't have our eyes on Christ's appearing—together. In other words, encouragement is vital.

If your Christian community—church, family, or other ministry—is not an encouraging environment, be bold. Live counterculturally yourself and help others do the same. Your ability to shine in the darkness will soon dispel the darkness altogether.

> Take courage. We walk in the wilderness today
> and in the Promised Land tomorrow.
> —D. L. MOODY

Where He Dwells

. . . so that Christ may dwell in your hearts through faith.
EPHESIANS 3:17

In Word

We're taught that Jesus lives in the heart of anyone who believes. When we come into His Kingdom by faith, when we accept Him as Lord and Savior, He comes to dwell within us. But here Paul prays an unexpected prayer for those who have already believed: that God would strengthen them with His Spirit *in order that* Jesus might dwell in their hearts.

Is the apostle implying that Jesus isn't in these people who have already been filled with the Spirit? That somehow they have received the promises of God and tasted the inheritance of Jesus' glory, but their hearts aren't yet inhabited by their Savior? No, the prayer is for something more than the simple presence of Jesus. It's that these believers would, by faith and the Spirit's strength, allow Jesus to live out His life within them. Not that He would simply exist within them, but that He would truly *live* within them—actively and powerfully.

There's a huge difference between being born of the Spirit and living in the Spirit's power. We often assume that if Jesus is living within us, then we have all we need. And it's true—in a sense, we do. But we aren't accessing all we need if Jesus is present but latent within us. Faith and prayer bring Him to the forefront and give Him prominence in our lives. When His Spirit strengthens us with power in our inner being (v. 16), Jesus isn't just there, He's alive and active.

In Deed

Don't be content with the simple fact that Jesus is within you. He is within you for a purpose. He doesn't want to just sit there; He wants to fill you with His love and power. He wants to work out His life within you, to inspire and empower your works and words. He wants to fill your spirit and your relationships and your activities with Himself. He wants your life to be an exhibition of His presence. Ask Him to fulfill His every desire within you.

> One person works upon another person from outside inwards, but God alone comes to us from within outwards.
> —JAN VAN RUYSBROECK

All of God

*. . . that you may be filled to the measure
of all the fullness of God.*
EPHESIANS 3:19

In Word

It sounds arrogant to some, simply impossible to others. How can human beings be
filled with all the fullness of God? After all, God is infinite; we aren't. The human can
contain *some* of the divine, but surely Paul is overstating a promise by using words like
"all" and "fullness." Maybe he means we can be filled to our capacity with God, assuming that our capacity has a limit. Or maybe he only means that our lives can overflow
with God, though it's our smallness and God's greatness that creates the overflow. But
literally "filled to the measure of all the fullness of God"? Those are words no mortal
can live up to. That's far too much to expect.

But the words of Scripture aren't accidental. The Spirit who inspired them had
something specific in mind with Paul's words. Our minds stretch to figure out what
it is, and we usually give up our literalism over statements like this and chalk them
up to spiritual hyperbole. Still, the incomprehensibility of this verse is challenging.
The claim is astounding. We're left with the sense that life in Christ is way over our
heads.

That seems to be exactly what Paul and the Spirit who inspired him intended to
convey. Maybe this verse really is an overstatement, the product of an apostle over-
flowing with the magnitude of Jesus, or maybe it has some plausible explanation we
haven't figured out yet. Regardless, if it keeps us from complacency by making us
realize that we haven't yet reached the ideal in our relationship with God, then it has
done its work. This ideal won't let us be satisfied with where we are. That's the way
it should be.

In Deed

However much you have grown in your relationship with God, however long you
have walked with Him, realize that you have barely scratched the surface. You were
designed to host His Spirit within you—that's a relationship without an imposed
limit. There is no ending point, no constraint. However full of Him you are, He offers
more. Accept it. Never be satisfied with "enough" of Him.

God is especially present in the hearts
of His people by His Holy Spirit.
—JEREMY TAYLOR

All about Attitude

Your attitude should be the same as that of Christ Jesus.
PHILIPPIANS 2:5

In Word

Attitude. Everyone has one—or more. There are good attitudes and bad ones, positive attitudes and negative ones, contagious attitudes and barely noticeable ones. There are attitudes that guide our entire lives and others that come and go as often as the wind changes. They are part of who we are.

We usually get our attitudes from others. The family we were raised in, the culture we live in, and the influential people in our lives have all shaped the way we think and feel. Kids imitate the attitudes of the athletes and entertainers they admire. So do adults, but we're more subtle about it. We can pick up an attitude from a community, a trend, or an event. We're often easily influenced.

We may not realize it, but our attitudes are a matter of choice. Yes, circumstances and people can influence them, and often those influences are overwhelming. Still, we can choose how we will react in any given situation or to any particular person. We can determine to be positive or negative, accepting or bitter. We are not victims of our impulses.

In Deed

Paul directs the Philippians to choose the attitude of Jesus. The next few days we'll look closely at His attitude, but we know the essentials already: gentleness, joy, zeal for the Kingdom of God, love for people, and as this passage in Philippians emphasizes, humility. Jesus exemplified all the fruits of the Spirit perfectly, and though elements of those fruits go beyond mental attitude, that's where many of them begin. If we want to be like Jesus, we have to think like Him.

We may think our discipleship is mainly a matter of imitating Jesus' powerful faith or His good works. Those are important, even essential, but following Jesus begins with His attitudes. If His mind-set isn't formed in us by His Spirit—if it isn't our foundation—the faith and the works will always be an impossible uphill climb. As you follow Him today, think about His attitudes, and ask God to cultivate them within you. Having an attitude is inevitable. Scripture says to choose His.

> For those who would learn God's ways, humility is the first thing, humility is the second, humility is the third.
> — AUGUSTINE

The Ultimate Humility

Who, being in very nature God, did not consider
equality with God something to be grasped.
PHILIPPIANS 2:6

In Word

The equality between God and Jesus is a solid scriptural truth. Jesus is called the "exact representation" of God (Hebrews 1:3) and "the image of the invisible God" (Colossians 1:15). Jesus Himself said, "I and the Father are one" (John 10:30). So there's no question, biblically, about who Jesus really is. He is God the Son, incarnate deity. He is King of all creation.

Jesus made a mind-boggling statement by entering the womb of a Jewish teenager. He refused to cling to what was rightfully His: a permanent position on the throne of heaven, the worship of myriads of created beings, all glory and honor from all things at all times. He left the position of deity and embraced the position of fallen humanity. No greater condescension has ever been made, nor can it be. There is no higher exaltation than where Jesus came from, and there is no lower depth than that to which He went for us. Jesus forsook equality with God, and He did it for a reason.

That should speak volumes to us. If the Son of God could have such humility, such a sense of sacrifice and love, then we are misguided if we think God would not ask us to make sacrifices. If Jesus wasn't above a birth in a stable and a death on a cross, we are not above any humble act God calls us to. If God led us into ghettos and garbage dumps, we'd have no right to refuse. Our unwillingness would be confronted—and sternly rebuked—by the humility of Jesus.

In Deed

How does your attitude measure up to Jesus'? If you're not willing to touch lepers, be ridiculed for the sake of the Kingdom, endure the attacks of the enemy, and tirelessly serve others, then it doesn't—not at all. That's not news to us, of course; we have a long history of not measuring up to Him. But that doesn't excuse us from trying. If we love Jesus, we'll love His attitude. We'll do whatever God calls us to do.

> Because Jesus Christ came into the world clothed
> in humility, He will always be found among
> those who are clothed with humility.
> —A. W. TOZER

Servants at Heart

. . . taking the very nature of a servant.
PHILIPPIANS 2:7

In Word

Christians are told to be humble, to be joyful, to be loving, to be . . . well, to be other than what we are. We are encouraged over and over again in Scripture and in our Christian communities to change. For many of us, that translates into a better performance. We become disciples to the extent we do what disciples do and act however disciples are supposed to act. We try to become Christlike by behaving like Christ.

That's good, and our motives for doing so are usually right. But there will be a certain amount of futility and frustration in such attempts, and there comes a time when we have to ask: Why aren't we displaying humility or joy or love because we actually are humble or joyful or loving? Why do they often depend on our acting ability rather than the condition of our hearts? Why can't we be like Jesus because we are like Jesus?

The difference is what's really in the heart. There's nothing wrong with being a servant because we believe Christians are supposed to be servants. But we want to go further than that. We want to be servants not because it's the prescription for discipleship but because we're servant hearted. Ideally, we want our attitudes to be our core, not our clothing. We want to be authentic.

In Deed

Jesus was and is thoroughly authentic, of course, and Paul has instructed these early Christians to be like Him. Their attitudes are to be authentic, as are their lifestyles, their works, and their worship. A close connection between the inner life and the outer life is a mark of Christian maturity. That kind of integrity and genuineness is God's design for us.

How do we get there? By lots of prayer, by deep searching, and by constant efforts to integrate the Scriptures into our hearts by the power of the Holy Spirit. In other words, we'll fail if it depends entirely on us. But it doesn't. God will help. Make His work in your heart be your prayer today.

I just wanna be real.
—MARK HEARD

Not Our Own

He humbled himself and became obedient to death.
PHILIPPIANS 2:8

In Word

If we're honest, we'll admit that there are limits to our obedience. We may say that there is nothing we wouldn't do for God, and we may say it sincerely. But most of us, somewhere deep inside us, have a bottom line, a line we would hardly dare to cross. We like to choose our areas of sacrifice.

We can't. Discipleship doesn't work that way. We can't be "a living sacrifice" according to Romans 12:1 and then choose how to live. If we have offered ourselves up to God, we are His. We have been bought with a price, as 1 Corinthians 6:20 says. We have no more say over our circumstances or our future than a piece of pottery has over its final shape. Our lives are in the hands of the Potter. Thank God.

Our problem with servanthood and obedience usually begins in our minds. Do we consider ourselves as important in God's Kingdom? Do we feel indispensable? Did we think we had some sort of leverage over the Father that allowed us to tell Him how He may use us and how He may not? If so, we were mistaken. We were completely dead, and He resurrected us. That means we owe Him everything. We have no claim to ourselves.

In Deed

When that really sinks in, we begin to live differently. We can serve others freely because we've dropped the desire to make a name for ourselves and achieve the status we've always desired. We've given up our agendas; we are no longer driven by ambition; we have surrendered our desires and goals to Him. With all that self-directed clutter out of the way, we can do whatever He wants—love someone who is difficult to love, feed someone who is hungry, or serve someone in need. If our desire is to further the Kingdom of God, and the Kingdom of God is built on humility and service, there's nothing we won't do.

Think of some act of service you can do today—something unusual for you— and then do it. The Kingdom of God will benefit by your obedience. So will you.

He who knows himself best esteems himself least.
—HENRY G. BROWN

The Way to Honor

Therefore God exalted him to the highest place and
gave him the name that is above every name.
PHILIPPIANS 2:9

In Word

There's an amazing truth about humble service that most people, even many Christians, refuse to believe: God honors it. Oh, we know that He'll honor the servant-hearted one day when they get to heaven. But most of us aren't moved by such delayed gratification. We want a payoff here and now.

If verse 9 is any indication of how God feels about humble obedience—and it clearly is—we would do well to pursue it with all our energy. Why? Because the Kingdom of God is built on such things, and God's highest reward goes to those who bear the most Kingdom fruit. God is zealous about His servants, using them as a testimony to this world and drawing them closer to His throne. He did so with Jesus, giving Him the ultimate exaltation and turning the praises of every creature toward Him. And God shares that blessing with servant-hearted Christians. Those who are like Jesus in attitude and action will be with Jesus in position.

That's why Jesus so often taught His disciples to serve each other and to obey God. He stressed the fact that this is how the world will know that God and His people are real. Our humble obedience gives observers a taste of the Kingdom of God, and for many it's an irresistible taste. There's no way God would refuse honor for such Kingdom servants.

In Deed

If you ever want God to use your life to bring others into the Kingdom, be a servant. If you ever want God to honor your service, embrace the humility of Jesus. If you ever want to be fulfilled, empty yourself. There is no clearer way to God's blessing than the way Jesus chose: humility, service, and obedience. No wonder Paul tells the believers to have this attitude.

Ask yourself: Does my attitude reflect the attitude of Jesus? If the answer is no, ask yourself why not. "Losing" everything is the way to gain everything. It will change you and your world.

He who stays not in his littleness loses his greatness.
—FRANCIS DE SALES

Anxiety-Free

Do not be anxious about anything, but in everything, by prayer and petition, with thanksgiving, present your requests to God.
PHILIPPIANS 4:6

In Word

It's one of the most straightforward commands in Scripture, but one of the hardest to fulfill. "Do not be anxious about anything." What unreasonable person came up with such a naive instruction? What primitive thinker was so uneducated in the ways of the human psyche? If we believe in the inspiration of Scripture, the originator of this verse is none other than the Holy Spirit. He's the one who gives us such a seemingly impossible order to desist from all anxious thoughts.

How can God expect us to be anxiety free? He must have a reason. He wouldn't tell us to do something that's impossible to do. No, the rationale for this imperative comes in the words that follow. The reason we can be anxious for nothing is that our prayers, petitions, and requests can be given over to God in a spirit of gratitude. If this accomplished little, or if this were even a hit-and-miss exercise, our anxiety would still be well-founded. But it isn't. Prayer with thanksgiving gives us rock-solid assurance that our fears are unfounded.

God would never tell us to cease from our anxieties and then give us an only sometimes-effective reason that we can. If He tells us that our prayers and petitions are the antidote to fearfulness, it isn't because He *might* answer us. It's because He guarantees that our anxiety is unreasonable. Our fears are completely unnecessary.

In Deed

If we only knew what God knows—if we only understood how He plans to respond to our thankful prayers and requests—then we wouldn't fear at all. But do we really need to know the specifics of how He plans to answer? Perhaps just knowing who He is should be enough for us. We may not always know *how* He will respond to our prayers, but we know He will—and that He will do so in a way that wouldn't make us nervous if we knew. If God tells us to talk to Him about our problems and then relax, we can. Whatever makes us anxious is safe in His hands.

Pray, and let God worry.
—MARTIN LUTHER

Our Mental Diet

*Whatever is true, whatever is noble, whatever
is right, whatever is pure, whatever is lovely,
whatever is admirable—if anything is excellent
or praiseworthy—think about such things.*
PHILIPPIANS 4:8

In Word

We may not always be conscious of it as we go through the normal course of our day, but we're surrounded with poisons. The air we breathe—at least figuratively, if not literally—is polluted with toxins of inaccurate belief systems, inappropriate visual images, pervasive doses of fear and doubt and discouragement, unholy lifestyles, slanderous words against God and others, and more. We like to think we aren't affected by such constant exposure, but how could we avoid being affected? When you're swimming in water, you can't help but get wet. And when you're swimming in polluted water, it can't be healthy.

When we hear ourselves talking in destructive or careless ways; when we start to look at life through dark-colored lenses, though we don't know why; when our relationship patterns seem to be self-defeating; and when our thoughts toward God seem dull and lifeless—then we know we've been influenced by a poisonous world.

That's why our thought life is such a critical battlefield. The world and the enemy have conspired to undermine the spiritual vitality of numerous Christians, and the strategy works. We can go from joyful to depressed without even noticing the decline. We can shift from selfless to selfish before we're even aware of what happened. We can move from fruitfulness to futility without knowing how we got there. The effects of the world's pollution can be so gradual or imperceptible that we're defeated unless we decide not to be. All it takes is a careful assessment of our thoughts at frequent intervals. We have to know how we think. More than that, we have to know *what* to think.

In Deed

Be proactive. Make sure you are feeding your mind with healthy food. Refuse to let the seeds of bad thinking infiltrate your thought processes. Choose a mental diet of whatever is true, noble, right, pure, lovely, admirable, excellent, and praiseworthy. Let the battlefield of your mind be dominated by the things of God.

Our life is what our thoughts make it.
—CATHERINE OF SIENA

A Long and Winding Road

Be strong in the grace that is in Christ Jesus.
2 TIMOTHY 2:1

In Word

Life as a Christian isn't easy. Actually, life isn't easy for anyone. But if we thought that becoming a Christian was going to make for smooth sailing, we were wrong. We've encountered rough waters, and land is not in sight. We're in this for the long haul.

That's hard to swallow for people who know we came from the Garden of Eden and are headed for the City of God. We live in the in-between time, and while we see the beauty of the past and the glory of the future, we don't see it clearly enough to keep us always encouraged. Sometimes we grow faint, and sometimes we just want to give up. Life is hard, and the reality of God's promises sometimes seems very distant. We struggle to keep going. Or at least to keep going faithfully.

So Paul reminds his protégé that there is grace to keep going. He never tells Timothy that grace will make things easy, and oh, how we wish he did. But he doesn't. Grace sustains, but it does not simplify. It doesn't tell us to relax; it gives us strength. It urges endurance more often than it gives us miraculous escape. But when it's all we have, it's more than enough.

In Deed

You need grace to keep going. You know that. You may even be acutely aware of that fact today. Whether you feel like you're walking on air—a wonderful rarity for most people—or climbing up Everest, you know deep down that what Paul writes to Timothy is vital for you as well. The life God has called you to requires extraordinary endurance, and only grace can give it.

Resist the urge to give up. Many Christians do, in fact, wave the white flag and walk away, at least internally if not externally. That's always a danger, especially when life is tough. If that's your temptation, dwell on this passage deeply this week. Memorize it if you can. Let its truths sink down into your heart. The walk of faith is a hard road—endure it well. And never forget that in your weakness, grace will make you strong.

> Grace grows best in the winter.
> —SAMUEL RUTHERFORD

God's Encouragement

Reflect on what I am saying, for the Lord
will give you insight into all this.
2 TIMOTHY 2:7

In Word

It's God's will for us to endure. We may have trouble believing that sometimes; it may seem that He is out to make things more difficult for us. But that's not God. That's the way of the world and the strategy of the enemy, and a weak prayer life and lukewarm discipleship will ensure that we are victims of both. But God—He is zealous about our ability to endure and persevere until final glory. He is with us each step of the way, encouraging and urging us forward.

You haven't noticed? Yes, our view of Him is sometimes obscured. We believe lies from the enemy—you may remember that the serpent started lying about God very early on in his conversation with Eve—and we believe reality is defined by the circumstances we see. But our eyes and the serpent deceive us. God is aware of our need, and He is always available to help us through it. He promised, and His promises are more real than anything else we can believe.

This letter to Timothy is further guarantee of the fact that God is on our side. He made a world in which soldiers must endure hardship, athletes must train rigorously, and farmers must wait and wait. And if He built patience into the movements of this world, why would believers expect a quick-fix solution to their problems? Just like the soldier, the athlete, and the farmer, we are urged to endure. To wait. To tough it out and look toward the prize. That's what Jesus exemplified, and that's what we are called to do.

In Deed

That's hard to remember in a microwave society, where the other coast of the continent is only hours away, where a thirty-second traffic light is excruciatingly long, and where dinner will be ready in ten minutes. But discipleship? No, that's hard. It's long. It's not for the faint of heart.

Do what Paul says: Reflect on what he is saying. And God—the God who is on our side, cheering us on from the throne of heaven and spurring us on from within—will convince us to never give up.

We conquer not in any brilliant fashion;
we conquer by endurance.
—GEORGE MATHESON

The Example

Remember Jesus Christ, raised from the dead.
2 TIMOTHY 2:8

In Word

We forget rather easily that Jesus endured hardship. Somehow we got the notion that He suffered so that we wouldn't have to. But that's not what He told His disciples. He suffered the penalty of sin so that we wouldn't have to, but He never told us we wouldn't have trials. In fact, just the opposite. He guaranteed tribulation (John 16:33), and He assured the disciples that they would follow in His painful footsteps (Matthew 10:22-25). If we wanted comfort, this was the wrong Master to follow.

But if we look into eternity, if we want glory and blessing in spite of whatever hardships it costs, this is the right Master to follow. We are told that He endured the cross for the joy that was set before Him (Hebrews 12:2). And that joy should keep us going too. If we've gotten discouraged, if we've lost heart, we've lost sight of the joy. There's a promise at the end of this long, hard road, and it's worthwhile. The glory, says Paul, will outweigh the trouble (2 Corinthians 4:17). The benefits will outweigh the cost.

We have no trouble, at least in principle, in applying that truth to saving money for a future purchase, dieting for better health, studying for a degree, or training for a competition. But when it comes to the hardships of life on a fallen planet and the glory that will follow, we focus on the hardship and forget the glory. We forget that the prize at the end is magnificent beyond our wildest dreams.

In Deed

If you want to be like Jesus, set your heart on the joy that is to come. If you really get a glimpse of that, no hardship will weigh you down, not for long. If you find yourself living for comfort and peace right now, you will find yourself constantly frustrated. But if you have set your heart on the joy of eternity, the momentary frustrations will be just that—momentary. And you will have become more like your Lord.

> Jesus promised His disciples three things: that they would be completely fearless, absurdly happy, and in constant trouble.
> —F. R. MALTBY

Never Give Up

Endure hardship with us like a good soldier.
2 TIMOTHY 2:3

In Word

A lot goes into making a good soldier. Training includes extensive study in weapons usage, skill development, enemy strategies, and logistical tactics. Physically, it includes rigorous exercise, stringent diets, and hardship conditioning. Some training programs put soldiers through extreme deprivation of sleep and food. Why? Because they might need such endurance in battle. The war is intense.

Our war is intense too. It doesn't usually have the physical dangers of military combat—although many Christians around the world do suffer and lose their lives—but the emotional and psychological fatigue can be debilitating. The spiritual effort can be draining. Those who thought the Christian life was for wimps bailed out early on. We who stuck it out know the truth: the faith is a life-and-death fight.

Have you considered that the life you are experiencing right now—the hardship you face today—is like training camp? You must learn your weapons, expect dangers, analyze strategies, and employ tactics. You must get into proper spiritual shape, eat a healthy spiritual diet, and condition yourself for extreme hardship. You must even have times of deprivation; you will need to know how to do without in the field. And above all, of highest importance: you must not bail out!

In Deed

Paul wrote to Timothy in a day when Christians were bailing out. Some were deceived by false doctrines and philosophies, some couldn't handle the persecution, and some had just been experimenting with the fad of this new religion. His words in 2 Timothy 4:9-11 are alarming: "Do your best to come to me quickly, for Demas, because he loved this world, has deserted me and has gone to Thessalonica. . . . Only Luke is with me."

In your training, where do you stand? Or are you even standing? Life is tough. The war is on. Endure hardship like a good soldier.

The Lord gets His best soldiers out of the highlands of affliction.
—CHARLES SPURGEON

Beyond Casual

I endure everything for the sake of the elect,
that they too may obtain the salvation that
is in Christ Jesus, with eternal glory.
2 TIMOTHY 2:10

In Word

Imagine being in a desperate situation, held hostage by terrorists in a building under siege. Your life is in the hands of the enemy unless someone comes to rescue you. Now imagine a rescue raid designed to free you and the other hostages. How would you feel when the rescuers burst in if they were out of shape, gasping for air, fumbling with their weapons, and confused as to who should take charge? How would you feel if they turned and ran at the first sight of resistance?

That's often the position we put our lost world in. They are held hostage by the enemy of God—a terrorist of the worst sort—and our rescue missions are sometimes pitiful. A few of us are motivated to save them, but many more are not all that concerned. And if we do get recruited, we sometimes engage in battle as untrained soldiers. We give the impression of being casual observers in the middle of a cross fire. It just doesn't make sense.

God didn't call us to be casual observers. He called us to endure hardship, to make sacrifices, and like Paul, to suffer anything for the elect in order for them to obtain salvation. We've been spiritually saved from the ghetto to glory, but now we avoid the ghetto at all costs. Meanwhile, God says the battle isn't done. He urges us to go back and bring more to Him. And He tells us it won't be easy.

In Deed

Ask yourself a hard question: How much do you sacrifice for the gospel? Do you send a few dollars, pray a few prayers, and take an occasional trip? Or do you give until it hurts, pray until your knees ache, and lay down your life for the Kingdom?

Our callings, of course, are not all the same. Our level of commitment, however, should be. And that's where we are weak. Paul endured everything for the gospel. Why can't we?

> Some like to live within the sound of church or chapel bell; I'd rather run a rescue shop within a yard of hell.
> —WILLIAM BOOTH

Alive

Just as you received Christ Jesus as
Lord, continue to live in him.
COLOSSIANS 2:6

In Word

It seems simple enough. If we receive Jesus by faith, then we live the Christian life by faith. But a strange thing happens between salvation and sanctification, and a lot of Christians forget what their new life is all about. We revert to old methods, the ones that seem most natural, the ones that fit perfectly with human tendencies to rely on self. The result is a body of Christ that isn't attached to its head. We turn our relationship with Him into a very pious but ineffective religion.

Does that sound harsh? Consider what Paul has been writing about—the unmatchable supremacy of Jesus. This Savior died for us while we were dead in our sins and imparted His own life to us (v. 13). It is by His life that we're saved to begin with. Is there any reason we would stop relying on that life and go back to our own strength—which, in fact, was thoroughly dead? Yet that's what many of Paul's readers did, or at least were tempted to do.

The fact is that we have been given the life of "the image of the invisible God, the firstborn over all creation" (1:15), the life of the one in whom the fullness of God dwells (1:19). The unblemished one lives within us, His perfect presence and awesome strength available to us any moment of any day. And what do we do? Try our best. Work hard at being righteous. Come up with a set of rules and principles that will keep us on track. All without regard for the Spirit who lives—and who *delights* to live—within us.

In Word

Think of the unimaginable gift we've been given—the life of the Holy One in place of our own. Think of the power that accompanies that gift. What keeps us from living in that power? What keeps dragging us down and making us indistinguishable from all the other religious people in the world? Forgetfulness and old habits. Never exchange the power of God for the strength of the flesh. Learn to rest in the life that has already been given.

> Without the power of the Holy Spirit, all human efforts,
> methods, and plans are as futile as attempting to propel
> a boat by puffing at the sails with our own breath.
>
> —D. M. DAWSON

A New Nature

Since you died with Christ to the basic principles
of this world, why, as though you still belonged
to it, do you submit to its rules?
COLOSSIANS 2:20

In Word

Something remarkable happened when we accepted Christ. It sounds trite to say we went from death to life, but the change was really that radical. God had long ago breathed His own life into Adam, and when humanity fell in Eden, we returned to being creatures of dust. But when Jesus breathed again into His disciples (John 20:22), the divine life filled human beings once more. The Spirit fell at Pentecost, and the new creation rapidly began to grow. It was clearly empowered by a supernatural source. A new humanity—God's original design—had been born.

That's why Paul was so frustrated with the people in his churches who had taken a religious approach to this new life. Other teachers had come along, especially in the Galatian churches, and told new Christians all the proper rules for righteous living. It made no sense—like telling lightbulbs to shine brightly or instructing dogs in the ways of barking. Lightbulbs simply need to be plugged into a power source, and dogs simply need to be dogs in order to bark. With the life of God Himself within him or her, why would anyone rely on anything else? In other words, why would anyone simply be religious when he or she could have a relationship with Jesus?

In Deed

That's still a mystery today. We forget what Scripture tells us. We have a new *nature*, not a new practice. We act as if we're trying to reform the old nature rather than letting the new nature have its way. In fact, sometimes we have to look really hard for the new nature within us because we've learned to ignore it. Depending on rules and regulations is much more clear and comfortable.

But that, according to the New Testament, isn't the substance of our lives. Our new nature is actually Jesus' nature, and we can trust it. In the life of faith, always look for the person of Christ within you. His Spirit lives—even thrives—in those who rely on Him.

It is always safer for you to be led by the Spirit into gospel liberty than to wear legal handcuffs.
—CHARLES SPURGEON

The Case for Jesus

You will be my witnesses.
ACTS 1:8

In Word

Jesus' disciples had been asking Him about the Kingdom of God—when it was going to be established and when Israel was going to be restored to its former glory. It wasn't the right question to ask, apparently, because Jesus answered in the way He often did: indirectly. They weren't to be preoccupied with the times and dates of the Kingdom. They were to be preoccupied with the King.

That's probably how Jesus would respond to us too. We spend a lot of time speculating about the end—how it will happen, when it will happen, the signs that we should be looking for (or that we might have already missed). But our focus on the Kingdom isn't really about times and places, it's about the King. Where does He reign in this world? What are we doing and how are we praying where His reign is not visible? Are we asking God that His will would be done on earth as it is in heaven? Are we concerned with God's agenda for pouring His mercy and healing into all areas of this wounded creation? Are we making the mistake of watching for His second coming instead of being evidence for His first coming?

The disciples were focused on the end, and sometimes so are we. Jesus points all of us back to Himself. "You will be my witnesses," He says. Is that a command or a prediction? Or both? Regardless, it's true. We are either good witnesses or bad ones, but if we have claimed the name of Christ, we are witnesses nonetheless. We are the primary evidence that He came.

In Deed

Being a witness for Jesus is more than a calling; it's an identity. He shows Himself to this world through the people who have called on Him as Savior. We may reflect Him well, or we may reflect Him poorly; either way, people will usually make their decision about Him based on what they see in those who follow Him.

Be aware of that. Be an authentic witness, not only for your own sake, but also for His. Don't just live for the Kingdom; live for the King.

> A witness in a court of law has to give evidence;
> a Christian witness has to be evidence.
> —GEOFFREY R. KING

A Needed Dependence

Wait for the gift my Father promised.
ACTS 1:4

In Word

We might not realize it now, after two thousand years of Christian history behind us, but the thought of the Spirit of God dwelling within human hearts was amazing to Jesus' disciples. They surely knew that some of the heroes of Old Testament times had been inspired by the Spirit—as needed. And perhaps they knew that John the Baptist had been filled with the Spirit from birth—as an exception. But the Spirit of God being so accessible as to occupy multiple hearts at once? Such an uncommon gift now so commonly available? That was earth-shattering.

Even so, Jesus had stressed this gift on the night before His crucifixion, and He stressed it on the day of His ascension. He made it clear that He was not speaking in parables, but that the actual Spirit of the living God was going to dwell in living people rather than in a stone temple. No longer would inquiring seekers from abroad need to come to Jerusalem, as the queen of Sheba had done, in order to meet God. God would be scattered throughout the world in a practical, powerful way through His people. The witnesses would be indwelt by the One about whom they witnessed.

That makes a huge difference. When we point to Jesus as a historical fact, we have the same resources the skeptic does. We've come to a different conclusion, but we've used the same historical evidence. But when we point to Jesus as a living reality, He is involved. We become intimately acquainted with the One about whom we speak. Our words can be used as His expression because He inspires and empowers them. We are living witnesses of a living Lord.

In Deed

Pray daily that you would be filled with the gift. The Spirit's coming was not a one-time event; Paul tells his readers to be filled continually (Ephesians 5:18). The apostles were filled repeatedly in the book of Acts. Your fellowship with God's Spirit depends on your daily interaction with Him. In your life as a witness, never forget the gift.

The Holy Spirit is God the evangelist.

—J. I. PACKER

Changed Expectations

*Lord, are you at this time going to
restore the kingdom to Israel?*
ACTS 1:6

In Word

You've been waiting for God to restore your kingdom. That's probably not how you understand your deepest longings, but that's what they amount to, in a sense. You have desires for fruitful and satisfying work, deep and lasting relationships, peace and purpose in your heart, and fulfillment of your visions and dreams. Much of what you do in life is based on realizing these goals. You know deep down that you were built for fulfillment, and you are waiting for God to fulfill. In other words, you are waiting for Him to restore the kingdom you envision.

Jesus' answer to you will probably be as indirect as the one He gave the disciples. "It is not for you to know" (v. 7), He will say about whatever specifics fill your heart. What we are to know is that He is at work and we are His coworkers. We are to be about His agenda. The Kingdom is in His hands, and our fulfillment will come in its proper time. Meanwhile, by taking our eyes off our own agendas and fixing them on His, we find that He fulfills us anyway.

That's almost always the way of Jesus. That's why He told His disciples to "lose" themselves in order to "find" true life. That's how they can carry their cross of death and still truly live. The paradox is consistent throughout Scripture: those who abandon themselves to God find themselves completely embraced.

In Deed

What kingdom have you been expecting? Whatever it is, stop striving for it. Live instead for the agenda of Jesus' Kingdom. Be His witness, live in His Spirit, seek His will on earth as it is in heaven. One day down the road, you may notice a startling phenomenon. In abandoning your own idea of the Kingdom for His, you'll find that His includes everything you deeply desired anyway. That may be a long way down the road, or it may be soon. Either way, you'll be satisfied. The real Kingdom will be much more fulfilling than your own.

> Before we can pray "Thy kingdom come," we
> must be willing to pray, "My kingdom go."
> —ALAN REDPATH

A Single Focus

Why do you stand here looking into the sky?
ACTS 1:11

In Word

Christians often have a dual focus. We want both "the American dream" and the King-dom of God. We plan our careers, marry our spouses, buy our land, build our houses, save for our futures, give our children the best, and establish ourselves in security as well as we can. Meanwhile, we devote ourselves to church and some form of personal ministry, reminding ourselves of the cross we bear and the sacrifices we make. Our two allegiances don't always contradict—theoretically, it's possible to have both—but they do frequently split our attention between them. We become halfhearted about one or the other. And often the one we become halfhearted about is the Kingdom.

The disciples had a split focus too. They were standing there looking into the sky, amazed at the ascending Lord. They are perfect symbols of Christians who believe in the coming Kingdom but who aren't busy investing in it. They believed this Jesus would come again, but they weren't yet involved in His mission. They had forgotten the task at hand.

God might well ask us the same question spoken by the angels: "Why do you stand here looking into the sky?" There's work to be done, there's a Kingdom in pro-cess, and there's a commandment to obey. There's an enormous difference between waiting for the Lord who will come and witnessing the Lord who is now at work. The Christian life isn't a gaze into the sky, it's an activity in the world.

In Deed

Which description fits your life better? Where has your focus been? Are you investing in the dream of temporal peace and material prosperity, or are you investing in the dream of eternal peace and ultimate prosperity? Or like most Christians, do you split your attention between them?

Spend some time evaluating your focus. Let your life be marked with Kingdom purposes above all else. Those are the investments that last. When heaven asks you where you are looking, be able to answer well.

The body has two eyes, but the soul must have but one.
—WILLIAM SECKER

An Urgent Purpose

*This same Jesus, who has been taken from
you into heaven, will come back in the same
way you have seen him go into heaven.*
ACTS 1:11

In Word

You have a mission in life. You may be conscious of it, or you may not, but it's there.
And you've spent years defining it. For some people, it's a mission to get rich. For
others, it's a mission to solve humanity's problems. It can show up as a drive to win a
gold medal or as an obsession to fit in with the crowd. Regardless of the shape it takes
or the level of awareness you have of it, it's there.

When Jesus ascended, He redefined the disciples' mission for them. The mission
was no longer about their personal agendas, it was about Him. And the angels' words
about His return put a period on the end of the mission; Jesus would be coming back
at a particular point in time when the mission is done. There's an ending. The situation is urgent.

We've lost that sense of urgency over the years. Weeks turned into months, months
turned into years, years turned into decades, then centuries, and then millennia. The
ends of the earth were farther away and harder to reach than anyone had thought. The
mission was going to be more than announcing the Good News; it would be a matter
of discipling people from every language and tribe. Sometime between the beginning
of Acts and the fulfillment of Revelation, we set in for the long haul.

In Deed

What can we do to get that sense of urgency back? Speculation about the time of
Jesus' return may help, but the real key is to understand the lostness of our world and
the ends of it that have yet to be reached. As long as there are undiscipled pockets of
people out there, the mission isn't complete.

Not only has your mission in life changed from what you first thought—Jesus
has given all His followers the same ultimate purpose—your mission also has a designated time frame. We could be casual with an open-ended mission, but not with this
one. Never forget that the situation is urgent.

> Christ has told us He will come, but not when, that we
> might never put off our clothes or put out the candle.
> —WILLIAM GURNALL

Things Above

Since, then, you have been raised with Christ,
set your hearts on things above, where Christ
is seated at the right hand of God.
COLOSSIANS 3:1

In Word

Paul once told a group of Christians to fill their minds with everything good, true, noble, pure, and worthy of praise (Philippians 4:8). Now he tells the Colossians where to set their hearts—or more literally, what to seek. They are to gaze at things above, where Christ is. Why? Because that's where we, as believers, have been raised to live.

Many readers of this verse think Paul meant for Christians to ignore the world and focus only on heaven, but that's not what he says. Because we have been raised with Christ, we have access to heaven's blessings. We are no longer slaves to the sinful ways that once held us down. We are no longer powerless to meet the needs of a hurting world. We are no longer victims of circumstance, or ordinary people who are just trying to get by. We are companions of the King, seated with Him at the Father's right hand. It's His life that works within us, if we'll give Him the freedom to do so. We are fundamentally different creatures than we used to be. Our hearts should reflect that reality.

In Deed

Our new nature doesn't mean that we'll never have trouble or get discouraged. Neither does it mean we'll walk on water or always have instant answers to our prayers. It does, however, mean that our lives are rearranged around an eternal purpose and empowered by an invincible Spirit. We can hinder the Spirit's work within us if we set our hearts in the wrong direction and focus on unworthy things, but why would we? If we seek the things above—His will, His strength, His work, and His ways—we'll reap the blessings of the Kingdom.

Determine to do that. Not many people consistently set their hearts on things above and live according to their new nature, so you may have to go against the flow. But do it anyway. Be intentional about it. Fix your focus on eternity, and your life will bear eternity's fruit.

Time is short. Eternity is long. It is only reasonable
that this short life be lived in the light of eternity.
—CHARLES SPURGEON

Hidden for Glory

*You died, and your life is now hidden with Christ
in God. When Christ, who is your life, appears,
then you also will appear with him in glory.*
COLOSSIANS 3:3-4

In Word

The Christian life on this earth is a process of exchanging. It began with Jesus exchanging His life for ours, dying in our place. By faith, we trade in our sins for His righteous life. From there, we begin exchanging our ways for His ways, our agenda for His will, and our weakness for His strength. That doesn't happen instantly; we have to learn how to give up the only way of life we've ever known. What Paul says is already a fact—that we died and rose again to new life—takes a process for us to experience.

That's part of the reason many Christians aren't actually living the Christian life—that is, depending on the life of Jesus within them. Processes are long. We can get distracted from our focus. We can forget the truths we were taught. We can get frustrated and give up. Somewhere along the way, we stop exchanging the old self for the new creation, and before long, we've forgotten there's a difference.

The result is that though Christians are seated with Christ in heavenly places, many are stuck in the mud. We know our identity in theological terms but rarely experience it in daily life. That's one reason so many Christians are discouraged. The glorious truths of the New Testament have often become theory rather than practice.

In Deed

Does that describe your experience? If so, let your mind dwell on the reality of this truth today: You have died, you were hidden in Jesus' burial, and you are awaiting the full and final revelation of the exchange you once made when you came to Him. When He returns—when the fact of His rising is revealed for all to see—you will be seen with Him in glory. Once that begins to sink in, the exchange grows more into a matter of experience than theory. Life truly becomes new.

A Christian has union with Jesus Christ more noble,
more intimate, and more perfect than the members
of a human body have with their head.
—JOHN EUDES

A Reconciling Mission

All this is from God, who reconciled us to himself through
Christ and gave us the ministry of reconciliation.
2 CORINTHIANS 5:18

In Word

This world is fragmented. That wasn't the case in Eden, where creation was new and complete. But sin has far-reaching effects, severing multiple relationships in multiple ways. It disconnected human beings from their Creator, it put enmity between man and woman, it created rivalries among siblings, and it made our relationship with the earth a matter of hard labor rather than joyful abundance. It even separated us from ourselves, causing the image of God and a heart of sin to dwell in the same body. The result is brokenness and fragmentation. We are a disunited world.

The redemption offered by Jesus addresses this problem. In Christ, we are reconciled with God. In Christ, we become one body of believers. In Christ, the whole world that groans for its redemption gets a taste of it now. Whatever was broken in the Fall can be healed at the Cross and redeemed for a purpose. That's what salvation is all about.

Even so, Christians still struggle with the effects of broken relationships and a fragmented society. We aren't always sure how to reconcile people alienated from God and at odds with one another. Conflict is still part of our lives. And what this week's passage tells us is that such conflict is the stage for God's redemption. This is the battleground where His mercy is seen.

In Deed

Do you see your mission as one of reconciliation? There are many sides of that: we help people get reconciled to God through Jesus, we assist reconciliation between warring parties, and we proclaim healing to whatever is broken in this world. But if we don't see reconciliation as our primary purpose, we won't be active in bringing it about.

Learn to see the ministry of reconciliation as your God-given role. He has called us to apply His redemption everywhere we can. Our salvation isn't just between us and Him; it's intended to reconnect a fragmented creation with its Creator and with itself.

God, and not the world, can give peace.
—BILLY GRAHAM

A Reconciling God

God was reconciling the world to himself in Christ,
not counting men's sins against them.
2 CORINTHIANS 5:19

In Word

God made the world for His own glory. We've seen how tragically short of His glory we've fallen; there is much on this earth that is ugly and ungodly. God knew this would happen before He spoke light into darkness and crafted the heavens and the earth, and He made us anyway. Why? Because His glory can come out of the shame.

We wonder how that might be possible. How can the depravity we've seen and participated in—the genocides and injustices, the crimes of society and of the human heart—how can any of it reflect well on God? That is where we see His mercy. We know the tender side of God through such tragedy. We've tasted the sweetness of forgiveness and watched the power of healing overcome the power of sin. We've seen ultimate mercy in a bloody Savior on a hill.

Don't let that thought pass too quickly. The purpose of all creation, it seems—the point of this horribly fallen world—is to demonstrate a God of reconciliation and grace. Our broken world highlights the compassions that are new every morning and the faithfulness that never sets with the sun. The God who reconciles isn't clearly seen in His holiness and perfection, at least not until He reaches down in mercy. God becomes visible in the Cross.

In Deed

If the heart of God in this world revolves around redemption and reconciliation, we are at odds with Him if our hearts don't do the same. God was reconciling the world to Himself in Jesus; He wasn't counting sins against us because He was counting them against the Scapegoat sent from heaven. What we deserved, He bore. That speaks marvelous wonders about our Creator.

That's the heart of our mission—to speak marvelous wonders about our Creator. Reconciliation is the purpose for which we were created. Let it become your lifestyle.

The Spirit of Christ is the spirit of missions, and the nearer we get to Him the more intensely missionary we must become.

—HENRY MARTYN

A Reconciling Love

Christ's love compels us.
2 CORINTHIANS 5:14

In Word

Most of us don't enjoy conflict. We don't enjoy the distance that separates us from God when we've sinned, and we don't enjoy the enmity between us and other people when our relationships are laden with misunderstandings and offenses. Most of us want to live at peace with those around us. Life is easier that way.

In fact, an easy life is often our motivation. We want to be reconciled with so-and-so not because of our deep and burdened love for that person, but because life would be much more manageable if conflict with that person didn't exist. That feeling that something is not quite right, that unsettled sensation that comes from discord, would go away and we would feel better. We are often driven to reconcile—or else to flee the relationship—by such discomfort.

The mission of the believer is driven by a different motive. It's the love of Christ that compels. The love of Jesus, when it is living and thriving within us, will not be content to let broken relationships remain broken. It will urge us to seek the other person's benefit as well as our own. It will crave the wholeness that can only come through grace and forgiveness.

In Deed

What governs your relationships? Do you flee from conflict and let it lie unresolved? Or do you seek reconciliation as a means to make life easier? There's a better way. The love of Jesus—that love that prompted Him to leave the glories of heaven and live in a grossly corrupt world in order to reconcile it—is a love that we can build all of our relationships on. In fact, if we want to be a part of Jesus' mission in this world, that's a love that we *must* build our relationships on. It's what true reconciliation is all about.

How do we get it? First, ask God for it. It's a divine love, and it does not spring naturally from human hearts. It comes from His Spirit alone. Second, consciously apply such amazing love to your relationships. Substitute selfish motives with selfless ones. Seek the good of others above all else. That's what Jesus did. If His love compels us, it's what we will do too.

> Love, like warmth, should beam forth on every side, and bend to every necessity of our brethren.
>
> —MARTIN LUTHER

A Reconciling View

From now on we regard no one from a worldly point of view.
2 CORINTHIANS 5:16

In Word

You size people up. We all do. We make snap judgments about people's attitudes and personalities based on what they wear, the expression on their faces, the look in their eyes, the social groups they come from, or any other criteria we can get a handle on.

Most of our efforts are aimed at putting people in categories we can easily understand. There's no shame in that; it's how our minds work. The problem is that our categories are not God's. When we use our own judgments, we end up associating with people who are a lot like us in terms of skin color, economic status, political opinions, religious views, etc. We are most comfortable with similar people because we are most familiar with their characteristics. We have a lot in common with them—at least on the surface.

But such associations don't spring exclusively from the love of Christ. They don't take us on an adventure of reconciliation. They don't always lead us where God wants us to go. They see people in terms of the kingdom of this world, not in terms of the Kingdom of God.

According to God, there are two kinds of people in the world: those who are in Christ and those who are not. Those who are in Christ are one with us—no distinctions of language, economy, race, gender, or heritage. We are united in a common Savior. Those who are not in Christ are sought by God. And if they are sought by God, they ought to be sought by God's ministers of reconciliation.

In Deed

If you are a Christian, then you are a minister of reconciliation. It's your calling to go to the people God seeks. There are no biblical distinctions between them. Jew, Greek, black, white, male, female, rich, poor—all are sought by God. You may be more effective among some, but all are potential believers. God wants reconciliation with everyone. And God's point of view is to be ours.

> His love enables me to call every country my country, and every man my brother.
> —DANIEL WHEELER

A Reconciling Appeal

We are therefore Christ's ambassadors, as though
God were making his appeal through us.
2 CORINTHIANS 5:20

In Word

An ambassador is a bridge between two nations. He or she represents one country in the territory of another. It's a difficult job, demanding sensitivity and tact. It requires a balance between respect for the host culture and allegiance to the home culture. By definition, an ambassador represents the agenda of his or her homeland. Though he or she lives in a foreign land, the interests of home are paramount.

We live in a foreign land. We belong to another Kingdom, as the Bible makes clear; it calls us citizens of heaven (Philippians 3:20) and members of a holy nation (1 Peter 2:9). But we are assigned a role in the land of our birth. Sometimes that land is hostile territory, and sometimes its familiarity lingers within us. Either way, our agenda is clear: we are to represent the interests of our King and to do so winsomely.

Most of us are simply trying to get by from one day to the next in this life. We see ourselves more as survivors than as ambassadors. Nevertheless, we have a higher calling than survival. We are not simply saved out of this world, we are called to go back into it, proclaiming the fullness of the coming Kingdom. We are to take the reconciliation of God into a dazed and confused generation. We are to live a holy lifestyle in the midst of an unholy culture. We are representatives of God.

In Deed

If that doesn't give purpose to your day, nothing will. Ambassadors are often people who are particularly special to the president or prime minister who appoints them. In our case, we are appointed by the Most High God. It is a sacred assignment with lives at stake.

Immerse yourself in the values of the Kingdom of God, then make your appeal to your culture. Go to individuals, to governments, to social organizations, to economic entities—go everywhere. The task of an ambassador is broad, and the purpose is clear: affect one kingdom for the sake of another.

The way from God to a human heart
is through a human heart.
—S. D. GORDON

A Faithful Guardian

*The Lord is faithful, and he will strengthen
and protect you from the evil one.*
2 THESSALONIANS 3:3

In Word

Everyone has had those days. From dawn to late at night, you feel like you're under attack, as though all the forces of the universe have conspired against you. You find yourself with an overwhelming load of responsibilities, and one more major project gets added to the pile. You find yourself swirling in the midst of conflict, and one more person adds his or her dysfunction to the mix. You find yourself under relentless financial pressure, and another major expense pops up out of the blue. Or in one of life's perfect storms, all of the above converge until you can't stand the pressure any longer.

These are the times that try our faith. We know God is sufficient for all of our needs in the good times, or even in the mediocre or slightly uncomfortable times, but what about in the insufferably overwhelming times? Is Jesus really able to calm storms? Is His grace really greater than all our sins? Does God still part huge bodies of water? Does He still send a deliverer into our moments of greatest need? We know the right answers to these questions, of course. But if there's any delay in experiencing those answers, we're tempted to start doubting whether God really behaves the way He used to in the Bible or whether He cares about our current situation or even notices it. We start to feel pretty obscure in His plans.

In Deed

God gives us reassurances even in those times when we feel most helpless and He seems farthest away. We have not been abandoned. He is not one of those invisible forces that seem to have conspired against us. We may not see the end of the crisis, but we do know this: (1) His strength is available—in fact, He often brings us to a point of complete vulnerability so we'll depend on that strength. And (2) He is protecting us—in fact, He often shows us the enemy's hand just so we can see what His protection involves. You can count on the fact that He is faithful—even in the midst of your greatest storms.

God's investment in us is so great He
could not possibly abandon us.
—ERWIN LUTZER

Anchored

May the Lord direct your hearts into the love of God and into the steadfastness of Christ.
2 THESSALONIANS 3:5 (NASB)

In Word

It seems like such generic blessing, but it's really a pointed prayer. The Thessalonians had suffered persecution for their faith, and now false teachers were coming in with alarming doctrines and creating a stir. The believers' hearts had been beaten down and misdirected. If anyone needed the Lord Himself to direct their hearts into God's love and the steadfastness or perseverance of Jesus, they did.

But the Thessalonian situation isn't all that unusual, is it? We live in a world that beats us down and throws all kinds of deception at us. Even if we live in a free society and our faith has no outward opponents, circumstances and false perspectives attack our beliefs relentlessly. When we try to direct our own hearts, sometimes they don't find the right path into God's love or Jesus' faithfulness. Sometimes they get tossed around by every wind and wave and miss the mark altogether.

Not knowing the love of God in a deep-down, rock-solid assurance kind of way will cause us to question Him in every adversity and pray to Him with faith-killing suspicion. And not knowing the faithfulness of Jesus will put us on a spiritual roller coaster, causing us to deviate from our pure and simple devotion to Him and doubt His pure and simple devotion to us. That kind of aimless spirituality is no way to live.

In Deed

Many of us live in a fragile state. The enemy says "Boo," and we jump. Life throws us a curveball, and we panic. God says, "I love you," and our hearts say, "Are You sure?" We need to be anchored in truth, and we aren't always the most reliable managers of that process. In other words, we need someone else to anchor us in truth. We need the God who saved us to also keep us.

Ask Him to do that. Do your part, but trust that He and His Word will oversee the direction of your heart if you let Him. In whatever you face today, ask to be driven further into His love and faithfulness. Whatever else happens, let Him anchor your soul in Him.

Though men are false, God is faithful.
—MATTHEW HENRY

The Necessity of Prayer

After they prayed, the place where they were meeting
was shaken. And they were all filled with the Holy
Spirit and spoke the word of God boldly.
ACTS 4:31

In Word

As followers of Jesus, we do well to embrace the mission to which we're called. But if we don't understand what makes the mission effective, we're destined for frustration. Every step of the way in Acts, after Jesus told His disciples they would be His witnesses, we find people praying. Behind all of the amazing works of the Holy Spirit in that book are prayers of people filled with the Spirit. The prayers and the works are inseparable.

We forget that sometimes. We pray a little and work a lot, then wonder why God hasn't blessed our efforts. We need to remember that the work of the Spirit cannot be done in the strength of the flesh; only God can accomplish His mission. He uses us in that mission, but He doesn't depend on our ingenuity and our talents. He breathes life into what we are able to contribute. The effectiveness is His.

That should drive us to our knees. If we are on a mission with Jesus, fulfilling His calling to be witnesses, living a ministry of reconciliation, we will soon realize how utterly dependent we are on His power. Nothing we do in itself can accomplish God's purposes if it isn't backed by His Spirit. And the way to make sure we are backed by His Spirit is to commune with Him often.

In Deed

Take a look at what prompted the first missionary journey in Acts 13:2-3. It was the voice of the Spirit in response to worship and prayer. It was a God-ordained mission. Paul and Barnabas didn't decide to go evangelize, asking the Spirit to bless them on the way. They got directions first. The trip was inspired and anointed.

Do you want your mission to be inspired and anointed? Then pray. Pray often, pray deeply, pray dependently. Everything you do depends on the Spirit's work.

> Prayer is a shield to the soul, a sacrifice
> to God, and a scourge to Satan.
> —JOHN BUNYAN

The Vision of Prayer

*Stretch out your hand to heal and perform miraculous signs
and wonders through the name of your holy servant Jesus.*
ACTS 4:30

In Word

Sometimes we pray small prayers. Is it that we question God's ability to answer the big ones? Or do we believe we're only worthy to receive small answers? Either way, we're misunderstanding the heart of God. He is able to do "immeasurably more than all we ask or imagine" (Ephesians 3:20), and He doesn't base His answers on our worthiness. When we pray small prayers, we are underestimating God.

God has big plans. His mission began with a handful of disciples and a vision as big as the world. Big prayers were essential to accomplish such all-encompassing plans. The disciples knew they were not equal to the task, but they also knew that God was more than equal to it. Those two pieces of knowledge are the fuel for any prayer life. If we understand who we are and what we've been called to do, and we understand the God who has redeemed us and commissioned us, then we will spend much of our time on our knees. We will ask for a lot because God promises a lot.

The disciples did that in Acts 4. They asked for healing and miraculous signs and wonders in the name of Jesus. They wanted Him to be glorified and for people to believe. They wanted the Kingdom of God to cover the territory of earth. And they knew that only God could do such a thing.

In Deed

How big is your prayer life? That's not a question that asks how long or how passionately you pray. It's a question that asks how much faith is involved when you talk to your Father. Do you seek Him with huge tasks and for huge answers? Or do you ask only for small, personal victories that will make your life easier but do little to further His Kingdom?

Develop a vision for the Kingdom of God. See how enormous and sweeping His mission is, and ask accordingly. Be prepared for Him to use you far beyond your capabilities. Why? Because a God of miracles delights in making a miracle of His people.

God shapes the world by prayer.
—E. M. BOUNDS

The Priority of Prayer

When they heard this, they raised their
voices together in prayer to God.
ACTS 4:24

In Word

We've all heard it before; many of us have even said it. It usually comes after all efforts have been tried and all ideas exhausted. It is almost a statement of despair, when hope is fading fast: "All we can do now is pray."

That's usually our expression of last resort. We don't mean to make God's assistance a backup plan, but that's what we often do in effect. Rather than calling Him into the situation up front, seeking His guidance and following His lead, we stress and strain over our own solutions. When they fail, we resort to God. We see if He can bail us out.

The early believers didn't do that. In Acts 4, we read that Peter and John had just come from the Sanhedrin where they were rebuked for teaching in the name of Jesus. The elders ignored the fact that a miraculous healing had taken place and unschooled men were preaching powerfully. The court commanded them to keep quiet and threatened punishment if they did not. Peter and John affirmed their obligation to obey God rather than men, and they left. Still, the situation wasn't resolved. Persecution of the new faith was clearly on the rise. The first response of the new believers—their immediate reaction—was to pray.

In Deed

What's your immediate reaction in a difficult situation? What's the remedy of first resort in your heart? What's your last resort? Where does prayer fit in the spectrum between the two? If God is a means to bail us out when all else has failed, then we have tried to tap into the most powerful force in the universe as a secondary measure after our own efforts. We have made our solutions the priority. We have put God on the back shelf.

There's a better way, especially where the mission is involved. God is to be sought first, during, and after. If we don't have His direction and His backing in a crisis, then we are destined for futility. The God of miracles and compassion would rather hear us say up front: "All we can do now is pray."

> We need more Christians for whom prayer
> is the first resort, not the last.
> —JOHN BLANCHARD

The Agenda of Prayer

Enable your servants to speak your word with great boldness.
ACTS 4:29

In Word

Try an experiment. For one week, write down every petition that you offer up to your Father. At the end of the week, go back and categorize them. How many of them were related to the necessities of life? How many of them were on behalf of other people? How many were about your own dreams and plans? How many were about the mission of Jesus to this world?

That last question may convict us. We perhaps pray for missionaries, nations, and our communities at church, but usually only as a brief mention. And in our personal mission—yes, we all have one—our prayers are often a reaction to opportunities that God has put upon us rather than requests for those opportunities to abound. Most of us rarely ask God to make us bold witnesses for Him, either in our lifestyles or in our words. But such prayers honor Him; they were the substance of the New Testament mission.

For examples of the Bible's priorities for our prayers, try reading through the prayers of Paul sometime. Many of his letters contain a prayer in the first few verses, and they are almost always that his readers would better know God and better represent Him to the world. There are few hospital lists among them, few requests for personal schedules, and few individual petitions that did not also include the community of faith as a whole. There is certainly nothing wrong with personal requests for health and wholeness, and the Bible does give us some examples of such. But the emphasis is the mission. Always.

In Deed

Seek a prayer life that lines up with the main emphasis in the New Testament's prayers. Examine what was most important to the early believers and the apostles who wrote letters to the churches. Ask God what's first on His agenda, then pray for that. You'll find your life becoming more and more of a witness for your Savior. And you'll find yourself in the middle of an exciting mission.

Prayer meetings are the throbbing machinery of the church.
—CHARLES SPURGEON

The Power of Prayer

The kings of the earth take their stand and the rulers gather
together against the Lord and against his Anointed One.
ACTS 4:26

In Word

We live in hostile territory. That's no surprise; the difficulties of this world get us down often, and they frequently seem designed to do exactly that. There's nothing random about our trials when we're on mission with God. A world system inspired by the evil one stands against us.

That may seem intimidating, but John reminds us that the One who lives in us is greater than the one who lives in the world (1 John 4:4). Our opposition is really an opportunity to call on the God who saves and delivers and establishes His Kingdom. When the authorities of this world stand against us, as they did with Peter and John, we can appeal to a higher authority. Prayer is a mighty weapon, not because it is powerful in itself, but because of the power of the One to whom we pray.

Remember that as you go through life in this world. Obeying God and living as His servant are difficult tasks. There are many obstacles to faithfulness. But Jesus told His disciples that faith could move obstacles as big as mountains. We can do whatever He calls us to do in the power of prayer.

In Deed

It's easy to take prayer for granted. It's so commonly encouraged and God is so readily accessible that we treat prayer like a favor we do for Him; it becomes trivial to us. But the right to communicate with God was bought with a heavy price, and there's nothing trivial about it. It is a privilege, and it is powerful. It is the most effective thing a Christian can do.

Resolve to recommit to prayer. Let it form the foundation of every day. Begin with it in the morning and end with it at night. Come back to it frequently in every task and every decision required of you. You'll find that the opposition offered by this world remains fierce; but the victory over it becomes greater and greater.

> None can believe how powerful prayer is and what it is able
> to effect, but those who have learned it by experience.
> —MARTIN LUTHER

Crucified

I resolved to know nothing while I was with you
except Jesus Christ and him crucified.
1 CORINTHIANS 2:2

In Word

Paul had just come to Corinth from Athens, where he had preached a very philosophical sermon without mentioning the name of Jesus (Acts 17:22-34). It made sense, considering his audience—Athenians were known for their sophisticated philosophies and scholarly pursuits. But the sermon didn't exactly shake the city, as only a handful of people believed while most laughed at the idea of a resurrection. A man who rose from the grave didn't seem to fit into an intellectual debate.

So Paul arrived in Corinth with a different agenda: a singular message about the Cross of Christ. This message alone was life changing; other ideas were simply words. The real power of the gospel is in the holy transaction that took place on a hill outside of Jerusalem when someone perceived as a religious deviant was executed at the request of the reigning priesthood. The depravity of human beings was paid for, and lives were exchanged. He became what we were and took the consequences of our sin so that we might become what He is and inherit the Kingdom of God. It's an absurd message, a far-fetched rescue with behind-the-scenes meaning that we barely understand, but it's truth. And when that message is lived and preached, it is accompanied by the supernatural power of God.

In Deed

We frequently get too fancy with our faith. We develop sophisticated theology that tries to account for every nuance of God and explain everything we don't understand. But the bottom line is that the deep mysteries of God aren't explained by our reasoning; they are embodied in a Person. To the degree that this Person is present in our actions, our discussion, our prayers, and our lives, there's power. And to the degree that this Person is only a philosophy or an idea, there isn't. He's the key.

Make the same resolution Paul made: to live as though you know nothing but Jesus Christ and Him crucified. The power of God abides in the life of the One He sent to us.

> To know Jesus and Him crucified is my
> philosophy, and there is none higher.
> —BERNARD OF CLAIRVAUX

Raised

My message and my preaching were not
with wise and persuasive words, but with
a demonstration of the Spirit's power.
1 CORINTHIANS 2:4

In Word

Paul described his own presence as weak, fearful, and trembling. It's hard to imagine the bold apostle in such terms, but he was apparently much more impressive in letters than he was in person. He certainly preached with earnestness and zeal, and he knew how to reason from the Hebrew Scriptures to prove that Jesus was the Messiah—his first strategy in the synagogues of every city he visited. But pure reasoning wasn't enough, and neither was zeal. Why did people believe his message? A repeated theme throughout Acts is perhaps captured best in his visit to Iconium: "Paul and Barnabas spent considerable time there, speaking boldly for the Lord, who confirmed the message of his grace by enabling them to do miraculous signs and wonders" (Acts 14:3). In other words, God supernaturally proved His own truth.

We often forget that God is even more interested in spreading the gospel than we are. We think we do it "for" Him as a task that comes either from raw obedience or as a favor to Him. We treat the great commission simply as an assignment that Jesus gave, and now it's our responsibility to go and fulfill it while He waits for the results. As a result, we come up with our best apologetics, our most persuasive appeals, and our most up-to-date marketing techniques—none of which are bad in themselves. But we need to remember that a message without the power of God is a message that will ultimately fail.

In Deed

It's true that the power of God doesn't convince everyone to believe the gospel. When Jesus did miracles, many people came to faith and many others refused to believe. But for the truth to impact people's lives, we need to remember that God's power is the key. No amount of persuasion or wise tactics will really make an eternal difference. We need to remember whose message it is. A witness who reflects trust in Christ as the difference maker will be accompanied by His power. Nothing else can change lives.

> Only Jesus Christ by His Holy Spirit can open blind eyes, give
> life to the dead, and rescue slaves from satanic bondage.
> —JOHN STOTT

Full of Hope

Always be prepared to give an answer to everyone who asks you to give the reason for the hope that you have.
1 PETER 3:15

In Word

This is a comforting verse for those of us who are not extroverted evangelists by nature. It simply tells us to be prepared to answer those who ask us about the gospel. We're comfortable with that; it puts the initiative onto the seeker and requires much less relational risk for us. We don't have to put ourselves out on a limb.

But there's a troublesome implication here too. Peter's instruction assumes that people will ask us about the hope we have. That means that the hope we have will be something other people are able to pick up on. They will see something distinctive about believers and be prompted to ask what the distinction is. They will notice we're different.

Most of us don't have people coming up to us asking about the hope we display. Part of the reason for that is that Peter was writing to a persecuted group of believers, and their hope was remarkable. We aren't usually persecuted for our faith, so a context for hope may be less visible with us. But we do live in a fallen world with all of its disappointments and difficulties. And God has given us a multitude of hopeful promises about the kind of faith that overcomes the world. If people are looking for hope, we certainly have plenty of opportunities to demonstrate it.

In Deed

Is your hope noticeable? If not, why not? What keeps people from seeing eternal life in your eyes in the midst of trials? What about your hardships makes it difficult for you to take hold of the eternal promises of God?

For most people, an absence of hope means they have placed too many expectations in what this temporal life has to offer and not enough in what eternal life affords us. There's a simple remedy for that: spend a lot of time thinking about the fullness of the coming Kingdom. Understand that your fulfillment will be eternal, even if you don't see it right now. In order to display hope, cultivate hope. And be prepared to answer those who ask you about it.

> Hope is the power of being cheerful in circumstances which we know to be desperate.
> —G. K. CHESTERTON

Blessed by God

To this you were called so that you may inherit a blessing.
1 PETER 3:9

In Word

God called us to live a countercultural, hope-filled life for a reason: to be blessed. Peter's instructions to his persecuted readers encompass a whole array of behaviors and attitudes—brotherly love, sympathy, returning good for evil, hopefulness, suffering for doing good, and more. The picture he gives is of a spiritual oddity in the midst of oppressive circumstances. He describes a people who will not cave in to the culture of selfishness and victimization. He urges his readers to stand out as nonconforming beacons of hope and goodness. And he reminds them that God blesses such nonconformists.

That has been true throughout Scripture. Noah, for example, lived in the midst of a twisted generation, and he lived differently. God blessed him. The same can be said of Abraham, Elijah, Esther, Daniel, and a host of other biblical characters. That's God's methodology; those who conform to His character rather than to the world around them will be at odds with the world but at home in the heart of God. And there's no place of greater blessing than that.

Most Christians are hungry for a life that is blessed. We pray for it and try to feed ourselves with blessing after blessing, often not realizing that the key is an attitude that fits God's character. God has designed His people to be like Him in order to be visible witnesses of His glory. And though there are few blessings offered by the world for that, the blessings of God outweigh the world's offerings enormously.

In Deed

Do you want to be blessed? Then live with a countercultural attitude. Conform your expectations, your lifestyle, and your very heart to the person of God. Refuse to fit the world's standards for behavior; have a higher one. As you do, you will fit right in with the mission of God. And you will be blessed.

> Blessed is he who does good to others and desires not that others should do good to him.
> —BROTHER GILES OF ASSISI

Devoted to Jesus

In your hearts set apart Christ as Lord.
1 PETER 3:15

In Word

Our hearts have many lords. We may deny it, but we find that our allegiances are often split. Jesus warned against trying to serve two masters for a reason: that's the tendency of human beings with multiple desires.

You've probably encountered that tendency in yourself at some time or another. It's the anguish that arises when God's will and yours diverge, when obedience is difficult, when you make your plans to fulfill your goals and God vetoes them. It's the sense of entitlement that arises when we want to nurse our grudges or damage the reputation of those who have offended us. We may end up compliant with our one true Lord, but if we're honest, we'll admit that we struggled to submit to Him. The truth is that we want to call Him Lord and follow our own agenda at the same time. That's easy to do when our will and His converge. But when they don't? We have divided hearts.

That's why Peter tells his readers to set apart Christ as Lord. If they are to live lifestyles and demonstrate attitudes that are consistent with God's character and that further His mission in this world, they are going to have to dispense with divided hearts. They will have to forsake the natural tendency to return evil for evil, to fight against their suffering, or to demonstrate anger instead of hope. The natural attitudes of a person in pain are going to have to give way to supernatural attitudes. And the only way for that to happen is for Jesus to reign in the heart.

In Deed

Which lords reign in your heart? If you are a committed believer, Jesus is surely there. But you've probably noticed rivals as well. You know that natural reactions to the problems of life come much too . . . well, naturally. If you are like most of us, you are filled with supernatural love and hope far too infrequently.

The remedy is to set apart Jesus as Lord in your heart. It's a conscious, daily, even hourly process. Whenever something inconsistent with Jesus arises in your heart, replace it with the Lord Himself. Your heart will never be the same.

> The Holy Spirit cannot be located as a guest in a house. He invades everything.
> —OSWALD CHAMBERS

Gentle with Others

Live in harmony with one another; be sympathetic,
love as brothers, be compassionate and humble.
1 PETER 3:8

In Word

There is considerable historical evidence that early Christians handled the Roman Empire's crises better than their peers. They took care of each other (and outsiders) during epidemics; they withstood the pressures of persecution with an eternity-minded outlook; they conducted their trade honestly and generously; and they cared for the needy, especially in crowded cities, often adopting orphans and outcasts into their own homes and churches.

There is also considerable historical evidence that such behavior had a dramatic impact on society. Many people became Christians simply because of the higher ethic displayed by these early believers. Seekers dissatisfied with the utilitarian and often brutal aspects of Greco-Roman religions saw a more satisfying option. They saw evidence of renewed hearts.

That's God's design for our lives. We are to live decidedly different lives than our non-Christian peers. Early Christians made huge sacrifices in order to demonstrate the love of Jesus, and in many ways we've lost that sense of sacrifice over the centuries. As a result, our lives do not give off the aroma of Christ. We are not the witnesses we could be.

In Deed

Peter told his readers to live in harmony, to be sympathetic, to love as brothers, and to be compassionate and humble. Both he and his readers knew that these instructions were at extreme odds with the people who were persecuting them. These attitudes did not fit with society at large. But fitting with society wasn't the point. Displaying Jesus was.

Examine how much your life displays Jesus. Is it filled with extraordinary love and compassion? Is it marked with humility and harmony? If not, you may need to reexamine the degree to which Jesus is Lord in your heart. His lordship will come out in our lifestyles. When it does, we and the world around us are changed.

Sanctify yourself and you will sanctify society.
—FRANCIS OF ASSISI

Able to Endure

*[Keep] a clear conscience, so that those who
speak maliciously against your good behavior
in Christ may be ashamed of their slander.*
1 PETER 3:16

In Word

Many early Christian communities had a well-developed theology of suffering. Their purpose was not to live as peaceable and comfortable a life as possible; it was to display the character of Christ in whatever circumstances they were in. And one of the best opportunities to do so was in the context of persecution. Bearing pain with the attitude of Jesus is a powerful testimony.

Many Christians have lost that perspective. Our reaction to slander or misrepresentation is to fight back and set the record straight. Our sensibilities have been cultivated in a society of individual rights, and we are very conscious of our own. Like secular culture, we demand that our rights be respected. In so doing, we often miss out on an opportunity to respond to malice with the patience of Jesus.

That's not an easy path to take, but it's a fruitful one. Jesus' crucifixion was a powerful witness to many onlookers, as the reaction of a Roman soldier indicates (Luke 23:47). We, too, are witnesses of the way of the Cross. We have multiple opportunities to bear injustices with peace and patience, and so display the Spirit of Christ. We can impact our world in powerful ways.

In Deed

No one wants his or her good behavior to be ridiculed or misrepresented. No one wants to stand out from his or her culture in a highly conspicuous way. Nevertheless, that's our calling. Though we are not persecuted like the believers to whom Peter wrote, we experience hardship and pain. Sometimes those experiences are unjust. And when they are, we have an opportunity to be just like Jesus.

In the eternal scheme of things, that's an opportunity we just can't pass up. It powerfully impacts the world—in the long run, if not the short—and is rewarded with the blessing of God.

Endurance is not just the ability to bear a
hard thing, but to turn it into glory.
—WILLIAM BARCLAY

The Battle

Fight the good fight of the faith.
1 TIMOTHY 6:12

In Word

Anyone who thinks the Christian life is for the weak at heart is sadly mistaken. Nowhere is that more evident than in areas of faith—i.e., believing what is unseen. People who think of faith simply as hoping for a positive outcome in the future or expecting heaven when they die can perhaps be passive and complacent about it. But those who truly live as though invisible realities are real are in for a fight. We are tested daily. Do we take the next step according to what we see, or do we base it on an unseen promise? Do we listen to the second-guessing—whether from others or in our own minds—or do we press ahead stubbornly into what God has said but not yet shown? These are not easy battles. We have to fight to live by faith.

And it can be a nasty fight. The enemy hurls lies at us that would undermine what God says or bend us toward compromise. The world often ridicules or even perse- cutes those who stake their lives on what is unseen. That's why Hebrews 11 lifts up those who displayed great faith and honors them as examples. People like Noah and Abraham and Moses paid a high price for believing God. Faith cost them dearly. They based their lives on eternal hope and on specific words from God, and few people understood them. Anyone who chooses to live by faith will have to fight—against competing claims, against contrary advice, and even against their own doubts—to do so.

In Deed

To believe in God and hope in heaven is perfectly acceptable and inoffensive to most of the people around us. But to base our daily decisions on what God has specifically spoken? That's another matter entirely. That kind of faith has to endure relentless assaults. We will have to fight enormous battles, both internally and externally, to defend actions based on unseen truths. It can unsettle the people who support us and offend the people who don't. But that's what we're called to do. We're to fight the good fight, at all costs, to hang on to what God has said.

> You are but a poor soldier of Christ if you think you can overcome without fighting.
> —JOHN CHRYSOSTOM

A Rich Provider

Command those who are rich in this present world not to be arrogant nor to put their hope in wealth, which is so uncertain, but to put their hope in God, who richly provides us with everything for our enjoyment.
1 TIMOTHY 6:17

In Word

Markets crash, banks close, and scams and scandals undermine the whole financial system. That's life in a commercial world, and there's really no way around it. Those who have a lot of money may lose a higher percentage of their comfort than those who have little, but we all experience the same uncertainty. Those who put their hope in riches are woefully misguided.

Paul's words to Timothy concern "those who are rich in this present world," which applies to nearly everyone in Europe and North America in this century. Globally, we are the most affluent generation in history. It's easy, even in an economic downturn, to rest in a certain standard of living or to offer complacent prayers of thanks before each meal. All of our needs—our real physical needs—have been taken care of for a long time. God's steady provision has turned from a cause of gratitude to a presumption. That attitude is a breeding ground for faithlessness and arrogance.

In Deed

We have to guard against that. Complacency is an archenemy of the life of faith. It's possible to *have* wealth and great faith simultaneously, but it isn't possible to *trust* wealth and have great faith simultaneously. Paul doesn't tell rich people that they are wrong to be rich; he simply tells them to be careful where they put their trust. And he reminds them of a truth we often forget: God richly provides us with things to enjoy. He isn't holding out on us. We don't have to turn to wealth because we already have the owner of all things on our side. No matter how much we think we need today, money won't step in and give us peace. Only God can do that. And we can trust Him no matter how uncertain our economic situation becomes.

> The real measure of our wealth is how much we'd be worth if we lost all our money.
> —JOHN HENRY JOWETT

Sent to Serve

I make myself a slave to everyone, to
win as many as possible.
1 CORINTHIANS 9:19

In Word

Not many people are standing in line to become servants. Submission is not a valued commodity in our society. We honor people more for their independence and authority than for the abandonment of their personal rights for the sake of others. Servant-hood is not a common ambition.

But people aren't exactly standing in line to share in God's mission either. Paul's attitude toward nonbelievers was rare, even among the Corinthians to whom he wrote. In a world of ambitious people striving to go higher and do better, Paul was climbing down the ladder in order to reach more souls. He had tapped into the humility of Jesus, and it was a powerful motivator. Paul understood what it meant to lose oneself in order to win others.

We need more of that. When we survey the ladders of success in this world, we need to get a glimpse, not of the glory of the climb, but of the glory of the descent. We need to learn to walk the way of Jesus. He came into this world from the glories of heaven—an amazing descent we can scarcely understand—and clothed Himself in human flesh. Why? Because that's where He could meet us. And then He told His disciples He was sending them out in the same way that He had been sent (John 20:21). He called them to descend into every deep corner of their world.

In Deed

How much of your life is spent climbing ladders? If you are aiming for success, what kind? The sort of success that God calls us to has little to do with status or income; it's about fruitfulness. And the best way to fruitfulness, in the pattern of Scripture and the Incarnation, is servanthood.

Yes, we have freedom in Christ, but only because we have first submitted to the lordship of Christ. And His lordship will always lead us into humble, Cross-centered ways. That doesn't mean we can't have success in this world; it simply means that our success will be an opportunity for service. The Lord who came to serve calls us to be just like Him.

The only life that counts is the life that costs.
—FREDERICK P. WOOD

Just like Jesus

*I have become all things to all men so that by
all possible means I might save some.*
1 CORINTHIANS 9:22

In Word

God never changes. His character has no impurities in it, no variation from one day to the next. Perfect and complete in the beginning, He does not grow. There is never anything to add to who He is. As He is now, He will always be.

How amazing it is, then, that the God who does not change once clothed Himself in human flesh and walked among us. His character remained unchanging, but His appearance did not. He became what we are in order to redeem what we were and to change us into what we can be. The unchanging God came to change us forever.

The result is a people that is remarkably like-minded with God—that's the goal, at least. It takes us time to get there, perhaps, but we should be growing toward the unchanging character of God. And as we do, we become like Him in this respect: we are willing to clothe ourselves in the form of people who need Him in order to reach them. We come alongside the needy—the spiritually, materially, emotionally needy—rubbing shoulders with them and sharing their needs, all in order to bring them to God. That's what Jesus did for us, and that's what Paul did for others. That's the heart of God.

In Deed

Our ability to identify with those who need God will, in large part, accurately measure how close we are to the heart of God. The Incarnation expressed His will perfectly. As we grow to be like Jesus, we will embrace the spirit of the Incarnation. We will incarnate the Spirit of God in places where the Spirit is most needed.

Yes, that's an uncomfortable life. It was uncomfortable for Jesus, and it will be uncomfortable for us. But God never called us to comfort, did He? There's nothing in the commissioning words of Jesus that promises us ease. We are promised fruitfulness, however, and that's a much greater treasure. There is no greater blessing than being like Jesus.

Christ became what we are that He might make us what He is.
—ATHANASIUS

The Mystery of the Mission

I do all this for the sake of the gospel,
that I may share in its blessings.
1 CORINTHIANS 9:23

In Word

Most church members have heard the appeal many times before: "Join God in His mission." It comes in many forms, from personal evangelism classes to annual missions giving to regular prayer meetings for those who are on "the front lines." Churches can often be wonderfully mission focused.

But there's a deep mystery to the Christian's mission that isn't always expressed. We don't often hear it in appeals to go to the lost or in requests for funding those who do. We hear a lot about sacrifice and inconvenience, but we sometimes miss the mystery. The truth is that there is a magnificent benefit to the believer who is on mission with God. It leads into His heart in a profound way, and we cannot get there otherwise.

Just as Jesus endured the Cross for "the joy set before him" (Hebrews 12:2), so can the believer endure the sacrifice of the mission for a little-understood blessing. In taking up the Son's mission, we become like Him. And in becoming like Him, we share in the glory He will receive at the end of the age.

Is sharing in Jesus' glory an uncomfortable concept? After all, we've heard that God will not share His glory with another (Isaiah 48:11). And when it comes to idols, He won't. But with His own people? The Bible is full of such promises. Jesus prayed that His disciples would share His glory (John 17:22). Paul and Peter promised that if we suffer with Him we will share His glory (Romans 8:17; 1 Peter 5:1). And salvation itself allows us to share in God's glory (2 Thessalonians 2:14). There's a side of this mission we've only begun to understand.

In Deed

In the mission of God, we can never sacrifice more than we will receive. That's hard to understand this side of eternity, but it's true. There's a blessing for those in Jesus' mission. Paul knew it, Peter knew it, and Jesus prayed that we might know it too. Remember that when it's time to give, pray, or go. The mystery of the mission is waiting to be discovered.

Faith in God will always be crowned.
—WILLIAM PLUMMER

Press toward the Goal

Run in such a way as to get the prize.
1 CORINTHIANS 9:24

In Word

The Christian life is never casual. It has casual moments, of course, and it can be full of joy and lightheartedness. But it can never be approached as a casual matter. The stakes are too high. Nothing that involves the Kingdom of God is insignificant.

Even so, our lives often seem rambling and reactive. We're just trying to get by, much less win a prize in the process. We feel more like we're running on a treadmill than in a medal competition. The rat race is all too familiar, and it never offers a prize.

Paul urges his readers, through his own example, to run with purpose. Christians are to have a goal and to train for it, never randomly or aimlessly, but always pointed toward the finish line. The crown that waits for us is not perishable like the one a marathoner might receive. It's imperishable, eternal, and more glorious than we can imagine.

If today's athletes religiously pursue gold medals and world records, sacrificing years of their lives just for the temporary honors, why wouldn't we demonstrate such zeal for more lasting prizes? What is it about their motivation that gets them going so much more persistently and passionately than us? Why do the visible treasures of this world often weigh more to us than the invisible treasures of the Kingdom?

In Deed

Go into training. Pray for God to guide you, and then plan out your goals under His guidance. Ask Him what He wants you to accomplish in life, and then train yourself to reach for it. It will involve discipline and perseverance, but much of life does. We learn such things for mundane purposes, so we should be able to practice them for eternal purposes. Always press toward the finish line; a prize awaits, and it is glorious. It is enough to keep us running passionately, persistently, and purposefully for a very long time.

> What is needed is not mere present professions, but perseverance to the end in the power of faith.
> —IGNATIUS OF ANTIOCH

Living Purposefully

I do not run like a man running aimlessly.
1 CORINTHIANS 9:26

In Word

Striving for success in a secular society is an aimless endeavor. Few people, other than last century's existentialists, perceive that, but it's true. Though secular-minded people set their goals of economic prosperity, political power, social status, cultural influence, and more, there's little rhyme or reason at the end for most of them. They want to do well in this life, but they've rarely thought beyond it. They may think they're aiming somewhere, but they are falling far short of the true direction of history.

We know history's outcome, of course. Jesus is coming back, and the Kingdom of God will be established. Creation is being redeemed, and the King will rule when He comes. There will be mercy for those who confessed Him in truth and judgment for those who refused. We live our lives with an eye on the point of it all.

We're supposed to, anyway. We forget to do that sometimes, but God reminds us every once in a while what it's all about. When He does, it's usually not a reminder simply for ourselves. We are witnesses of the direction of history because others need to know it. Aimlessness won't prepare people for the Kingdom and the judgment to come.

In Deed

Do you see your role in preparing people for the Kingdom and the judgment? Our roles may differ, but we all have one. For some, it's preparing their children to meet their God. For others, it's bringing the gospel to hidden tribes in faraway lands. Some are called to live the gospel in the business world, and some are called to express it through the arts. The possibilities are nearly limitless, but the point is the same. In an aimless society, we are to live with a purpose.

If you have felt purposeless lately, consider the goal of history and the ways God has gifted you to help others prepare for it. Live with an eye on the Kingdom, pressing toward it with passion and purpose. An aimless world needs to see you do that. Run like you know where you're going.

> Purpose is what gives life meaning. A drifting boat always drifts downstream.
> —CHARLES PARKHURST

A Single Master

*If I were still trying to please men, I would
not be a servant of Christ.*
GALATIANS 1:10

In Word

The opinions of human beings can have a powerful effect. During Jesus' ministry, many people would not publicly acknowledge their faith for fear of the repercussions (John 7:13; 9:22; 12:42). The Jewish leaders could not arrest Him once because of His popularity (Mark 12:12); yet because of His popularity, they wanted even more zealously to seize Him (John 7:32). And ultimately Jesus was crucified because Pilate wanted to make the people happy, keep the peace, and give Rome no reason to worry about his territory. In each of these cases, people's responses to Jesus were shaped by the opinions of other people. And in each case, their responses were off base.

That happens when the people around us seem big and our God seems small. They have a more powerful voice in our lives than He does. Paul frames that dilemma in stark terms: "If I were still trying to please men, I would not be a servant of Christ." It's one or the other. Please Jesus or please people. Stand up for Him or cave in to them. Do what's right or do what's popular. Believe truth or compromise with public opinion. And while Paul's black-and-white view of the situation seems to fit his personality, the point for the rest of us is clear. When we choose to follow Jesus, we choose not to follow anyone else.

That's easier said than done. Many of us are people pleasers by nature, always wanting to make everyone happy. And though the desire to please others is admirable, the practice is pure torture. We're tossed around between one opinion and another and another. Eventually, no one is pleased—including ourselves, and especially our one true Master.

In Deed

The apostle who penned the above verse also wrote, "If possible, as far as it depends on you, live at peace with everyone" (Romans 12:18). But peace does not mean compliance. We are called to serve an uncompromising Lord. Anything in our life that doesn't fit His will, His character, or His ways must bow to Him.

He values not Christ at all who does not value Him above all.
—AUGUSTINE

Looking Back

*I have fought the good fight, I have finished
the race, I have kept the faith.*
2 TIMOTHY 4:7

In Word

The night before He was crucified, Jesus prayed a lengthy and majestic prayer for His disciples and their future ministry. As He began that conversation with the Father, He remarked on the status of His mission: "I have brought you glory on earth by completing the work you gave me to do" (John 17:4). It's a statement every believer would love to be able to make at the end of his or her life. There is no higher achievement than completing the assignment our Father gives us.

More than three decades after Jesus was crucified, Paul was able to make a similar remark about his ministry. He had fought the good fight, finished his course, and firmly clung to the faith he had been given. In his first letter to Timothy, he had twice encouraged his protégé to fight the good fight (1:18 and 6:12). Now he was able to say that he had followed his own advice. He had done the most any Christian can be expected to do. He had completed his assignment, and it had been satisfying.

The question we have to ask ourselves is whether we are living in such a way today that we will be able to make a similar claim at the time of our death. Are we completing the task God has set before us? Are we being diligent about our assignment? Are we fighting the good fight? It isn't that we can't make mistakes—Paul certainly did, and he regretted them deeply. But when we look back, will we be able to say that we have finished well?

In Deed

None of us knows exactly when we will finish our race. So if we are to be certain of finishing well, we need to be living well now. We can't afford to be slack about how we fight the good fight. As you go through your day today, look ahead to how you will look back at this moment in your life. Run your race now in a way that you'll be satisfied with later.

When I have learned to do the Father's will, I shall
have fully realized my vocation on earth.
—CARLO CARRETTO

Looking Ahead

Now there is in store for me the crown of righteousness,
which the Lord, the righteous Judge, will award
to me on that day—and not only to me, but also
to all who have longed for his appearing.
2 TIMOTHY 4:8

In Word

The Bible is clear that we will be rewarded in heaven. Though many Christians are uncomfortable with the idea of seeking rewards, Jesus often spoke of them as an incentive for how we live (Matthew 6:4-6, for example). Paul spoke of rewards in other letters too (1 Corinthians 3:8 and 3:14, for example). In fact, the word shows up nearly thirty times in the New Testament as the specific result of what we do during our lives. Though we are saved by nothing but grace through faith, we are rewarded as a condition of how we live.

But what kind of rewards? We don't know exactly—knowing God, they are probably multifaceted—but Paul was focused on only one kind of crown: righteousness. He hadn't placed his hopes in a greater degree of authority or privilege; he wanted to finally be done with the fallenness and brokenness of human nature and life in this world. He wanted the righteousness that comes from Jesus. That was his goal in fighting the good fight and finishing his race.

Of all the things human beings long for—health, wealth, pleasure, and more—righteousness is probably further down on most people's lists. Maybe that's because we're satisfied with being "good enough," or maybe we just don't see the benefit of being totally pure and just. But being perfectly in sync with the Father's heart is paramount. Seeing life with His sense of integrity and justice and love leads to greater blessings than we think. Righteousness—that "rightness" toward Him and others—is worthy of our longings.

In Deed

Jesus promised satisfaction for those who hunger and thirst for righteousness. Paul hungered and thirsted and fully expected to wear righteousness as his crown. It's a promised gift for all who have longed for Jesus' appearing. Let the longing shape your mind and your heart today.

My hope is built on nothing less than
Jesus' blood and righteousness.
—EDWARD MOTE

Unapologetic

*It is because of my hope in what God has
promised our fathers that I am on trial today.*
ACTS 26:6

In Word

In the arena of ideas, Christians are often passive listeners. Our society generally lifts up the sciences as factual and only humors the faithful as opinionated. But God has called us into the courtroom of this world, wherever we find ourselves in it, to give a defense of the hope we have within us. We have answers, even when the world doesn't ask the right questions. We are authorized by heaven to speak.

That doesn't mean that we have all the answers, of course. No one does, except for God. But we can point people in the right direction. And where we start is where Paul focused his argument in Acts 26. He defended his faith in the promises of God.

God's promises really are unique in the wide world of religions. His prophecies have never proven false, often being fulfilled centuries later with amazing accuracy. His comfort and assurance in times of trial have spared the sanity of many a believer throughout the centuries. His power to save has come through time and time again. Other religions are founded on codes and principles. Ours is founded on promises. There's an enormous difference.

We should claim that difference. We may not understand all of God's promises thoroughly—why He sometimes heals and sometimes doesn't, or how everything will pan out at the end of time—but His track record is solid enough for us to present it as evidence in the court of public opinion. We can point to fulfilled prophecies and powerful prayers as case studies in the reality of God. Yes, we have something to prove.

In Deed

Arm yourself in Christian apologetics. That's how we can engage a skeptical world in discussions about truth. As long as they think our faith is wishful thinking and personal opinion, they can discredit it easily. But when we can show how it is founded in real history—actual people and places—it is convincing. When you find yourself on trial, defend your hope well.

> [Apologetics is] the task of commending Christianity to thinking people as needed truth.
> —J. I. PACKER

Believing

*Why should any of you consider it incredible
that God raises the dead?*
ACTS 26:8

In Word

Séances have long been celebrated as ways to contact the dead. Television shows about witches and vampire slayers regularly probe the underworld. A recent popular movie features communication with people who have died. Yet if a Christian mentions the Resurrection to a skeptic, it is considered a wild fantasy or ancient folklore.

Why is that? Because a bodily resurrection is considered an impossible phenomenon. People have relatively little trouble conceiving of the souls of the dead remaining in some living form, but a physical resurrection? That's highly improbable. Few people, historically, have seen such a thing. Even the ancient Greeks laughed at Paul for suggesting it. Ancient or modern, skeptics aren't very open to the idea of a dead man coming to life again.

That's inconsistent logic, if we think about it. Many believe in a God who created this world, breathing life into it. Such a Creator would have to be unimaginably powerful and intelligent, larger than all our known galaxies combined and able to govern them with His incomprehensible mind. Such power is conceivable to modern humanity, even those who are secular minded, but the thought of one man being raised from the dead? The skeptics laugh. They forget that the undeniably vast, complicated miracle of creation makes resurrection a fairly simple concept.

In Deed

In defending your faith, never back down from the Resurrection. Paul said our faith depends on it; if it didn't happen, our faith is worthless and we are above all people to be most pitied (1 Corinthians 15:19). By the Resurrection, Christianity stands or falls. It is nothing to be ashamed of.

Even so, it will sound like an outrageous claim to many. But God honors faith in the resurrection of His Son. That is what salvation hinges on, and He has a way of powerfully convincing people through His Holy Spirit that Jesus is alive. Don't just believe the resurrection of Jesus, boldly defend it. It's the power of God to save.

Belief in the resurrection is not an appendage to
the Christian faith; it is the Christian faith.
—JOHN S. WHALE

Transparent

I too was convinced that I ought to do all that was
possible to oppose the name of Jesus of Nazareth.
ACTS 26:9

In Word

Nothing damages a Christian witness more than a perception of inauthenticity. People don't want to hear just what we believe, and they don't want to see what we pretend to be. What they want is a genuine testimony that there is a God and that He is working. If that is real, lives are changed.

Paul was authentic. He never hesitated to tell of his background. We might be ashamed to reveal such details about our past, but to Paul, those details highlighted the glory of Jesus. They showed His power to save. Paul's past mistakes weren't the issue; the redemption found in the cross of Christ was everything.

If that's the kind of testimony we have, people will be open to us. That doesn't mean that we have to come from a Christian-killing, legalistic background like Paul. It does mean, though, that we'll be pretty honest about the kind of people we were before we were saved, and even about the kind of struggles we still have. If, through those things, people see how Jesus saves and how He is helping us now, they'll be much more likely to believe.

In Deed

The tendency of our hearts is to justify ourselves and to rationalize our behavior. But as Christians, we've already confessed our sinfulness. Why do we need to deny it? Jesus came for sinners, and we qualify. There's no need to impress.

Let your testimony point not to how good you are or how faithfully you are living. Let it point to Jesus and His power to save. Tell people honestly where you came from and how Jesus changed you. Let them know your flaws and weaknesses so they can know how God has met you there. When Jesus is the object of your testimony, all pretense is pointless. An authentic witness makes an authentic impact.

Jesus Christ makes us real, not merely sincere.
—OSWALD CHAMBERS

Honest

*I saw a light from heaven, brighter than the sun,
blazing around me and my companions.*
ACTS 26:13

In Word

Many Christians feel pressured into keeping quiet about their faith. A society zealous about separating religion from the public arena has been effective at guarding itself from Christian "intrusions." It's a more subtle message than the one given to Peter and John by the authorities when they ordered the disciples to stop preaching in the name of Jesus, but it carries the same intent. Those who are offended at the name of Jesus have done a good job of intimidating those who claim it.

Claim it anyway. If God has done a work in your life, there's no reason to keep it quiet. The work that He does is for Him to use however He chooses, and if He chooses to make us witnesses of it, an unbelieving world has no business forcing us into a quiet, inoffensive piety. We don't need to be tactless and forceful in present- ing the work of God in our lives, but we can certainly be honest. He usually changes people through the ones He has already changed.

How does that translate into our everyday conversations? When we've been blessed, we don't need to attribute the blessing to good luck or our own efforts. When we're going through trials, we don't need to attribute our perseverance to willpower or good psychology. When we've borne fruit, we don't need to classify it as personal influence or self-help techniques. All of these things may be used by God, but if God is behind them, we can say so.

In Deed

Paul could have attributed the dramatic change in his life to sunstroke, a guilty con- science, or a logical realization of truth. He didn't. He told people over and over again exactly what happened. Jesus appeared to him, and it affected him forever.

How has Jesus affected you? However He's done it, the information is unique to you and able to affect others. There's no need to hide it. Just be honest.

If he has faith, the believer cannot be restrained.
—MARTIN LUTHER

Rational

What I am saying is true and reasonable.
ACTS 26:25

In Word

Somehow, the world has gotten the impression that faith is an opinion, and a super-stitious one at that. The secular mind perceives math and science as objective and religion as highly subjective—and highly suspect. Our society has long lacked enough coherent expressions of the sheer logic of Christianity.

Logic alone won't convince many people, of course. They'll need the witness of the Holy Spirit to bring them to faith. But believers who are able to articulate their reasons for believing can remove serious obstacles for the open-minded seeker. We can explain historical facts of Jesus and the Scriptures, we can explain the necessity of a sacrifice for sins, and we can give example after example of lives that have changed because of the power of the gospel. When the skeptics tell us our faith is subjective and irrational, we can give them clear evidence that it is not.

That's what Paul did. Everywhere he went, he laid out a logical foundation for faith. To Jews, he argued from their Scriptures. To Greeks, he argued from their phi-losophers. To everyone, he defended the "foolishness" of the Cross over the "wisdom" of the world. In the minds of many hearers, the Cross won.

In Deed

What will it take to convince those around you that the gospel is true? Only God knows, but you can participate in His work. Arm yourself with the truth of the gospel, understanding how it fits logically with humanity's need for redemption and how it can be defended historically. Belief in Jesus and the Bible are far less superstitious than most skeptics think. Many of them simply have never heard a Christian articulate a valid reason for believing.

That's part of our calling: to articulate a rational faith. We won't convince every-one, but we can help others jump some of the hurdles that have kept them from believing. What we believe is true and reasonable.

> Be to the world a sign that, while we do not have all the answers, we do know and care about the questions.
> —BILLY GRAHAM

Perspective

. . . while we wait for the blessed hope.
TITUS 2:13

In Word

Everyone has a blessed hope. For many, it's a peaceful and prosperous retirement. Others have a more immediate desire to live in the perfect setup—the right location, the right vocation, the right partner to share it with . . . the right everything. In fact, most of us spend at least some of our time and energy trying to bring the blessed hope into the present. As Proverbs 13:12 tells us, "Hope deferred makes the heart sick, but a longing fulfilled is a tree of life." We're tired of sick hearts. We want the tree of life as soon as we can get it.

That's why waiting is so hard. There's a gap between the promise of a future blessing and the blessing itself—a very long one sometimes—and the interim period can be excruciating. But there's design in that delay. God uses the hope of future blessings to shape how we live. When we're looking forward to nothing in particular, we become aimless. But when our eye is on the prize, we live accordingly. We discipline ourselves to press ahead, we develop the characteristics we will need in order to fit the calling, and we grow into the future God has for us as He increases our capacity to receive it. We become fit for the blessing by longing for it.

Paul writes of the ultimate blessed hope. It's "the glorious appearing of our great God and Savior, Jesus Christ," and it shapes who we are today. How? It causes us to say no to ungodliness and to live uprightly in this present age (v. 11). We have an amazing knack for finding the right road when our sights are truly set on a goal. Our perspective defines how we live.

In Deed

It's extremely important to guard your perspective. A clear focus on the blessed hope you've been promised will profoundly affect what you do today. A lack of focus will also profoundly affect what you do today, but for the worse. Fix your eyes on the goal, and your feet will find the right path.

> I thank You, O Lord, that You have so set eternity within my heart that no earthly thing can ever satisfy me wholly.
> —JOHN BAILLIE

Purified

[He] gave himself for us to redeem us from all
wickedness and to purify for himself a people that
are his very own, eager to do what is good.
TITUS 2:14

In Word

Purity isn't exciting—at least not for most people. We think of it as an ideal we should strive for but are unlikely to attain. Unless we happen to be in one of those moments of being completely frustrated with our impurity, it's a "have to," not a "want to." Purity is not usually what we enthusiastically put at the top of our personal prayer requests.

But if we look at purity from the perspective of a groom waiting for his bride, it takes on a whole different meaning. Purity *is* exciting to a couple in love. Even in the case of our Bridegroom, who knew exactly how impure we were when He found us, His goal is a bride who has been made pure. He delights in those who have been set apart completely for Him, those who are no longer stained with past mistakes and have no other lovers in sight. He wants those who belong only to Him.

Jesus paid a lot for us to be that kind of people. He gave all of Himself in order to extract a people all for Himself. He took us out of wickedness to make us holy. We talk a lot about our hope in eternity and what we look forward to in heaven, but the truth is that we aren't the only ones looking forward in hope. Jesus is zealous about His bride.

In Deed

That's why it's important not only for us to do good because we should, but to do good because we're eager about it. There's a special union taking place between Jesus and those who realize they are being set apart especially for Him. He takes great pleasure in those who want nothing to do with former ways and look only to Him to be satisfied. He's eager about purifying that kind of person. We should be eager about being one of them.

If there is joy in the world, surely the
man of pure heart possesses it.
—THOMAS À KEMPIS

God of Miracles

The apostles performed many miraculous
signs and wonders among the people.
ACTS 5:12

In Word

"The LORD is with you," an angel once told Gideon. Gideon's response was revealing: "If the LORD is with us . . . where are all his wonders that our fathers told us about?" (Judges 6:11-13). To Gideon, God seemed mightier in the past than He was in the present. Gideon asked a question we are often tempted to ask.

Our Bible is full of miracles. Sometimes, it feels as if our lives are not. The difference between the two can be disheartening, especially when a miracle is the only thing that can help us through a time of need. We pray to God and hope that He will answer, wondering where the miracles have gone. If we really listen, we will hear Him tell us to open our eyes.

God's dramatic miracles are scattered throughout history, sometimes in clusters (as in Acts), and sometimes spread out over painfully long years. But even when we don't see the drama, God is always doing miracles. He redeemed us, after all—that was a miracle in itself. And He continues to work in our lives. Sometimes we see His hand, and sometimes we don't. But the fact that He is working, whether behind the scenes or in plain view, should always fill us with hope.

In Deed

One of our problems is that we often anticipate the ordinary from God. We pray with realistic expectations, hoping He will answer us with obvious answers. Our minds confine Him to the predictable, forgetting that He is able to do infinitely more than we can even imagine (Ephesians 3:20). We underestimate Him.

When you pray, trust that God is working. He may be working behind the scenes, or radically changing hearts in the midst of our circumstances, or waiting for the plot to unfold a little further before He intervenes in a visible way. But the key to seeing God work is to expect Him to work. He is—and has always been—the God of miracles.

> Miracles are the great bell of the universe,
> which draws men to God's sermon.
> —JOHN FOSTER

God of Relationship

More and more men and women believed in
the Lord and were added to their number.
ACTS 5:14

In Word

God desires to be known. That's why He made a world full of human beings formed in His image, and that's why He sent His Son into this world to redeem us. He wants to be known in His compassion, in His mercy, and in all His wonderful attributes. His Spirit is a master cultivator of relationships. When He works, it is toward that end.

When we ask for the power of God, we should ask with that in mind. We frequently petition Him for things that have little to do with a revelation of His character, or that do little to further His mission to be known. We sometimes treat Him as our heavenly butler, requesting this or that favor. And while He is always open to whatever we ask Him, there's an agenda in His answers. He seeks a deeper relationship.

For that reason, the Christian's life should first and foremost revolve around the relationship agenda of God. Our ministry in His name should deepen His relationship with us and with others, and our prayers should be directed toward His goals. When God worked in the early church, whether to demonstrate His holiness (see the first part of Acts 5) or to save and to heal, He worked to reveal who He is. His plan hasn't changed at all.

In Deed

The early believers were filled with awe and devoted to prayer because they had seen God work. God worked because they were filled with awe and devoted to prayer. It was an upward cycle of blessing through which God continued to reveal more and more of His attributes. Many people believed and were gathered into the church because the Spirit of Jesus was visibly alive and active. God's power is evident where people are caught up in who He is.

The way to experience God, then, is to be caught up in who He is. Major on relationship—His relationship with you and with others—and His power will be displayed. The God who wants to be known will always be near to those who want to know Him.

God is continually drawing us to Himself
in everything we experience.
—GERARD HUGHES

God of Fellowship

*All the believers used to meet together
in Solomon's Colonnade.*

ACTS 5:12

In Word

When God works powerfully and visibly, His people want to get together to share their experiences. When the Spirit fills His servants with love and awe, there's rarely an urge to be isolated. We want to celebrate the drama unfolding around us, and we usually like to enjoy our celebration together. If we don't like being around other Christians, something is wrong.

But that's sometimes the case, isn't it? There are times when God's people have a tendency to distance themselves from one another rather than come together in fellowship. When a church is struggling, when life is hard, when trials abound, or whenever it seems that God is not as near as we'd like Him to be, staying away from the fellowship is often easier than getting deeper into it.

The problem isn't with other people. We frequently think it is; we project a disenchantment with God onto those around us. But deep in our hearts, we may feel that we're missing something. If we feel far from God, we don't want to be around a bunch of people who can't relate. We don't want to be reminded that there's a closer relationship with Him that we're missing. The fellowship of saints is uncomfortable to those who don't feel like one.

In Deed

If it has seemed easy to stay away from the fellowship lately, resist the urge to do so. Realize that the problem may be nothing more than a deep wish to see more of God in your life and a reluctance to be around those who do see more of Him. But the way to see more of Him is for you to come together with fellow believers. When God shows up, it's usually a community experience.

God did miracles in Acts, and the people celebrated. As they came together, God did more miracles. There's a connection between the gathering and the glory. Do everything you can to tap into it.

> Be eager for more frequent gatherings for
> thanksgiving to God and for His glory.
> —IGNATIUS OF ANTIOCH

God of Favor

They were highly regarded by the people.
ACTS 5:13

In Word

The early Christians who were in awe of God were "highly regarded by the people." That may not ring true to those who recall the persecution in chapter 4, but that persecution came from authorities who felt threatened. Their status quo was being challenged because God was working. The average person on the street, however, had nothing to lose and everything to gain by a great move of God. They watched in awe from a distance.

That should be the dynamic at work in our lives as well. Whether God's miracles in our lives are highly visible or subtly at work behind the scenes, they should produce a love and awe in us that people are drawn to. Those who feed off the status quo will always be opposed to the gospel; there's nothing status quo about it. But those who have nothing to lose and everything to gain by a great move of God will be attracted to those who seem to know Him. Like moths to a flame, people honest about their needs love getting a glimpse of God.

The question we believers need to ask ourselves is whether people are getting a glimpse of God through us. That's not an issue of success and a problem-free life; it's a question of whether we are experiencing God wherever we are, even when deeply in need. If we are fulfilled by God, people hungry for fulfillment are more likely to eventually notice.

In Deed

What in your life indicates that God is working? Is He making Himself visible not only to you, but through you? There may be seasons when He seems far away, but there should also be seasons when His power is clear to you. And when it is clear to you, somehow and some way it can become clearer to others.

Pray about God's mission in your life. Spend some time asking Him to show His power in the ways that He wants to show it. Ask that your life line up with His will. And when it does, be prepared for people to notice.

Miracles are not the proofs, but the
necessary results, of revelation.
—SAMUEL TAYLOR COLERIDGE

God of Authority

*Crowds gathered also from the towns around
Jerusalem, bringing their sick and those tormented
by evil spirits, and all of them were healed.*
ACTS 5:16

In Word

God has not worked so clearly in every age of church history. We wish the miracles of Acts were an everyday experience, but they are rarer than we hoped. We long for God's power to be visible all the time in miraculous ways.

Or do we? We forget that these early days were about more than miracles. Yes, the onlooking world was drawn to Christians, but that was not a one-dimensional attraction. Before the miracles of Acts 5, there was the persecution of Acts 4 and the harsh elimination of Ananias and Sapphira for their dishonesty before God (Acts 5:1-11). The believers were in awe of God, not just because He healed a few people, but because His presence defined their lives. And His presence was more than a supernatural sideshow; it was holiness and love, power and purpose, an overwhelming sense that they were under authority from above. We often long for God's miracles without His holiness and authority. We are on a futile search for a one-sided coin.

When God works in our lives visibly, it's in His complete presence. He doesn't show up in power without showing up in authority. His love and His holiness are inseparable. If we want God, we have to want all of Him.

In Deed

If you want to impact your world for the mission of Jesus, don't forget the terms of the calling. We aren't called simply to display His power; we are called to represent all of His attributes. In order to do so, we have to live them. In our desire for a miracle-working Lord, we have to take the "Lord" with the "miracle-working." Otherwise, we're searching for a God who doesn't exist. We really desire an idol.

Awe and submission are prerequisites to seeing the power of God. And seeing the power of God is a prerequisite to affecting your world for Him. When we respect the progression, God works. He may not work the way we expect Him to—that's where the awe comes from—but He will work. And it will always, in one way or another, be miraculous.

Obedience is the key to every door.
—GEORGE MACDONALD

Counterfeit Mercy

Certain men whose condemnation was written about
long ago have secretly slipped in among you.
JUDE 1:4

In Word

The mission of God has its counterfeits. That should be no surprise. When God does a new work in the world, it will be contested; we can see that in Acts 4 and every opposition thereafter. But when opposition doesn't accomplish the enemy's purposes—and it never does, when God's people remain faithful—then deception is the next strategy. If the people who are coming to God are given subtly deceptive alternatives, they can be fooled into a false understanding of salvation and led into unbiblical ministries.

That's why there are so many pseudo-Christian teachings in the world. God's enemy has hoped to confuse the matter so people will throw their hands up in frustration or will be led astray into false doctrine. And if he can't keep them out of the Kingdom, he will at least try to minimize their effectiveness. Christians who have lost sight of the purity and simplicity of devotion to Jesus are usually the products of false teaching, and the enemy is pleased.

Jude wrote against false teachers for exactly that reason. Wherever God's Word is bearing fruit, counterfeits will be found. They aren't always obvious—counterfeits never are—and many of them are sincere. But sincerity does little to distinguish truth from error. Christians need to be discerning.

In Deed

The abundance of passages in the Bible regarding false teachers should cause us great alarm. We should be diligent to maintain devotion to Jesus in truth. When we aren't, the mission suffers; people are deceived, and the Kingdom is misrepresented. In a sobering, ultimate sense, lives are at stake.

Our culture of relativism would bristle at such diligence, but we aren't called to obey our culture. We are called to obey Jesus and to understand His Word. The church must be a zealous guardian of the truth of the gospel of grace. That's a necessary part of our mission.

We like to be deceived.
—BLAISE PASCAL

Real Judgment

The Lord delivered his people out of Egypt, but
later destroyed those who did not believe.
JUDE 1:5

In Word

There's a certain comfort believers find in the Lord of deliverance. It can be an appropriate comfort when we stand in awe of the One who saved us. But when comfort
turns to complacency—when we take God's grace for granted and use it as a license
for careless morals—we have fallen into the trap that Jude condemns. We have misrepresented the gospel.

That's what the false teachers of Jude's day did, so Jude urged the church to
remember who God is. Their God did, in fact, deliver His people out of Egypt and
into the Promised Land. But on the way, there were many who rejected the Land of
Promise because it seemed so unpromising. To the community of faith, Canaan's
inhabitants seemed bigger than God. So God let a generation die in the wilderness.

What's the point of Jude's reminder? The God of salvation is also the God of judgment. He majors in grace, but He doesn't tolerate its abuse. The false teachers who
were advocating casual morals and a take-it-easy approach to obedience were distorting the character of God. They were counting on the God of salvation while ignoring
the God of holy judgment. They were teaching things they didn't really understand.

In Deed

God's will for believers is for us to be saturated in grace and to live in holiness. Teachers
who lean too far to one side or the other have skewed the gospel. They have become
missionaries of a false mission.

It is up to each Christian to be vigilant about such distortions. We have a sacred
calling, not only to know both the grace and righteousness of Jesus, but also to communicate them to others in a balanced way. We were saved from sin—given grace to
counter its penalty and the Spirit of truth to counter its presence—and we dare not
treat it casually. God's Son didn't die on a cross for a casual matter. Never give the
impression that He did.

> There is a danger of forgetting that the Bible reveals not first
> the love of God, but the intense, blazing holiness of God.
> —OSWALD CHAMBERS

Keys to Survival

Build yourselves up in your most holy
faith and pray in the Holy Spirit.
JUDE 1:20

In Word

Your heart is a battleground. Perhaps you knew that already; you've probably witnessed the war within. If so, you know how easily human beings distort the gospel, and
you know how unlimited are the tangents we can get off on. Having been redeemed
by the God of grace through the Cross of Christ, we can be alarmingly unfocused.
We take our eyes off the basics and follow the nuances of the world, the flesh, and the
enemy of God.

Jude tells his readers the best way to avoid the tangents and twists of an unfocused
heart. We are to build ourselves up and pray in the Spirit. In other words, fellowship
with others and fellowship with God are the keys. Encouragement from others and
petitions to God are the safeguards against deception. When we are accountable to a
larger body and in daily communion with God, the enemy doesn't stand a chance.

It's no surprise, then, that Satan targets our relationships with others and with
God. If he can cultivate discord and disunity in the fellowship, and if he can get our
eyes off Jesus and onto laws, principles, and hairsplitting doctrines, he can open up
an opportunity for deception. If he can get our hearts out of sync with the body and
Spirit of Christ, he can set foot on the battleground with optimism.

In Deed

It takes courage to live for God in this world, but even courage isn't enough. The
most courageous soldiers on the battlefield are generally helpless without weapons,
a strategy, and their fellow soldiers. If we want to resist the subtle deceptions of the
enemy of God, we must put ourselves in a place of safety. And the only way to do that
is by maintaining the fellowship of prayer and of the body.

Never fall for any deceptions that would move your eyes off Jesus and your feet
out of the community of faith. Both are essential to a healthy spiritual life, and both
are key to the mission of God. To be effective for Him, we have to be effective with
Him and with each other.

Satan watches for those vessels that sail without convoy.
—GEORGE SWINNOCK

Understanding Love

*Keep yourselves in God's love as you wait for the mercy
of our Lord Jesus Christ to bring you to eternal life.*
JUDE 1:21

In Word

To modern ears, Jude's instruction in verse 21 sounds remarkably similar to the licentiousness he condemns in verse 4. That's because we interpret God's love as permissiveness and His mercy as a sin-doesn't-really-matter-anymore kind of forgiveness. But Jude would not have written of God's love as a license to abandon the character of Christ for the pleasures of worldliness. He would have defined love entirely differently.

That's one of the ways our false teachers have been successful over the years. The god who is acceptable to the culture at large is the god who exists for our purposes. His love for us means that he endorses everything we do or tells us not to worry about our sins. He is a very indulgent god, full of understanding and compassion. His love isn't much more than a feeling.

To us, the love of God is truer and harder. He tells us that we've sinned and He won't let us get away with denying it. He forgives us, not by saying "never mind" about our sin, but by paying an excruciating price to deliver us from it. Why? Because it is real and tragic. His love is filled with mercy, not because we're really okay to begin with, but because we actually need it. His love tells the truth.

In Deed

Our lives need to reflect His truth. More than that, our mission needs to reflect His truth. We can't follow the call of Christ—the great commission that He gave and elaborated on at the end of each Gospel and the beginning of Acts—if we don't understand why He came into this world to begin with. We must insist that Jesus died for our sin.

Yes, God loves us; we are unimaginably worthwhile to Him. No, that doesn't mean He always endorses our agenda and soothes our ego. Christians are called to stand up for the difference, to become teachers of God's true love and exposers of the counterfeits. We are to represent God as He really is.

> The Holy Spirit has promised to lead us step
> by step into the fullness of truth.
> —LEON JOSEPH SUENENS

Mercy and Fear

*Be merciful to those who doubt; snatch others from the
fire and save them; to others show mercy, mixed with
fear—hating even the clothing stained by corrupted flesh.*
JUDE 1:22-23

In Word

Mercy mixed with fear. That's a strange combination to a lot of non-Christians, but not to those of us who understand both the holiness of God and the condition of this world. We know God loves this fallen planet enough to have suffered for it intensely. We also know that the price He paid wasn't meaningless. If the cost was that enormous, the rebellion was that offensive. If we understand that, we will be merciful and fearful, both at the same time.

Jude would not have fit well into an I'm-okay-you're-okay culture. Nothing in his letter indicates a casual approach to disobedience. He understood the gravity of our corruption as well as the enormity of God's grace. If grace were not there, the situation would be hopeless. The fact that it is inspires both terror and gratitude.

That combination—fear and gratitude for God's mercy—should pervade our relationships with nonbelievers. We are not advocates of a better way of life; we are lifeguards on duty. We are to be always merciful and patient with those who doubt, never forgetting the dire outlook of those who refuse to turn from corruption. We are priests between a thoroughly stained people and an unimaginably pure God.

In Deed

How much godly fear do you have for the world around you? How much mercy do you have for it? Those two attitudes may seem like two competing ends of a spectrum, but they are not. If you're weak in one, you'll be weak in the other. The deeper you grow in one, the deeper you are likely to grow in the other. The truth of God's Word calls you to be extreme in both, always aware of the fires of judgment as well as the mercy of God. In other words, you are to tell the truth to the world around you.

Mercy imitates God and disappoints Satan.
—JOHN CHRYSOSTOM

The Sympathetic Priest

Every high priest . . . is able to deal gently with
those who are ignorant and are going astray,
since he himself is subject to weakness.
HEBREWS 5:1-2

In Word

Because of what sin did to humanity, we need an intermediary between God and us. It needs to be someone who can represent human beings to God and also God to human beings. The Jewish priesthood that God established did that, purifying men to stand between the human and the divine. God's intention was, according to Hebrews 5:1, for us to have sympathetic mediators who understand our issues because they have had them too.

The writer of Hebrews said a few verses earlier that Jesus is just such a high priest. It's hard to understand how the Holy One could relate to us; He's unique, right? But the whole point of the Incarnation was for God to become like one of us—someone who meets us where we are. Though the eternal Son of God is not subject to weakness in His glory, He became subject to the elements and temptations of this world. He chose to experience our weakness so we could know and trust Him. His compassion means more to us when we realize that He was tempted like we are and understands what we face.

That's vital to remember. You may think you are going through unique trials and temptations and that God is waiting for you to get it all right. But whatever angst or crisis you are up against today, Jesus has been there—or somewhere very similar. He isn't on the other side of the fence trying to pull you into His will; He's on the same side walking with you into the places you need to go. Whatever the "big question" of your life is today, He has faced some form of it and is determined to help you do the same.

In Deed

Accept the very personal ministry of your High Priest today. He isn't just with you for moral support. He's with you to help in a powerful and effective way. You cannot walk a path that is unfamiliar to Him. Let Him guide you in the way He already knows.

> Christ has taken our nature into heaven to represent us,
> and has left us on earth with His nature to represent Him.
> —JOHN NEWTON

Be Real

During the days of Jesus' life on earth, he offered
up prayers and petitions with loud cries and tears
to the one who could save him from death, and he
was heard because of his reverent submission.
HEBREWS 5:7

In Word

This verse doesn't seem to describe an invincible, unshakable Messiah. It sounds more like a human being in great distress who was completely dependent on God's mercy. But in Jesus, the contrasts of the last two sentences are blended. He *is* the invincible, unshakeable Messiah, and He *was* in great distress and completely dependent on His Father. He was not like us at all in His home in glory, but He became exactly like us in human form. And according to Hebrews 5:7, He wasn't entirely dignified about it.

Can you picture Jesus praying with loud cries and tears? shouting at the top of His lungs for His Father's mercy? facing a crisis and losing His outward composure? Not if the Jesus of Hollywood films has influenced you very much. The stone-faced mystic in the movies would never yell or cry. But the real Jesus did. He spent an agonizing evening in the garden of Gethsemane; He wept—probably more than a subtle trickle—at the tomb of his friend Lazarus; He spoke of leaping for joy when suffering persecution; and He compared His Kingdom to a wedding feast, which in Jewish culture is hardly an understated affair. The Jesus of Scripture seems to have worn His heart on His sleeve.

In Deed

Jesus wept loudly, and Scripture calls it "reverent submission." That means at least two things for us: (1) we may need to revise our definition of "reverent submission" to include emotional outpourings; and (2) we need to revise our perception of Jesus to include the idea of a real man with real feelings and a real connection with the human condition. In other words, if we are being conformed to the image of our Savior, we can be real. No posing, no masks, no false dignity. Authentically human. Just like Him.

Never apologize for showing feeling. When
you do so, you apologize for truth.
—BENJAMIN DISRAELI

Be Direct

Saul, who was also called Paul, filled with the Holy Spirit, looked straight at Elymas and said, "You are a child of the devil and an enemy of everything that is right!"
ACTS 13:9-10

In Word

Confrontation is not an admired trait in our society. It is often necessary, but it is rarely aspired to. We prefer to live and let live, to not rock the boat, to avoid conflict whenever we can. The words of Paul are uncomfortable for us. We who have been cultivated in a tolerant culture don't want to think of Christians speaking that harshly.

But Paul, full of God's Spirit, was only telling the truth. He realized that subtlety was often a friend of the enemy's lies. A soft approach to deception could let it remain unexposed and fertile. So Paul confronted a sorcerer who was turning people from the faith, and he confronted him harshly. Elymas was a false prophet who presumed to speak for God. Paul didn't approach the problem as if he were blowing out a match; he attacked it as if it were a wildfire.

That doesn't go over well today in our culture, but we are citizens of the Kingdom of God, not of this world. Sometimes we simply will not fit in. There's no need to try not to fit in; it will just happen sometimes. The trick for the Christian is to confront error without being personally offensive. We walk a fine line between attacking falsehood and attacking the personalities that embrace it.

In Deed

We live in a culture of relativity. To society at large, almost anything is acceptable. Truth and error are considered matters of opinion, and being rigid about such opinions is a major faux pas. The only "sin" our culture rejects is intolerance. The world doesn't look kindly on self-appointed judges.

Our contention is that we're not self-appointed. We've been given a mission by a high authority. Jesus confronted false teachers harshly, and we are His followers. When lies are told about Him, it's all right to be blunt. Not offensive, but blunt. If we represent the Lord of truth, we are to become truth's most ardent defenders.

Truth demands confrontation; loving confrontation, but confrontation nonetheless.
—FRANCIS SCHAEFFER

Be Truthful

Now the hand of the Lord is against you.
ACTS 13:11

In Word

God opposes the deception of the enemy. We're much more tolerant of spiritual lies than He is. We want to be tolerant and forgiving, both admirable qualities in themselves; but we confuse gentleness and patience with compromise and passivity. We don't draw lines that God would have us draw. But Paul did. He understood how God feels about active rebellion in this world. He knew that God has an archenemy intent on slandering His name and distorting His truth. And he realized that lives were at stake. He didn't compromise his message, and he didn't ignore the threat to it. He represented God well.

Does that mean we should go through life harshly condemning everyone who disagrees with us? Or worse yet, condemning everyone who doesn't quite embrace the whole of biblical truth? Hardly. That's not what God calls us to do. We are given the responsibility of pointing out those who actively oppose the work of the Spirit of God—gently when the offense is unintentional, bluntly when it is not. Most of all, we are to tell the truth.

In Deed

That's hard for us to do. The truth can hurt, and we often want to run from it. We hesitate to challenge the distortions that secular society makes about Christians and our faith. Sometimes, we'd rather just let it drop.

But God is a truth-telling God. He told us the truth when it hurt—read any one of the prophets for a case study—and He has never compromised His ways. He has been patient without resigning to passivity. His integrity remains untainted.

That's the call of the Christian—to let our integrity remain untainted. We are to live in a corrupt, truth-twisting world without getting caught up in its deceptions. The hand of the Lord is against those who oppose the gospel, even while His love for them calls them to Himself. If we can live with that balance, opposing falsehood while loving the deceived, we will be a lot like our God.

> Truth and love are wings that cannot be separated, for truth cannot fly without love, nor love soar aloft without truth.
> —EPHRAIM THE SYRIAN

Be Discerning

You are full of all kinds of deceit and trickery.
ACTS 13:10

In Word

The truth tellers of God need to be able to recognize falsehood. In order to do that, we first need to be well acquainted with truth. The common illustration of how bank tellers learn to recognize counterfeits is a good reminder: if we handle the real thing constantly, the fakes will become obvious whenever we encounter them. Discernment begins with a good foundation.

We might not be quite as blunt as Paul in calling the spades of our culture the spades that they really are, but we are to be just as discerning. If we become confused about the gospel, it's probably because we've allowed our hearts to flirt with its rivals. We've taken a subtle turn here and a simple twist there, calling it all a search for truth or spiritual fulfillment. But those subtle and simple deviations are often a willful resistance to the Word disguised as an open mind. Our deceptions spring from a desire to make God's truth a little easier to embrace, and those deceptions begin when we aren't discerning. A little bluntness might serve us well.

It helps to remember that the enemy of God will not appear as an offensive, obvious deceiver. He comes as an angel of light with no warning badge on his sleeve. His lies are designed to be attractive and appealing. They aren't always easy to see.

In Deed

The heart of the believer needs to be well trained in seeing deception, whether it comes from our own tendencies or the philosophies of this age. Regardless of how easily we confront others, we need to confront our own misperceptions. Our hearts must be tuned in to God's. That requires a deep commitment to prayer and honesty.

Let the Spirit be your guide. He will take you into the Word of God and illumine its truths. He will glorify the Son and draw you closer to Him. God is able to protect His people from deception and keep them from falling. The source of discernment is the God of truth Himself.

The truths I know best I have learned on my knees.
—JOHN BUNYAN

Be Available

Immediately mist and darkness came over him, and he
groped about, seeking someone to lead him by the hand.
ACTS 13:11

In Word

What a great description of our culture. It is in mist and darkness, groping about for direction. Paul had confronted a sorcerer and false prophet, and his confrontation seemed very harsh—much harsher than a politically correct society would tolerate. Even so, his response was inspired by the Holy Spirit (v. 9). Calling a deceiver "a child of the devil and an enemy of everything that is right" (v. 10) is apparently an authentic approach of a loving God. It may not fit our perceptions of God very well, but it does fit the revelation we've been given.

But while the initial declaration was harsh—Paul even declared blindness upon Elymas—the result put the sorcerer exactly where God wanted him: "seeking someone to lead him by the hand." And that's what God's judgment is still designed to do. It isn't to punish. That comes later, after all opportunities for repentance have been rejected. No, this judgment is for redemption. It puts the deceivers and the deceived in the position of knowing their deception. They have to either acknowledge a need for God or continue in their blindness. It's a harsh judgment toward a merciful end.

In Deed

This passage captures well a truth that we have a hard time understanding. It shows us on one hand that God is violently, zealously opposed to sin, and on the other hand that He is always working redemption into the rebellion of this world.

The implications for us should be clear. We are to oppose sin and embrace sinners. We once wandered in mist and darkness ourselves, and God spoke the truth to us. He guided us out. There's nothing wrong with confronting a deceiver, but if that deceiver ends up aware of his confusion and blindness, we are to grab the hand that gropes about. We are to be available to others as God was available to us, leading convicted wanderers by the hand.

> The real mark of a saint is that he makes it
> easier for others to believe in God.
> —ANONYMOUS

Be Visible

When the proconsul saw what had happened, he believed,
for he was amazed at the teaching about the Lord.
ACTS 13:12

In Word

The proconsul, "an intelligent man" (v. 7), was caught between two options. He had summoned Paul to hear the word of God, but a false teacher was trying to undermine Paul's teaching. It was a tense situation, similar to the predicament of many people today. Intelligent people, faced with a choice, are caught in a battle between truth and error.

The clincher for the proconsul was that he "saw what had happened." That influenced him and made it easy to believe in God. The truth that Paul preached was backed up with a lifestyle, a message, and a sign, all testifying to the authenticity of Paul's claims. A gospel without power may not have won the proconsul over, but a gospel that so clearly confounded its naysayers made the right choice obvious. A seeker of God in an important position was impressed by the hand of God.

The hand of God shows up in many ways. Sometimes it's a deep impression in the heart, a timely word for someone's need, or even a supernatural phenomenon like this one. But a mission that is not backed by the hand of God will be fruitless. People simply don't believe in a radically new way unless there's evidence for the belief itself.

In Deed

For us, that means that we have to be people of evidence. No one believes a message that has not visibly changed our lives or that is not perceptibly affecting the people around us. Whether our evidence is a lifestyle or a miracle, something needs to be there for people to see. They won't just accept an assertion about truth if it seems comparable to all the other opinions out there.

The proconsul was amazed. Are you living in a way that amazes others? Are your words and your ways backed by God's hand? If not, why not? Get to the root of the problem. Intelligent people, seekers of God, need something, somewhere, to see.

We are not only to renounce evil, but to manifest the truth.
—HUDSON TAYLOR

A Hostile Context

This girl followed Paul and the rest of us, shouting,
"These men are servants of the Most High God,
who are telling you the way to be saved."
ACTS 16:17

In Word

She was telling the truth, for the most part. She told it to the point of being annoying, but she still pointed out Paul and his entourage accurately as servants of the Most High God. She even let everyone around her know that these men had the way of salvation. Still, she was the mouthpiece of a demonic entity. She was telling the truth in the wrong way and in the wrong spirit.

Paul rebuked the spirit within her and commanded it to come out, much in the same way that Jesus rebuked evil spirits for truthfully pointing Him out as the Son of God (e.g., Mark 1:25, 34; Luke 4:35, 41). Both Jesus and Paul—the Truth Incarnate and one of His greatest advocates—spent a lot of energy preaching heavenly realities to people, but they silenced demons who agreed with them. Why? Because we aren't to get our truth from demons. It doesn't matter how accurately the girl portrayed Paul, Silas, and Luke; she wasn't the right spokesperson for the job. In the Kingdom of God, the source counts.

Evil masquerading as truth is a common dynamic in this Kingdom that Jesus brought us into. We live out our salvation in a hostile context, and sometimes the hostilities are very, very subtle. Satan doesn't always use a frontal assault. He sends his own prophets—teachers who tell almost all of the truth, mixed with a little error and a lot of confusion. What they say isn't as important as the spirit in which they say it.

In Deed

We have to understand the spirits of the age. We are citizens of an invincible Kingdom, but we are at its foreign outposts, surrounded by a hostile culture. The new life we have in Christ will be contested. The message we share will be counterfeited. The unauthorized variations on God's true theme will be subtle and dangerous. The most important thing we can do today—and every day—is to arm ourselves with truth and live in the true Spirit of God.

Satan accomplishes more by imitation
than by outright opposition.
—VANCE HAVNER

A Firm Response

Finally Paul became so troubled that he turned around and said to the spirit, "In the name of Jesus Christ I command you to come out of her!"
ACTS 16:18

In Word

God isn't interested in the confessions of demons. His Spirit is fully capable of leading people to salvation in Jesus without the help of competing voices. He wants a clear separation between His servants and the servants of the underworld.

Paul knew that, so when a possessed girl followed him around for days shouting out his message—on demonic terms—he put an end to it. We don't know if the demon was mocking, setting the stage for deception, or just cheapening the truth by making it annoying. Regardless, it was in the way. Paul ordered the spirit to come out of her. He confronted this subtle act of hostility with the power of God. And God won.

We need to have that sense of anger toward the interfering spirits of our age. We may think we are being peaceful and compassionate by tolerating rivals to the gospel, but we are not consistent with the heart of God when we do. If we truly want to be Christlike—to be in sync with God's Spirit—we need to be disturbed by false voices masquerading as truth. Jesus certainly was, and His servants are to be consistent with His heart.

That doesn't mean we can insult and attack the people who voice the lies of the enemy. Our responsibility is to love them and resist the enemy. Like God, we are to be angry toward deception, but forgiving of deceivers.

In Deed

How do you respond to your hostile environment? Are you able to discern false voices and stand against them? Are you able to do so without wounding the people who serve as their mouthpieces? It's a hard balance to find, but Paul gives us a good example. Be strong in your message, confront its rivals, and stick to your mission. Speak very firm truths in very assertive love. That's exactly how Jesus lived the gospel in a hostile world.

> Let us arm ourselves against our spiritual enemies with courage. They think twice about engaging with one who fights boldly.
> —JOHN CLIMACUS

A Deeper Worship

About midnight Paul and Silas were praying
and singing hymns to God, and the other
prisoners were listening to them.
ACTS 16:25

In Word

What do you do when your hostile environment seems to get the best of you? If you're like most people, you fight back, lament your losses, or just get depressed. Not Paul and Silas. They sat in a dirty Philippian jail in the dark of night singing hymns to God.

The reason they were in jail to begin with was because they were obedient to God. They cast the demon out of the servant girl, but in doing so, they undermined an entire fortune-telling enterprise. Those who had been exploiting the girl's "talent" set them up on false charges—a reaction many people have when losing money. So Paul and Silas sat in a cell with a song in their hearts.

They could worship enthusiastically because they realized that their opponents had only seemed to get the best of them. They knew that circumstances can be misleading. They understood that the enemy's tactics are superficial scare tactics. Satan can create all kinds of situational havoc, but he cannot disturb the Spirit within us. If that's where we dwell—if we are immersed in the Spirit of God—the difference between a five-star hotel and a Greek jail cell is minimal.

In Deed

Where do you dwell? If you are easily swayed by your circumstances, your quality of life will be manipulated by the enemy of God. If you live at a deeper level than that, grounded in the Word of God and filled with His Spirit, your quality of life cannot be shaken. Every situation will be an opportunity to worship, or at least to acknowledge the sovereignty of the Father.

This is a crucial principle to grasp if you are going to maintain your sanity in the hostile environment of a fallen world. You cannot live zealously for Jesus while living as a victim of circumstance. You have to read between the lines of your life and recognize both the enemy's surface tactics and the underlying will of God. The spiritual war requires great focus—and the ability to worship in dark places.

The worship of God is not a rule of safety—it
is an adventure of the spirit.
—ALFRED NORTH WHITEHEAD

A Fruitful Sacrifice

Paul shouted, "Don't harm yourself! We are all here!"
ACTS 16:28

In Word

A violent earthquake shook the foundations of the prison, and the doors flew open. The jailer woke up—apparently, he usually slept through the uneventful night shift—and, seeing the open doors and broken chains, prepared to kill himself. A self-inflicted fate would have been better than the punishment awaiting a jailer who let prisoners escape. But Paul wouldn't let either happen. He shouted to get the jailer's attention and let him know that all the prisoners were still there.

Why? Most of us would have seen the earthquake as God's provision for our escape, but not Paul. He was still reading between the lines of his life. He could tell that God was more interested in the jailer than in Paul and Silas's rights. He could have fled, and no one would have blamed him. He was, after all, on a God-appointed mission to preach the gospel. Surely God would want him free to fulfill His calling.

A believer who understands spiritual warfare, however, will care more about the people he meets than the suffering he's experiencing. He will be more concerned with giving a godly response than using God's resources for personal gain. The spiritual battle will be at the top of his agenda. He will desire fruit more than freedom.

In Deed

What drives your agenda? Do you live your life for personal fruitfulness or for personal fulfillment? Though they go hand in hand, fruitfulness should always lead the way. For Paul it did; he seized an opportunity to share the gospel rather than split the scene. As a result, an entire household was saved.

Few of us really live life that way. We want to fulfill God's plan and our own, balancing both at the same time. Eventually, something has to give. When your moment of decision comes, which will it be? Will your response to the spiritual war drive you out of a chaotic situation? Or will it keep you there as a witness? One response is easier; one is more fruitful. And only one can bring the Kingdom of God into hostile places.

> To be a witness . . . means to live in such a way that one's life would not make sense if God did not exist.
> —EMMANUEL SUHARD

A Painful Dynamic

He was filled with joy because he had come to
believe in God—he and his whole family.
ACTS 16:34

In Word

It's an uncomfortable dynamic, and we are reluctant to embrace it. Nevertheless, it's a consistent theme in Scripture. The good news of salvation is traumatic. New life begins in pain. Always.

Think about that. Jesus suffered on a cross to give us life. The Spirit convicts us of our sins—and often subjects us to futility and despair—before we come to Christ. The mission of Jesus involves intense prayer, hard work, and spiritual opposition before bearing fruit. God has even woven the principle into physical life: ground is brutally plowed before planting, seeds die before sprouting, and rains pound before harvest. And women writhe in agony before birthing a beautiful child. The joy of life always has its roots in the sacrifice of pain.

That is the dynamic Paul and Silas embraced in a Philippian prison. Because they were faithful, an unjust imprisonment, a violent earthquake, chaos among criminals, and a suicidal guard led to a family's salvation and a citywide testimony. The conduit for grace is often despair, and those who are tuned in to the conflict between the Spirit and the adversary will leverage the despair for the grace. That's how God changes the world.

In Deed

If you became a Christian thinking that life would be easy, you may be disillusioned by the war you entered. As a believer, you have probably encountered counterfeits, injustices, and chaos, and wondered why God was absent. The answer from Acts 16 is that He isn't. In fact, He is never more present. He allows desperate times as a platform for His grace. All He asks is for His servants to seize the platform.

Try that next time you're in a difficult situation. Somewhere around you is the equivalent of a Philippian jailer—someone who is ready to give up because of the chaos around him or her. You can seize the opportunity for grace, both for yourself and for those you see.

We must meet the uncertainties of this world
with the certainty of the world to come.
—A. W. TOZER

Waiting Patiently

*So after waiting patiently, Abraham
received what was promised.*
HEBREWS 6:15

In Word

Scripture is fascinating in how it deals with its heroes. On one hand, it deals with them warts and all, never hiding some of their most embarrassing moments from the eyes that will read their story for all eternity. On the other hand, when the retrospective view is given, it's clear that people like Abraham waited patiently. This is the same Abraham who suggested that his servant Eliezer might be his best chance at an heir (Genesis 15:2-3); the same Abraham who listened to Sarah's advice to try for a miracle son the natural way through her servant Hagar (Genesis 16); and the same Abraham who laughed when God repeated the promise well after childbearing years (Genesis 17:17). Yes, we are told, this is the Abraham who "did not waver through unbelief" (Romans 4:20) and waited patiently.

That's encouraging for those of us who have tried to hold on to a promise, stumbled, wavered, held on some more, questioned, wondered, and ended up holding on in the end. The view in God's rearview mirror is that we never wavered, that we waited patiently. And, of course, the happy result of that patient waiting is the same as for Abraham. We receive what was promised. If we end with faith, faith has prevailed, no matter what attacks and wavering it has suffered before. Such faith bears fruit for enduring. It receives promises.

In Deed

Know that even when your faith goes through ups and downs, it's still faith. The verdict is how well your faith survives, not what it endures along the way. Whatever promise you have been waiting for God to fulfill, trust that the payoff is coming. When? He rarely tells us that. But He does assure us that the kind of faith that perseveres is the kind of faith that is rewarded. Like Abraham, hang on. Look ahead. Believe in spite of obstacles and appearances. Never let go of what God has said.

Teach us, O Lord, the disciplines of patience,
for to wait is often harder than to work.
—PETER MARSHALL

A Sure Thing

It is impossible for God to lie.
HEBREWS 6:18

In Word

God has given us a multitude of promises in His Word. Some of them are for the biggest issues of all—eternal life and a relationship with Him. Others are for the prayers we pray or the blessings we seek. But regardless of the scope, the truth is unwavering. Whether we're talking about a big-ticket promise like eternal life or a smaller promise during this age, the principle is the same. God can't lie.

Those who have clung to a promise of God know where our minds take us at this point. Sure, God can't lie, but we can misunderstand Him. We can hear a promise that isn't there. We can misinterpret what He has said. We can make assumptions about what His will is. We know *He* is infallible, but we certainly aren't. So underneath all His promises in Scripture, we mentally fill in the blanks with fine print and legal caveats just so we'll have a good theological explanation in case we get let down. The result is a God who cannot lie trying to communicate with people who won't let themselves accept His truth.

It's true that we can misunderstand God, but the theological gymnastics we go through to explain why His promises mean something other than what He said are completely unnecessary. What He has said is true. The promises He has given us for eternal life are inviolable. The assurances that He will answer our prayers of faith are rock solid. The God who expects us to have unwavering faith would not give us wavering covenants. When He has spoken, we can trust that we have heard and that He will do what He said.

In Deed

God isn't like us. He doesn't say one thing and mean another. He doesn't waffle on His plans. He doesn't change His mind with every shifting circumstance. He speaks and then waits for those with real faith to step into the truth He has spoken. The question is whether we will take His words as the reality they are.

> God is the God of promise. He keeps His word, even when that seems impossible; even when the circumstances seem to point to the opposite.
>
> —COLIN URQUHART

The Spiritual War

Be strong in the Lord and in his mighty power.
EPHESIANS 6:10

In Word

The truth we discover soon after becoming Christians is that we are in the middle of a war. If the restoration of all things had come instantly after the Resurrection, there would be no conflict. The whole world would have been made new, the evil serpent would have been bound and cast into hell, and believers would be living in a perfect environment. But all of those future realities were secured by the Cross and empty tomb, not enforced by them. Not yet. We've set our faith on those promises, but for now, life is a struggle. It is a struggle because we were born into the middle of a war.

We have two options: fight or flee. The option to flee is an illusion—the war exists whether we want to acknowledge it or not. If we ignore it, we've lost already. But the option to fight—that's where we get confused. We charge into battle and then quickly wind up defeated. We forget rule of engagement number one in the spiritual war: be strong in His mighty power.

That's easy to say, but hard to live out. It isn't complicated, just unnatural. We pray for God's strength and live by faith for a while, and then any success puts us in our default mode: self-reliance. Only after failing in our self-reliance do we learn to rely again on His strength.

In Deed

A battle mentality is essential for the Christian life. We cannot bear spiritual fruit, internally or externally, if we are not alert and equipped for the conflict that inevitably comes. But our alertness is not to lead us to our own strategies and resources; it must lead us to dependence. Faith means casting ourselves unreservedly into the hands of God. We, like Jesus and the apostles, will pray God's authority against evil and live for God's Kingdom, but the power behind the prayers and the life is not ours. It belongs to the Spirit within us. If we aren't vitally related to Him, we will lose. The only way to win—the only way even to survive—is to be strong in His mighty power.

> You were rubbed with oil like an athlete—Christ's athlete—and you agreed to take on your opponent.
> — AMBROSE

Be Aware

*Our struggle is not against flesh and blood, but
against . . . the powers of this dark world and against
the spiritual forces of evil in the heavenly realms.*
EPHESIANS 6:12

In Word

Most Christians know that our struggle is not against flesh and blood. Few Christians actually live like they know it. We tend to assign naturalistic explanations to the many personal and social difficulties of the spiritual life: early childhood issues, relationship dynamics, emotional quirks, personal charisma (or lack thereof)—the options available to us are limited only by the number of social and psychological theories out there. And all of those issues can be genuine factors in our struggles. Meanwhile, the Bible assures us that there is more going on behind the scenes.

Many people will raise their eyebrows at the thought of evil spirits at war against the Kingdom of God. Ancient people could accept such superstitions, but we're full of scientific knowledge and modern perspectives, aren't we? But the Son of God Himself attests to the reality of an archenemy of God who is bent on defacing God's creation and the people He has redeemed. Jesus spoke to demons, and they spoke back—and there's no hint of metaphor in the text. God incarnate would not have interacted with unseen spirits if they didn't exist. And He wouldn't have given His disciples authority over the enemy if they didn't need it.

In Deed

Let the reality of the unseen world sink in. Don't be paranoid; just be alert. Awareness of those who dwell in dark realms will explain a lot of the challenges to your faith. Whenever you are compelled to doubt God's goodness or violate His character, you can be pretty sure there's a malicious presence at work.

God wants you to live with an awareness of the war. Your faith will not go uncontested. The service you offer in God's Kingdom will not remain unchallenged. The growth you so desperately want and need will not be a walk in the park. It will be a walk through a battlefield. Why? Because our struggle is not against flesh and blood.

The existence of the devil is so clearly taught in the
Bible that to doubt it is to doubt the Bible itself.
—ARCHIBALD BROWN

Stand Firm

Stand firm then.
EPHESIANS 6:14

In Word

Some people respond to the spiritual war with paranoia. Others respond with aggressive yet extrabiblical strategies. Some choose to ignore it, to their own detriment, and others choose to obsess about it, also to their own detriment. The propensity of believers to get out of balance on this issue is alarming. Meanwhile, all Scripture really tells us to do is stand firm.

There are a lot of ways to do that: pray for God's Kingdom to come rather than the enemy's; refuse to be swayed by false philosophies or unbiblical ideas about God; resist temptation; cling to truth and unshakable faith; know Scripture and use your knowledge often; and ground yourself thoroughly in the gospel and share it readily. But all of these aspects of standing firm still amount to one basic stance. If we are rooted in the gospel—and all its implications—we will not be moved.

That's the antithesis of the enemy's agenda. Satan would have us fall for his lies, listen to his whispers of doubt, trip over his temptations, allow his accusations to wound us, wallow in our guilt, and accept his alluring counterfeits. There is nothing he can do to us spiritually that cannot be thwarted by digging our feet into the rock of the gospel.

In Deed

When we fail to stand firm, we usually do so for one of two reasons: ignorance or feelings. We either don't know the truths of Scripture or we do not know how to cling to them when we don't feel like it. When we let God's Word fall several steps on our list of priorities, we lose our sense of alertness and our knowledge is deficient. When we base our faith on moods and situations rather than on facts, we are blown by every changing wind.

Our best approach to the spiritual war is to immerse ourselves in truth and cling to it regardless of our emotions and circumstances. Some things change by the hour; God's Word doesn't. When the battle comes, know where to stand. Above all, stand firm.

> The devil wrestles with God, and the field
> of battle is the human heart.
> —FYODOR DOSTOEVSKY

Always Pray

*Pray in the Spirit on all occasions with all kinds
of prayers and requests . . . be alert.*
EPHESIANS 6:18

In Word

Imagine a battalion in the heat of conflict without any communication between the field and central command. Some success may be won right there in that spot, but if no one knows where other enemy troops are positioned and no one is coordinating the next move, the gains will be very temporary. Communication is critical in a time of war.

A life that is aware of the spiritual war will wield its God-given weapons liberally—including the crucial communication we need in order to advance. We sometimes act as if we have a shortage of ammunition; we forget that God is our supplier. There is no need—or conceivable reason—to skimp on prayer. It is our only means of communication with central command. It is also our link to the power of God and our only real means to "be strong in the Lord and in his mighty power," as verse 10 tells us. When we sense the enemy at work and we pray, we are bringing invincible power against invisible evil. Why would we ever use such a weapon sparingly?

The only reasons we have—and they aren't very good—are lack of time, a short attention span, ignorance of how vital prayer is, and similar flimsy excuses. Jesus told His disciples that if they were in Him and He was in them, they could ask whatever they wished and it would be done. If those simple conditions are met, a believer will understand the battle and the critical need for prayer—and its amazing power. If not, our senses are dulled. Prayerlessness is a refusal to wake up.

In Deed

Pray often, pray hard, pray for everything . . . just pray. It is no coincidence that Paul ends a discourse on spiritual warfare with repeated commands to pray. This is where the battle is truly fought—on our knees. Fighting the war without much prayer is like casually strolling into battle with no flak jacket, no gun, and no means of communication. It just shouldn't happen. Make sure it doesn't happen today.

Prayer is that mightiest of all weapons
that created natures can wield.
—MARTIN LUTHER

Ultimate Stakes

Pray also for me, that whenever I open my mouth, words may be given me so that I will fearlessly make known the mystery of the gospel, for which I am an ambassador in chains.
EPHESIANS 6:19-20

In Word

Those who do not believe in the truth have been blinded. That's what 2 Corinthians 4:4 says. The "god of this age," Satan, has shrouded this planet in a dark haze of confusion. The gospel, as free and simple as it is, remains a mystery to billions. People don't see it because they are spiritually disoriented. Information usually isn't the issue; Satan is.

Do you understand the implications of that? The stakes of the spiritual war are eternal. If we do not stand firm in our faith and wield our weapons, people die and go to hell. Yes, God is sovereign. But the sovereign God commanded us to pray and to take the gospel into a lost world. The tasks we are called to do are the very tasks the enemy resists most fiercely. This is a high-stakes war, and the faint of heart are not helping.

That's why Paul asks for prayer. Evangelism is not a game, it is not a career, and it is not an option. It's the task of the whole church, and only prayer can make it fruitful.

In Deed

You may not have realized that you enlisted for a war with eternal consequences, but it's part of your decision to follow Jesus. You can't have Him without His mission, and you can't be part of His mission without coming face-to-face with an evil adversary. Your discipleship will be contentious because it can have devastating consequences for the powers of darkness. You are more of a threat than you think.

Most of us don't live as though we are threats to the kingdom of darkness. Even though we are children of the King and seated with Him in heavenly places (Ephesians 1 and 2), we assume that our part in the battle is very small. That may be humble, but it's unbiblical. God has called us to war. Those who do not fight—aggressively and persistently—are missing part of their calling. A blinded world needs us to stand, to fight, and to pray.

Evangelism is not a human enterprise; it is a divine operation.
—ARTHUR SKEVINGTON WOOD

Blessed Assurance

*Now faith is being sure of what we hope for
and certain of what we do not see.*
HEBREWS 11:1

In Word

Jesus gave His disciples a remarkable promise about prayer: "Whatever you ask for in prayer, believe that you have received it, and it will be yours" (Mark 11:24). It's the summary statement following His wild claim that those who have faith in God can move mountains. But this verse is not only a promise; it contains a command that few people notice. Before the extravagant assurance that "it will be yours" is an imperative: "Whatever you ask for in prayer, believe that you have received it."

The writer of Hebrews says this is what faith is all about. His primary purpose is to assure Jewish Christians that the new covenant is true—that the history of God's chosen people portrayed only a shadow of what Jesus now offers us. But the principle is the same whether we are talking about eternal life in the heavenly Kingdom or a short-term promise about prayer. The way of the Kingdom is faith, and faith is being sure of what we hope for and certain of what we don't see.

That means that when we request something God has promised but don't see it yet, it's still reality. It means that when the evidence isn't visible yet, we shouldn't be surprised. If faith is the way of the Kingdom, then the way of the Kingdom involves invisible realities. Of course we can't see the object of our faith yet. That would remove it from the realm of faith.

We will eventually see what we've believed and hoped for, of course; faith results in sight at some point. But it usually doesn't until our faith has become mature. That's why God often delays the answers to our prayers. He's waiting for faith to be truer and more certain. When it is, He rewards it with His favor.

In Deed

Whatever you ask for, believe that you have received it. Don't be surprised that you don't see it yet; you couldn't have faith if you did. You could only have sight. But God honors faith. He keeps His Word and blesses those who know that with certainty.

> Praying without faith is like trying to cut with a blunt knife—much labor expended to little purpose.
> —JAMES O. FRASER

Pleasing God

Without faith it is impossible to please God.
HEBREWS 11:6

In Word

It's a startling claim, isn't it? We're told not only that God is pleased with our faith. That would be simple and encouraging enough. No, we're told that it's impossible to please God without faith. If we don't allow ourselves to be in a position to believe what we can't see, we can't experience His pleasure.

We have a lot of subtle (or not-so-subtle) ways of rebelling against faith. We get discouraged and frustrated when we have to wait for answers to our prayers. We assume God hasn't answered us when we hear nothing but silence. We base our decisions on the evidence before us rather than the promises and wisdom of God. But when we demand to see those things we're supposed to believe in, we're really demanding to move from a state that pleases Him into a state that doesn't seem to affect Him at all. We're revolting against an opportunity to please Him.

That's why it's essential to become comfortable with waiting on God, with trusting in His character when circumstances would pressure us not to, and with disregarding any evidence contrary to His promises. Life gives us plenty of opportunities to make a statement about who God is and about the integrity of His Word. When confronted with tension between what we see and what He says, which will we choose? The way of faith pleases Him. Anything less than faith doesn't.

In Deed

Maintaining faith can be extremely difficult, but it's absolutely necessary if we are to please God. The tension between faith and sight becomes our testing ground to demonstrate what we believe about God. Will we hang on to what we know to be true, or will we live under the tyranny of all things visible? The line between the two can become very fuzzy sometimes, but the choices we make on our testing ground can be monumental. Regardless of what you see, choose faith. It always pleases God.

> Faith is blind—except upward. It is blind to impossibilities and deaf to doubt.
> —S. D. GORDON

Not Afraid

*When they heard this, they were furious
and gnashed their teeth at him.*
ACTS 7:54

In Word

Stephen was bold and very blunt. He had been charged with preaching that Jesus
would change the customs handed down by Moses (Acts 6:14), and that wasn't a very
popular message to authorities steeped in centuries-old traditions. So at his trial, he
reviewed Jewish history and pointed out how Israel's leaders had always persecuted
the prophets and resisted God's Spirit. It wasn't a very politically correct message. In
fact, it got him killed.

Death was no surprise to Stephen. Persecution of the early believers had already
begun, and Stephen knew he had already been accused of blasphemy. Still, he didn't
back down. He knew that the Spirit of God and the traditions of men stand in opposition when the Spirit moves and men don't. The Spirit moves and people don't. In
hearts of fallen flesh, the status quo is more comfortable—and more sacred—than
the will of God. But Stephen chose to bow out in the will of God rather than bend
down to the judgments of men.

Stephen is an important example for us, not because we often face stoning for
our faith, but because the same conflict still rages. Man-made institutions always resist
the movements of God, and we are repeatedly put in a position of having to choose
between them. The ways of the world and the ways of the Spirit are opposed, and the
result can be heated and fierce. In the intensity of the opposition, we should remember Stephen.

In Deed

Every Christian must come to a decision in life. For some it's a daily, incremental
direction, and for others it's a life-changing moment of crisis. Either way, the decision
must be made. Will we plant both our feet in eternity and face up to God's opponents,
even at great risk? Or will we try to live with one foot in the world and one in the
Kingdom, hoping the two will converge comfortably in our lives? It's a monumental
decision, even when we barely notice that we made it. It defines the level of victory in
our lives. It determines whether we will honor God as Stephen did.

> Christ's followers cannot expect better treatment
> in the world than their Master had.
> —MATTHEW HENRY

Not Alone

Stephen, full of the Holy Spirit, looked up to heaven and saw the glory of God, and Jesus standing at the right hand of God.
ACTS 7:55

In Word

God could have looked at Stephen and thought: *What a fool. He had his whole life in front of him. He could have been a great witness for Me. I was hoping he would go back to serving the church, where he belonged.* But we know God doesn't think such things. Nowhere in Scripture does He rebuke someone for making too great a sacrifice for His glory. Extravagant gifts are pleasing to Him. He may guide people to spend their lives differently, but He never tells them not to spend them for Him. He welcomes ultimate sacrifice.

We know that because as Stephen ended his fateful speech, he saw Jesus standing at the right hand of God. The ascended Lord is seen elsewhere as seated in heaven, but not here. Here He stood for one of His own. He smelled the pleasing aroma of a dying sacrifice and honored Stephen's gift. He welcomed His servant into the fullness of the Kingdom.

Most of us look at Stephen as a superhero of the faith: amazing in his example, but impossible for normal people to follow. We think that only an exceptional Christian life is so sacrificial. We forget that lukewarmness and mediocrity nauseate God (Revelation 3:15-16). We forget the honor bestowed on the prophets and apostles—and regular, unknown Christians—who died in the spiritual war.

In Deed

God loves a heart fully dedicated to Him, even when dedication results in deep wounds. The Healer isn't devastated by our suffering; the resurrected Lord isn't fearful of our death. In God's Kingdom, life and death aren't ultimate. Love and faithfulness are.

Ask God to help you see your life differently—as a daily offering that is ready to be fully spent for Him. Pray that He would inspire in you both extravagant grace and brutal honesty in your interactions with the spiritual opposition. Do whatever you can to get to the point where you can say, "Lord, whatever my offering costs, I want to see You stand."

> God will be our compensation for every sacrifice we have made.
> —F. B. MEYER

Not Intimidated

"I see heaven open and the Son of Man standing at the right hand of God." At this they covered their ears and . . . dragged him out of the city and began to stone him.
ACTS 7:56-58

In Word

He knew it wasn't going to go over well. You don't just walk into a lions' den and impugn the character of lions. A mob mentality is never calmed by condemning it. It only rages stronger. Stephen understood what happens when you accuse the self-righteous of unrighteousness.

From a practical standpoint, Stephen's decision to go out in a blaze of glory seems pointless. He had no chance of appeasing his rabid opponents, and his lonely, dissenting voice would never speak again. His sacrifice wasn't going to change anything, and it ensured that he would never have another chance to change anything. The whole event appears futile to us. It seems like such a waste.

But Stephen's witness stands for us today, some two thousand years later. After he preached a searing message that day in Jerusalem, he preached a visual message with his death, and the latter message still moves us. We are reminded that truth is more important than life, that the Spirit is poured out through uncompromising faith, and that our love for God must always be stronger than our fear of human beings.

Jewish leaders were convinced Stephen was a blind fool. But Stephen saw heaven opened. He had already made a decision about what would fill his gaze: the approval of God, not the approval of men. He knew where to fix his sight.

In Deed

What fills your sight in this world—a vision of God or the opinions of human beings? Which has a greater influence on you, especially in moments of crisis? It is normal for Christians to experience opposition to their faith. It is sad when that opposition alters their stand. It comes down to a choice between the power of intimidation and the power of a bold witness. Whichever looms larger to us will dictate our choices. Stephen traded his life for truth and a strong witness, and it was worth it. It always is.

> Men who fear God face life fearlessly. Men who do not fear God end up fearing everything.
> —RICHARD HALVERSON

Not Hopeless

While they were stoning him, Stephen
prayed, "Lord Jesus, receive my spirit."
ACTS 7:59

In Word

The invisible war that is integral to the Christian life can be brutal. There are spiritual attacks of doubt, deception, temptation, and condemnation, and every godly act and attitude is challenged. There are psychological attacks of emotional distress, discouragement, and despair, and sanity isn't as easy as it looks. There are relational attacks of conflict, misunderstandings, bitterness, betrayal, and persecution, and peace is often a distant ideal. And there can even be physical attacks of fatigue, disease, and injury. On every front in our battles against the world, the flesh, and the devil, we can be awfully beaten down.

It is impossible to live this new life in Christ without hope. Christians who spend little time thinking about the Kingdom of God will fall helplessly into despair. Life in this fallen world can be beautiful, but it is never easy. It is not as it was first created, and it is not as it will be when Jesus comes again. Without a firm gaze on eternity, our temporal trials consume us. We have to invest our hopes in the coming Kingdom; otherwise, we are most pitiable among all humanity (1 Corinthians 15:19). If we don't see beyond the grave, we despair.

Stephen prayed to Jesus essentially the same prayer that Jesus prayed to the Father: "Receive my spirit." Both knew that the war against evil in this world is deadly in the flesh but alive in the Spirit. Both had abandoned all hope in setting up their lives and their treasures in the visible world for the greater glory of setting up life and treasure in the invisible world.

In Deed

The early Christians had that focus on eternity. So do persecuted Christians around the world today. Many of us have lost this perspective; we don't yearn for heaven, we just kind of wait to be taken there against our will. But there's no hope in that. Our faith has no need to cling to a fallen world. We have a deeper ambition. We have hope.

Hope is the struggle of the soul, breaking loose from
what is perishable, and attesting her eternity.
—HERMAN MELVILLE

Not Vengeful

He fell on his knees and cried out, "Lord,
do not hold this sin against them."
ACTS 7:60

In Word

We live in a culture of personal rights. The goal of most of our laws is to make sure that no one is even slightly defrauded or deprived of his or her assumed rights—ever. Though that's a wonderful ideal, it will never be realized in a fallen world, especially among those who fight in the spiritual war. Our detachment from trivial things means we will not cling to them when others fight us for them. We have deeper values. Children of God don't need to enforce their rights.

Jesus challenged this human obsession with personal rights. "Love your enemies, do good to those who hate you, bless those who curse you, pray for those who mistreat you. If someone strikes you on one cheek, turn to him the other also. If someone takes your cloak, do not stop him from taking your tunic" (Luke 6:27-29). Believers who are firmly focused on eternity are radically detached from the things that consume most people's hearts. Those who are abundantly supplied by God in all things have no need for greed or grudges. We can give and forgive recklessly.

Stephen did that. Ravenous wolves were murdering him, and he pleaded with God not to punish them but to forgive them. Stephen already had everything he would ever need, and more. He was entering glory. His persecutors were far from it—and headed for disaster.

In Deed

How do you respond when the world turns vicious? Do you get bitter? resentful? vengeful? angry and withdrawn? Or do you take the Stephen option, blessing those who persecute you and praying for those who slight you? How you respond to persecution—or any kind of hardship—speaks volumes about your faith.

Vengeance doesn't change the world. It's the way of the world from the Fall, and no one notices anything unusual about it. But a merciful response to injustice? Forgiveness that is clearly supernatural? That can impact society with surprising power. That kind of grace can change the world. In fact, it already has.

> You never touch the ocean of God's love as
> when you forgive and love your enemies.
> —CORRIE TEN BOOM

How to Run

Let us throw off everything that hinders and the sin that so easily entangles, and let us run with perseverance the race marked out for us.
HEBREWS 12:1

In Word

Sometimes life is a breeze. More often, it feels like walking through mud. We're bombarded with setbacks, distractions, obstacles, and, unfortunately, even our own sin. Or perhaps *especially* our own sin. Though we know our ultimate destination as believers, we let a lot of other things hinder a life of faith. It isn't the simple endeavor we wish it could be. It gets pretty complicated, and we allow it.

The writer of Hebrews encourages us to look at people who lived by faith and endured numerous obstacles in the process—that's what all of chapter 11 is about—and now urges us to do as they did. We are reminded that a great cloud of witnesses has traveled this path before us, and many of those trailblazers of faith suffered great hardship or overcame enormous odds in their journey. There's no reason we can't do the same.

We need that reminder because in our trials and tribulations, we can get very introspective and turn to self-pity and a sense of futility. We feel insulated from the encouragement of the Spirit and other believers. When we add to that sense of isolation an acute awareness of our own sins, we're soon floundering in frustration. We feel stuck in the mud and far away from the life of faith we were called to live.

In Deed

God called us to run a race, to soar like eagles on the wind of His Spirit, to overcome the entanglements and weights that would conspire to hold us back. Faithlessness has no place in that kind of life. One of the prevailing truths of the Kingdom of God is that at any moment, we can have the kind of faith that overcomes. Though we feel trapped by circumstances and sin, we aren't. Our burdens are no match for our God. Faith sees the reality of that truth and allows us to keep running our race to the end.

My strength lies solely in my perseverance.
—LOUIS PASTEUR

All for Joy

Let us fix our eyes on Jesus, the author and perfecter of our faith, who for the joy set before him endured the cross.
HEBREWS 12:2

In Word

Many Christians have the perception that God's rescue mission for the human race was a reluctant venture. We blew it, so He resorted to plan B, at enormous expense, and did what He had to do to save us. His Son suffered excruciating agony to bring us into His Kingdom. He died for lowly, undeserving sinners like us because He had to.

But He didn't have to, and it wasn't a chore. It was a sacrifice, to be sure, but it wasn't a reluctant one. Though the night in Gethsemane was tearful and painful—no one wants to suffer unspeakable pain, after all—the Cross was a willing choice. Jesus didn't save unworthy sinners because He was obligated to do so. He did it for the joy set before Him.

Think of the great lengths a man deeply in love would go in order to win his beloved's heart. Whatever price he had to pay, however long he had to wait, whatever obstacles he had to overcome would not seem like a sacrifice. Why? Because of the inestimable worth of the prize. Love goes to any length to be fulfilled. The cost is irrelevant. Only the fulfillment matters.

In Deed

That's how Scripture describes the rescue mission Jesus went on to redeem humanity. It was—and still is—like a bridegroom seeking a bride. No cost is too high, no sacrifice too great, no wait too long. The joy in the end will be worth it.

This is the role model we are told to fix our eyes on. Because of His great love, Jesus became the author and perfecter of our faith. Just as He endured every obstacle and hindrance because of the joy set before Him, so can we. When we realize our ultimate destination, no cost seems too great. Whatever we face in life today, we can keep going because the goal is worth more than anything we will ever have to endure.

The principle of sacrifice is that we choose to do or suffer what apart from our love we should not choose to do or suffer.
—WILLIAM TEMPLE

Lord above All

He is the image of the invisible God.
COLOSSIANS 1:15

In Word

Romanus was a fourth-century Christian who was willingly tortured for his faith. Brutally beaten, hung naked from a tree, and gouged by iron hooks, he still confessed the honor and glory of Jesus. He declared that a young Christian in the crowd had more wisdom than any of the torturers, because the youth knew the true God. For his incessant preaching, even on the verge of death, Romanus's tongue was cut out. He died a faithful witness.

That doesn't happen much in America today. Maybe it does in parts of the world, but we rarely hear the details. We more often experience small moments of decision, those times when we are given a choice between Jesus and the ways of the world. For some of us, it would be easier to choose Jesus if our lives were at stake than it is to choose Him in daily decisions. But the choice is still required. In the little things and in the big things, day in and day out, we decide who will be Lord in our lives.

In a world of conflict, that's a crucial awareness to have. The spiritual war, however it manifests itself, compels us to ask ourselves a vital question: Whom will I serve? When we compare all the world's philosophies and religions, the trends and the movements, the political causes and the economic interests, one Lord should stand above the rest. Jesus is the image of the invisible God.

In Deed

We always pursue an image, whether we realize it or not—the image of a celebrity, the image of a fad, the image of a generation, or perhaps the image of a certain status. The world is full of choices, but God has given us the image that is to guide our lives. Jesus embodies God perfectly, and there is no one more worthy of our allegiance.

Think about your daily choices. When life is hard, when faith is weak, when relationships are tense, or when injustice comes, you have a choice. You can believe what Jesus says about hope and heaven, the fruit of His Spirit, and the glory to come; or you can measure your experiences and base your decisions on lesser promises. The choice should be clear. The image of the invisible God is infinitely worthwhile.

Christ is either Lord of all or He is not Lord at all.
—HUDSON TAYLOR

Lord behind All

God was pleased to have all his fullness dwell in him,
and through him to reconcile to himself all things.
COLOSSIANS 1:19-20

In Word

God was pleased. That's an intriguing verse, if we think about it. The infinite God, who lacks nothing and satisfies Himself in His own person and in His creation, was notably pleased to dwell in Jesus. The Ancient of Days, who has never had a problem with contentment, took special pleasure in the Incarnation. It wasn't a whim, it wasn't a chore, and it wasn't a mild interest. It was a passion.

When we understand that God takes pleasure in saving the world, we approach life with a much deeper perspective. Our struggles seem less exhausting, our trials seem more tolerable, and our obsessions become subordinate to a greater purpose. Like parents who rejoice in a child's growing pains—not for the pain they cause, but for the maturity they signal—God rejoices in the process that is bringing us into full maturity in Christ. He knows the end result, and it is glorious. A joyful God is much easier to embrace as Lord than a reluctant God. When we get a taste of His values regarding our struggles, we can live through them more zealously. We may even enjoy wondering how they will be used for eternal gain.

In Deed

Immerse yourself in the pleasure of God. Meditate on the passion with which He redeemed us. He was pleased in the Incarnation. He didn't enjoy the Cross, but He was excited about its result. Jesus endured the Cross for the joy that was set before Him (Hebrews 12:2). He doesn't just tolerate the new creation; He delights in it. God looks at this broken world, in all of its problems and pain, and is enthusiastic about what's coming. He knows what He has in store for us.

You'll find that bathing in the pleasure of God—really understanding the beauty and joy behind His redemptive work—will rub off on you. You will begin to experience the same joy. You'll see hardships from an eternal perspective, and you'll soon discover a strange sensation: not only does God take pleasure in His difficult work, so do you.

> It pleases the Father that all fullness should be in Christ;
> therefore, there is nothing but emptiness anywhere else.
> —WILLIAM GADSBY

Lord before All

He is before all things.
COLOSSIANS 1:17

In Word

The rhythm of Scripture is steady. Cain and Abel were taught to give their first portions to God. Abraham was taught to honor God above all things, even his son. The Israelites were taught to keep the law first and foremost on their lips and in their lives. The first day of the feasts were sacred, the firstfruits of the harvest were offered up, and the first sons were set apart. In everything, God came first.

When we get to the New Testament, we find that Jesus comes first. Those who say that the Bible never claims deity for Jesus have missed the not-so-subtle implications of scriptural reverence for Him. Colossians spells it out in this passage: Jesus "is before all things." That has two meanings: He was before all things chronologically, and He is before all things positionally. Either way, He is clearly preeminent in all of existence, and He is clearly to be preeminent in our lives.

In Deed

Take comfort in that. The news of His rightful lordship in our lives is not the hard news we make it out to be. We often hear the word Lord and cringe at the difficulties it implies. We want Him to be Lord in our hearts, but we know the pain of obedience and submission. Lord seems harsh and heavy.

It isn't. Yes, obedience can be difficult, and we inevitably fall short of its demands. But that's only when we focus on ourselves. When we focus on the Son of God who didn't even withhold His own life from us, we realize that the preeminence of Jesus benefits us. It means that the greatest power in the universe is on our side.

Think through that today. In each difficult situation you face, consider what it's like to have the All-powerful on your side. Let your heart be filled with faith in the One who is before all things. And be glad that He is.

> The world appears very little to a soul that contemplates the greatness of God.
> —BROTHER LAWRENCE

Lord over All

. . . so that in everything he might have the supremacy.
COLOSSIANS 1:18

In Word

Groups of Chinese students regularly leave their homeland on a march to Jerusalem. Why? Because the route goes through strongholds of every major religion in the world, and the students' passion for telling the story of Jesus is strong. They know that many of them will die from persecution along the way. They know that they aren't allowed to turn back, even if their family members need them. Regardless of health and hardship, they will continue until they reach Jerusalem or die. In their lives, Christ is supreme.

Most of us won't be called to go on such extreme adventures of faith, but we must still wrestle with the reality of Jesus' supremacy. Is He first only in our thinking and our beliefs? Or is He first in our lifestyles? There's a difference. Intellectual faith in the deity of Jesus requires little risk. Lifestyle faith in the deity of Jesus requires everything.

Our spiritual opposition knows that too. Satan and his forces will do whatever they can to keep our faith in our minds and out of our lives. They can exploit a deficient lifestyle easily. What we think is not nearly as strategic to them as what we actually do.

In Deed

In which areas of your life does Jesus have the supremacy? In which areas does He not? Once you've answered those questions, you'll notice an interesting correlation: the areas in which you have not submitted to Jesus as Lord are the areas most easily exploited. They aren't just sins; they are platforms for the powers of darkness to rest on.

Let Jesus reign supreme in your life—not just because He wants to, but because you want Him to. Realize that His lordship is in your best interests. No one ever lost out in submitting to God, not in any real terms of value and eternity. In a moment of crisis, the question of whom we serve has a powerful answer: we serve the supreme Lord of all.

The devil fears a soul united to God as he does God Himself.
—JOHN OF THE CROSS

Lord for All

All things were created by him and for him.
COLOSSIANS 1:16

In Word

There are people who hate Christianity and Christians, spewing bitter insults at all who claim Jesus' name. But they were created by Jesus for Himself. There are wicked thieves and murderers who will crush a life easier than we swat a mosquito. But they were created by Jesus for Himself. There are slaves of all sorts of sexual perversities who would spit in God's face before obeying His plan. But they, too, were created by Jesus for Himself.

In fact, all things were created by Jesus for Himself. Sometimes we approach the spiritual war with anger and hatred, forgetting that the battle is for the glory of God and that flesh and blood are not the warriors. And sometimes we just let it slide. Evil can have its way in its own corners of the world, as long as it doesn't invade our neighborhoods. All the while, God would point us to one unarguable fact: those who commit evil in this world and war against the faith are those who were created by Jesus for Himself.

This means that whenever we approach the victims or the aggressors of this war casually, we are treating as profane people whom Jesus created for Himself. Whenever we respond to attacks or injustices with hatred toward the human agents involved, we are rejecting a work that Jesus intends for His own purposes—and we are rejecting any part He might have planned for us in their redemption. We are treating sacred objects profanely.

In Deed

Approach your world as the potentially sacred environment that it is. Be bold and firm against evil, but do not hate its representatives. They were designed for a purpose, and for all we know, they will be redeemed before the last day. When our plans for people don't match God's, we need to make an adjustment, and sometimes the adjustment will be huge; His plans are often beyond our imagination. The important thing to remember in all of our encounters in this world is this: everyone we meet was created by Jesus for Himself.

Though our Savior's passion is over, His compassion is not.
—WILLIAM PENN

What Really Counts

What counts is a new creation.
GALATIANS 6:15

In Word

Pressure. No one likes it; everyone feels it. It can come from deadlines, society at large, TV commercials, or people very close to us. One of the enemy's most effective weapons is to pressure people to conform to something other than the image of Christ. That kind of oppression seeks to manipulate people when the stakes are ultimate. No Christian really wants to compromise his or her convictions.

That's what was happening in the church in Galatia. Paul had taught his church one thing, and false teachers were infiltrating, using high-pressure tactics to push another message. Paul's letter is an example of a bold stance in the face of spiritual opposition.

The issues we face are not exactly the same as in first-century Galatia, but the principles are the same. Not only do Christians face contempt from outside the church, we face pressure from others within the faith who diverge from the gospel in one sense or another. As God breathes His will and His plan into the church, those who aren't sensitive to the Spirit aren't able to focus on the new creation. They often miss what counts.

Last week's readings asked a question of those in crisis-of-faith situations: "Whom will you serve?" This week's readings ask a slightly different question: "Whom will you love?" Service and love should always go hand in hand, but in fallen human beings, they often don't. Galatians 6 teaches us how early believers handled internal opposition. Paul pointed them back to their first love and the true gospel of salvation.

In Deed

"What counts is a new creation." That's where our focus should be. The new life is about a radical rebirth into love and faith. When the Spirit has done a new work, we don't love Him by falling back on the old one, at least as we perceive it. We love Him by following His lead confidently and boldly. The key to handling pressure is to always remember what really counts—in God's eyes.

> Christianity is not a system of doctrine but a new creature.
> —JOHN NEWTON

Blessed by Grace

Peace and mercy to all who follow this rule.
GALATIANS 6:16

In Word

We understand the plan of salvation. Jesus died on a cross to pay the penalty for our sins, and whoever believes in Him is forgiven and blessed with the privilege of being resurrected with Him for eternity. We've heard more times than we can count the basis of this salvation: it comes to us by grace through faith alone. As believers in Jesus, we hold the doctrine of the new birth firmly in our minds.

The distortions of the gospel are many and varied, however, and history is full of counterfeits. Some of those counterfeits prosper even within the church. The new life is lived against opposition from our internal sinful nature and the powers of darkness in this world, but it is also lived in the context of shifting beliefs and variations away from God's theme. Wherever we face attacks, whether in the mundane details of life or in the life-or-death struggle against the enemy of God, there's a blessing we need to grasp tightly: "Peace and mercy to all who follow this rule."

What rule is Paul writing about? Living as new creatures deeply changed from within. Pressure to modify the gospel is a constraint placed around us; God's truth is birthed deep inside us. The Christian who can tell the difference—and live by it—is blessed.

In Deed

This benediction from Paul expresses God's grace to those who come to Him on the basis of His truth, regardless of the attacks they are facing. Pressure from those who oppose us spiritually is completely undermined by a firm grip on the truth of the gospel of grace.

In the heat of the spiritual war, peace and mercy are two of the sweetest words we could hear. Peace is promised to those who cling to grace, even when the battle rages, and mercy won't let us lose. The rule of the new creation wins the war. The God of peace and mercy guarantees it.

They travel lightly whom God's grace carries.
—THOMAS À KEMPIS

Dying to Live

*May I never boast except in the cross of our
Lord Jesus Christ, through which the world has
been crucified to me, and I to the world.*
GALATIANS 6:14

In Word

There is one war strategy that will force the enemy to lay down his arms. No, it isn't an all-out assault. It isn't even a nuclear attack. Any aggression, no matter how forceful, may lead to an aggressive counterattack. The only strategy that is exclusively up to us and guarantees that the enemy will stop fighting is death. Not his. Ours.

Military tacticians don't normally advocate this approach. Apart from desperate suicides like those at Masada, few people end the fighting by taking their own lives. But in the new creation, we have that option. We are crucified with Christ, and the world has no hold on us. If we really believe this—if we really live this way—what territory is left for the enemy to invade?

Think about the ways you feel attacked in the spiritual war: your health, your relationships, your work, your dreams and desires, your emotional stability—you know your vulnerabilities. What if those areas were completely surrendered to God? What if you were already dead to the possibility of losing the things that are important to you, as long as you don't lose what is most important to you? What if your security and identity were not wrapped up in the props around you, and you could just submit them all to the glory of God?

Armies that destroy their own airfields and production facilities before the enemy arrives have left very little for the enemy to attack. In worldly military strategy, such actions signal retreat. In the spiritual war, this is the key to victory.

In Deed

Again, it all comes down to one question: Whom do you love? If you love the things that are prone to enemy attack—whether from outside or within the community of faith—you will spend a lot of energy fighting for those things. But if you love the King Himself above all other loves, the rest is extra. The enemy will only be able to exploit what matters least to you. Being crucified to the world and in love with God is an invincible combination.

> He is no fool who gives what he cannot
> keep to gain what he cannot lose.
> —JIM ELLIOT

Compulsive Superficiality

*Those who want to make a good impression outwardly
are trying to compel you to be circumcised.*
GALATIANS 6:12

In Word

Everyone wants to make a good impression. That's why we dress the way we do, shave or put makeup on, work our positive traits into our conversations, drop names, rub shoulders with the elite, speak authoritatively about topics we know little about, work our way up the ladder, or whatever else we can think of to make ourselves look better. For some people, making an impression defines their life.

For some people, making a good impression defines their faith. It's sad when that happens, but it often does. The church is full of posers, people who are there not for the love of God, but for the love of duty or influence. We've done a marvelous job over the centuries of making the one institution based on crucifixion and selflessness a place of power and status. All too often, we conform to the traditions of men instead of the image of Christ because men express their approval more immediately. And in embracing the trappings of the age, we lose the war of the ages.

In the spiritual battle, the enemy always tempts us to live Christian lives that are fueled by externals rather than by the indwelling Spirit. That enemy has influence over the externals. If he can get us to base our lives on them, he can keep us fruitless and frustrated. If not, he doesn't stand a chance.

In Deed

Many Galatians had fallen prey to the enemy's schemes. They were focused on the externals of the faith without getting the heart of it. They put pressure on others to approve of them. For those who desire to make a good impression, validation is critical.

How important is validation to you? Or more precisely, how important is human validation to you? We are to seek the pleasure of the only opinion that matters—and only His. Anything else spells defeat.

God is not deceived by externals.
—C. S. LEWIS

The Offensive Gospel

*The only reason they do this is to avoid being
persecuted for the cross of Christ.*
GALATIANS 6:12

In Word

The desire to avoid persecution is one of the most natural and understandable desires we have. We can be thankful that we don't live under the emperor Nero, who enjoyed tormenting Christians. But we do often feel pressure to keep our faith private and inoffensive. If we can dress it up as a time-honored tradition or a preference among many options, we can live comfortably in a politically correct world. But Christianity has never been about living comfortably, has it?

No, the Christian faith is about living for the glory of God in Christ, regardless of the consequences. That's the only way the world can see the difference between Jesus and religion. For some, the world's understanding comes at too great a cost; for others, there's no cost too great.

Our enemy doesn't mind Christianity when there's no cross in it. He inspires a world that places expectations on us to modify our faith to make it as palatable as possible. But Jesus said He would be a stumbling block; we have no right to compromise Him. We should remove all offensiveness from ourselves, but if we take the offensiveness out of the gospel, we don't have the gospel.

In Deed

The enemy's tactics are subtle. He tries to water down the truth. He tempts us to love Christianity rather than Christ. He turns us against one another over details so we will divide over the basics. And when it comes to pressure, he hopes we will not cling to our love. Satan loves a conformist to anything other than the image of Christ.

Don't conform to anything or anyone but Jesus. Don't cross the line from being a Christian in the world to being a Christian of the world. Ask yourself daily: whom do I love most? Invest your love in Jesus, then follow Him zealously. Even when it costs.

Persecution for righteousness' sake is what
every child of God must expect.
—CHARLES SIMEON

Increased Authority

To him who overcomes and does my will to the
end, I will give authority over the nations.
REVELATION 2:26

In Word

Jesus has told the church at Thyatira that they will learn that He is the One who searches hearts and minds. He does not let the evil in their midst run rampant. Those abuses that have been hidden will be exposed. He is zealous about purifying His people.

Because of His zeal for His church, Christ will reward those who overcome the evil among them and who continue to follow His will to the end. How? He will give them authority over the peoples of the world. And though the promise seems to be particularly relevant to the new earth of Jesus' reign, it highlights a spiritual principle in operation even now. Those who remain in the will of God and overcome the assaults against their faith are given expanded roles in His Kingdom. Greater faithfulness results in greater influence.

Jesus made that principle clear in His parable of the talents. Those who responsibly handled what they had been given found themselves with greater gifts to manage. They had proven themselves worthy of increase. "Everyone who has will be given more, and he will have an abundance. Whoever does not have, even what he has will be taken from him" (Matthew 25:29). Not only does it apply to churches like Thyatira in Revelation, it applies to our churches and to us as individuals today. If we want greater spiritual influence, we need to handle responsibly what we've already been given.

In Deed

If you are seeking more from God, consider how well you have managed your current responsibilities and gifts. If you are overcoming the world's assaults on your faith and running the race with perseverance, you can trust the Lord to increase both your privileges and responsibilities in His Kingdom in due time. He honors those who have been faithful, especially when their faithfulness has come in the face of opposition, temptations, and hardships. You will be raised up to higher levels of influence. Ultimately you, along with other believers, will rule nations with Him.

> People trust good stewards with larger and
> larger sums, and so it is with the Lord.
> —CHARLES SPURGEON

Staying Alive

Remember, therefore, what you have received
and heard; obey it, and repent.
REVELATION 3:3

In Word

The community of Christians at Sardis received an alarming assessment from the Lord. They had a reputation for being alive, but they were dead (v. 1). What gave them this reputation? Was it their enthusiasm? their busyness? their seeming effectiveness in ministry? Regardless, this verdict should be just as alarming to us as it was to them. It's entirely possible for us to appear lively—busy, enthusiastic, even "on fire" for the Lord—and still not be operating from the life of Jesus within us.

Plenty of churches and Christians mistake their own zeal for the power of the Holy Spirit. While it's true that the Spirit will often produce zeal, that doesn't mean that all zeal comes from the Spirit. Paul wrote that Jewish leaders had a zeal for God, but "not based on knowledge" (Romans 10:2). Likewise, many mistake religious activity for the Spirit, but while the Spirit prompts us to be active, a lot of activity doesn't spring from Him. The church at Ephesus learned that in its message from Jesus; they were commended for hard work and perseverance but rebuked for losing their first love (Revelation 2:2-4). What we consider "alive," Jesus often calls "dead." Only the life that comes from the Spirit Himself is truly alive.

What's the remedy when Jesus calls us dead? Go back to the beginning. Remember how we were saved—by grace through faith. Return to "Christ in you, the hope of glory" (Colossians 1:27). The Christian life is not religious activity or even truly serving Jesus in the strength of the flesh. It is Jesus working out His life in us and through us. That's the message that we received and heard. That's the truth we obey.

In Deed

Never mistake zeal and activity as the essence of life in the Spirit. Those are His by-products, not His substance. Too many believers try to manufacture evidence of being alive when they aren't functioning in the Spirit, and the result is eventually frustration and burnout. Remember that you aren't simply trying to live for Christ; He is actually living in you. Return to that truth daily.

The Spirit of God is given to the true saints . . . as a
divine supernatural spring of life and action.
—JONATHAN EDWARDS

No Surprise

Dear friends, do not be surprised at the painful trial you are suffering, as though something strange were happening to you.
1 PETER 4:12

In Word

Peter wrote to a group of people who were being persecuted for their faith, but his words of wisdom apply to believers going through any kind of crisis. We know this because he tells his readers that they are participating in the sufferings of Christ (v. 13), who suffered more than the Cross—including temptation, grief, hunger, and more. We often use this passage for faith-related suffering exclusively. But for people whose faith is their life, everything is faith related. When we hurt, we should not be surprised.

Jesus walked through a fallen world, and so do we. His paths led Him through minefields of sin, temptation, pain, ridicule, abandonment, doubt, and rejection, and so do ours. He encountered the tendencies of His own human flesh, He encountered the world's twisted systems of values and beliefs, and He encountered the enemy. So do we.

Even with a long track record of trials and tribulations in this world, we still manage to be surprised when we have them, as though we expected them to gradually fade away as life progresses. But no disciple of Jesus ever experienced such a trend. In fact, most of them experienced the opposite.

In Deed

That may not sound very comforting on the surface, but it does help to know that difficulties are normal. They do not necessarily indicate that we have fallen out of favor with God or are suffering the consequences of our own sin (although we need to ask God if either is the case). Even a life lived perfectly will encounter extreme opposition and hardship. Jesus proved that, and He called us to follow the same path.

The beautiful truth behind this calling is that we can overcome suffering as Jesus did. We live deeper than it can reach. The normal Christian life may be a painful one, but it is also a victorious one. And one day, the victory will end the pain.

> A Christian is someone who shares the sufferings of God in the world.
> —DIETRICH BONHOEFFER

Blessed Rejection

*If you are insulted because of the name of Christ, you are
blessed, for the Spirit of glory and of God rests on you.*
1 PETER 4:14

In Word

No one likes rejection. It's one of our worst fears. Nearly everyone can tell a story of
being rejected early in life by peers or parents, and the wounds are still deep. Many of
us never get over them. In fact, we spend much of our lives trying to avoid rejection
altogether.

That avoidance can lead to three extremes: (1) trying to please everyone all the
time; (2) trying to control other people to keep them in our circles of communication; or (3) forming a habit of rejecting people before they have a chance to reject
us. And if you look at all three of those tendencies carefully, you'll notice a common
spiritual denominator: none of them are acceptable for a Christian.

Look at Jesus. He didn't try to please everyone, He didn't dominate, and He didn't
reject others. Then He taught His disciples to follow His lead. They were to bear the
brunt of humanity's rejection of God, but never to reject others. They had to learn to
take the abuse without dishing it out. They had to learn the blessing of being rejected
by human beings and accepted by God.

In Deed

The only way for us to do that is to find our identity and our security completely in
God. The Father loves us unconditionally, the Son died because of His love for us,
and the Spirit birthed us with His own spiritual DNA—and He continues to live in
us and sustain us. With all of that to our name, what possible concern could we have
about the rejection of others? What does the child of a King suffer when citizens of
an enemy kingdom taunt him or her? We have nothing to lose and everything to gain
if we are rejected by those outside the gospel. There is nothing they can do to destroy
our identity.

Remember that when you think about past rejections or current affronts. The
people who caused them were deceived, or at least unaware. They need to know the
King—the King who accepts you forever and without reservation.

> Christianity is about acceptance, and if God accepts
> me as I am, then I had better do the same.
> —HUGH MONTEFIORE

Rational Joy

Rejoice that you participate in the sufferings of Christ, so that you may be overjoyed when his glory is revealed.
1 PETER 4:13

In Word

Skeptics throughout history have considered verses like this one to be clear evidence that Christianity is rooted in insanity. They don't say it quite like that, but human nature has very little interest in a faith that includes joyful self-denial and hardship. Our beliefs don't seem rational to those who think the here and now is all there is, or who think God's love equals comfort. When we rejoice because of what our sufferings mean, we look crazy.

That's okay. Nowhere does the Bible tell us to appear respectable to all people. In fact, Jesus thanked God for making the gospel evident to the simple and obscure to the wise (Luke 10:21), and Paul said we were the "foolish" in this world (1 Corinthians 1:27). We can go through our battles confidently and even joyfully because we know the outcome. We understand what it means to follow a Lord who suffered.

Jesus faced all those battles, too, so we can see what it means to have joy in them. It doesn't mean that every trial is pleasant. Jesus wasn't having much fun in the garden of Gethsemane the night before His crucifixion, or especially during the crucifixion itself. He was, however, focused on the joy that His trials would lead to (Hebrews 12:2).

Jesus won every battle He ever faced. On the surface, it doesn't seem so. It looks like He lost on several occasions, most notably on a hill outside of Jerusalem. But appearances can be deceiving, can't they? Reality doesn't always come to the surface.

In Deed

That's the lens through which we should look at our trials. Appearances are deceiving. What seems to be defeat is often the path to victory—especially when God is involved. If that were not true, Jesus could never have told His disciples to rejoice when they were persecuted, and Peter could never have repeated the command in verse 13. Rejoicing is a viable option for a hurting believer. And in the end, it will prove entirely rational.

In shunning a trial, we are seeking to avoid a blessing.
—CHARLES SPURGEON

Bearing the Name

*If you suffer as a Christian, do not be ashamed,
but praise God that you bear that name.*
1 PETER 4:16

In Word

Bearing the name of Jesus is a powerful concept. It means not that we simply believe in Jesus, that He is a part of our lives, or that He is an obligation we must live up to. It means that He is our life and that we find our identity in Him. It means that our identity and His merge into one, and that when He suffers, we suffer.

Paul had this concept down. He considered his heritage, his accomplishments, and his entire pedigree a pile of rubbish compared to his simple identity in Jesus. He even desired—not tolerated, but desired—to share in Jesus' sufferings and to be like Him in death (Philippians 3:10). Why? Because he couldn't mentally separate Jesus' resurrection and power from His suffering. To embrace Jesus meant to embrace all of Him—even His pain.

When we are consumed with a desire to be like Jesus, we cease to be picky believers who want a little patience, a little love, and a lot of forgiveness. We want all the fruits of His Spirit, even the ones that cost a lot, because in becoming like Jesus, the costs never exceed the benefits. No one has ever become Christlike and then said, "You know, I think that was too hard. I wish I had never started down this path." It just doesn't happen. No matter how much hardship we face, it is always worthwhile.

In Deed

We know what Jesus' pain led to: resurrection, ascension, an eternal seat next to the Father, and glory fulfilled. Do we not realize that our pain leads to the same thing? It comes in different forms and it seems so pointless sometimes, but there is a final product that we should be jumping up and down to embrace.

Jump up and down today. Maybe not literally (though you can if you want), but at least in spirit. The Bible repeatedly tells us not to tolerate our trials but to rejoice in them, with real joy. Be a person who understands what this difficult life leads to. Bear the name of Jesus gladly—and all it entails.

He that rides to be crowned will not think much of a rainy day.
—JOHN TRAPP

Eternity in Your Eyes

Those who suffer according to God's will should commit themselves to their faithful Creator and continue to do good.
1 PETER 4:19

In Word

Some Christians say that it is never God's will that we suffer. Others say that anytime we suffer, it must have been God's will. Somewhere between those two extremes is a biblical perspective: sometimes when we are living faithfully and obediently, God brings suffering into our lives through the hands of others.

Why? We know the standard answers. It's to conform us to His image; it's to keep us humble, as He did with Paul's thorn in the flesh; it's to force us to depend on Him; it's to work out His will in our lives in mysterious ways; it's to help us identify with our Lord. All of those are valid, biblical answers, but they aren't the only ones. Sometimes God brings suffering into our lives to show us—and the world around us—what an eternal perspective looks like.

We have to know that kind of perspective. A here-and-now perspective doesn't do anything to demonstrate the Kingdom of God. It doesn't point to anything that a nonbeliever doesn't already know. Worldly understandings are common in this world; eternal ones are not. God wants us to display the right perspective. Suffering gives us the stage to do it on.

In Deed

Suffering should bring this out in us, but we don't always let it. We turn inward, asking God why this is happening to us, why He is letting us go through this situation, how He will deliver us, or sustain us, or change us. We assume that our suffering is entirely about our own lives—individualists do that—and we rarely realize that our suffering is for the world. It's for others to see our response, to get a glimpse of an eternal perspective, and to notice what peace the Father can give. We aren't forbidden to grieve or ask questions, but we are forbidden to become completely self-absorbed.

If you are going through a hard time, try to avoid too much introspection. Look at what God might do through your situation for others. Let the world see eternity in your eyes.

> No man is fit to comprehend heavenly things who has not resigned himself to suffer adversities for Christ.
> —THOMAS À KEMPIS

Open Doors

*See, I have placed before you an open
door that no one can shut.*
REVELATION 3:8

In Word

Jesus had both encouragements and rebukes for most of the congregations He
addressed in Revelation, but not for Philadelphia. There are no rebukes for these
persevering, faithful believers. Jesus promises to make their enemies fall at their feet
and acknowledge that He has loved them (v. 9). Because they have already passed
so many tests, He will keep them from the trial that is coming upon the whole earth
(v. 10). Those among them who overcome will be made pillars in the eternal temple
of God (v. 12). And because He has seen their works and faithfulness, He has placed
before them an open door that can't be shut.

It's a promise we all long for. We love open doors of opportunity, but we know
that most opportunities in life have an expiration date. They are "limited time only."
So if God places before us an open door—*and* assures us that no one can shut it—we
feel invincible. All we have to do is recognize the door and walk through it. Few promises could encourage us more than that.

It's important to notice the kind of believers to whom Jesus gave this offer. They
are people who have little strength but have held on anyway; they have not denied
Jesus' name in spite of intense opposition; and they have kept His Word (v. 8). These
are not believers who have simply asked for an open door. They aren't demanding
greater opportunity. They are exemplary in their faithful endurance. They are true
servants of God.

In Deed

As you seek God for open doors, ask yourself if you are the kind of believer whom
God can trust with them. Have you proven your endurance? held on to His Word
despite intense opposition? demonstrated faithfulness with the opportunities He has
already given? If so, you are the kind of person for whom God is glad to open more
doors. Expect Him to. And when you see them, walk through them with the same
faithfulness you have already shown.

Faithfulness in little things is a big thing.
—JOHN CHRYSOSTOM

Love and Discipline

Those whom I love I rebuke and discipline.
So be earnest, and repent.
REVELATION 3:19

In Word

The Lord has no harsh words for the church at Philadelphia, but now that He is speaking to the Laodiceans, His tone has changed. He has no compliments for them, no affirmation of their faith and works. No, their lukewarmness repulses Him; their self-satisfaction is unfounded. They are complacent and far too content with the status quo. They are on very dangerous ground.

But Jesus still encourages them. He reminds them that His harsh words of correction come only to those He loves. He would not discipline them if they were too far gone. God's message to the church is that of a Father to His children, not of a Judge to the guilty. He is not putting them away; He is giving them an opportunity to repent.

But that isn't the only encouragement Jesus has for them. There are profound benefits to repentance. Jesus is standing at the door and knocking, imploring the church to open its fellowship to Him. And if they do, He will come in and eat with them. He will meet them in their meals—in the Lord's Supper when they worship, as well as at the table of their individual hearts. If they will respond to His rebuke and discipline humbly and maturely, they will reap unfathomable blessings. If they don't . . . well, who wouldn't? Fellowship with Jesus is what being a Christian is all about.

In Deed

Nobody likes being rebuked. We shy away from the Lord's discipline. But all of God's children need chastening at times. The distinguishing mark of those who go on into greater maturity is how they respond to His correction. The common denominator of those who remain stagnant is their insensitivity to His discipline.

It's impossible to grow spiritually without humility. Listen to the Lord, even when it hurts. Respond to whatever He says, even when it's hard. The fact that He is still speaking is confirmation of His love and your relationship with Him. And the rewards will be greater than you can imagine.

> When God chastens His children, He does not
> punish as a judge does but chastens as a father.
> —CHARLES SPURGEON

The Great Contest

*Remember those earlier days after you had
received the light, when you stood your ground
in a great contest in the face of suffering.*
HEBREWS 10:32

In Word

"A great contest." The writer of Hebrews had seen a lot of suffering: persecution, humiliation, injustice, and death. He had even seen people walk away from their faith in Jesus, simply because they couldn't take the heat anymore. His sympathies might have led him to say, "You've been through a lot. God understands when you need to back off a little." But his convictions and the Spirit within him wouldn't take such an angle. He called his readers to remember and to stand their ground.

Perseverance is an unwelcome word in many of our situations. By and large, we aren't a persevering people. Drive-through windows, ATMs, and microwaves haven't taught us to be very patient. When we're in trouble, we want out. Soon.

God calls us deeper in. He wants us to look at the big picture: where we came from (dead and lost); how He saved us (by blood and grace); and where we're going (Kingdom and glory). In light of all that, a sacrificial life isn't that demanding. Our life span is but a tiny, tiny window in the vista of eternity. If that window fogs up—even if it gets shattered—eternity remains the same. Whatever we have to persevere through, in the grand scheme of things, won't last very long.

In Deed

Life is a great contest, and the stakes are really high. But we don't see athletes give up when their strength is fading and the game is on the line. We don't see runners slack off toward the end of the race to catch their breath. We don't see women decide in the twelfth hour of labor that the product isn't worth the process. We know what it means to endure.

Our problem is that we see perseverance as a mountain and our reward as a molehill. We need corrective lenses that will make the reward seem monumental and the perseverance seem minimal. In God's eyes they are. The great contest is already won.

> When a train goes through a tunnel and it gets
> dark, you don't throw away your ticket and jump
> off. You sit still and trust the engineer.
> —CORRIE TEN BOOM

The Great Reward

My righteous one will live by faith. And if he
shrinks back, I will not be pleased with him.
HEBREWS 10:38

In Word

The quote is from Habakkuk 2. Paul used it in Romans 1 to indicate how sinners are justified. Here, the writer of Hebrews uses it to launch into his famous passage on faith. For centuries, Christians have treasured Hebrews 11 because of its implications for our trust and hopefulness. In isolation, it can be rightfully applied to all sorts of situations. But it wasn't written in isolation; it was written in the context of Christians under fire.

It sounds harsh, doesn't it? Here these Jewish Christians are being beaten and bullied for trusting in the Messiah, and the writer urges them not to shrink back because God "will not be pleased." That in itself could come across as intimidation, except for one wonderful fact: this passage isn't just about God being displeased with shrinking faith; it's also about God being delighted with persevering faith. Behind the prohibition is an amazing blessing. Those who believe until the end will enjoy all the treasures of God.

In Deed

What kind of faith do you have in a hardship? The issue really isn't how disappointed God will be if you fail (although He will be, because He cares). The issue is how much you'll miss if you don't persevere. God wants us to remain steady because He knows what joys He will trust us with when we do. He wants us to persevere, not for our pain, but for our ultimate pleasure.

The kind of faith that is birthed in us is an enduring faith. It has to be—it comes from God. It doesn't fade away easily, even when people or circumstances rail against it. It enjoys the highs of discipleship, and it plows through the lows. It is focused on two things: the Rewarder and the reward.

Faith is the sight of the inward eye.
—ALEXANDER MACLAREN

The Great Revision

You sympathized with those in prison and joyfully accepted the confiscation of your property, because you knew that you yourselves had better and lasting possessions.
HEBREWS 10:34

In Word

A scene in *Doctor Zhivago* shows the main character coming home from war to his rather large house in Moscow. But his rather large house has been filled with several families, because as a communist official tells him, it was too large for just one family. "Wasted space." Despite the fact that his family now occupies only a corner of the house—once his own possession—he nods his head casually and responds that the new arrangement is certainly more efficient. It wasn't that he agreed with communist redistribution of property. He just had a higher agenda—like seeing his family after a long absence.

Though a thoroughly secular movie, it gives us a taste of the dynamic Hebrews refers to in this verse. If we find that we've been slighted, or even that the enemy is trying to steal our lives away, we can nod and get on to greater things—like the "better and lasting possessions" we have. It all depends on what's at the top of our agenda.

In Deed

Reassessing our values requires an enormous revision. We stop trying to fulfill ourselves with people, possessions, or positions, and place all our emotional investments in a more enduring account. While those who are steeped in the ways of the world run around after this toy and that property, acquiring and consuming because they can't find fulfillment anywhere else, we can stand back and let them. Why? Because we know that kind of life will never lead to fulfillment. At the end, such a lifestyle is comparable to a dog chasing his tail or a donkey driven by a carrot dangled a foot in front of him. It's an endless chase that never satisfies.

Our chase is satisfied. We can sympathize with those in prison and joyfully—yes, joyfully—accept the confiscation of our property (or rights, or dreams, or whatever) because we know a secret. We have better and lasting possessions.

Desire only God, and your heart will be satisfied.
— AUGUSTINE

The Great Promise

Do not throw away your confidence; it will be richly rewarded.
You need to persevere so that when you have done the
will of God, you will receive what he has promised.
HEBREWS 10:35-36

In Word

In *Charlie and the Chocolate Factory*, the young hero is one of five fortunate children to tour an enigmatic candy maker's well-guarded factory. But there are many temptations on this tour, and all of the children except Charlie fall prey to them. For his unwavering commitment to both the rules and the wonder of the factory, Charlie is rewarded in the end with a prize that far exceeds his expectations. He receives what was promised—and then some.

That's a pretty good parable of the Christian life. On our tour through this world, we are promised great things for following our Leader well. Along the way, comrades may fall one way or another to an endless array of temptations. But there are extraordinary promises for those who persevere. If we don't throw away our confidence, it will be richly rewarded.

A lot of Christians are uncomfortable with the thought of rewards, but the Bible mentions them often. Jesus Himself told His disciples on several occasions, "Great will be your reward." God would not have promised them if He didn't want us to think about them. Sometimes thinking about them is the only thing that helps us hang on.

In Deed

Don't be afraid to think about the promises and rewards of the Kingdom. God revealed them to us for a reason. He doesn't want us to be self-absorbed about them, but He does want us to persevere with hope. We need to have perspective, and the promises give it to us.

Practically, how can you apply hope to your life? Memorize the promises and review them often; stop listening to the lies in your head about how desperate your situation is; or share hope with those around you. Be creative. Let hope be "room temperature" for you, and persevering will become a lot easier.

> God's promises are like the stars; the darker
> the night, the brighter they shine.
> —DAVID NICHOLAS

The Great Divide

*We are not of those who shrink back and are
destroyed, but of those who believe and are saved.*
HEBREWS 10:39

In Word

Hebrews has some terrifying verses in it. This is one of them. Those who shrink back
are destroyed. Those who believe are saved. There is no in-between.

After thanking God that we are in the believing category, it soon becomes painfully alarming to us that we know plenty of people who are not. We who count on
the promises of God cannot be content to keep them to ourselves. That would be
like dining at a never-ending, everyone's-invited buffet, but keeping it a secret from
starving people lingering around us. There's a word for those who are content to be
well fed while those around them starve: selfish.

The Christian life is anything but selfish. The Father who went to great lengths
to save us isn't selfish. The Son who commanded His disciples to go into the world
with the gospel isn't selfish. The Holy Spirit who lives within us isn't selfish. God
didn't hand us the ball for us to drop it. He wants us to run with it. He has a plan—a
very unselfish plan.

In Deed

Take time regularly to measure your participation in God's plan. Take an inventory of
your attitudes and actions. Does the great divide between those headed for destruc-
tion and those headed for redemption get under your skin? Or have you grown numb
to the reality? Do you pray for, give to, and pursue lost people persistently? Or are they
an afterthought? In other words, do you share your food?

The gospel is about sharing. Always has been, always will be. There's nothing in
Scripture about embracing all of the gospel except the missions part. No, the gospel
is a package deal, and evangelism is in the package. We may not be gifted in the same
ways, but we're all called to participate in the mission zealously. It's important to God
because of the terrifying divide we read about, and if it's important to God, it has to
be important to those who love Him. Love compels us to do something about the
divide—to share our food.

> Evangelism is one beggar telling another
> beggar where to get bread.
> —D. T. NILES

Pure Gold

The testing of your faith develops perseverance.
JAMES 1:3

In Word

Faith is the currency of God's Kingdom. It's the precious commodity through which we receive salvation by grace, fellowship with God, answers to prayer, and more. Throughout Scripture, we are urged to have faith and to persevere in it. And according to Hebrews 11:6, it's impossible to please God without it.

But faith is like a precious metal—it comes in varying degrees of purity. It is valuable in any form, but God's desire is for the purest gold. It's true that we can move mountains with faith the size of a mustard seed (Matthew 17:20), but size isn't the only issue. Our faith, no matter how small, has to be undiluted and uncorrupted with doubts and fears. It needs to be the real thing.

The only way for our faith to get from its raw state to refined beauty is for it to be tested. Like a precious metal in a crucible, the impurities must be burned with fire. It's a painful process—our faith gets reshaped in the harsh treatment—but it's worth it. Once circumstances, trials, the enemy's lies, and our own doubts are through assaulting it, whatever remains is precious and pure. That's the kind of faith that God loves to see in His people. He showers His power and love on those who truly and purely believe.

In Deed

That's why the Bible places so much emphasis on persevering. James is very clear about the results: perseverance brings us into maturity and causes us to lack nothing (v. 4). We don't just endure the trials of faith for the sake of enduring; we keep going because we are in a process of refinement. The trials we face are producing in us a precious quality fit for eternity.

Don't rebel against the process. No one relishes trials, but James tells us to rejoice in them anyway (v. 2). Why? Because of what they do for us. They fit us for the Kingdom. They purify our faith and make it powerfully effective.

> The trials of the saint are a "divine pruning" by which he grows and brings forth abundant fruit.
> —CHARLES SPURGEON

Tossed

*He who doubts is like a wave of the sea,
blown and tossed by the wind.*
JAMES 1:6

In Word

In the storms of life, people without solid faith are at the mercy of the winds. They can't see where God is leading them because it takes faith to hear His voice and discern His will. They can't see how Jesus is protecting them because it takes faith to know that He is the Son of God and that His Spirit is real. They can't receive many answers to prayer because faith is usually a prerequisite to receiving. In the midst of a storm, that's a problem. There's nothing to do but be tossed.

James says that anyone who asks God for wisdom—or anything else, for that matter—must believe and not doubt. Why? Because God often responds to us according to how we see Him. Those who believe Him to be a hard Master often find Him so. Those who don't believe He heals will rarely see Him heal. Those who believe He is distant will rarely find Him close. And those who don't realize that He speaks will rarely hear His voice. If we want His wisdom, we have to believe we will receive it when we ask. Otherwise, we may not recognize it when He gives it. And we'll continue to drift aimlessly.

If faith is the currency of the Kingdom of God, doubt is economic instability. It undermines the primary means of communication between God and His people. While faith sets us up to receive God's blessings, to recognize that they came from Him, and to give Him thanks for them, doubt prods us to question whether a blessing was a divine gift or a mere coincidence. God interacts with us much more fluidly and openly when we are conscious of the interaction. Doubt wonders whether interaction with God is even a likely possibility.

In Deed

When you ask God for wisdom, direction, or any other need, refuse to doubt that He will answer. His desire is to meet with you, speak to you, and fellowship with you. Faith will be able to find Him doing so. It will keep you anchored in the worst of storms.

Believe your beliefs and doubt your doubts; do not make the mistake of doubting your beliefs and believing your doubts.
—CHARLES F. DEEMS

A Secret Wisdom

*We speak of God's secret wisdom, a wisdom
that has been hidden and that God destined
for our glory before time began.*
1 CORINTHIANS 2:7

In Word

It's a confusing world. We have seen how the believer can be bombarded with false teaching, blatant persecution, subtle deception, alluring temptations, and so much more. We are on a path that leads to the fullness of God's Kingdom, but the path takes us through well-disguised minefields. When we walk through this dangerous territory, we are assured of safety when we cling to the Word and the will of the Father. If we will but stay on the path, we will get to where we're going unharmed.

Staying on the path isn't as easy as it seems. That's why God has given us a Guide. When false teachers come at us with their persuasive words, we have a Spirit within us who can cut through them. If we are persecuted—or just beaten down by the world—the Spirit within us fills us with hope. When we are assaulted with almost imperceptible lies, the Spirit can expose them for us. And when the seductions of this age tempt us, He can turn our weakness into strength.

How? By revealing His secret wisdom, a wisdom that has been hidden for ages past and that the world considers foolishness. This wisdom was destined—planned out and zealously pursued—for our glory, even before time began. The Spirit in our hearts is not a happy accident. It is an intentional gift that God planned to give, even before we rebelled. Our treason against Him was figured into the plan. The secret depended on it.

In Deed

Do you realize how much God wants to guide you through this world? Learning His will is not akin to pulling divine teeth. We don't have to twist the strong arm of the Lord to get wisdom out of Him. It is in the pages of the Word, in the Spirit in our hearts, and in the sovereignty protecting us all. Yes, this war is intense. God's zeal for us is so much more intense. He is on our side, offering wisdom and glory.

> There is a deep wisdom inaccessible to the wise
> and prudent, but disclosed to babes.
> —CHRISTOPHER BRYANT

A Divine Revelation

God has revealed it to us by his Spirit.
1 CORINTHIANS 2:10

In Word

The world is fascinated with secret wisdom. From the Gnostics of antiquity to the guiding force of a galaxy far, far away, human religions and stories are filled with some-one who knows some specially revealed truth and uses it to overcome extreme odds and deathly enemies. Most times, such knowledge is spurious, the product of active imaginations or spiritual deceptions. In one case, however, it is true. The God who knows all has given us some of His knowledge. He has revealed His will to us by His Spirit.

This is not a movie or a game. God doesn't tell us secrets for us to feel the special status of being "in the loop" or above others. The Gnostics were very exclusive in their secrets, with initiation rituals that guarded their spiritual gates. With God, the secrets are available to anyone who seeks Him. But not otherwise. Those who do not have His Spirit simply will not understand.

Why does God so desire that we have intimate knowledge of His plan? We might think it's because He insists on our obedience, or because He has a special task for us to do, or some other action-oriented reason. That's part of it, but only part. The ultimate reason God delights in imparting the secrets of His heart to His people is that He enjoys the intimacy. He has called us to be partners and friends. In His great mercy and descent, He wants us to share His mind and His passions. He is a God who loves to reveal.

In Deed

We have a hard time accepting that. Perhaps we think we're not worthy. We're right, but that's not the point. Perhaps we think we're too dense to "get it." We're right again, but that isn't the point either. God's revelation doesn't depend on our worthiness or our intellectual capacities. It depends on our love for Him. If we draw close to Him, He whispers secrets into our ears.

We can walk through dangerous territory on those terms. Intimacy with the divine can get us through a lot. The secret wisdom the world has long craved is finally ours.

> Human salvation demands the divine disclosure of truths surpassing reason.
> —THOMAS AQUINAS

A New Understanding

We have not received the spirit of the world
but the Spirit who is from God, that we may
understand what God has freely given us.
1 CORINTHIANS 2:12

In Word

One of the greatest deficiencies in contemporary Christianity is that we don't under-stand what God has given us. We've turned salvation into a one-day, for-the-spirit-only kind of dream that God will fulfill for us. And it's true that there are extravagant promises for our future. But we don't really understand them. The thought of heaven seems boring to some and its realization distant. We forget that God has freely given us promises for right here and right now. The Kingdom will come one day, but it is already coming.

Did you notice that when Jesus was teaching His disciples to pray, He didn't say, "Your Kingdom come, Your will be done one day when the earth is ancient history"? No, He told them to pray God's Kingdom and will into earth as it already is in heaven. Right now. The beauty and glory of heaven—as it actually is—into the fallen world—as it could be when touched by God. The promises for doing that have been freely given. We often don't understand that.

That kind of understanding would transform us from a people defeated and dis-couraged by the world to a people representing the King of the new creation. Read Ephesians 1:17-23 sometime, and try to feel defeated. The only way you can is if you simply don't believe what it says.

In Deed

Believe what it says. Don't resist the Spirit of God when He urges you to pray and to live with all the hope of the Kingdom. This is one of many cases where God com-mands us to believe something that sounds too good to be true. But not to believe would be disobedient. When God promises access to the Kingdom of Heaven, He means it. Who would pass up such a gift?

Paul writes that the Spirit who is from God, not the spirit of the world, is to fill your mind and heart. He calls you to embrace truth. You can do that without apology. It depends only on what you choose to understand.

> The promises of God are just as good
> as ready money any day.
> —BILLY BRAY

A Personal Teacher

*This is what we speak, not in words taught us by
human wisdom but in words taught by the Spirit.*
1 CORINTHIANS 2:13

In Word

In many homes, the television is on more than six hours a day. Statistics have shown that even in faithful, church-attending families, our children will have watched 24,000 hours of TV by the time they are eighteen. By contrast, they will probably have been in church less than 3,000 hours. The statistics don't change much for Christian adults, who by some accounts are saturated in media five times more than in Bible study, prayer, and fellowship. The subtle voices of the world have ample time to drown out the voice of the Spirit.

We're in a spiritual war, trying to keep a straight path through a vast array of deceptions. If we're having trouble doing so, we may want to look at the teachers we expose ourselves to. If we are being fed by the philosophies behind media news and programming—and yes, everything has a philosophy behind it—then it's harder to be nourished by the Spirit. Like healthy plants, we tend to grow toward the closest light. We need to be careful which light shines on us most directly.

The Spirit is more than willing to teach us the words of God Himself. He is available with guidance, revelation, comfort, and support. But if we are tuning in to other frequencies, we won't hear Him very easily.

In Deed

If we want to enjoy the awesome privilege of being taught by God, the only source of truth, we must actually allow ourselves to be taught by Him. Careful communication with the Spirit will be far more penetrating than our absorption of false philosophies, but only when we take time to cultivate that communication. If we want God to speak, we need to have ears to hear.

The result of a hearing ear is a mouth that can speak the words of the Spirit. Like Paul, we can minister in truth if we are fed by it. Our door to divine secrets is right in front of us. The only condition is our willingness to open it.

The words of God which you receive by your ear, hold fast
in your heart; for the Word of God is the food of the soul.
—GREGORY I

A Beautiful Mind

We have the mind of Christ.
1 CORINTHIANS 2:16

In Word

Our world is awfully confused about what is right and wrong. Worse yet, it is largely ignorant of the way to God. If ever there was a time to speak up, this is it. Our needy planet is desperate for a word from God.

Paul tells us that no one knows the thoughts of God except the Spirit of God, which by the way, we have (vv. 11-12). The Spirit doesn't just know the general will of God; He "searches all things, even the deep things of God" (v. 10). In a world hungry for truth, we have been given free access to it, and it is wonderful. Truth is far more fulfilling and amazing than we could ever have imagined, but it is lacking in voices. There are plenty of opinions out there, but few words with the power of the Spirit behind them. A shallow world needs to hear the deep things of God.

That doesn't mean our message will be gladly accepted by all. Like children who are hungry at mealtime, but reluctant to eat what is set in front of them, the dazed and confused seekers of our generation may not recognize the deep things of God when they see them. But the Spirit who reveals them is powerful. He can penetrate any heart He chooses. Our job is not to convince people of the deep things of God, but simply to declare them. The Spirit of God does the rest.

In Deed

We have the mind of Christ. The Word says so. That places two equal responsibilities on us. The first is to be filled with, steeped in, and standing firm on the deep secrets of God. He didn't give us His mind for us to vacillate on His will. Wishy-washy Christians are called "unstable" and "double-minded" in James 1:5-8. The mind of Christ is not indecisive.

Our second responsibility is to give the world the wisdom it so desperately needs. We can't force it on anyone, and we can't expect people without the Spirit to understand spiritual realities. But we can make sure they hear, and the Spirit will help some see the wisdom in His truths. We have clarity where the world has confusion. We have the mind of Christ.

> The things He has written on our hearts are not doubts or opinions, but assertions—surer and more certain than sense or life itself.
> —MARTIN LUTHER

Choosing Sides

Anyone who chooses to be a friend of the
world becomes an enemy of God.
JAMES 4:4

In Word

In some wars, neutrality is a sensible stance. Perhaps it's easy to see both sides of the issue, so a country chooses to seek mediation. Maybe we have well-established relations with both parties and don't want to offend either. Or perhaps the issues don't really affect us, so we choose to keep our distance. Regardless of the reason, picking sides isn't always necessary or advisable.

That certainly isn't true spiritually. In the cosmic war, a rebellious world stands defiantly against the Kingdom of God. It's an absurd position, but those who have orchestrated the world's systems—its philosophies, perspectives, values, and methods—are blinded to spiritual truth. The result is a network of societies, economies, governments, and cultures that don't recognize God and, in fact, work against His agenda. In such a clear case of right and wrong, neutrality is not a sane option. Trying to get along with both God's Kingdom and the world's ways is impossible. To declare allegiance to one is to declare hostility against the other.

That's why James calls friendship with the world "adultery." That's a graphic metaphor for spiritual unfaithfulness. To fit right into the world's rebellious ways without any real discomfort is akin to sleeping with the enemy. The bride of Christ has no business cozying up to other suitors.

In Deed

The Spirit of God is jealous for His people. That should come as no surprise; God declared early on in Scripture that His name is "Jealous" (Exodus 34:14), and He has made it clear ever since that our hearts should belong only to Him. We can't operate smoothly in sinful realms without offending the One who made and redeemed us for Himself.

Be careful how you live with respect to the world around you. God's love for the world He created is unwavering, but so is His hatred for the world's rebellious ways. If you're being conformed to His character, the same will be true for you. Always be aware that your love for God will compel you to forsake all rival loves.

Do not let the false delights of a deceptive world deceive you.
—CLARE OF ASSISI

The Higher Way

Humble yourselves before the Lord, and he will lift you up.
JAMES 4:10

In Word

The Kingdom of God is full of paradoxes. The first will be last, and the last will be first. The way to become great is to become a servant. Those who lose their life will save it, but those who seek to save their life will lose it. And the only way to really live is to die.

So it's no surprise that the way up in the Kingdom of God is to go down. Though our human nature is always striving to reach higher and boost ourselves up, the way of God is to forsake natural ambitions and embrace humility. The Kingdom doesn't have a ladder of success that we can climb. It only has a floor on which we can kneel. In order to be lifted up, we must descend into a position of complete dependence. Such humility is an affront to our pride, but it's the only way to be lifted up.

Having godly humility means being unassuming—resisting the urge to seek every advantage for ourselves, promote our interests, or defend our rights. We have to choose whether to be our own advocates or let God advocate for us; to defend ourselves or let God defend us; to force doors open or to let God open them in His way and in His time. Resting in His ability and timing to "promote" us spiritually or otherwise grates against our nature. It's extremely counterintuitive. But so is virtually everything in God's Kingdom. To adopt His ways, we have to forsake our own.

In Deed

Whatever advancement you seek in God's Kingdom, lay it before Him in humility. Trust Him with it. Fulfill your responsibilities toward that end, but don't rely on what you can do. God has promised to put you where He wants you whenever He wants you to be there. The straightest path to that place is humble obedience—an attitude of submission that refuses to take matters into your own hands. In His wisdom, He will lift you up.

> The door of God is humility.
> —JOHN THE SHORT

The End of Pain

The day of the Lord will come like a thief.
2 PETER 3:10

In Word

The best thing about the spiritual war—the opposition that we now face as citizens of the new creation—is that it has an ending point. It won't last forever, and neither will it just fade away. It will be cut off at a particular point in time, when few people expect it. The days of the enemy are numbered.

That means all of the conflict we face, all of the tension in our relationships and in our own hearts, and all of the brokenness of this world will be done away with. The new creation is exactly that—a new creation. There will be a new earth that will not be corrupted by any evil or death. There will be no crime, no natural disasters, no emptiness deep within us, no pitiful attempts at finding fulfillment in the trinkets of the old world, no crying ourselves to sleep, and no suffering. The adage "no pain, no gain" will be completed. The pain will be over, and the gain will be eternal.

Meanwhile, the days of distress will intensify. Jesus said, "If the Lord had not cut short those days, no one would survive. But for the sake of the elect, whom he has chosen, he has shortened them" (Mark 13:20). But we can take the intensity if we know He has cut short the days. The enemy, in spite of his wide range, is still on a leash. Those who trust God cannot be fatally wounded.

In Deed

When you hear that Jesus is coming again, what reaction do you have? Exhilaration? Panic? Something in between? Those who realize the brutal nature of the conflict now and the peace of the Kingdom then will welcome the advent of the eternal Lord. He will come and establish His reign, and it will be perfect. The utopia that we have instinctively longed for from ages past will be realized, but it will be better than we thought.

Remember that in the heat of battle. Your fight won't last much longer. The peace treaty has already been drafted. Jesus is going to come.

> We are not a post-war generation, but a pre-peace generation. Jesus is coming.
> —CORRIE TEN BOOM

The Reason for Time

He is patient with you, not wanting anyone to perish, but everyone to come to repentance.
2 PETER 3:9

In Word

We spend our lives looking forward to the great promise: the re-genesis, when all things are made new and the groaning of creation becomes a joyful shout. Jesus started that new creation on Resurrection Day, and we've been tasting it ever since. One day, these foretastes of glory will be fully and finally satisfied at a festive banquet table, and Jesus Himself will show us our seat. And the party will never end.

Sounds wonderful, doesn't it? It sounds so wonderful, in fact, that we don't understand why God doesn't just go ahead and accomplish it. If that's the ultimate goal and history is hurtling toward that final day, it seems reasonable to expect Him to anticipate it as highly as we do. We know we would not be able to resist the urge to go ahead and usher in the Kingdom. How can God resist? Why would He delay bringing about something so incredibly good?

So it can be incredibly better. In the Kingdom of God, the more the merrier. God did not send Jesus into the world to die a criminal's death just to close the gates later on those who might benefit from the sacrifice. There is a fullness to be achieved before God is ready to restore this world. The Redeemer isn't done with His redeeming.

In Deed

That's why the Day of the Lord hasn't come yet. It isn't that God is slow in keeping His promises; He is patient because many for whom Jesus died haven't repented yet. To end history prematurely would, in effect, squander some of the fruit of Jesus' sacrifice. God would never do such a thing. His amazing love translates into amazing patience.

Many believers today pray for the urgent return of Jesus. That isn't wrong; Revelation ends with such a prayer. But imagine that sort of prayer being answered the day before you accepted Christ. Such a thought should compel us to pray desperately for the lost. God waits for them for a reason.

Repentance is the golden key that
opens the palace of eternity.
—JOHN MILTON

Our New Home

In keeping with his promise we are looking forward to a new heaven and a new earth, the home of righteousness.
2 PETER 3:13

In Word

Many Christians aren't excitedly anticipating the day of Jesus' return. There are too many plans to achieve and dreams to fulfill. Some of us are so busy building our own little heaven on earth that we aren't very interested in the one that is infinitely better. When it comes down to it, we are more infatuated with our agendas than in love with God.

That comes from a lack of understanding. If we really knew the promise of God, we would, like Peter, be looking forward to the new heaven and new earth. And one of the reasons we would be looking forward to it is that it is "the home of righteousness." Righteousness, as Jesus once said, is worth hungering and thirsting for (Matthew 5:6). If we aren't hungering and thirsting for it—especially in its completion—we don't really understand the promise.

Think about what God has told us: All of those news reports that make us sick to our stomachs will become ancient history. All of the illnesses we and our loved ones have suffered will vanish silently into the dark. All of the conflicts we've experienced, the wars we've waged, and the stress we've endured will be over. There are no broken hearts in heaven, because there is no hint of unrighteousness there. One dismal, ravaged creation will become suddenly ravishing.

In Deed

How do your emotions respond to that? Does it thrill your heart when you think of that day? It should. That's one reason Paul tells you to set your heart on the things above (Colossians 3:1). You can get through a lot of trials with an eye on the prize. An intense desire for the day of Christ shines light in the darkest caverns and breaks the seductions of your idols. You don't plant your feet in the kingdoms of this world when you understand the Kingdom of your Lord. People who relish their true citizenship never forget it.

Set your heart on the Kingdom. Seek it above all else. Let it stir your passions. And never forget the promise.

> He who provides for this life, but takes no care for eternity, is wise for a moment, but a fool forever.
> —JOHN TILLOTSON

Look Forward

You ought to live holy and godly lives as you look
forward to the day of God and speed its coming.
2 PETER 3:11-12

In Word

An athlete focused on a gold medal will train rigorously and uncompromisingly. An entrepreneur building a business will strategize and invest wisely. A couple planning to get married will begin to unite their dreams, their finances, and their possessions. Those with an eye on the goal will change their lifestyle today in order to reach it.

It's no different for a Christian. If we have our eye on the end result—the Day of the Lord and the consummation of this age—we will live in light of that day today. We will begin to adopt the attitudes and actions appropriate to His Kingdom. Our character will conform to our understanding of heaven if we are looking forward to that day.

You can tell when a believer isn't highly anticipating the Lord's return. He or she has not conformed to His image and seems to have little interest in doing so. When that's the case, there's little awareness of the glory of the Kingdom and little interest in its fulfillment. People who do that probably invest most of their time, talents, and resources in the here and now and allow their characters to be shaped by this age.

In Deed

Does that describe you? If so, it may be helpful to spend some time focusing on the final revelation of Jesus and the coming of His Kingdom. He spoke a lot about those who were not ready for His return, and there were always negative consequences. The Master, He made it clear, is pleased with those who are living according to His Kingdom before it is completely unveiled.

If you do need to make that adjustment, use Peter's admonition as a barometer of your eternal focus. A holy and godly life will accurately indicate the desire you have for the Second Coming. Your ultimate goals will be revealed in your lifestyle today.

> He who has no vision of eternity will
> never get a true hold of time.
> —THOMAS CARLYLE

Hold Out

You must understand that in the last days scoffers will
come, scoffing and following their own evil desires.
2 PETER 3:3

In Word

The non-Christian world sees our belief in the return of Jesus as ludicrous—if they are even aware that we believe that. The thought is so far-fetched that it doesn't even enter the mind of the unredeemed unless we bring it up. In fact, it could be seen simply as wishful thinking—people from several religions believe their founder will return—except for the fact that Jesus was quite explicit about it. He was not vague when it came to the consummation of the age. He emphatically said He would come again.

It won't be possible to convince our world that Jesus is coming again unless we live like He is coming again. That doesn't mean that we should stand gazing into the sky; it means that we should be conforming to His image daily, enthusiastically, and rapidly. Those who envision and anticipate His return will grow to be like Him and reflect His glory even before that day. We can be evidence that He is alive. In other words, we should give the scoffers no reason to scoff.

In Deed

If they continue to do so, it is a deliberate choice (v. 5). Even so, our calling remains the same. There is nothing in Jesus' teachings, nothing even in all of Scripture, that tells us to be affected by the opinions of those who don't believe. We may find ourselves in a hostile environment from time to time, but our response is to look toward God, not toward the hostility. No matter how evil our surroundings, no matter how contemptuous the world is of our beliefs, we, like Noah as he built the ark, are to hold out for the truth of the coming judgment and redemption. Our faith is to see what the world doesn't see.

If that's a struggle, be encouraged. Read some of the passages where Jesus describes His second coming. Realize that it will come like a thief, that He expected people to scoff, and that His return is a certainty. Live in light of that day in the midst of a world that needs to be aware of it.

> The fact that Jesus Christ is to come again is not a reason for
> star-gazing, but for working in the power of the Holy Ghost.
> —CHARLES SPURGEON

In Due Season

See how the farmer waits for the land to yield its valuable crop and how patient he is for the autumn and spring rains. You too, be patient and stand firm, because the Lord's coming is near.
JAMES 5:7-8

In Word

Farmers do a lot of work to yield a crop. They prepare the ground, sow the seeds, water and fertilize them, and protect them against pests. But there's one thing farmers can't do: make something grow. After all the time and energy and hard labor, ultimately the yield is dictated by weather patterns and natural processes. All that's left is the waiting.

God works in seasons. Nearly everyone who has prayed for something or waited on Him to fulfill a promise can testify that He can be excruciatingly slow. It isn't that He lacks speed; when He finally acts, He can turn the course of events in lightning-fast time. But He's very, very thorough in His processes. We have certain responsibilities in His Kingdom to work faithfully, but in spite of all our labor, we are ultimately dependent on His timing. In many spiritual endeavors, all that's left is the waiting.

That's why James illustrates faithful perseverance with a growing season. There's work involved, but extreme patience is required. His readers were going through hardship and opposition, and many were looking for the Lord's return. And while the promises of His intervention in our lives and of His ultimate return are certain, they aren't necessarily immediate. God isn't a vending machine, a drive-through window, or a microwave. We don't just pop in our contribution and receive His response right away. Faith almost always involves waiting.

In Deed

So we wait. We don't always like God's seasons; His delays can be pretty uncomfortable. But we wait on the Lord just as the farmer waits on processes beyond his control. In fact, our faith is purified in the waiting. We become convinced in the interim season that God will come to us. In response to our faith, His answers to our prayers will be timely, and His intervention in our circumstances will be perfectly orchestrated.

> Patience and diligence, like faith, remove mountains.
> —WILLIAM PENN

Blessed Endurance

*As you know, we consider blessed
those who have persevered.*
JAMES 5:11

In Word

We look back at the biblical heroes of faith with enormous admiration. They heard God's voice and overcame doubts and discouragement to obey. They endured in their faith in spite of being misunderstood, insulted, beaten, imprisoned, and killed. We honor them for the risks they took and the obstacles they faced. This kind of faith, we tell ourselves, is what life in God's Kingdom is all about.

But when we find ourselves in the midst of trials, we often begin to question God. The perseverance of biblical heroes is the stuff of the Kingdom, but the need for perseverance in our lives? Perhaps that's a sign of God's disfavor, or maybe it means our prayers just aren't working. We must have neglected some act of obedience or committed some unintentional sin. Otherwise, life would be working out the way it should. Our trials wouldn't be happening, right?

We forget that the ways of God's Kingdom haven't changed. We can't expect that the perseverance so admirable in others would be irrelevant to us. Those things that we honor in retrospect are still applicable today. If God allowed the people of faith to overcome trials in ages past, He will allow us to face them now. Faith and the power of God are proven in such trials. His people will always be called to endure them.

In Deed

Peter once told his readers not to be surprised at the painful trials they were facing as though something strange were happening to them (1 Peter 4:12). In fact, they were to rejoice in the face of trials—the same instruction James gave earlier in his letter (1:2). Even so, we're often surprised at the trials we go through. As people who have been chosen by God and adopted into His family, we don't expect them. They don't seem like signs of His favor.

Appearances can be deceiving. Our trials are actually opportunities to press ahead and demonstrate how God's people overcome the world. Embrace them when they come. Resolve to endure. Remember that we consider blessed those who have persevered—even today.

All our difficulties are only platforms for the manifestations of His grace, power, and love.
—HUDSON TAYLOR

Shalom

He himself is our peace.
EPHESIANS 2:14

In Word

Shalom. Most people know that it's a Hebrew word for peace, but few know what kind of peace it refers to. It implies not just lack of conflict within and with others, but a fullness, abundance, health, and prosperity of all of life that comes from being with God. The Greek word that Paul used in Ephesians has similar connotations, though not as comprehensive. But Paul the Jewish believer would not have been able to think of peace without thinking shalom. The shalom of God is a picture of the Kingdom.

That's what Jesus is: the Shalom. He doesn't just bring peace to us, He is our peace. That applies to the division between Jew and Gentile in this passage—a division that exists no more in Christ—but it also applies more broadly.

The coming Kingdom is a matter of bringing together all who believe into one body. The barriers come down, reconciliation is made perfect, the Spirit is poured out, and we bask in the shalom of God's Kingdom.

This peace that comes to the believer is often seen by some as an individual gift, the peace of our own personal domain. By others, it is seen as a political and institutional mandate, either among churches or among nations. And while both of those are certainly desirable under God's domain, there's more going on with the Prince of Peace than that. He has come into our hearts, into our churches, and into our world in order to establish His reign. And His reign is where all blessings abound. The peace of God is the place of blessing.

In Deed

That's where we are to live: in the place of blessing. That's why Jesus came. He did not come for us only to think of the peace that will one day be established; He came for us to experience the shalom of God everywhere we go. In fact, we are to be vessels of that shalom. Our character, our attitudes, our faith, our works, our countenance, our relationships—everything we embody should represent such peace and fullness. Like Jesus, we are to be pictures of the Kingdom of God.

Peace reigns where our Lord reigns.
—JULIAN OF NORWICH

The Union

His purpose was to create in himself one new
man out of the two, thus making peace.
EPHESIANS 2:15

In Word

"In himself." It's an important concept with a lot of power. While institutions, peace projects, international treaties, and goodwill ambassadors try to make one people out of two (or many), the purpose of Jesus was to create in Himself one new kind of person. This is not a matter of putting a bunch of diverse people together and telling them to get along. It isn't even about rallying everyone together around a common cause. It's about a new creation that is spiritually, integrally, intrinsically wrapped up in the incarnation of God Himself. It's better than harmony; it's complete union.

The tragedy of Christendom today is that God's people are a shattered fellowship. God doesn't have a fragmented heart, but He has a fragmented people. The organic union of the body of Christ still exists, but it exists among people who don't like each other and don't even know they're united to each other. Somewhere along the way, many Christians forgot how to distinguish between the essentials of the faith and the minor details. We've split fellowships over the details, never realizing that the body of Jesus cannot be broken again. There is only one Spirit who lives in every believer.

In Deed

Imagine how parents feel when their children don't get along and don't care to try. Then imagine an infinite heart of love with that same feeling. That's God. When the church has failed at peace, the church has failed at the Christian faith.

The good news is that Jesus is the Prince of Peace. He restores it. Wherever He reigns, the peace of God—the shalom of the Kingdom—springs up. When it does, the purpose of God is fulfilled. Human beings become one in Him. They don't just learn to coexist, they don't play nice, they don't have to bite their tongues as they painfully try to get along. They become one. A new creation. A completely different kind of human being. A people marked by and living in peace.

There is only one organism of the new creation, and
we are members of that organism, which is Christ.
—LIONEL THORNTON

God's Household

*You are no longer foreigners and aliens, but fellow citizens
with God's people and members of God's household.*
EPHESIANS 2:19

In Word

The entire direction of history is moving toward building a household, an eternal dwelling place of God among His creation. It began with a few chosen people, planted, cultivated, pruned, and tended with the greatest care. From a tiny seed, a Kingdom of enormous branches has grown. And there will come a time when that growth has reached its full maturity. When it does, the Kingdom has come.

It's a blessing to be a part of that. Many people aren't. In fact, there was a time in history when only a handful of individuals even had access, geographically and spiritually, to the people of the King. Even today, many people remain isolated from the truth, barred by ideological constraints, linguistic barriers, and cultural taboos. When the Bible tells us we are no longer foreigners and aliens to God's household, it's a truth worth falling down in worship over.

We'll be amazed in heaven by all the barriers to the truth that were overcome. We will worship next to people of languages we have never even heard of and tribes most of us didn't know existed. We may even find that people who lived next door to each other for decades without speaking will embrace each other in the final celebration. If only they had known before what they found out when Jesus came, the Kingdom could have been a much more present reality.

In Deed

It can be, you know. If history is heading in this direction, we might as well try to get there before everyone else. The destination is to be reflected in the journey; the unity of the Kingdom is to be found in our hearts today.

Examine your motives, your dreams, your relationships, your work—everything. Do they point toward the direction of history? If not, why not? And is there anything you can do about it today?

> The whole Christian life is that we are totally
> one with each other in His church.
> —PETER BALL

A Holy Temple

In him the whole building is joined together and
rises to become a holy temple in the Lord.
EPHESIANS 2:21

In Word

We are witnessing in our day the raising of a temple. We read about it in the book of Acts, and have heard of it throughout the ages. But it is bigger now than ever. It has the potential to be the most glorious thing this world has ever seen except for Jesus Himself, and it will be. All those years we've prayed that the Father's will be done on earth as it is in heaven, this was the answer we were receiving. The holy, eternal temple is the passionate work of God.

You may not feel that way when you pull into the church parking lot on Sunday. It may feel like a routine or an obligation, or perhaps an enjoyable time with God and others. You may think of all sorts of ways you'll be edified and educated, built up by the fellowship and inspired by the music. But the temple is bigger than that. It's a divine movement, the ultimate countercultural statement against the kingdoms of this world. Being a part of that temple is the role you were created for.

In Deed

If you don't see the church that way, ask God to give you a vision of His holy temple in progress. As He does, you will begin to see how the parts fit together as a whole and point toward His glory. Avenues of service will open up to you, and they won't seem like needs to be filled but a passion to be pursued. The excitement that comes from being part of an eternal building will add new dimensions to your day.

Maybe you don't need new dimensions. Maybe the routine is fine, and you'd prefer the alarm clock get you up rather than the adventure beckoning from inside you. Maybe you're just interested in the house payment, not the temple offering. But if an eternal building excites you—if you want not only to be a worker but one of its living stones—rise up and thrive. The Lord of the holy temple calls you.

The church is the only institution
supernaturally endowed by God.
—CHARLES COLSON

The Dwelling

In him you too are being built together to become
a dwelling in which God lives by his Spirit.
EPHESIANS 2:22

In Word

The Temple of God in the Old Testament was to be a place where outsiders could come and recognize the presence of God (2 Chronicles 6:32). The world was to know that God dwelled in that place. Indeed, foreign kings and dignitaries visited Solomon and marveled at both his wisdom and the structure. But there's no evidence that Israel let the Temple become the shining light that it was supposed to be. And when judgment came, the Temple was destroyed.

The living temple has the same purpose. We are to be a magnet to the nations. With the Holy Spirit dwelling in us and among us, we are the final evidence for this world of the salvation that is offered. We follow the way of Israel sometimes, turning inward rather than outward, and obscure the presence of God, but our purpose is to display Him.

Perhaps it will help to envision the final display. Meditating on the glorious presence of God in the multitudes of heaven will give us tastes of that presence now. More than that, it will give the world tastes of that presence now. And there's nothing the world needs more.

In Deed

Creation displays God's glory. The heavens speak forth His glory. Israel was chosen for glory. The church is being built as a monument to God's glory. Everything God does points toward that purpose. God has chosen to display His glory in remarkable ways. The most remarkable is His desire to inhabit His own creation. In order to do that, He redeemed sinners and poured out His Spirit into them. The infinite God lives in finite beings. That's amazing.

That's so amazing, in fact, that we should spend the better part of our days soaking in the Spirit, operating in His gifts and by His strength. The world needs the presence of God, and we're called to be the presence of God. We exist to give everyone a glimpse of what the glory of the Kingdom will be like.

> According to the New Testament, God wills that the
> church be a people who show what God is like.
> —STANLEY GRENZ

Pray and Praise

*Is any one of you in trouble? He should pray. Is
anyone happy? Let him sing songs of praise.*
JAMES 5:13

In Word

In some Christian circles, the advice for those in trouble is to worship their way out
of it. It's good advice—praising God is always appropriate, and words of praise have
a remarkable power to change our attitudes and even outward circumstances. The
first and last phrases of the verse above would fit nicely together. But the "praise God
anyway" approach often comes across as superficial. It fails to acknowledge that we
do go through deep distress sometimes. Though we always want to acknowledge
God's glory even in the depths of a crisis, there's no point in denying that the crisis
even exists. When we're in trouble, it's okay to admit it. God insists on honesty in our
relationship with Him.

But God doesn't leave us in our crisis. When we're in trouble, our first response
is to pray. Why? Because prayer connects us with Him. It's the line of communication
between helpless humanity and supernatural power. Like a battlefield soldier calling
headquarters for support, we can appeal to God in any circumstance of life. Like a
child crying out for a parent's attention, we can cry out to our Father at any time for
any need. God has not left us alone in this world. In fact, Jesus came to prove just the
opposite. He was, and always will be, Immanuel—God with us.

In Deed

Most of us don't need to be told to pray when we're in trouble. James's readers probably
didn't either. What we do need is a reminder that prayer isn't an appeal to unknown
gods, a wishful hope hurled upward like a random shot in the dark. No, there's a
reason we should pray when we're in trouble. Prayer effectively invites God into our
trouble to do something about it—to be present with us in it, to redeem it, to teach
us in the midst of it, to guide us out of it, and ultimately to fix it. We don't pray simply
as a spiritual exercise. We pray because prayer accomplishes something. In your crisis,
hang on to that.

> Prayer is a powerful thing, for God has
> bound and tied Himself thereto.
> —MARTIN LUTHER

Righteous Power

The prayer of a righteous man is powerful and effective.
JAMES 5:16

In Word

"Elijah was a man just like us" (v. 17). That's the example James gives us to prove that prayer is powerful and effective. While we might question how far one can press this illustration—Elijah seems to have been a man unlike any other—the fact is that he was still just a human being. The prayers he prayed were not under some special dispensation of grace or power. He came before God and uttered bold requests, and there's no reason we can't do the same. In fact, there's every reason we should. God tells us to.

Still, we're frightened away from full faith in the power of prayer by James's use of one adjective: righteous. It isn't the prayer of just anyone that is powerful and effective; it's the prayer of a *righteous* person. Deep down inside, most of us know we don't qualify. We pray, but not as those who are as righteous as Elijah. We don't pray from a position of radical opposition to ungodly influences. We aren't lone voices in the wilderness crying out against false worship in spite of rabid persecution against us. We aren't biblical icons like the hairy prophet of fiery chariots and mysterious whirlwinds. We aren't sure our prayers receive the same hearing that Elijah's did.

But that's only because we don't understand the righteousness we've been given. Jesus said that no one before Him was greater than John the Baptist, who came in the spirit of Elijah. Yet the least in the Kingdom of God—those born of the Spirit—were greater than John. The righteousness of the new birth is greater than the righteousness of bold prophets of old. If we understood that righteousness and lived in it, James's words would be no mystery to us.

In Deed

In Jesus, we have all the righteousness we need to pray bold, powerful, effective prayers. We need to be reminded of that; otherwise, we lack faith to pray anything beyond the ordinary. But our prayers are to be anything but ordinary. Ample promises from God and the righteousness of Jesus Himself assure us of that. We can pray with the power of Elijah.

> Prayer is the secret of power.
> —EVAN ROBERTS

Peaceful Faith

*Since we have been justified through faith, we have
peace with God through our Lord Jesus Christ.*
ROMANS 5:1

In Word

Faith equals peace. That's the principle God gives us, even centuries before Jesus justified us through His Cross. God had made the equation especially clear to us in Abraham, who believed God's promise, and it was counted as righteousness. "Against all hope," we are told in Romans 4:18, "Abraham in hope believed." And because of that—because of Abraham's simple insistence on the fact that God was telling the truth, though all appearances contradicted the promise—he was considered righteous.

That's the key to the "shalom" of God, the peace and wholeness that saturate His Kingdom. When we believe what God has said, regardless of what people and circumstances tell us, we are righteous in God's eyes. That hinges on the Cross, of course, the central event in all of salvation history. If we don't believe Jesus paid for our sins and was raised from the dead, it does no good to believe all of God's other promises. We can't logically reject the big one and cling to the little ones. But if we believe the big one, we can believe all the others. And that kind of faith equals peace. Shalom can saturate our lives.

That's the life of the believer who has his or her eyes on the fullness of God's Kingdom. That now-invisible Kingdom starts to become visible. Those who walk by faith, not by sight, will begin to see. While others declare that they will not believe it until they see it, we declare that we will not see it until we believe it. Our faith in the things that make for peace and wholeness actually leads to peace and wholeness.

In Deed

Remember that. The Christian life is built on faith. Never agree with people or circumstances that contradict God's revelation of reality. The truth of a situation is always what God says about it—not emotions, not rationalism, and not apparent impossibilities. God's many promises, including the promise of your justification, will bring you peace.

If the basis of peace is God, the secret of peace is trust.
—J. N. FIGGIS

Flowing Love

*God has poured out his love into our hearts by
the Holy Spirit, whom he has given us.*
ROMANS 5:5

In Word

The Kingdom of God, with all its peace and abundance, is a Kingdom in which God's Spirit freely reigns. That's why His Kingdom is so desirable; it is full of everything our hearts were shaped for. Where the Spirit of God rules, there is freedom and life. Where He doesn't, there's captivity and death.

There is also love wherever the Spirit of God dwells. John tells us in one of his letters that God is love (1 John 4:8), so if He has given us His Spirit, He has filled us with love. Our hope is built on the foundation of a love that has been poured into us, a pure and holy passion that comes straight from the heart of God Himself. If we want to know what the Kingdom looks like, that's the best place to start.

Our problem is that we try to cultivate love. But if we look carefully at Scripture, we see that the source is the Spirit. As with all other fruits of the Spirit, we don't cultivate love by determining to get more of it. We get it by cultivating our communion with Him. That river of life flows through our hearts already (John 7:38-39); we just need to learn to tap into the flow. Just as there's no need to turn on a water hose when you're neck deep in a river, there's no need to concentrate on love when you're neck deep in the Spirit. If He rules in your heart, God's love flourishes there.

In Deed

Do you want to rest in the hope of the Kingdom? First, believe God with every fiber of your being (v. 1). Then live in love. It's no coincidence that Paul linked faith, hope, and love in his first letter to the Corinthians (13:13). The Kingdom becomes visible in our midst when these three virtues, especially God's love, characterize our lives. Faith lasts only until it becomes sight, and hope lasts only until it's fulfilled, but love lasts forever. Draw close to the One who gives it.

God's love is always supernatural, always a
miracle, always the last thing we deserve.
—ROBERT HORN

Anticipated Glory

We rejoice in the hope of the glory of God.
ROMANS 5:2

In Word

How do you feel about the glory of God? Is it exciting or boring? important or irrelevant? at the center of your heart or in the back of your mind? Paul said that believers rejoice in the hope of God's glory. It's something to be fulfilled in our lives, the resolution to all the devastation and disappointments that have surrounded us in this world. When the glory of God is revealed, the Kingdom has come in its fullness. It's something to hope for deeply.

Paul takes this hope even further. We can go ahead and rejoice in our tribulations, he says, because they will lead to perseverance, proven character, and hope. And because hope does not disappoint, our joy can be a current reality (vv. 3-5). The glory that God has—and that He shares with us (John 17:22)—will always outweigh the trials we go through. It is inconceivable that we will get to the heavenly Kingdom and say, "You know, I'm just not sure this was worth all the trouble." Glory will blow our minds.

Our afflictions are "light and momentary," according to 2 Corinthians 4:17. In our everyday experience, our hope is to be larger to us than our trials are. We are to see the difficulties in life as anthills and the glory to be revealed as a vast mountain range. When it comes to the Kingdom, we are not to be nearsighted. God's reign is much bigger than the troubles in front of our eyes.

In Deed

Spend some time today rejoicing. It doesn't matter what is going on in full view in your life; what matters is what's going on in your heart. If you dread today's activities or lament the tragedies that threaten, you are filling your vision with anthills. They aren't unimportant—they may be wounding you deeply—but they don't dominate the eternal landscape. Something far greater, far more beautiful, and far more powerful makes them small. It's glory. Let your heart hope for it—and rejoice in it—today.

> Hope springs eternal in the human breast.
> —ALEXANDER POPE

Contagious Joy

We also rejoice in God through our Lord Jesus Christ,
through whom we have now received reconciliation.
ROMANS 5:11

In Word

Is your joy contagious? If not, there may be a spiritual reason. The problem a lot of Christians have is mentally believing the coming glory without emotionally embracing it. It remains a mind principle, not a heart faith. You may have noticed that academic understanding doesn't bring us any sense of joy. Only a deeply held belief in the heart can do that. We are made joyful not by the things we comprehend, but by the things we treasure.

So the question remains: Is your joy contagious? Are the promises of God the treasures of your heart? If they are, nothing can quench your faith. If we really knew and fully believed all the promises of God in Christ, the thought of His glory, His Kingdom, and His peace would bring spontaneous songs and praises to our mouths. We never see people who just won a multimillion-dollar lottery sweating about their next credit card bill, and we should never see people who have been promised the Kingdom and glory of God sweating the day's challenges. When we realize what we have, joy abounds.

Not only does it abound, it overflows. Just as complaining and discouragement spread rapidly to the people exposed to them, so does joy. It dismisses those who think we are delusional, it runs deeper than the constant exhortations to "get in touch with reality," and it transcends the "facts" of a situation. True joy sees the whole picture, the reality behind the appearance, the truth behind the facts. It's based on eternal blessing.

In Deed

If you struggle with discouragement and depression, consider the truth. God's promises are more real than anything you see, any circumstantial assault on your senses, or any lie your mind or anyone else tells you. The Spirit of God is not limited by your circumstances today or the people around you. But your own thought patterns? Guard them well. If you do, joy can thrive in your life. And it can spread to everyone around you.

Joy is the serious business of heaven.
—C. S. LEWIS

Supernatural Evidence

God demonstrates his own love for us in this:
While we were still sinners, Christ died for us.
ROMANS 5:8

In Word

God demonstrated His own love for us in a rather remarkable way: He sent His beloved Son into the world to die for people who had long rebelled against and insulted Him. You don't normally see that kind of love in this world. It isn't natural. In fact, it's supernatural.

Paul has already told us in verse 5 that God has poured out His love into our hearts. Now he tells us what kind of love. This is it—sacrificial, unexpected, out-of-this-world love. God has loved us in this way and then given us the Spirit who loves in this way. What we have freely received, we can freely give. We can be the visible evidence of an invisible Kingdom.

In fact, that's our calling. We are evidence. That's what a "witness" is, isn't it? We talk about witnessing to others as though it's a conversation, and that is certainly part of our task. But we are the kind of witness that does more than tell the evidence. We are the evidence. When people look at us, they are to see faith, hope, love, joy, and all the other beautiful signs of a beautiful Kingdom. They are to see the things their hearts deeply long for.

In Deed

How do you do that? Go back and read the full passage again. Romans 5:1-11 gives us the keys of the Kingdom: a sacrificial Savior, a faith in His promises, a love from above, a hope in the present and future glory, and a joyful purpose to fulfill. All the temporal things people crave are some shadow of the real thing. If we show them the real thing, we are signposts to eternity.

The only way to get those things—faith, hope, love, and all other spiritual fruit—is to drink deeply from the fountain of life. The fruit of a tree is always drawn from its roots. Grow your roots in eternity, and your life will always point to it.

Unless a life is lived for others, it is not worthwhile.
—MOTHER TERESA

Inside and Out

If we claim to have fellowship with him yet walk in the darkness, we lie and do not live by the truth.

1 JOHN 1:6

In Word

One of the most astounding truths realized by early believers is that it was now possible for those who once lived in darkness to have deep-down, internal fellowship with the Holy Spirit of God. This was no longer simply a Master-servant or Father-child relationship. It was both of those things and more—an intimate union between the infinite and the finite, between the holy and the corrupt. Behavior could not earn the presence of God. The obstacles to this internal union had been removed, and the fellowship had begun.

Such fellowship can lead to false assumptions, though, especially on the part of those who accept it as doctrinal truth without knowing it by experience. If the union is given freely and unconditionally, it must remain free and unconditional; otherwise, it isn't a gift at all. And though this understanding is true, it misses a crucial point: if the union is real, it will have profound implications for all of life. It isn't possible to have intimate fellowship with a Spirit who is pure and holy and to live a life that isn't.

John recognized the inconsistency among many early Christians and called it what it was: a lie. Those who claim to have fellowship with God but live as though they don't are lying. Unintentionally lying and very sadly mistaken, perhaps, but lying nonetheless. He makes that abundantly clear, emphasizing that Jesus is "the Righteous One" (2:1) and declaring that "whoever claims to live in him must walk as Jesus did" (2:6). There is no room for misunderstanding there. Those whose spirits have been born of God, who have become one substance with the Holy One, will be transformed. They will become like Him. If they don't, something is seriously wrong with the fellowship they claim to have.

In Deed

Your outward life will always eventually conform to your inner condition. When there seems to be a discrepancy between your walk and your inward fellowship with God, check the vitality of your fellowship. Let your walk reflect the Spirit He has put within you.

> Study universal holiness of life. Your whole usefulness depends on this.
>
> —ROBERT MURRAY M'CHEYNE

Deep Forgiveness

*If we confess our sins, he is faithful and just and will forgive
us our sins and purify us from all unrighteousness.*
1 JOHN 1:9

In Word

Most of us know what it's like to depend on this verse regularly. Our lives sound as predictable as instructions on a shampoo bottle: sin, confess, repeat. Our sin cycle contains a wonderful promise from God to wipe the slate clean whenever we ask, but we still know there's a problem. We know the cycle isn't over simply because our sin is forgiven. We're familiar enough with ourselves to realize that unless the source of the sin is dealt with, it will come up again and again.

In dealing with our sin, God promises more than a "get out of jail free" card. He doesn't just wipe the slate clean, He deals with the root. We have to cooperate with the process for it to be effective, but it can be. His promise in 1 John 1:9 is not only that He will forgive us but that He will purify us. Our confession can be simply an acknowledgment that we need forgiveness, but it really should be much more than that. It should be a statement of our utter dependence on His Spirit to work out His righteousness within us.

Knowing God's desire to deal with the root of our sin leads to a glaring question: why doesn't He? Why do we still have sins that easily plague us time after time? The answer is implied in verse 6: only real, deep, lasting fellowship with His Spirit can transform us. Superficial confessions and forgiveness can't. We have to be immersed in the Holy One in order to live like Him.

In Deed

God is zealous about our inner transformation, and in His mercy He is also very patient about it. But His only solution for repeated cycles of sin is to insert Himself thoroughly into the process. For our new nature to actually function as a new nature, we need to submit the deepest core of our being to His work. Don't be satisfied with simple confessions. Invite Him to radically change you from within. Because He is faithful and just, He will.

> The renewal of our natures is a work of great
> importance. It is not to be done in a day.
> —GEORGE WHITEFIELD

The Future Glory

*It is God who has made us for this very
purpose and has given us the Spirit as a
deposit, guaranteeing what is to come.*
2 CORINTHIANS 5:5

In Word

"We do not wish to be unclothed but to be clothed with our heavenly dwelling" (5:4).
Deep down, that's the desire of every person. Every layer of makeup, every plastic
surgery, every new style of clothes—all are expressions of the hunger deep within to
be clothed with something other than mortal flesh. It has been written into our being
from the sixth day of creation. Humanity wasn't designed to die.

That's why many people experience a pang of sadness with every new wrinkle or
bifocal prescription. We know what these things signal. No matter how disappointed
some of us may have been with our lives, we still don't want to die, at least not in the
ultimate sense. We know life has its pleasures and beautiful moments, and we want
them to last. We crave the eternal.

The glorious promise of Scripture is that the craving can be satisfied. We often
have a hard time embracing the promise wholeheartedly; it seems too good to be true.
Paradise is a figment of desperate imaginations, we think, and we assume God is more
realistic than that. But to God, realism is beautiful. He offers the ultimate utopia, the
infinite pleasures of His presence to all those who will be cleansed enough to join Him
there. And He has already given us a deposit.

In Deed

Perhaps you don't think of the Holy Spirit as the down payment on an eternal transaction, but that's how Scripture describes Him. He guarantees what is to come. If we will
let Him do His work in our lives, we will begin to see the evidence of eternal glory.
The life that begins to spring up within us and overflow into our surroundings will
forever increase. Redemption is not going to end.

Meditate on that thought today. You may have a hard schedule or a difficult problem facing you, but hardship is actually the context of this passage. Even so, it points
to glory. Remember today that glory never wrinkles or fades. And trust the Holy
"Deposit" to help you.

> All of the Holy Spirit's influences are heaven
> begun, glory in the seed and bud.
> —MATTHEW HENRY

The Ultimate Trust

We know that the one who raised the Lord
Jesus from the dead will also raise us with Jesus
and present us with you in his presence.
2 CORINTHIANS 4:14

In Word

Would you trust Leonardo da Vinci to paint your portrait? Abraham Lincoln to write a speech for you? Mother Teresa to feed you if you were starving? Most rational people would answer yes to all three. We appreciate excellence when we see it. We want the best.

If you wanted to overcome tribulation and death, whom would you trust? You would turn to someone who has proven His healing and resurrection power and goodness to others. You would want the God who has done this before.

Paul tells us how to view our own resurrection. It's in the hands of the same God who resurrected Jesus. If we ever lose heart about the prospects of eternal life, we need only remember that God has a perfect résumé. The power that raised Jesus from the dead has been birthed within us. When we need an expert to do the job that concerns us most—and every one of us will—then we know where to turn. The artistry of the resurrection masterpiece is available to commoners like us.

In Deed

This passage of Scripture draws us out of current difficulties and into the ultimate Kingdom. It doesn't promise immediate deliverance from everything that concerns us, but it does deliver us from an obsession with temporal trials to a faith in everlasting fulfillment. Whenever we get discouraged about today's predicaments, we need, like Paul, to lift our eyes to a higher view of them.

That takes practice. It doesn't come naturally. We have to train ourselves to see things from a heavenly point of view rather than from ground level. But God will help us. It's His desire to encourage us, and He urges a mental transformation that keeps our thoughts on things above. If you ask, God will give you His perspective on things. And He'll remind you of His rather impressive résumé.

> It is not our trust that keeps us, but the God
> in whom we trust who keeps us.
> —OSWALD CHAMBERS

The Inner Renewal

We do not lose heart. Though outwardly we are wasting away, yet inwardly we are being renewed day by day.
2 CORINTHIANS 4:16

In Word

Not many people are able to say that they are wasting away, yet not losing heart. In fact, that's an indication of delusion in most cases. There's only one exception: when the one who is wasting away on the outside has Jesus thriving on the inside.

That was Paul's situation. He had suffered much in his ministry, describing his recent experience as a matter of carrying around the death of Jesus in his body. He was feeling very much like a "jar of clay" (2 Corinthians 4:7). Still, he was able to describe this life of daily death as "light and momentary troubles" (4:17). What mattered most was not what physical suffering his body was going through but the renewing presence of the Spirit within. If Jesus was working in Paul's ministry, Paul was satisfied.

Why was Paul able to say that? Because he had set his heart on the glory to come, a glory that would far outweigh whatever this world could dish out. In other words, when someone is faithful to God, the benefits will far outweigh the costs.

In Deed

A lot of people believe they have gotten a raw deal in life. They don't think they've lived up to God's expectations or that He has lived up to theirs. When it really sinks in that this is a fallen world, the disillusionment can be devastating. The disappointments of this age can condition us to keep our hopes in check. So when God promises extravagance, we sometimes avoid a complete emotional investment.

For a Christian, there's no reason to water down hope. We are given ample reason to go ahead and dream big. Comparing the trials of today to the glories of eternity is like comparing a one-hundred-dollar investment with zillion-dollar returns. It makes the up-front cost look a lot better.

So don't lose heart. Jesus didn't, even during that long night before the Cross. Stephen didn't, even while he was being stoned. John didn't, even during a long exile on Patmos. That's the normal Christian attitude, and it's strongly encouraged. Let your heart dream of glory.

To live without hope is to cease to live.
—FYODOR DOSTOEVSKY

The Big Picture

We fix our eyes not on what is seen, but on what is unseen.
For what is seen is temporary, but what is unseen is eternal.
2 CORINTHIANS 4:18

In Word

A hiker walked a lonely path in a driving rainstorm. Around him were magnificent mountains and lush valleys, but he couldn't see the scene. The clouds were too dense and the rain too relentless. It was slow going, and all the hiker could go by were his map and compass. He certainly couldn't walk by sight.

Meanwhile, an airplane passed overhead. From six miles up, a traveler in a window seat could see a gorgeous vista. There was a small cloud down below, but it didn't cover much territory and certainly didn't mar the scene. In fact, it accented the landscape's color and form. It was a beautiful sight.

An essential key to the joyful Christian life is perspective. People who are able to fix their eyes on the unseen, as Paul instructs, are able to weather the storms at ground level. If we know that the landscape is gorgeous and that the rain will pass, we can enjoy the process and look forward to the view from above. If not, we will suffer miserably.

In Deed

Few people enjoy misery, but we follow its recipe often. We lose our focus, fixing our eyes on what is seen and neglecting what is unseen. We become absorbed in "now" and oblivious to "forever," and our hearts suffer from the wounds. We easily give up hope.

But a life that is filled with hope is a blessing to those around it. It breathes life into deathly situations, binding wounds and healing emotions. It is a source of encouragement and strength. Those who hope have understood the reality of the Kingdom of God. Their attitudes are a statement about eternity and a picture of heaven.

If you have a negative attitude, repent. That may seem harsh, but nowhere in Scripture are we instructed to agree with the visible and ignore the invisible. We are taught remarkable truths that can only give life when embraced by faith. A negative attitude is a refusal to believe them. When we turn to hope, we agree with heaven. There's no better way to live.

Faith tells us of things we have never seen, and cannot come to know by our natural senses.
—JOHN OF THE CROSS

The Shared Promise

*We make it our goal to please him, whether we are
at home in the body or away from it. For we must
all appear before the judgment seat of Christ.*
2 CORINTHIANS 5:9-10

In Word

Knowing what we know about eternity, we have every reason to live for it today. We aim to please the One who gave us the blessing of our destiny, regardless of our current situation. Our feet are to be rooted not in the reality of the moment but in the reality that never ends.

There's another aspect to eternity that we need to consider. The fact that we will all appear before the judgment seat of Christ should help shape our decisions today, but it should also shape our relationships. The alarming truth is that many people we know do not desire to please the Lord and are not aware that they will appear before His judgment seat. For those of us for whom there is now no condemnation (Romans 8:1), that day will not be a life-or-death matter. But for those who have not accepted Him, there will be an altogether different kind of judgment. Unlike Paul, they will not "prefer to be away from the body and at home with the Lord" (5:8). They will wish they had met Him much earlier.

We can help them with that. In fact, if we have an eternal perspective, we will. It simply isn't possible to know what we know and remain unconcerned about those who don't. And when Jesus is giving us "what is due . . . for the things done while in the body, whether good or bad" (5:10), He will consider our level of concern. More than that, He will consider whether our concern prompted us to action.

In Deed

Evaluate your concern for those outside of Christ. Does it reflect the reality of the coming judgment? Or are you more a passive observer of God's grace than an active distributor of it? If your assessment reveals anything lacking in your attitude toward the lost, deal with it quickly. Ask Jesus to work Himself into your relationships. Let the promise of redemption guide your interactions. The eternity you look forward to should be a shared experience.

We are the Bibles the world is reading.
—BILLY GRAHAM

Extraordinary Love

Dear friends, let us love one another,
for love comes from God.
1 JOHN 4:7

In Word

Perhaps the Beatles overstated the case a little—and probably according to a skewed definition of love—but "All You Need Is Love" isn't too far from the truth. After all, Jesus identified the two greatest commandments as loving God and loving others. Paul declared that even the greatest spiritual gifts and most impressive works are meaningless without love. And John made the radical assertion that those who lack love don't know God (v. 8). On God's list of priorities, love ranks very, very high.

It's surprising, then, that plenty of Christians seem to lack a generous spirit and a gracious attitude. We can get so zealous about serving God and fulfilling our calling that we step on anyone who gets in our way. In between all our worship services and Bible studies and devotional readings, we leave casualties of our lovelessness everywhere. The Christian church is known in our culture for particular doctrines and busy agendas, but we are not known for our love—even though Jesus told His disciples they would be. Though individual Christians may demonstrate remarkable love from time to time, as a worldwide community of believers we have failed priority number one. Love is not the church's most recognizable characteristic.

That's sad. It isn't that we don't have love—ministries all over the world have sprung up because love has prompted believers to make great sacrifices and address deep needs. But in our one-on-one relationships, we are often indistinguishable from the culture around us. We are not as noted for radical love as God wants us to be.

In Deed

John's instruction to love one another is more than a gentle nicety. There's urgency in it. Those who have been born of God are loving, and those who aren't loving may not even be born of God. In your life today, give love the same rank on your list of priorities that God does. Because God is love, we must be love too.

You learn to love by loving.
—FRANCIS DE SALES

The Spirit's Mark

We know that we live in him and he in us,
because he has given us of his Spirit.
1 JOHN 4:13

In Word

Soon after Pentecost, there was a huge debate in the early church over the salvation of Gentiles. Did they need to become Jews first? Or could God save unrighteous sinners directly before they had embraced His law? It was a hotly contested dispute at times, but one argument seemed to decisively end it. Whether it made theological sense or not, the Spirit had fallen on Gentiles. God had witnessed to the right side of the argument Himself.

Why did this reason effectively sway opinions? Because the Spirit came with evidence. There were signs. Lives had changed, miracles had occurred, and a new nature had sprung up in people's hearts. The Spirit wasn't an intangible reality. This was no subtle change of attitude or spiritual philosophy. It was palpable and real.

John essentially carries on the same argument in his letter. How do we know we are of God? Because He has given us His Spirit. John has just identified the prevailing characteristic of the Spirit as love, and he gives no indication that this love is a subtle sign. No, when the Spirit comes into a life, it should be apparent. Changes happen. A love we didn't have before rises up within us.

In Deed

Sometimes the new evidence of love—and any other change the Spirit brings—is sudden and dramatic, but sometimes it isn't. In either case, however, it should be noticeable. If it isn't, we need to ask why.

Examine yourself today to see how freely the Spirit's love and character flows through you. If His presence is hard to discern, don't despair. Simply confess any obstacles to His love, any failure to live in it and express it, and then ask Him to fill you with it. Filling lives with His love is one of His favorite activities. Any prayer that He would do so will surely be answered. Accept the love He showers on you. Then shower it on those around you.

We share in the divine nature through
our sharing of the Spirit.
—ATHANASIUS

The Accounting

Each of us will give an account of himself to God.
ROMANS 14:12

In Word

A young baseball player dreamed of the big leagues. All through his high school years, he trained for hours a day. He maintained a strict diet and a rigid exercise program on top-of-the-line equipment. He watched every televised game and took every opportunity to speak with coaches and professional players, learning every nuance of every game situation. Whenever the local field had activity on it, he was there. He was preparing for a day when his talents would be measured.

In a way, that's what believers must do. We aren't quite so performance oriented; Jesus is not going to base His judgments on raw talent and training regimens. He will be looking instead for how the heart has been shaped by the Spirit and is bearing its fruit. As the baseball player assumed all the characteristics of a big leaguer long before his opportunity to be one, we are to assume all the characteristics of a Kingdom citizen long before the Kingdom is made visible. Our identity is shaped by who we want to be. Or better yet, by whom we want to be like.

That's the sort of thing we will give an account for. We will have to explain what we did with what we were given. We will be shown the profitability of our eternal investments, and if they are lacking, we will have to confess why. Our entire lives as believers are leading up to a final assessment.

In Deed

That's sobering. Jesus once told His disciples that everyone would have to give an account for every careless word (Matthew 12:36), and He told parables about making the most of the Master's resources. Those of us who are steeped in grace are jolted into diligence by such words. We know we aren't saved by our works, but we learn that our salvation is to produce a lot of them. According to Jesus, fruit matters.

Live your life in view of the final accounting. Don't fear failure; God is full of mercy. Rather, fear the kind of caution that buries God's gifts. Take risks in faith and sow seeds liberally. Then you'll be able to tell Jesus you gave it everything you had.

It ought to be our business every day
to prepare for our last day.
—MATTHEW HENRY

The Judge

*Every knee will bow before me; every
tongue will confess to God.*
ROMANS 14:11

In Word

The felon knew before the trial ever began that he would be found guilty. As soon as he stepped into the courtroom, he could see it in the judge's face. This was a man who embodied the law—not just the letter of the law, but the spirit of it too. He would not compromise society by sending a criminal back into it. The character of the culture had to be preserved.

That's how Scripture describes our God. He overflows with such mercy on our fallen world that, in this case, the Judge served the sentence so the felons wouldn't have to. But He didn't just let sin slide. It had to be dealt with. The character of the Kingdom had to be preserved.

It will always be preserved. In the last day, everything in all of creation that points to the glory of God will be saved, and everything else will be condemned. For the Christian, we need not fear condemnation, but we do need to be mindful that God will dispense with whatever we did outside the bounds of His glory. If we have borne fruit in the power of His Spirit for the glory of His name, that fruit will remain. The rest will not. Everything will bow to God.

In Deed

History is hurtling toward that day of separation. All that is pure and perfect will be revealed as Kingdom reality, and all that does not conform to the Kingdom culture will be set aside. There will be no waffling, no ambiguity, and no delay. It will be decisive and final. The revelation of ultimate glory will have nothing inglorious in it.

Keep that in mind as you approach that day. The Judge is pulling for you, sifting your life to fill it with as much glory as possible. But what doesn't get sifted out now will be eliminated then. If that's a lot, it could be pretty traumatic. Know the love of the Father, but bear in mind His ultimate goal. Conform to the culture of the Kingdom.

> Tomorrow's history has already been written. At
> the name of Jesus every knee must bow.
> —PAUL E. KAUFFMAN

The Jury

Why do you look down on your brother? For we
will all stand before God's judgment seat.
ROMANS 14:10

In Word

It's common for the community of the saved to take on an attitude of the community of the superior. We don't intend to do that, but when we feel that God has revealed to us His will, we often develop contempt for everything that doesn't fit it. We forget that we were once ignorant of God's will and outside His Kingdom. He gave us mercy, not contempt. If we are to be like Him, we'll do the same.

We seem to have trouble with that. If other Christians understand Him differently, whether it's a matter of minor theology or a practical approach to living, we often see them as less enlightened citizens of the Kingdom. According to Scripture, we will see soon enough how God sorts it all out. Meanwhile, we have no business making sweeping judgments about things the Bible leaves unclear.

That's the situation Paul addresses in this passage. One group of people is making judgments about another group because the second group interprets God's standards differently. And the second group is flaunting its sense of freedom in a way that causes those in the first group to stumble. Underlying the tension is a sense of superiority on all sides, an innate tendency to judge others by our own opinions. And that tendency implies a lack of trust in God's ability to handle His people.

In Deed

If the practices of other believers bother you, realize that they will have to give an account to God for them. That has two implications: God has the understanding to deal with it; and you don't. When it comes down to it, the Kingdom of God is a spiritual Kingdom consisting of the deep things of the heart, and only God can see those deep things. What manifests itself on the outside of a believer isn't always easily interpreted. Only God knows if it comes from good motives.

Guard your heart. No one is ever judged for the decisions of another; plenty of people are judged for a lack of mercy. Let your heart be shaped by grace.

Do not think of the faults of others but of what
is good in them and faulty in yourself.
—TERESA OF AVILA

The Sentence

Let us stop passing judgment on one another.
ROMANS 14:13

In Word

We are called to be blind. Well, not in most areas; God wants us to have keen spiritual sight. But when it comes to our differences with other Christians, we're not to notice them. We are given plenty of permission in the New Testament to focus on the gifts and graces of other believers, and no permission to go hunting for their faults. Our attention toward others should cultivate the Spirit within them and ignore the fading reality of their fallenness.

As people who would love to be treated in this manner, we can understand why Jesus would have us treat others that way. It's one of the surest ways to spread God's blessing to those around us. That kind of attitude would set us apart from the world—it is completely alien to the spirit of this age—and it would powerfully declare the nature of God's Kingdom.

Many believers are not aware of how heavy the burden of judgment is. It's hard work holding people to our standard of fairness. If we mentally try to make people pay for their violations—whether through our visible anger or passive-aggressive tactics—we can exhaust ourselves quickly. Our fatigue is often a product of our grudges. God intends for us to bless, be generous, and be merciful, even in the recesses of our minds. The sentence handed down in our spiritual courtroom should always be a relief.

In Deed

This seems like a difficult task, but it can actually be fun. Try spending a full day—today would be a good start—thinking nothing but good of others. If they smile at you, bless them. If they curse you, bless them. Where normally you would feel offended, determine to be free of any hostility whatsoever. Let people cut in front of you in traffic, apologize for any hint of transgression, and bend over backward to be at peace. After a full day of being radically magnanimous, you'll start to feel light and liberated. Your blindness to faults will make your world appear much brighter.

No man can justify, censure, or condemn another, because no man truly knows another.
—THOMAS BROWNE

The Witnesses

*Christ died and returned to life so that he might
be the Lord of both the dead and the living.*
ROMANS 14:9

In Word

Jesus is Lord of all. That seems like an easy confession for us to make until we realize a sobering implication. If Jesus is Lord of all, that means we are lord of nothing. Nothing is ever completely under our own domain. Whatever authority we might have in life, it's always under His higher authority. We can never say "the buck stops here" unless we are pointing at Him.

In principle, we would never disagree with that. In practice, we often do. We exercise authority, judgment, control, and all sorts of lordly rights without first submitting them to Jesus. As parents, we don't always take our cues from the Father. As believers, we don't always operate in faith. As servants, we don't always follow the pattern of Jesus' sacrifice. Whatever role we play, we sometimes play it in our own wisdom. And that leads to distorted relationships in the body of Christ.

Jesus died and was raised for a better way. His exaltation makes Him Lord of every person we shun, every responsibility we avoid or abuse, every brother or sister we disdain, every truth we distort, and every task we foul up. Most of all, from our personal perspective, He is Lord of us.

In Deed

One of the greatest problems in the church today, and one of the biggest reasons the world doesn't trust our testimony, is that we say Jesus is Lord and live like He isn't. That's not an intentional snub; it's a matter of simple neglect. And when relationships among Christians are characterized by criticism and complaint, as Paul indicates they were, the picture of the Kingdom of God gets terribly out of focus.

Christians should be the most wildly magnanimous, generous, and merciful people on the planet. The world should be compelled to marvel at us. If that's not happening in your personal arena today, do whatever it takes to change. Let your life throw the Kingdom of God into sharp focus.

> Wherever God rules over the human heart as King,
> there is the kingdom of God established.
> —PAUL W. HARRISON

Full Assurance

*Let us draw near to God with a sincere
heart in full assurance of faith.*
HEBREWS 10:22

In Word

People who have been abused or neglected as children are likely to go through life
tentatively, never knowing whom they can trust. Over time, they may develop hard
and assertive exteriors that give them an air of confidence, but deep inside they are
desperately insecure. They learn to cope, but they may never learn to fully trust.

The same could be said for many of us who have never been abused or neglected.
Life has a way of beating us around, and people have a way of letting us down. We learn
certain safeguards that allow us to relate to people well, but relationships with them
are usually guarded. Only those who have earned our trust over time, with whom
we have gradually grown to feel safe and free to let down our guards, are allowed to
see our vulnerability. Those are the relationships in which we can function in full
assurance.

That's the kind of relationship God has provided for us, but few Christians are
able to enjoy it. Many of us really feel safe with God only when we can keep Him
at an emotional distance. We dress ourselves up in a pose of piety because we just
couldn't approach Him as unclean sinners. We frame our prayer requests in terms
of a purely "spiritual" agenda because we are afraid He won't be concerned with the
personal needs of our hearts. And though He sees right through us, we still don't want
to appear vulnerable. We want to fit the culture of heaven before we dare step up to
His throne.

In Deed

Hebrews tells us we have no reason to do that. We can come to God in full assurance—
completely vulnerable and exposed. Though His holy presence has been dangerous to
many, we can trust Him completely. Why? Because He has made us absolutely clean,
and He has declared that He is fully, irrevocably on our side. If there is any hindrance
keeping you from a full, vulnerable, open stance at His throne, let Him deal with it.
His desire is to meet you in the awesome but safe place of His presence.

> The greater and more persistent your confidence in God,
> the more abundantly you will receive all that you ask.
> —ALBERT THE GREAT

Broken Sight

*Let us hold unswervingly to the hope we
profess, for he who promised is faithful.*
HEBREWS 10:23

In Word

The life of faith can be excruciating. Why? Because it's a continual process of breaking
us from what we see. In order to live by faith, we have to redefine what we call "reality."
Is it the evidence our eyes and ears perceive? Or is it what God has said? We'd like to
think those two pictures blend, but they often don't. Faith is the assurance of what
we hope for and the evidence of what we *don't* see (Hebrews 11:1). It's embracing
the invisible.

   Consider Abraham, for example. For years he lived with the promise of a multitude of descendants, even though he was childless. Even after he had fathered a son by
his wife's maid, he was told that the promise would come through another son—and
he continued to be told so after he and his wife were old and wrinkled. It's hard to
live confidently with the word of God when it sounds so absurd. But after decades of
the reality being invisible, it became visible. Abraham became the father of those who
believe because he accepted an "impossibility" as reality.

   That's hard to do. Every natural impulse we have tells us to accept what we see as
the clearest evidence of reality. Somehow we got it in our minds that the testimony of
circumstances is the most truthful one we can hear. But if we want to follow an invisible God, if we want to walk in faith as He calls us to do, we have to be broken of that
assumption. The testimony of circumstances often lies. When God says one thing and
visible evidence says another, we have to choose which "reality" we'll believe.

In Deed

You may be faced with impossible circumstances today. Perhaps you're barely hanging
on to hope but questioning whether it's faith or wishful thinking. God doesn't give us
blanket statements about those situations, but He does make one thing clear: if He
has promised something, it's a greater reality than any other evidence you face. When
He has spoken, it's true. Let nothing persuade you otherwise.

> There is a living God. . . . He means what He
> says and will do all He has promised.
> —HUDSON TAYLOR

Edify

*Let us consider how we may spur one another
on toward love and good deeds.*
HEBREWS 10:24

In Word

Look around you. You probably see a lot of people who have it made, who seem to be getting along fine in life. Many of them have everything handed to them on a platter, while others succeed at pushing and shoving to get what they want. And people who are having a hard time . . . well, it's probably only temporary. Everyone goes through a hard time. But surely they know it will all work out in the end.

Illusions aside, nearly everyone you see is wounded in one way or another. Those who don't exhibit external crises may very well have deep insecurities or epic internal struggles with issues we don't see. Those who are struggling may wonder if life will ever get better, if God has lost sight of them or withdrawn His favor. Though hope is out there, they wonder if it applies to them. Across the board, people carry dysfunctions and hurts and grief that we rarely see.

This truth may be less pronounced in the church—a lot of healing has taken place in those who come to Jesus—but it's still there. Christians aren't immune from these issues; we have our struggles. In fact, sometimes those struggles are less openly discussed among believers than in the world because we're supposed to be healthy and whole. To bare our souls could shatter the church's image or our own. Sadly, the walking wounded often need to walk less openly in the place where redemption should occur.

In Deed

The truth is that everyone needs encouragement at a deeper level and more often than most of us imagine. Everyone we run into has a story, and each story most likely has involved some pain. One of the primary functions of the body of believers is to offer words of affirmation and healing to each of its members. Our fellowships should be marked by encouragement, even to the point of sounding excessive. That's how people get strengthened. Take every opportunity, even today, to build someone up.

> The really great man is the man who
> makes every man feel great.
> —G. K. CHESTERTON

Under Construction

Each one should be careful how he builds.
1 CORINTHIANS 3:10

In Word

You are in the midst of a building project. You may feel like a building project yourself some days, but you are actually a contributor to one. The building is the eternal Kingdom of God, and it's a privilege to have been chosen to participate. You have many coworkers joining in, and it may be tempting to slack off and let them do the heavy work. But that's not how eternal buildings are built. Your job, according to Scripture, is to be a very diligent member of the construction team.

Your job is also to cooperate with the rest of the team. The Foreman loves a well-coordinated effort, so departing from the general design framework is frowned upon. There's room for your own creativity, of course, but not for drawing up your own plans. In Paul's day, back when the architectural design was finally unveiled, team leaders often attracted personal loyalties that distracted from the Foreman's leadership. Things haven't changed much. We have a lot of leaders working independently of one another, not realizing they are working on the same project as other construction teams. There are so many interpreters of the design that the Foreman's megaphone is often indiscernible.

That's no way to build. Paul had a problem with the idea that this ultimate, eternal project could be subdivided. When the King is overseeing the work, there's really no room for other contenders. Every thought, strategy, and material should reflect His purpose.

In Deed

The body of Christ cannot be a makeshift project. It has to be excellent, it has to be coordinated, and it has to endure. If we are building in a way that falls short, we need to be careful how we work.

What does that mean in your life? At the very least, it means a firm commitment to the ultimate design and a willingness to sacrifice anything to complete it. Such devotion will pass any stress test before the ribbon cutting. The Foreman notices how you build.

> When the world asks, "What is God like?" we should be able to say, "Look at the church."
> —WILLIAM R. L. HALEY

A Solid Foundation

*No one can lay any foundation other than the
one already laid, which is Jesus Christ.*
1 CORINTHIANS 3:11

In Word

The quality of a building is largely dependent on the strength of its foundation. When the groundwork isn't solid, no degree of quality will substantially increase the value of the structure. But if the foundation is sure, the rest of the building can only add to its value.

Jesus is a sure foundation. Not only that, He is the only foundation. There is no other. Any faith that stresses a different approach to God other than the gospel is destined to crumble. It is not worth building on. It will never stand the test of time.

So when God established His eternal plan, He based it on His Son. The human project—the creation of a temple of God in living flesh—had to be forever unshakable. Adam and Eve proved that they were not a trustworthy foundation, and we would have done the same. Divinity had to inhabit humanity in order to undergird an everlasting race, so God clothed Himself in flesh. The result is a temple that cannot be moved.

In Deed

God's favor rests on the foundation of His Son. He thundered from heaven that He was well pleased with Jesus, and to the degree we love the Son, the Father's favor rests on us. As we approach the consummation of the age, we have to remember that. Whenever we evaluate our priorities, this should be the standard we use. God has given us a foundation worthy of our every effort. Whatever we do should be done on that plot of land and secured to the structure already laid, if we want it to last. If we engage in irrelevant projects, they will not stand in the city of God.

As this organic building grows, we have the privilege of investing our lives in a project of unimaginable worth. We make choices daily that will either last because they fit the plan or will land in the cosmic trash bin because they don't. Whatever you do today, keep your eyes on Jesus. Your work will never crumble on that foundation.

The church's one foundation is Jesus Christ her Lord;
she is His new creation, by Spirit and the Word.
—SAMUEL J. STONE

The Light of the Day

His work will be shown for what it is,
because the Day will bring it to light.
1 CORINTHIANS 3:13

In Word

"The Day" will bring your work to light. Your reaction to that statement will tell you a lot. If the thought of your work being brought to light alarms you, there's probably a reason. If the thought thrills you, there's also probably a reason.

Most Christians find cause for both alarm and excitement in the thought of that day. Most of us have enthusiastically contributed to the eternal building project in the power of the Spirit, and most of us have done some building with our own resources. We know that the brightness of the light will reveal mixed results, and we know the mercy of the Father will focus on the lasting ones. Even so, the light is a little intimidating.

That's because we know the Architect's standards. They are incredibly high. The materials He keeps can come only from a single spiritual source, and we fear we've corrupted our work with our own efforts. While that's a realistic concern, it fails to take into account the Architect's methods. His design is guaranteed to bring Him the right results. He has put the source within the worker. He is more than an observer; He's the power behind the job.

In Deed

Let that be of some comfort. Those who love and trust Him have nothing to fear on that day. The light will be a cause for celebration, not despair. We will see exactly how we reflect His glory.

If you want to feel secure heading into "the Day," follow a few simple instructions. Love Jesus with all your heart, above all other loves; keep your eyes on Him and follow His lead; do everything in faith, even when it takes you out of your comfort zone; depend on the power of the Spirit, through prayer and action, to accomplish His purposes; and be enormously grateful for the process and the results. Do those things, and the light will shine on you beautifully.

An inheritance is not only kept for us, but we are kept for it.
—RICHARD SIBBES

A Fiery Test

If what he has built survives, he will receive his reward.
1 CORINTHIANS 3:14

In Word

We don't like that word *if*. We would be more encouraged if Paul had said, "When what he has built survives, he will receive his reward." But he didn't. He knew that many who believe in Jesus will spend a lifetime trying to do the works of the Spirit in the strength of the flesh. They will depend on their own resources and wonder why God doesn't bless their efforts. They will be too cautious to step out in faith and begin an endeavor that only God can accomplish. They will attempt to build heaven according to the pattern of earth.

So Paul says "if." There's no guarantee that what we do as Christians will survive the test of God's fire. Whatever is of purely human effort and initiative will be burned up like dross, and whatever is of God's Spirit and divine initiative will be purified. In that day, the difference between the temporal and the eternal will be clear. And only the eternal will remain.

That "if" doesn't need to frighten us. There are some steps we can take to guarantee that what we have built will survive. If we build on the right foundation, if we follow God's initiative and depend on His resources, if we stick to the Word of God and obey His voice, our work will last forever. No fire will be able to burn it up because the building materials of God are eternally durable. If we ever wanted our lives to be characterized by quality, this is the way to get it.

In Deed

Practically, what does that mean for your life today? First, spend some time asking God what He wants to say to you. Listen to His voice in the depths of your spirit, pay attention to the Bible verses that leap off the page at you, and obey what He says. Bring your deepest needs and most pressing problems to Him. Whatever you are preoccupied with today, know that it matters to Him too. He wants to fill your life with glory.

> Before the judgment seat of Christ, my service
> will not be judged by how much I have done,
> but by how much of me there is in it.
> —A. W. TOZER

A Place of Presence

*Don't you know that you yourselves are God's
temple and that God's Spirit lives in you?*
1 CORINTHIANS 3:16

In Word

Nowhere in Scripture did God design a tabernacle or temple simply because He needed a comfortable place to dwell. The throne room of heaven and the glory of creation were plenty sufficient for that. No, God designed holy dwelling places because He wanted specific pointers to His presence. He did it to get the attention of His world.

He's still doing that, you know. God has chosen believing human hearts to inhabit so that His presence in this world might be seen. That's an incredible thought. Satan thought it was such a good idea that he counterfeits it with demon possession and a vast array of emotional and psychological oppressions. But the counterfeit should never distract us from the real thing. God has put His Spirit within redeemed human flesh in order to be seen, heard, and felt.

There are two implications to that thought: one is that we as individuals are filled with God's Spirit; the other is that the church as a whole is filled with His Spirit. In this verse, Paul addresses the latter dynamic. He is speaking of the church and rebuking those who would divide it. How dare anyone split the body of Christ into subsections, Paul argues. They are messing with a sacred, divine body. The dwelling place of God on this planet cannot be splintered without serious consequences (v. 17). No one has proprietary rights to God.

In Deed

Remember that. We love our categories, and they can be helpful for understanding God's truth, but they can never become anything other than descriptive. Among our denominations that adhere to the core of the gospel, we cannot define them in terms of "us and them." Everyone in the Kingdom of God is "us." There are no exceptions.

Learn to see the church as God's visible expression of Himself in this world, His dwelling place for the benefit of the lost and broken. Let the temple become sacred to you. And never, ever seek a division of the sacred.

> All His glory and beauty comes from within,
> and there He delights to dwell.
> —THOMAS À KEMPIS

No Weapon Forged

*Now have come the salvation and the power and the
kingdom of our God, and the authority of his Christ. For
the accuser of our brothers, who accuses them before
our God day and night, has been hurled down.*
REVELATION 12:10

In Word

One of the most exhilarating promises of Scripture is Isaiah 54:17: "No weapon forged against you will prevail, and you will refute every tongue that accuses you." In fact, this is the heritage of those who serve the Lord, says God through His prophet. His people will be vindicated. In spite of all our sin, accusations won't stick. As Paul put it, there is no condemnation for those in Christ (Romans 8:1). We are free from our sins.

That's what Scripture means when it says salvation has come. But though we may appreciate the promise as a guarantee of eternal life, we have a hard time applying it to ourselves today. Still, in spite of all the grace we've been given, in spite of all the assurances that our sins are no longer counted against us, we kick ourselves around for our failures. We perform in order to please God and lament how badly we do it. We know how to let our sins hang over our heads for years. Though God has declared us free, we—or someone else—declare ourselves guilty.

That judgmental voice sounds suspiciously like God's enemy. Satan is called the accuser for a reason. He relentlessly wields our list of offenses before God's judgment seat. God's answer to him is decisive; He points Satan to the blood of Jesus that paid for all those offenses. But that verdict often remains remarkably unacknowledged among those of us who believe. We bear the burden of our offenses much more than we ought to.

In Deed

Repeat it to yourself a thousand times if you have to. There is no condemnation for those in Jesus. None. The conviction we feel should lead us to repentance. Any guilt we sense after repentance is irrelevant. Refuse to live with the burden. The voice of the accuser has no power to pin our offenses on us. He has been hurled down. In your heart and mind, hurl his accusations away with him.

The best protection against Satan's
lies is to know God's truth.
—ANONYMOUS

Living Martyrdom

They overcame him by the blood of the Lamb and
by the word of their testimony; they did not love
their lives so much as to shrink from death.
REVELATION 12:11

In Word

One of the most stunning characteristics of many early Christians in the eyes of the
society around them was their reckless disregard for their own lives. They refused
to change their testimony when threatened with death. They gave hands-on care to
people with highly contagious plagues, even though they knew they would probably
die in the process. They faced eternity without any sense of fear because they knew
they had been cleansed to enter the holy Presence. They overcame vicious threats and
ominous obstacles to their faith because they did not love their own lives.

Jesus said, "Whoever wants to save his life will lose it, but whoever loses his life
for me will save it" (Luke 9:24). Christians who live in dangerous places come face-
to-face with that reality. They are confronted with the radical call of eternity and have
to make a choice. Many of them are living martyrs—people who know they could die
at a moment's notice, even though they haven't had to yet. Others have gone ahead,
absent from the body but present with the Lord. They have finished their race well
because they did not shrink when many others would have. They overcame a hostile
world by the blood of the Lamb and by the word of their testimony.

In Deed

Most of us are never put in the position of having to choose between the gospel and
death, but that doesn't exempt us from living with the attitude of sacrifice. Christians
who have already given up any claim they have to this life and set their sights on eternity are able to live with a sense of freedom few people ever know. It's liberating to
have nothing to lose. And we can, considering how thoroughly Jesus has already saved
us. Jesus calls us to grip our lives loosely. It's how we overcome.

Live as though you may die a martyr's death.
—CHARLES DE FOUCAULD

Hope

Behold, I will create new heavens and a new earth.
ISAIAH 65:17

In Word

Many religions aim at improving this world. Others aim at escaping it. Christianity does neither. A fallen world enslaved in corruption cannot be "improved"; it needs a re-creation. And a world created "very good" by a God with a strong sense of purpose cannot be abandoned. In between both extremes is the truth: God's plan is to create new heavens and a new earth. The rebellion's effects will be burned up, and the original purpose will be fulfilled. God makes all things new.

Isn't that exciting? Every time you find yourself dreading the to-do list of the day or lamenting the futility of the world around you, think about what it will be like to live in new heavens and earth. In this new creation there will be no frustration, no unsatisfied desires, no aimlessness, no corruption, no personal insults, no tedious tasks, no wondering if it's worth all the trouble. In *The Lion, the Witch and the Wardrobe*, C. S. Lewis described the curse as "always winter and never Christmas." In the new heavens and new earth, it will be always spring and never Good Friday. Mourning will be a thing of the past, and celebration will be the cultural norm. Life flourishes unthreatened in the new creation.

Somehow, the fact of that celebration needs to translate into our current lives. Our tendency is to put off our joy until the days of hardship are over, but God doesn't mean for the redeemed to suffer hardship untempered by joy. The promises of the Kingdom aren't meant to be a surprise gift we can't wait to open. They are meant to be an expected inheritance that can be borrowed against today. The new creation is now.

In Deed

This truth explains how Jesus can tell His disciples to be encouraged and joyful in the face of tribulation. He knows the end of the story, and He wants us to know it too. Not only does He want us to know it, He wants us to live as though it's real. Because according to His Word, it's more real than the world we see today.

> The main object of religion is not to get a man into heaven, but to get heaven into him.
> —THOMAS HARDY

Celebration

I will rejoice over Jerusalem and take delight in my people.
ISAIAH 65:19

In Word

Many religions portray God as stern and angry. Others portray Him as distant and detached. Not surprisingly, those that see Him as angry are the ones that aim at escaping the world, and those that see Him as distant are the ones that aim at improving it. In one case, God is about to lower the boom on all creation, and our best hope is to get out of the way. In the other case, God is too far removed to help, so we have to do the best we can. But in Scripture, God gives us a much more pleasant picture of Himself. He enjoys a good party, and He's not shy about inviting us to it.

The picture of God in Isaiah goes much deeper than that, of course. Not only is God enjoying the celebration of the new creation; He's one of the guests of honor. He is the Bridegroom at the wedding bash, the One who has the best reason to be thrilled about the event. He takes delight in His people, the apple of His eye and the treasure of His heart. This is not just any party. It's the consummation of eternal desires.

It's hard to fall in love with the gods of other religions, but the unbridled joy of our God is captivating and endearing. We can love a God who celebrates, who knows what hearts desire and how they feel when longings are fulfilled. Though we often minimize the emotions of God so we can do a better job of formulating tidy theology, Scripture makes no apologies for Him. He experiences a wide range of emotions, and He made us in His image so we could too. And all God's feelings will end with the picture of Isaiah 65. He—and we—will experience ecstatic joy.

In Deed

With that in mind, all pessimism among Christians should be viewed with suspicion. Those who walk in discouragement have not yet seen the big picture. The remedy is to fall in love with the God who celebrates at His own wedding party. Go ahead and taste of His banquet. As one in whom God delights, do not postpone your joy. Join the celebration as soon—and as often—as you can.

> No joy . . . can compare with the joy of
> God in beautifying His people.
> —JOHN PIPER

Joy

Be glad and rejoice forever in what I will create.
ISAIAH 65:18

In Word

Most of us are good at reactive emotions. We grieve when tragedy strikes, we get angry when injustice is done, we celebrate over good news, and we feel peaceful when all is well. But God asks us to do a strange thing in Scripture. He calls not only for our natural, reactive emotions, but also for supernatural, proactive emotions. He urges us to be glad and rejoice forever in something that has not yet taken place. He wants us to celebrate over what He will create.

We're so used to reactive feelings that this request is hard for us to fulfill. It's hard for us even to imagine fulfilling it. When it comes to our feelings, we take a wait-and-see attitude. We're afraid to invest our emotions in the future, to count our chickens before they're hatched, to get our hopes up only to have them disappointed later. We forget that God isn't guessing about the future. This isn't a speculation about probabilities. This is rock-solid certainty. There is nothing more inevitable in this world than the fact that there will be a new world. We are given full permission to go ahead and be joyful about this new creation.

This dynamic of rejoicing before something has happened is an integral part of faith. It's just as much an act of faith to celebrate a promise as it is to step out of the boat onto turbulent water or to set foot in a Red Sea that has not yet parted. Our emotions may not be quite as visible as these steps of faith, but they are based on unseen promises just the same. When we invest our hearts in God's future work, we're allowing ourselves to crawl out on a limb of faith. We're telling Him we believe what He says.

In Deed

What have you invested your emotions in? Are you holding some of them back, waiting to see what God will do about His promises? Too many Christians have mental faith without a heart investment. After all, heart investments are risky. We feel as if we're setting ourselves up for a letdown. But God never let anyone down—ever. Go ahead and rejoice in what you believe.

> God and eternal things are my only pleasure.
> —HENRY MARTYN

Answers

Before they call I will answer; while they
are still speaking I will hear.
ISAIAH 65:24

In Word

As a member of the human race, you have longed for answers. You have wondered what the meaning of life is, you've wanted to know why tragedy inevitably seems to interrupt our search for peace, and you've waited for the fulfillment of prayers express-ing the deep desires of your heart. You, like everyone around you, yearn for a God who seems strangely elusive at the most inopportune times.

God promises answers. Actually, He promises them long before the new heavens and earth come—most of us have embraced the truth of the gospel and have expe-rienced remarkable answers to prayer more often than we're prone to remember—but He especially pledges full disclosure in the age to come. We'll understand the mysteries of life and we'll hear His eager voice before we've had time to get anxious about our questions. In the end, not only will all things be made new; all things will be made clear.

In the meantime, we can count on the fact that God's answers are already avail-able to those who seek Him diligently. According to Proverbs 25:2, it is God's glory to conceal a matter and the glory of kings (including the royal priesthood of which we are a part) to search them out. The elusive nature of a concealed God provides the context for true believers to prove their faith in His promises and their love for His presence. The answers of eternity are available for those who believe God is a rewarder of those who diligently seek Him (Hebrews 11:6).

In Deed

Most of God's promises for eternity are meant to be enjoyed in some measure now by those who draw near to Him. This is one of them. Yes, there will be a day when all answers become clear. Life will be so much easier then, and stress will be so unneces-sary. But even now, God loves to reveal Himself to those who earnestly desire Him. Let your prayers be filled with that knowledge. Keep pressing into Him for answers. He longs to share them with those who long to know Him.

Large asking and large expectation on our part honor God.
—A. L. STONE

Peace

*The wolf and the lamb will feed together, and the lion will
eat straw like the ox, but dust will be the serpent's food.*
ISAIAH 65:25

In Word

Can you imagine a world without danger? Some write novels about utopia or make
science fiction movies about societies that have advanced beyond the threats of war
and disease. But no one considers these fictional civilizations to be anything other
than fantasy. Why? Because no one has seen anything even remotely resembling utopia since the Garden of Eden. The idea is so far-fetched that even the Garden of Eden
is considered by most to be fiction.

Still, God makes this outlandish claim through the prophecies of Isaiah and others. Mortal enemies will dine together in peace. Those who used to eat each other for
dinner will enjoy warm fellowship without fear. Evil instigators who have always fed
themselves on corruption and strife will have nothing to eat but dust.

As with the other promises of the new creation, this one is to be enjoyed in some
degree now. Those of us who are new creatures in Christ can partake of the blessings
of new creaturehood. Yes, we'll have tribulation in this world—Jesus said so—but He
also assured His disciples that not a hair of their heads would perish (Luke 21:18).
He gave them every reason to live in this world without fear of danger, no matter what
dangers they faced. They were to live as citizens of the new heavens and the new earth,
even in the midst of the old ones.

In Deed

God's new-creation promises are utterly contrary to the current condition of the
world on nearly every point. That's good news for all who are beaten down by the
old creation. It's such good news, in fact, that it's hard for us to believe.

Believe it anyway. Whatever you go through today, remember that the end result
will be your sitting down and enjoying eternal fellowship in a world with no hint of
fear and disappointment. You can go ahead and act the part now; one day, you will
live it completely.

> [The people of God] are to model the new
> heaven and new earth, and by so doing awaken
> longings for what God will bring to pass.
> —PHILIP YANCEY

Heavenly

You have come to Mount Zion, to the heavenly Jerusalem, the city of the living God.
HEBREWS 12:22

In Word

The city of the living God. Who among the redeemed wouldn't want to live there? The writer of Hebrews has already told us that Abraham lived in faith because he was looking ahead to that city, whose architect and builder is God Himself (11:10). In fact, quite a few Old Testament heroes lived with an eye on that city, but none of them saw its foundation being laid. That's a New Testament event, and we can still observe the growth of the city today. The faith of centuries is being fulfilled in our time. We only need eyes to see it.

The vision Hebrews gives us is graphic enough to send high levels of adrenaline pumping through our veins. "You have come to thousands upon thousands of angels in joyful assembly, to the church of the firstborn, whose names are written in heaven" (vv. 22-23). This mountain of Zion, where the heavenly Jerusalem sits, is far beyond the Sinai experience. At Sinai, the recently delivered Jews trembled in fear at the holiness of God's presence and the fire and darkness that surrounded them. Zion, though just as holy and frightening, is where redemption was achieved. In the presence where humanity once cowered in fear, the saved can now gather in celebration. The life based on faith is welcome there.

In Deed

The sobering news is that only the life of faith is welcome there. For those of us who cannot bring ourselves to walk on the path of future promises, the city of God will be an entirely foreign place. The writer of Hebrews has already told us that without faith, it is impossible to please God (11:6). That means that the only way to please God is to count on what we hope for and believe what we cannot see. It is to stake everything on invisibilities.

Is that how you live? If not, get busy practicing. You are coming to a city where faith is the common currency and unbelief is worse than worthless. The gates of that city only open to those who have eyes to see it.

No man may go to heaven who has not sent his heart there before.
—THOMAS WILSON

Earthshaking

*Now he has promised, "Once more I will shake
not only the earth but also the heavens."*
HEBREWS 12:26

In Word

Panning for gold is a process of elimination. You sift through a lot of silt to find a few glimmering flakes. Most of what you scoop up from the stream is going to be shaken back into it. Only the golden specks are kept.

God will also shake His creation for gold. Verse 27 of this passage tells us that the shaking of the earth and the heavens is for the purpose of removing all that doesn't shine with His glory. The fallen creation will be sifted out while the redeemed creation will be preserved. The Kingdom that remains will remain forever.

Why does God do this? What does He really want from His creation? The same thing He has wanted from day one: an eternal, intimate union with creatures made in His own image. Since there is no such thing as intimacy between the holy and the unholy, all that is unholy has to be shaken out. Without the Cross of Christ, that would be everything; creation would have been lost forever. But through redemption, some things have been turned to gold. Holiness and humanity can meet. Intimacy is restored.

In Deed

What remains between God and us in this Kingdom can never again be shaken (v. 28). The union is permanent. Whatever trials we are going through in our lives right now, they will one day be sifted out, and only gold will remain. Which leads us to a critical question about our relationship with God: to what degree are we focusing on the part that will last?

Think about that. If you are like most Christians, 95 percent of your communication with God deals with the problems of the day—problems that will eventually be sifted out. The remaining 5 percent deals with the praise and intimacy that He redeemed us for—the parts of the relationship that are eternal. As you look forward to the day when God shakes creation, look past your trials and enjoy His presence. That's what will last in the city where even the streets are paved with gold.

To sensible men, every day is a day of reckoning.
—JOHN WILLIAM GARDNER

Attentive

See to it that you do not refuse him who speaks.
HEBREWS 12:25

In Word

When applying for a job, we try to make sure we fit the expectations of the employer. If there are instructions to follow, we follow them. If there are skills to learn, we learn them. If there's a dress code, we adhere to it. We would be foolish to reject the words of the employer and still hope to do the work.

God's interview process is a little different—it's based on heart issues, not résumé issues—but the principle is the same. God has told us what His Kingdom is like. He has been quite specific about the character we will need to have and the instructions we need to follow to have it. He has emphasized the priority of faith and the new birth in the Spirit. It would be foolish—ludicrous, in fact—to think that we can reject those words and still fit in.

In Deed

God has offered you a total transformation of the heart. How zealously have you pursued it? Have you done everything you can to embrace the words of the One we all so desperately need? While nearly all Christians would affirm the need to internalize Jesus' words, quite a few don't spend much effort doing that. We accept the truth of our salvation and then move on with life, squeezing our discipleship in around more urgent matters. We forget that our discipleship is the most urgent matter.

Jesus said it more pointedly: "Seek first his kingdom and his righteousness, and all these things will be given to you as well" (Matthew 6:33). In other words, feel free to become completely absorbed in Kingdom issues, and daily life issues will be handled by God Himself. We get that backward, becoming completely absorbed in daily issues and hoping God will somehow steer us toward eternity. But hearts are not transformed like that, and everlasting Kingdoms are not built like that. We need to make a daily decision to focus on what matters. That's what God does, and He is very focused on you. Do not refuse Him who speaks.

Be not only attentive in hearing, but retentive after hearing.
—THOMAS WATSON

Unshakable

*Since we are receiving a kingdom that cannot
be shaken, let us be thankful, and so worship
God acceptably with reverence and awe.*
HEBREWS 12:28

In Word

The Kingdom we will be receiving is unshakable. We've never seen such a thing on earth. Egypt, Greece, Rome—all eventually fell. Earthly kingdoms may last a long time, but they are not eternal. But the city of God? It's invincible.

That means its walls cannot be penetrated, its defenses cannot fail, its government cannot be overthrown, its culture cannot be corrupted, and its people cannot be harmed. In the city we inherit, the lion will lie down with the lamb, swords will be beaten into plowshares, and no one will lock their doors. There won't even be night there, as the glory of the Lord will continuously shine. No one will cheat, lie, or steal—or even complain. Everything we want our neighborhoods and society to be, the city of God will be. And more.

That's a nice thought, but what does it mean today? Gratitude. Worship. Praise. Unbridled joy. The appropriate response to such extravagant blessing is extravagant appreciation. That's what results when people are given a gift beyond their wildest dreams. The euphoria is unrestrained.

In Deed

When we think of the Kingdom of God, though, we often restrain ourselves. But why? All our fear will be ancient history. We won't even remember how to be afraid. We'll laugh at the doubts we had, the anxieties we felt, and the stress we obsessed about. The problems that seemed so mountainous will suddenly look like molehills. The negative feelings that once consumed us will fade into oblivion.

All that's left is worship and gratitude. What will we do with ourselves? With no reason to plan things like how to insure our possessions, how to invest for the future, or how to squeeze in that much-needed vacation, we'll have a lot of time on our hands. More importantly, we'll have a lot of emotional freedom. We can fill hours and hours with praise. In fact, go ahead and do that now. The Kingdom is just as unshakable today as it will be then.

We are not only to sing the doxology, but to be the doxology.
—FRANCIS SCHAEFFER

Pure

*You have come to God, the judge of all men, to
the spirits of righteous men made perfect, to
Jesus the mediator of a new covenant.*
HEBREWS 12:23-24

In Word

We long to be complete. We seek completion in our work, our mate, our interests,
and our education; it's different for each person, but we all long for it. That's nothing
new; it began in the days of Eden, when God looked at Adam and said it wasn't good
for man to be alone. He needed a completer. Millennia later, we still need a completer.
The couple in the Garden was a picture of what would come: Jesus and His bride, the
seed of the Spirit in the heart of humanity, and, as this verse spells out, "the spirits of
righteous men made perfect." Our deep longing for completion is more than a longing
to be cultivated; it's a promise to be fulfilled.

The ways we try to fill that longing are at best humorous, and at worst sinful. But
in that day, when we have come to the Judge of all people and the Mediator who represents us to Him, there will be nothing humorous or sinful about it. The completion
of our souls will be glorious, intense, and pure. When the Bible speaks of being made
"perfect," it means being made "complete," "mature," and "whole." While we may learn
and explore and grow for eternity, we will not yearn for fulfillment. That will have
already been given to those who have faith in the Mediator of the new covenant.

In Deed

If you're looking for a practical application to this passage, consider this one: Your
attitude shapes everything about you. If you are expecting heaven to be boring, sti-
flingly pious, or irrelevant to your heart's passions, you'll live a depressed, unmoti-
vated existence. If, however, you expect the city of God to be exciting, full of wonders
and adventures, and where your needy heart is made complete, you'll live with energy
and zeal. What could be more practical than that?

Let this truth transform your attitude, knowing that your attitude will transform
your life. As a result, you'll be that much closer, at least in your affections, to the city
of God.

The best is yet to be.
—JOHN WESLEY

He's for Us

If God is for us, who can be against us?
ROMANS 8:31

In Word

It's a rhetorical question, designed to make us realize the folly of our thinking. The mountains of circumstance block our view of the expanse of heaven and, in the process, cause us to question whether God is on our side. Paul's argument points out the absurdity of the thought; if God has given us promises and His Son—while we were still sinners, no less—why would He abandon us now? What could possibly undermine His favor now? Why would anyone, especially the all-wise God, bail on such a priceless investment?

He wouldn't. Any doubt a believer has about God's intentions is the result of a lie. It's the same lie Satan told Eve in Eden: Has God really said what you think He said? Have you considered that He might be holding out on you? Are you sure He has your best interests in mind? For people who have accepted the sacrifice of the Son, there's no longer any barrier to His favor. If God is for us, there can't be anyone of any significance against us.

But we feel like life is against us sometimes, don't we? We see a repeated pattern of dashed dreams and annoying frustrations. We interpret them as evidence of God's hand, and our "evidence" makes us wonder how good He really is. We forget that Satan and circumstances are small in the eyes of God. Our obsession with small things reveals our lack of obsession with Him. And that leads to distorted thinking—like the idea of God not being on our side anymore.

In Deed

The best way to deal with that kind of thinking is to treat it as sin. Whether doubt is sin or not is debatable among Christians, but the treatment of it as such is highly effective. The Word of God repeatedly and emphatically declares His extravagant goodness and favor to those who believe. Any suggestion otherwise is a contradiction of the Word. Reject such folly, and live in faith. God is on your side.

Discouragement is to be resisted just like sin.
—J. O. FRASER

He's Generous

*He who did not spare his own Son, but gave
him up for us all—how will he not also, along
with him, graciously give us all things?*
ROMANS 8:32

In Word

Imagine one of your good friends suddenly revealing that he secretly inherited hundreds of millions of dollars a few weeks ago. Then imagine him giving you a million dollars this Christmas, just because he likes you and wants to share his wealth with you. To him, the gift was a drop in the bucket, hardly making a dent in his wealth. Now suppose the next time you went out to lunch together, you forgot your wallet, and he had to pay. Can you imagine him being outraged at having to fork over the price of your lunch? Is a person who gave you a million dollars the type to get angry over pocket change?

That's pretty easy to answer, isn't it? Even if you have no wealthy friends, you probably can't envision one being generous with a lot and stingy with a little. Generous hearts don't work that way. And our God has a very generous heart.

But we sometimes approach Him more as a stingy Lord than a generous Father. We feel as if we are twisting His arm when we pray, not realizing that the length and intensity of some of our prayers are designed to draw us closer to Him. The answers we seek are never withheld because God is reluctant. He who did not spare His own Son for us is clearly not a reluctant Father. He is a generous friend who would give us the world.

In Deed

Maybe understanding that is the first step in getting answered prayers. If we pray expecting Him to be a hard Master, we may find a hard Master. But if we pray expecting an extravagant Giver, we may find an extravagant Giver. After all, Jesus did say that we would receive according to our faith, and that without it, it is impossible to please God. If we feel that we have to twist God's arm, maybe it's because we believed we would have to.

God has graciously given us all things—His Kingdom and more. Believe that, and you'll see it more often.

> God is ever giving to His children, yet hath not the
> less. His riches are imparted, not impaired.
> —THOMAS WATSON

He's Immovable

Who shall separate us from the love of Christ?
ROMANS 8:35

In Word

God never changes. That's bad news for those who want to make up their own rules in life, but in all other respects, it's comforting. When God speaks of His favor toward us, His love, and His promises to the redeemed, we don't want Him to change. Ever.

The good news is that He assures us He won't. The love of Christ has already been amply displayed for those who will receive it, and there is nothing—absolutely nothing—that can ever diminish it. We cannot be moved from it—not by trials, adversaries, diseases, disasters, poverty, or even our own stupid mistakes. Whatever we think might be threatening to our relationship with God, it ultimately isn't. It may hinder our communion with Him and slow our growth, but it will not undo His love. It can't. His love is immovable.

Think of all the times you feel separated from the love of Christ. Is it when you're depressed? in the midst of a crisis? too sinful to face Him? too busy to care? Whatever the case, your feeling about the intensity of His love is an illusion. It isn't lukewarm, it isn't distant, and it isn't withheld. The love of Christ may manifest itself as parental discipline or a test of faith, but it is never withdrawn from your life. Nothing can separate you from infinite love.

In Deed

There will be times in your life when you'll need to know that, and to know it so well that your feelings can't convince you otherwise. They'll try, you know. Feelings do that. They masquerade as authorities on subjects that they know little about. They can take a promise of God and tell you that it's highly unlikely, and they can take His love and tell you it's an obligation He doesn't enjoy. Don't believe them. Feelings can lie.

Scripture doesn't, and it tells you that nothing can separate you from the love of Christ. In the context, that means nothing can. In the original Greek, that means nothing can. Even today, in your life, that means nothing can. Never forget it.

Jesus loves me, this I know, for the Bible tells me so.
—ANNA BARTLETT WARNER

He's Victorious

*In all these things we are more than
conquerors through him who loved us.*
ROMANS 8:37

In Word

If you were to take the most talented athlete in the world and put him or her in a room of liars and verbal abusers for two hours a day, you'd see the athlete's performance sharply decline. The level of talent remains the same, the training continues, but the ability to win vanishes. Why? Because no one can listen to constant discouragement and be encouraged. No one can have confidence undermined and still be confident. No one can doubt his or her ability and still use it effectively. What we believe matters a lot.

That also applies to the Christian life. When we listen to the feelings that tell us God is distant, the satanic lies that convince us our sins follow us everywhere, or the thought patterns that incorrectly interpret our circumstances and relationships, we end up like the athlete. We lose our confidence, doubt our abilities, and walk through life defeated. We don't live like citizens of the Kingdom of God.

A firm belief in the declarations of Scripture can change that. Paul had been through all sorts of persecution and hardship, both physical and relational, and he was still able to declare that we are more than conquerors through Christ. That's a powerful thought. It doesn't suggest that we might conquer, or that we barely conquer, or that we even deserve to conquer. It insists that we are more than conquerors because we are intimately united to the ultimate Conqueror. If the One who overcame death lives inside of us, what's left to fear?

In Deed

Live without fear. Do not be afraid to take bold risks for the gospel. The Kingdom of God is invincible, and it surrounds you. The hardships may come, the battles may be fierce, and the stresses may be real, but the love and power of Jesus remain undefeated. The key to living victoriously is to know that you can. Like an athlete in a room of trainers and encouragers, listen to the victory of Scripture as often as you can. Be more than a conqueror.

> God wants us to be victors, not victims; . . .
> to overcome, not to be overwhelmed.
> —WILLIAM ARTHUR WARD

He's Sovereign

*I am convinced that neither death nor life, . . . nor
anything else in all creation, will be able to separate us
from the love of God that is in Christ Jesus our Lord.*
ROMANS 8:38-39

In Word

One of the most persistent questions from atheists and agnostics is why a good God
would let bad things happen to good people. That question can't undermine the truth
of our faith, but when we are the good person to whom bad things happen, it wreaks
havoc with our intimacy with the Father. If we want our relationship with God to
impact the world, however, we can't be wavering between assurance and despair. We
have to be convinced that neither life nor death nor anything else can separate us
from His love.

A few verses earlier, Paul made an astounding statement about all things working
together for the good of those who love God and are called according to His purpose
(v. 28). That sweeping promise, coupled with that of verses 38 and 39, is the key to
constancy. There's no need to vacillate between assurance and despair when we truly
believe that all things are working toward a good purpose for us and that nothing can
separate us from Jesus' love. When we hold fast to those truths, the world cannot
move us away from our faith or our joy. We have a solid rock to stand on. Nothing can
come between us and the Kingdom.

In Deed

We need to remember that God watches over us with a love that cannot be quenched.
We alone have stability in an unstable world. We're blessed to know the King and the
Kingdom that last, being irreversibly attached to them. Whatever insecurity you feel
on that point, it's an illusion.

Don't fall for it. An uncertain world needs to see people living in certainty. That
doesn't mean that you aren't ever allowed to struggle or that you need to wear a mask
in public, but it's important to stop doubting what God has said is true. The opportunity a shattered world affords us to demonstrate an unshakable Kingdom is compelling. Take that opportunity. Trust the love of a sovereign God.

> Faith is a living and unshakeable confidence, a
> belief in the grace of God so assured that a man
> would die a thousand deaths for its sake.
> —MARTIN LUTHER

The Return of the King

The Lord himself will come down from heaven.
1 THESSALONIANS 4:16

In Word

"The Lord himself will come down from heaven." He did that once already, and we still celebrate it every December. But this will be an altogether different Advent—no baby in a manger, no years of growing up in obscurity, and no cultivation of disciples before the truth is found out. No, this time He will come with the clouds, revealing judgment and redemption all in one heavenly appearance. There will be a loud trumpet and shout. The bodies of those who have fallen asleep in death will be awakened in glory, and everyone—even those of us who expect it—will be astounded. It will be a day unlike any other.

There is confusion about that day, as theologians argue about when and how and the order of things, and the non-Christian world chalks it up to wishful thinking on our part. But the hope of the Kingdom is not a figment of our imagination. According to Jesus, "the Scripture cannot be broken" (John 10:35). The Son of Man, by His own promise, will return. All our confusion will be settled, and all our hopes will be fulfilled.

Count on that day. Our confidence as it approaches will shape how we live and how we die. It will shape our values, guide our spending, prioritize our schedules, and strengthen our resolve. Whatever we go through in this life, we look ahead to its completion. We are not aimless wanderers.

In Deed

That's the difference between Christians and others. Adherents of most religions speculate about what will happen to them after death. They wonder how many times they will have to die and be reborn before they are merged into some amorphous collective consciousness, or whether they will get a thumbs-up or a thumbs-down on the day of judgment, or whether this is all there is. Not so with us. We've been given promises by the most trustworthy Being in the universe. He will come again, and it will be perfect when He does.

> The primitive church thought more about the Second Coming of Jesus Christ than about death or about heaven.
>
> —ALEXANDER MACLAREN

Waking the Dead

We who are still alive, who are left till the coming of the Lord,
will certainly not precede those who have fallen asleep.
1 THESSALONIANS 4:15

In Word

God has no questions about the day of Jesus' return. He sees our speculations, our anxieties and fears, our hopes and wishes, and our ignorance, and He smiles. He knows that the thought of an end to history is alarming to us. He even knows how traumatized we will be on that day, even though we believe it will turn out well. He knows how He made us, and He remembers that we are frail creatures of dust (Psalm 103:14). He knows that He will never let us slip through His fingers.

We know that, too, but we're still a mixed bundle of nerves and anticipation. We can't imagine people rising up out of graves with new, eternal bodies. We don't know what it will be like to meet the Lord in the air, how we will be transformed, and whether we'll feel like we were ready. We don't know how it will all work out. The good news is that we don't have to. God already does, and we can trust Him.

If we realize that we can trust God to pull off the big event at the end of time, it should somehow sink in that we can trust Him with the details of today as well. We're sometimes inconsistent, trusting Him for salvation and resurrection while praying doubtfully about an individual problem on an individual day. But if God has our eternity in His hands, He also has our times in His hands. His care for us does not begin at the end of time. It began before the foundation of the world.

In Deed

We live in a day of wild speculation, on topics as diverse as global government, transitioning economies, social directions, and religious truths. In our lives, the speculation is all about our personal problems, our immediate future, and our eternal destiny. And the way God sees it, all of the questions have already been answered.

Take comfort in that. God has every moment of every day in His hands—even until the day He raises you up.

Our Lord has written the promise of the resurrection not in books alone, but in every leaf in springtime.
—MARTIN LUTHER

A Grief Observed

We do not want you to be ignorant about those who fall
asleep, or to grieve like the rest of men, who have no hope.
1 THESSALONIANS 4:13

In Word

You grieved when that special loved one died. You had to; it just about ripped your heart out. That event confronted you with the reality of death, and it deprived you of someone to whom you were rather attached. It was a traumatic event, even if you knew of the glory to come.

Many believers wonder if they will recognize their loved ones in heaven. The answer given by Scripture, at least by implication, if not explicitly, is emphatically yes. Abraham, Moses, Elijah, a pauper named Lazarus, martyrs, and a great cloud of witnesses all have a presence in the New Testament, and they are not presented anonymously as unknown entities. They are portrayed as distinguishable, knowable beings, just like the rest of heaven's multitudes. It's unthinkable that God would have made our DNA, our personality, and our experiences so unique and distinctive if He were planning to abandon that strategy in the Kingdom. We will be recognizable individuals in heaven. One might even argue that it wouldn't be heaven if we were not.

Of all the ideas about what the resurrection will be like, none of them have hit the mark. We know that because we are told that "no eye has seen, no ear has heard, no mind has conceived what God has prepared for those who love him" (1 Corinthians 2:9). The glories of heaven will be beyond our wildest dreams. There's no vision in the mind of a human being that can match what we will see there.

In Deed

That's what God wants us to remember when we are confronted with the death of a loved one. If that person was a believer, there's nothing ultimately sad about his or her passing. There's sadness for our loss, of course, but it's a temporary loss for us and an eternal gain for him or her. We may grieve, but not like those who have no hope. We know something the rest of the world doesn't know. It's more than a silver lining around a dark cloud; it's the dispersal of the cloud itself.

> Other men see only a hopeless end, but the
> Christian rejoices in an endless hope.
> —GILBERT BRENKEN

Practicing the Presence of God

We will be with the Lord forever.
1 THESSALONIANS 4:17

In Word

Forever is a long time. If we are going to be with someone forever, we want to be with someone worthy of the commitment. We would find no comfort in an eternity that is boring, painful, lonely, or without purpose. When it comes to forever, we want it to be good.

The Bible doesn't tell us a lot about our activity in heaven, but it does tell us that we will be with the Lord forever. We know we will be among the multitudes worshiping around His throne, but we also know that to be absent from the body is to be present with the Lord (2 Corinthians 5:8), and there's every indication in Scripture that this is a very personal presence. The God who knows us by name and has counted the hairs on our head is not going to assimilate us into the crowd in heaven. We will see Him face-to-face—personally.

That might be an awkward moment if we haven't spent much time in His presence in this age. If our prayer life is one-dimensional—our talking to Him and hoping He hears—then we may need to get acquainted with Him on that day. But if we are tuned to His voice, comfortable in the holy presence of His Spirit, and aware of His constant and affectionate attention, heaven will be a continuation of the theme. One way or another, how we know Him here will have a lot to do with how we know Him there.

In Deed

With that in mind, it might be helpful to practice His presence right now. There are many ways to do that, but one of the most basic is simply to be aware. Scripture has told us that He is always with us, so to imagine and to sense that He is with us is never inappropriate. Far from being an escapist fantasy, awareness of His presence gets us closer to reality than we normally live.

Do that today. As you drive, as you work, as you relax, in all the things you do, be aware of your constant Companion. Talk to Him and make time to listen. Enjoy His company. Remember that His loving eyes are on you and His loving hands hold you up. And realize that His companionship will never, ever end.

> I make it my priority to persevere in His holy presence, wherein I maintain a simple attention and a fond regard for God.
> —BROTHER LAWRENCE

A New Hope

Encourage each other with these words.
1 THESSALONIANS 4:18

In Word

We live in a world in pain. Even now, many people are being wounded deeply. Others are wondering if their scars will ever fade. Life is tough, especially for those who don't know its Source and for those who don't know how it will all be resolved. Anywhere you walk in public, you are likely to pass people who are depressed, bitter, hopeless, angry, confused, and even suicidal. You will likely pass someone who has been abused, someone who has been betrayed, and someone who has been forgotten. In this age, you always walk among the wounded.

Do you realize, though, that you have the antidote to human despair? It's more effective than therapy, more effective than medicine, and more effective than self-help techniques. It's the knowledge of the ultimate end of fallenness and the beginning of beauty and peace. When confronted with the angst of this world, you can promise purpose. When confronted with disease, you can offer healing. When confronted with death, you can offer life. Psychiatry can't do that, religions can't do that, and friendships can't even do that. Only the knowledge of the end can do that. And we have it.

"Therefore encourage each other with these words." There's more purpose in that statement than a better mood or a don't-worry-be-happy attitude. We are told to encourage each other—believers and unbelievers alike—with the promise of His coming. In a world desperate for hope, we have the only real promise there is. Even where death pretends to rule, these words can give life.

In Deed

Be a life giver. Jesus gave us life and then told His disciples, "Freely you have received, freely give" (Matthew 10:8). So freely give what you have received. If you are comforted by the fact that Jesus is coming again; if you are thrilled that all things will be made new; and if you are looking forward to living with Him forever; then encourage each other with these words.

Encouragement is oxygen to the soul.
—GEORGE M. ADAMS

Overcomers

Everyone born of God overcomes the world.
1 JOHN 5:4

In Word

The pattern was set long ago. A child born of God and woman entered this world as an overcomer. He looked as vulnerable as any other infant, and He soon became the target of a cosmic enemy's rampage. But no enemy could defeat, distract, or divert this overcomer's mission. Temptations were rebuffed. Opponents were refuted. And physical threats missed their mark . . . until, that is, the time of fulfillment came. Only then did He enter extreme shame and pain, suffer death, and disappear into the cold earth.

To most of us, that would appear to be the opposite of overcoming. But the well-known story didn't end there. Death was defeated in His resurrection, and He was exalted above every authority in heaven and earth. No power could—or ever will—defeat Him. In every sense, He has overcome.

We're thankful for the Incarnation as a unique act of God. But Jesus is more than our high and holy Savior. In many respects, He's also the prototype of what we are to become. Just as He was born into this world as an invincible child, we are born by His Spirit as invincible children. We won't live sinless lives as He did, but we will overcome in spite of our stumbling. Those who truly believe, who have truly been born from above, will end up beyond its corrupting and threatening reach. We are members of the family of God, and nothing that close to God's heart can be ultimately defeated.

In Deed

Remember that on this unusual day. We are born of imperishable seed (1 Corinthians 15:42). No matter how vulnerable we look or feel, our future is as secure as that of the infant in the manger. We can be attacked, hurt, tempted, bruised, discouraged, and beaten down, but we cannot be defeated. "We are hard pressed on every side, but not crushed; perplexed, but not in despair; persecuted, but not abandoned; struck down, but not destroyed" (2 Corinthians 4:8-9). We can live with complete confidence. Why? Because, like a special baby long ago, everyone born of God overcomes the world.

> God is never defeated. Though He may be opposed, attacked, and resisted, the ultimate outcome can never be in doubt.
> —BROTHER ANDREW

Believers

Who is it that overcomes the world? Only he
who believes that Jesus is the Son of God.
1 JOHN 5:5

In Word

Throughout history, people have tried to reach beyond the confines of our own humanity—to connect with a world beyond space and time, to rise above struggles, to understand beyond human wisdom, to live beyond death. But creatures of dust that we are, we all fall short. No human invention has allowed us to discover the transcendence we seek. We are, by nature, more limited than we want to be.

The promise of the gospel changes that. We are still finite creatures, but we are integrally connected with the life of our God. We are still human flesh, but we are filled with a supernatural Spirit. We still die, but we live forever. In profound and mysterious ways, we have overcome the world.

How? Not by the normal means human beings have always attempted. Not by magic or rituals, nor by education and experience, nor by simply persevering or praying or fighting for our lives. There is only one God-ordained way to overcome the world: by believing. And not just by believing, but by believing in Jesus as the Son of God.

In Deed

That seems simple enough, doesn't it? But surprisingly, we forsake simplicity for human effort. We still try to receive God's blessings by earning them. We still try to do the work of the Spirit in the strength of the flesh. We still try to overcome sin by fighting it. We have a multitude of ways to rely on techniques other than simple faith. Still, God insists. Those who overcome must believe.

When all else fails, simply believe. Believe what God promises, trust His strength, rest in His grace. Life is much less complicated than we try to make it. Our connection with God's presence is a matter not of striving but accepting. When you get to the end of your own efforts and still haven't overcome, remember the Overcomer. Believe and trust. The rest is up to Him.

Our life is grounded in faith, with hope and love besides.
—JULIAN OF NORWICH

Euphoria

*Then I saw a new heaven and a new earth, for
the first heaven and the first earth had passed
away, and there was no longer any sea.*
REVELATION 21:1

In Word

Every four years when a soccer team wins the World Cup, a nation erupts in delirium. In the arena of national pride, there is no greater euphoria than a world title in the planet's most popular sport. For years, the winning team's supporters have sung spirited, spontaneous anthems in crowded stadiums, zealously waved the nation's colors for all to see, and now their allegiance has proven profitable. For four years, the citizens of that nation can delight in the exclusive glory of victory.

Many years ago, a very new kind of humanity was born into a very old kind of stable. That didn't look like the beginnings of victory, and neither did His ignominious death some three decades later. But from that birth, death, and resurrection will come an entirely new order of creation: a new spiritual race, a new heaven, and a new earth. The old era will pass away, and the euphoria of victory will cause an entire planet full of redeemed people to erupt in wild celebration. The national pride of a World Cup winner will pale in comparison to the ultimate ecstasy of this eternal triumph. Elation will be the new everyday mood.

For many of God's people, the thrill of victory will be a shock. Many of us have sung the anthems of our allegiance in ritual boredom, scarcely realizing the weight of the lyrics they contain. We've held the national flag close to our side, giving it a half-hearted, almost-apologetic wave whenever a measure of success is evident. When the new heaven and earth are established in eternal supremacy, many of us may wonder what all the shouting is about.

In Deed

Don't be one of those halfhearted supporters. Begin celebrating for the victory that is coming. Wave the colors boldly and sing the anthems at the top of your lungs. This will be the greatest triumph ever—and the last.

The religion of Christ is the religion of joy.
—OCTAVIUS WINSLOW

Elation

*I saw the Holy City, the new Jerusalem, coming
down out of heaven from God, prepared as a
bride beautifully dressed for her husband.*
REVELATION 21:2

In Word

"A bride beautifully dressed for her husband." Is there any more emotionally satisfying picture than that? The gorgeous bride, dressed in splendor, radiantly smiling. The beaming groom, thrilled beyond description, his heart nearly leaping out of his chest with delight. It's a very human picture with very divine overtones; and it's the final and most graphic picture the Bible gives us of the consummation of redemption. When the battle is done, the wedding will overwhelm us all.

It's okay to look forward to that day. God does. Theologically, we have a hard time with the idea that He is greatly anticipating the fulfillment of His desires. That just sounds too human. If He told us personally of His expectancy, many of us would counsel Him to find contentment first and not stake His emotions on an event, as though that event would actually satisfy Him. After all, that's what we tell each other: "Your contentment should be in God alone, not the plans He has for your life." But God has quite a few plans of His own, and He never portrays Himself as subdued about their fulfillment. Neither does He urge us to be subdued about our excitement. This event should be highly anticipated.

The issues of life—yesterday's regrets, today's difficulties, tomorrow's fears—become much more tolerable when we understand the excited anticipation of God. When we really get a glimpse of His heart and how it beats with joy for His bride, ours starts to beat in the same rhythm. And the rest of life falls under the spell of hopeful anticipation.

In Deed

Is that where your heart lives—in a state of hopeful anticipation? Are the turbulent issues of life subdued under the excitement of the coming wedding day? One of the greatest offerings you can present to your Suitor is a heart that beats with His. If yours doesn't, ask Him to fill you with His desires. If it does, it's time to get dressed for the wedding.

With God, the honeymoon never ends.
—JOHN PIPER

Presence

I heard a loud voice from the throne saying, "Now the
dwelling of God is with men, and he will live with them."
REVELATION 21:3

In Word

There came a voice from the throne. Whose voice was it? Was it one of the four living creatures who surround the throne? Or was it the voice of Him who sits on the throne Himself? Either way, it wasn't just a voice; it was a *loud* voice. An emphatic voice. A voice with an air of authority and a sense of finality. What this voice declared was ultimate and permanent.

We live in a strange time of human history when the fallen, corrupt, sin-saturated world is overlaid with the redeemed who love God and are called according to His purpose. Our job as members of this bridge between the ages is to bring the future into the present, to exhibit all the characteristics of the Kingdom of light in this place of darkness, to pray that God's will be done on earth, right now, as it is done in heaven. Part of that role is to display the presence of God—to be the ambassadors of heaven and the temple of God's Spirit—in this world. We alone are able to demonstrate this truth that "the dwelling of God is with men, and he will live with them."

Jesus made it clear to His disciples that the dwelling of God would be with them, not just at the end of the age when the new Jerusalem descends from heaven, but also in the day-to-day trials of this world and the age of the great commission. This future glory has present foretastes, as evidenced on the day of Pentecost and thereafter when the Spirit filled the redeemed. Revelation 21:3 is not just a future hope; it's your present condition.

In Deed

Most Christians believe that intellectually without being conscious of it in their hearts. Whatever it takes, live today as though God's dwelling with you is the clearest reality you have. Faith in this truth will cause you to see life through new lenses and will make His presence manifest. Know in your heart: God lives with you and in you.

God is above, presiding; beneath, sustaining; within, filling.

—HILDEBERT OF LAVARDIN

Wealth

He who overcomes will inherit all this, and I
will be his God and he will be my son.
REVELATION 21:7

In Word

"All this." That's the short description of the inheritance of a child of God. But what exactly is "all this"? Is it the water of life mentioned in the previous verse? That's only one thing—an incredible thing, of course, but hardly plural enough to be called "all this." Or does "all this" refer to everything mentioned up to this point in the chapter?

It does, as can be proved by other Scripture references. Included in the inheritance of the children of God are the manifest presence of God, the end of tears and mourning, and, best of all, the "everything new" of verse 5. In other words, all of the possessions of the Father are the inheritance of His children. As much as we try to let that sink in, it won't. It can't. It's simply too astounding.

Think about it anyway. Your inheritance—which, by the way, is already being distributed little by little to those who are ready to receive it—consists of everything in the Father's possession. Jesus told His disciples over the course of His ministry that He gave them authority over the enemy, the mystery of the Kingdom, the word of truth, and the Holy Spirit. Most amazing, He told the Father this about His disciples: "I have given them the glory that you gave me, that they may be one as we are one" (John 17:22). God had given Jesus everything; Jesus gives us everything. We are joint heirs with Him (Romans 8:17). That's incredible.

In Deed

A good question to ask yourself each morning when you get up is, How shall I use my inheritance today? In fact, make that part of your prayers today. Ask God if there's any aspect of His authority, His Kingdom, His purposes, His resources that He wants to entrust you with today. Then watch for your opportunities. They will come. The owner of all that exists—your Father, who has promised everything to His Son and the Son's siblings—has no intention of hoarding "all this."

> For the saints in the world to come . . . their great
> possession is unchangeable, but also inexhaustible.
> —HENRY BARCLAY SWETE

Radiance

The nations will walk by its light, and the kings of the earth will bring their splendor into it. The glory and honor of the nations will be brought into it.
REVELATION 21:24, 26

In Word

The glory of God and the lamp of the Lamb (v. 23) are all the light the world will ever need. When Revelation speaks of the light of the new creation, this is what it's talking about: the radiance of God in Christ. No sun, stars, or moon will be needed. There will be no dark corners in the new Jerusalem, no shadowy alleyways and secret chambers of mischief. There will be no need; corruption will not be allowed into the city. Ever.

What will be brought to the city, however, is the glory and honor of all nations. All the wealth and power and glory that human governments and kings have sought—at great expense to the human race—will belong to the Savior who humbly forsook the form of deity in this world. While humanity tried to climb its way up, Jesus lowered Himself down. And in the end, the glory and honor of nations will be His. No crown, no treasure, no prestige, no accomplishment will be boasted in by human pride. All that we sought, He'll have. And He'll shine His glory on all who love Him.

That's reason number one for us not to get caught up in the world's ambitions. They won't achieve anything worthwhile, and they won't last. All the radiance of creation shines from a surprising lamp that faithless eyes cannot see: the Lamb of God who humbled Himself to the point of death. Whatever splendor, glory, or treasure you've sought, you won't find it unless you find it in Him.

In Deed

As this year comes to a close, measure your goals and plans. What are your ambitions? Do they fit better with the glory of the world or the glory of the Lamb? In other words, what light do you seek? Make sure every dream you have this coming year comes under the glow of the glory of the Kingdom of God.

> [God] has an inexhaustible enthusiasm for the fame of His name among the nations.
> —JOHN PIPER

SCRIPTURE INDEX

you've been told not to trust your emotions—

feeling
like

GOD

the emotional side
of discipleship—and why you can't
fully follow Jesus without it

chris tiegreen

to rely on what you know rather than what you feel.

Yet you were created in the image of God, which means that many of your feelings are echoes of his own. In *Feeling like God*, Chris Tiegreen traces the character of God throughout Scripture, showing how God reveals himself as a deeply emotional being who longs to connect closely with you. When men and women like Abraham, Hannah, David, and Paul opened their hearts to him, their lives were radically transformed. Discover how your emotions are a bridge drawing you closer to your Savior—and you'll experience the passion of feeling like God does.

"If you're longing to *feel* God's love—not just *know* it—read this book."—**Chip Ingram**, president, teaching pastor, *Living on the Edge*

CP0266

"ABRAHAM. LISTEN..."

Christians look to the Bible for inspiration and role models—but if actual biblical characters walked into our lives, we might not know how to handle them. For instance, how would you have reacted if Abraham told you that God said to sacrifice his son? If Ruth said God prompted her to sleep at a strange guy's feet? Or if Isaiah insisted the Lord commanded him to go naked for three years? Is it possible we've created a safe, tidy Christian culture that too often holds back from embracing the complete truth of God's character—and those of his people?

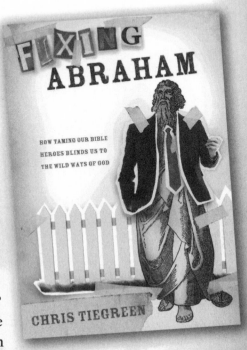

FIXING ABRAHAM

HOW TAMING OUR BIBLE
HEROES BLINDS US TO
THE WILD WAYS OF GOD

CHRIS TIEGREEN

In *FIXING ABRAHAM*, ACCLAIMED WRITER CHRIS TIEGREEN PROVIDES A FRESH INTRODUCTION TO THE BIBLICAL HEROES YOU THOUGHT YOU KNEW. IN THE PROCESS, YOU'LL BE CHALLENGED TO BREAK FREE OF FORMULAIC CHRISTIANITY AND OPEN YOUR EYES TO THE WILD AND HOLY WAYS OF GOD.

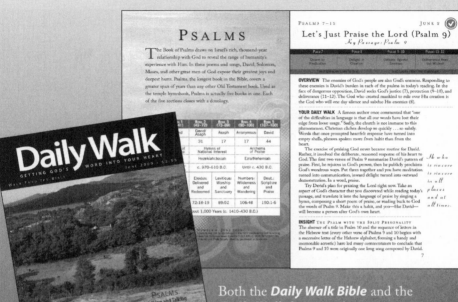

The devotionals in this book come from *indeed*—
a bimonthly magazine from Walk Thru the Bible
created specifically to help Christians
deepen their relationship with God.

indeed explores new depths of understanding and brings readers to new heights of spiritual insight. Each year covers a biblical theme—the words of Jesus, eternal wisdom, the heart of worship, and more. As children born of God's Spirit, we are called to an ever-growing understanding of God's Word and a clearer vision of His purposes. *indeed* can lead you as you explore the heart of God and seek to commune more intimately with Him.

Let *indeed* stimulate your faith and guide you as you meditate on the richness of God's Word. Each new issue will help you see His presence in your life, enhancing your prayers, your relationships, and your service in His name. Regardless of how long you've been a Christian, the Spirit of God longs for your spiritual growth. He has used *indeed* to bring many into a closer relationship with Him. To subscribe, visit our Web site at www.walkthru.org. Discounted bulk subscriptions are also available online.

WALK
THRU THE
BIBLE®

www.walkthru.org

Individual Orders: 800-877-5539   Bulk Orders: 800-998-0814   CP0109